# THE DYNAMICS
# OF FOLKLORE

# BARRE TOELKEN

UNIVERSITY OF OREGON

## HOUGHTON MIFFLIN COMPANY

### BOSTON

DALLAS     GENEVA, ILLINOIS

HOPEWELL, NEW JERSEY

PALO ALTO     LONDON

# THE
# DYNAMICS
## OF
# FOLKLORE

For Wayland D. Hand

The author wishes to make the following acknowledgments for permission to adapt and reprint previously published material included in this text:

Barre Toelken, "A Descriptive Nomenclature for the Study of Folklore: The Process of Tradition," *Western Folklore* 28 (1969): 91–100.

Adaptation of "Seeing with a Native Eye: How Many Sheep Will It Hold?" by Barre Toelken in *Seeing with a Native Eye: Essays on Native American Religion*, edited by Walter Holden Capps. Copyright © 1976 by Walter Holden Capps. Courtesy of Harper & Row, Publishers, Inc.

Some of the ideas developed in Chapter 7 were previously published in Barre Toelken, "World View, the University Establishment, and Cultural Annihilation," *The Journal of Ethnic Studies* 2:4 (Winter 1975): 1–21.

Barre Toelken, "A Circular World: The Vision of Navajo Crafts," *Parabola* 1:1 (Winter 1976): 30–37.

Printed in the U.S.A.

Library of Congress Catalog Card Number: 78–69536

ISBN: 0–395–27068–5

# ✹ CONTENTS ✺

CONTENTS

CONTENTS

# ❧ PREFACE ❧

Most folklorists, and most folklore textbooks, have paid more attention to the items of folklore than to the live processes by and through which folklore is produced. This has led at least one folklorist to lament recently that folklore scholarship tends to "dehumanize" folklore. Briefly put, this book is an attempt to provide a partial remedy for that situation by urging a basic attitude toward folklore study that stresses "the folk" and the dynamics of their traditional expressions. In this approach, my thinking is very much indebted to the works of Roger D. Abrahams, Richard Bauman, Dan Ben-Amos, Alan Dundes, Henry Glassie, Robert A. Georges, Dell Hymes, Albert Lord—in short, those who have focused on style, performance, event, and process, rather than on genre, structure, or text. However, the book does not attempt to do away with generic considerations. My hope is rather that it will constitute a theoretical complement to other works on folklore by providing a balance, or, to use another figure, by suggesting other equally valid axes along which the performances of tradition may be viewed.

No particular folklore school is espoused or represented here; indeed, the suggestions offered by this book should be palatable to a broad spectrum of theoretical positions, for in it I try to provide a fair, eclectic combination of the main trends in folklore today, with the focus admittedly on the active, live aspects of folk and their lore. Because it places its emphasis on the basic operation of folklore process, the book may be used by anyone from a student in an introductory course trying to find out about the internal mechanics of folklore to the advanced scholar interested in live perspectives in the profession. I do not assume that the reader has had extensive exposure to folklore previously; for this reason particularly, the bibliographies are meant to be basic and suggestive rather than exhaustive.

Students complain, often with justification, that literature is killed in the classroom, that social sciences in the academic setting can cause us nearly to overlook people, that the music in a book of technical analysis is nowhere near as interesting as music falling on the ear from a live source. The same kinds of objections have been made of folklore classes and folklore texts: Since it is possible to separate the lore from the "folk" and spend endless hours dissecting and studying the resultant texts, it is indeed possible for folklorists to overlook, or to avoid intentionally, those very dynamic human elements that make the field an exciting one to begin with. In view of this state of affairs in academia, I hope this book can present some views of the subject that have not been particularly characteristic of the academic approach. For one thing, where possible I have followed the lead of the tradition-bearers themselves, using their terms, topics, and perspectives. For another, I have not filtered out the so-called obscene elements that are so characteristic of folklore. In real life, and therefore in folklore, the ingenuous and friendly hospitality of old Mrs. Judkins stands side by side with the brash machismo of the logger, and next to the shy, home-oriented customs of the Japanese-American family there exists the open and exciting street jive of urban Black youths. Since folklore is not limited to rural environs, minority groups, and past times, I have looked as much as possible to all situations where we may see folklore in performance the way it is normally performed.

In so doing I have stressed groups with whom I have had considerable acquaintance (loggers, Navajos, Westerners, Japanese-Americans, farm families) so I could use anecdotal examples from my own experience to illustrate the main points of the book. For parallel ideas I have referred to the published work of others, but I have not pretended to scrape up extra fieldwork for this book just for rhetorical (or political) balance. For example, I have not done much work in folklore among Mexican-Americans; they are certainly one of the most dynamic folk groups in the United States today, but for that very reason I have decided not to "throw them in" for mere color. Their traditions are too important for that. But I have tried to indicate works to which the reader can refer so as not to be limited by the peculiarity of my experiences.

A picture may not be worth a thousand words in folklore, for we always want multiple pictures of any folk performance or event. Nonetheless, an attempt is made in this book for the first time to present pictures of those dynamic processes that are discussed. The pictures concentrate chiefly on folklore actually being performed, or folk traditions being passed directly from one person to another. In addition, a few pictures are provided only so that items discussed in the various chapters may be scrutinized by the interested reader.

In the task of compiling this book and providing analytical remarks about its contents, I am primarily indebted to the tradition-bearers who so graciously allowed me to use their most cherished customs, beliefs, and performances. Informants are identified in the notes to each chapter, but I must give particular thanks to the Yellowman family in southern Utah, the Damon and Howland families in Massachusetts, the Tabler family in Oregon, the Kubota family of Utah and California, and the Wasson-Hockema family in southwestern Oregon for allowing me to talk about them at such great length here. All whose words are quoted have given their permission either directly to me or to other fieldworkers who recorded the materials. Some people did not want their names mentioned but nonetheless allowed their remarks to be quoted or paraphrased. No one has received payment for materials used here, but neither have the folk expressions become mine or the publisher's by virtue of appearing in this book. Even if it were not for the new copyright law (which protects the ownership of spoken texts), the various folk "performances" offered here, mere fossils on the printed page, remain among the cultural property and under the personal proprietorship of those who are still telling stories, singing songs, building barns, and playing the dozens in complete (and admirable) disregard for the fortunes of textbooks, the passions of students, and the aspirations of university professors. The appearance of their folklore in these pages does not interrupt the regular traditional process, nor does it diminish the cultural possessions of tradition-bearers. On the other hand, it would certainly impoverish the student of culture if these texts and expressions and events were not available. The flesh, blood, and bones of the live folklore discussed here belong to those who have been the tradition carriers; the hot air is mine.

For assistance in fieldwork details and analysis leading to some of the passages in this book, I am indebted to Ray Scofield, who helped with logger folklore and with the songs sung by Mrs. Clarice Judkins; to George Wasson for his intermediary role with the Wassons and Hockemas;

to my wife, Miiko, and to Donna Misao Joo for guidance in interpreting Japanese-American cooking custom and symbolism; to Twilo Scofield for helping provide a full description of the Wodtli-Tabler Thanksgiving dinner; to Edwin L. Coleman, II, for suggestions and interpretations on Black folklore; to Joseph Epes Brown for unfailing wisdom in regard to Native American culture, religion, and worldview.

Photographers are identified in the captions of each photo, but I must mention here my sincere thanks to the following people for allowing me to use their fine pictures. Suzi Jones, Folk Arts Coordinator for the Oregon Arts Commission, let me pore through her extensive collection of Northwest traditions; Carl Fleischhauer and the American Folklife Center generously supplied a number of photographs from the center's collecting projects, and from Fleischhauer's work with the Hammons family; Ellen Waterston Bartow, of the Rafter Q Ranch in Central Oregon, provided pictures of traditional roundup chores virtually unavailable to outsiders; Edwin L. Coleman, II, volunteered to catch an exciting interchange of Black youths on film; Lucinda Mason allowed the use of pictures from her folklore field collection on a rural Black river baptism in Alabama; William Tabler, formerly a logger and scaler near Sweet Home, Oregon, lent me pictures he took of loggers in the woods during the 1940s; Brody Washburn combed the archives of the Special Collections of the University of Oregon Library for old turn-of-the-century logger pictures, and reproduced the prints beautifully from the original glass plates; Mrs. Chandler Stevens of Salem, Oregon, lent me the picture of her mother, Mrs. Clarice Mae Judkins, a talented traditional singer with an impressively wide repertoire; Oscar Palmquist performed the lab work, copying, and enlargements for most of the pictures used in this text with a remarkable talent that carries over to the pictures themselves.

Professors Louie Attebery of The College of Idaho, George Carey of the University of Massachusetts, Amherst, and Patrick Mullen of The Ohio State University were my distant Parcae during the writing of the book. They read all of it carefully and gently, indicating where they thought I was dull, where I was verbose, where I was wrong, where I was faking, and (best of all) where I was right. Their criticisms were detailed and just and I followed nearly all their suggestions for rethinking and revision. The book was very deeply affected by their help and would not be in its current state without their generous participation. Of course I accept the responsibility for the way it now stands, but that does not subordinate the really considerable role these colleagues played in shaping the final product and giving me reasons to believe it was worth doing.

The typing was done by Bonnie English, Charlene Gates, and Maren

Halvorsen. Far beyond their labor, which may make them hope never to hear of folklore again, I am sincerely in debt to them for catching innumerable slips and for the generous way with which they helped me confront the publisher's inexorable deadlines.

I am grateful to Twilo Scofield for extensive proofreading and for comments on early drafts of the text. Likewise, Karin Smith was a tremendous help with bibliographical data, and offered inestimably valuable advice, especially with regard to archiving practices and preservation concepts. My colleague, Sharon Sherman, told me all I know about film and gave me a good deal of helpful advice as I worked on later stages of the manuscript. Suzi Jones, my friend, graduate student, and now colleague, has been my most faithful and persistent critic throughout; without her honest advice, this book would contain many more blunders than it does. My son Hiroshi employed his artistic eye to suggest cropping and alignment of photographs.

Lastly, I would like to congratulate my family for leading an entirely normal life while this book was being written, even though to do so meant tripping over tape recorders, file cards, and father.

B. T.

# THE DYNAMICS
# OF FOLKLORE

# INTRODUCTION

## INTO FOLKLORISTICS

## WITH GUN AND CAMERA

**ANYONE LOOKING INTO THE** **SUBJECT OF FOLKLORE FOR THE FIRST TIME WILL NOTICE EARLY ON THAT THE SCHOLARLY DISCUSSION OF THE SUBJECT HAS BEEN** taking place for over a hundred years, mostly among people who have approached it from vantage points related to other interests and disciplines: language, religion, literature, anthropology, history, and even local nostalgia and ancestor worship. Indeed, the famous story of the blind men describing the elephant provides a vivid analogy for the field of folklore: The historian may see in folklore the common person's version of a sequence of grand events already charted; the anthropologist sees the oral expression of social systems, cultural meaning, and sacred relationships; the literary scholar looks for genres of oral literature, the psychologist for universal imprints, the art historian for primitive art, the linguist for folk speech and world view, and so on. The field of folklore as we know it today has been formed and defined by the very variety of its approaches, excited by the debate (and sometimes the rancor) brought about by inevitable clashes between opposed truths.

The earliest "schools" of folklore were mainly antiquarian; that is, they concerned themselves with the recording and study of customs, ideas, and expressions that were thought to be survivals of ancient cultural systems still existing in the modern world. Many early scholars were interested in religious systems and the ancient myths that may have informed their development. Still others were interested in the roots of language and in the study of the relationships between languages in far-flung families. Still others, often country parsons, busied themselves in noting quaint rural observances that might have hearkened back to pre-Christian times. Among the many encouragements to the study of tradition, not the least was the appearance of Darwinian theories in the middle 1800s; if life could be said to have developed from simple to complex forms, then, many argued, culture itself might have evolved in the same way. Folk observances and fragments of early rituals were taken as simple elements from an earlier stratum of civilization, studied because they would reveal to us the building blocks of our contemporary, complex society. The focus for these studies was primarily on lower classes, peasants, simple folk, "backward" cultures, and "primitives," for it was believed that these kinds of people had avoided or resisted longest the sophisticating influences of so-called advanced culture. Conversely, urban dwellers, immersed in literacy and sophistication, were thought to be immune to folklore. From their ranks came those who studied "the folk."

Under these circumstances, it is not surprising that the main arena for early folklore study was the rural environment. In fact, among the German folklorists, the term *Volkskunde* denoted the entire lifestyle of the rural people. The assumption seems to have been that only away from the influence of technology and modern civilization could one find those antique remnants of tradition that might reveal to us the early stages of our cultural existence. This basic assumption for the normal habitat of folklore still exists today in many European and South American countries, where folklore is understood to be by definition the traditions of rural people. In fact, up until very recently the rural scene has been the basis for most of the collecting and study of American folklore as well, for American culture itself has been defined—in its own terms—by a vanishing frontier, a disappearing pioneer tradition, a fading of the "good old days." Modern America has been thought by many to be totally lacking in folklore, almost in direct proportion to the time that separates Americans from their own rural frontier.

Since early American folklorists saw the rural atmosphere as one that might harbor fading remnants of folklore, they made their way to the Appalachian Mountains and other remote spots in search of the treasures of olden times. In tune with the feeling of the countryside in which the materials were sought, the accompanying descriptions were markedly bucolic: Folklorists spoke of reaping rich harvests of lore, gleaning last remnants of song, plowing narrow fields of folklore, tracking elusive genres in the nooks and byways of the back country; one heard about small eddies of ethnic groups, song catching in the mountains, and, inevitably, the nurturing of a field considered ripe for the picking.

Even though these words are still used, modern American folklorists do not limit their attention to the rural, quaint, or "backward" elements of the culture. Rather, they will study and discuss any expressive phenomena—urban or rural—that seem to act like other previously recognized folk traditions. This has led to the development of a field of inquiry with few formal boundaries, one with lots of feel but little definition, one both engaging and frustrating.

The person who wishes to look into this expanding discipline will want to have more detailed guides and maps for the terrain. It will come as neither a surprise nor a satisfaction to find that more than one folklorist has defined the field as being made up of those things that folklorists care to talk about. One will need to know that there are particular battle-grounds, heroes, and monuments. There was the Ballad War, in which a whole generation of scholars fought over the question of communal origins versus individual composition for the traditional ballad (modern scholars are inclined to view that battle as unfortunate and even needless, yet out of it came a mature field of ballad scholarship that one must master in order to proceed into fruitful areas of new folk song research and speculation). There was the Solar Mythology School of Max Müller and others, which related nearly all mythic phenomena to sun, moon, and stars (the Reverend R. F. Littledale, using Müller's own theories, subsequently proved that Müller himself was a sun god). There was the myth-ritual theory urged by Lord Raglan, among others, which insisted that the heroes of myth and folklore could only have derived from ritual characters and not from historical people (this view had been under attack for years when Francis Lee Utley finally proved, using Raglan's list of attributes for the hero, that Abraham Lincoln got a perfect score and therefore was a ritual character who had never really lived). And there have been skirmishes over the widespread view that folklore is simply (1) pagan *detritus*, stuff left over from previous, barbaric times, passed along by ignorant and illiterate peasants who didn't know any better, or (2) degenerated material from once courtly sources. J. G. Frazer felt that folk remnants could tell us what culture was like in earlier days, that the study of today's primitives could show us what we had been like at that stage of development. Others busied themselves to collect bits of folklore before it should degenerate altogether and cease to exist. These views obviously reflect the European-American premise of linear movement of time and history, and they represent thus a cultural view of tradition rather than a critical observation of how tradition really operates.

Perhaps the most subtle battle in modern folklore is the constant attempt of scholars to reform the widespread journalistic use of the words *folklore* and *myth*. In the newspapers, and in the common understanding of many people, the terms have come to mean "misinformation" or "misconception," or "outmoded (and by implication, naively accepted where believed) ideas." The misunderstanding and misapplication of these terms seem to stem from a modern continuation of that notion referred to previously, that only backward or illiterate people have folklore; where it exists among us, by implication, it represents backward or naive thinking. As subsequent chapters will show, this use of *folklore* to imply mental deficit is simply not borne out by the facts. At least something we call folklore is found on all levels of society, and scholars are at some pains to account for its persistence and development.

These wars, the struggles over definition, and the seemingly dizzy variety of critical approaches may initially put off the person newly interested in folklore. They need not be the occasion for fear, however, if put in a proper perspective. The great wars are over, anyhow, largely because there is now a profession of folklorists who talk to each other (sharply, at times, to be sure) and share perspectives and approaches. There are universities in which folklore is taught as an advanced undergraduate and graduate discipline, and many of America's leading folklorists are former classmates.

We have not become immune to the well-educated, well-intentioned myopia suffered by Müller and Raglan, however, so it is all to the good that each era of folklore study has continued to have its mavericks, young upstarts who do not accept present boundaries of the field. While one generation of established scholars studies texts and artifacts, a new group arises to call attention to the folk themselves; then others come forward to insist that a focus on context or communication or performance or structure would do better justice to the subject. The Young Turks of one era in turn become the middle-aged professors who teach folklore courses in the university, only to deal with the mavericks in their own classes.

Some leading folklorists have described the current state of the discipline in terms of schools, acknowledging that, in spite of widespread agreement about the field in general, there are distinct and well-structured methods of scrutinizing materials. The full account of these schools given by Richard Dorson in *Folklore and Folklife: An Introduction* is obligatory reading for anyone starting out in folklore. A characterization of these schools by their focus may help show their real differences in critical stance.

The most prominent single approach is that which asks us to look at the *artifacts* of folklore: the text, the final product of the folk performance, whether it be made of words (a ballad, a tale, a proverb) or of physical materials (a quilt, a barn, a chimney) or of music (a fiddle tune) or of physical movements (a dance, a gesture) or of culture-based thought and behavior (popular belief, custom). As long as we note the broadened use of the term, we may call this the *text* orientation to folklore. Usually, texts are grouped into genres and scrutinized for their content, their structure, and their kinship with other texts. Comparative approaches such as the historical-geographical method (sometimes referred to as the Finnish School, it is really more of a critical stance than a methodology) are based on the concept that a study of text or artifact variation can reveal the real contours and principal features of the folk item. The focus is thus on the folk expression as an object, and the processes of its development are inferred from a study of the range of features changed or retained in those variant items considered to be versions of the same item. No doubt one reason for the strength and wide development of this view is that many early folklorists were trained in literature, where the text is always central.

A different stance, one long familiar to anthropologists and now championed by many folklorists, may be called—for lack of a better term—the *ethnological* orientation. Its main focus is the group of people that produces the lore and provides the live cultural matrix within which a text is made manifest and understandable. Here, the text or artifact is still important, of course, but the principal features scrutinized by the scholar are the dynamics of the group: what it is, how it functions, how it perpetuates itself, what its coordinates for reality are, what its systems (subgroups, clans, status levels, moieties, kinship patterns) may be, and how all these functional societal realities find expression in folklore. While the basic question for the textual approach might be, "What is the item like, and how does it act?" the main question for the ethnographic approach might be phrased, "How does a particular culture express itself and its values in traditional ways?"

Another more recent orientation seizes on *performance* as the primary grouping of phenomena to be studied. Here the individual performer or creator of traditional artifacts is viewed operating in—and for—an audience made up of the group of people whose tastes and responses condition—and occasion—the performance. The primary question here is, "Who is expressing what for whom—and when, how, and why?"

Still another scholarly preference is a leaning toward the explanation of how and why certain kinds of folklore continue to operate in any given instance. This orientation may be termed the *functional* approach. Why do certain elements of folklore come into being? Why do we continue to pass them on? Observing that traditions can hardly exist when they make no sense or fulfill no purpose at all, the functionalists seek to account for folklore's generation and survival by studying particular instances and applications of traditional expression and behavior.

Probably the most prominent approach to folklore in recent years has been the *contextual*, which addresses itself to the details of the immediate surroundings in which folklore takes place and out of which folklore may grow. One of the most basic areas of scrutiny here has been the psychological: the immediate personal, biological, and psychosocial drives and constraints felt by an individual as a tradition is practiced. Drawing especially upon the work of Freud and Jung, folklorists have sought to relate basic mental processes to the kinds of idea sets that foster traditional behavior and expression from culture to culture. Beyond the psychological bearings of the individual, many folklorists explore the immediate physical context in which an artifact or a folk expression is produced: the group of people who may be present, the weather, the occupational situation, or any other setting that may induce or modify traditional behaviors or performances. On still another level, contextualists are interested in geographical factors, the extent to which region may exert an influence on the maintenance or development of traditional expressions. Broader yet is the interest in historical context, the ways in which certain periods of humanity's experience may occasion the development or the dismemberment of folk tradition. (Historical and geographical concerns expressed as contextual interests should not be confused with the historical-geographical method mentioned in connection with the first area of focus, in which the artifact itself is the main focus.)

Contextual perspectives are demanded of all folklorists today; most of the major practicing scholars can be found centering their interests on any one or several of the areas of focus previously mentioned, but they all take contextual evidence into consideration as a standard obligation.

Perhaps it is this recognition of the unavoidable effects of context that sets modern folklore scholarship apart from that of the late 1800s and early 1900s. Certainly, the very best works of folklore criticism are combinations of all the previous interests; Alan Dundes's and Alessandro Falassi's *La Terra in Piazza* is a prime example of a multidisciplinary approach to a particular folk tradition, the running of the Palio horserace in Siena, Italy.

Of other possible areas of focus that have not become very well defined yet, perhaps the most important is that which might be called folk *aesthetics*, a concern with the aesthetic ideas of folk performers and their communities. To what extent does the exercise of a personal aesthetic (taste) play a role in the performance of any traditional song, or the production of a folk play, or the construction of a quilt or a barn? Scholars are likely to pay attention to the community standards for what a barn or a quilt should look like, but they have been relatively hesitant to take seriously the aesthetic reflections of the performers themselves. There are exciting exceptions to this, and they will be discussed further in Chapter 5. Michael Owen Jones has spent some years trying to enlist the interest of other folklorists in this important consideration, but in general his call has not been adequately answered.

It is common for newcomers to the subject of folklore to see these varying orientations as pedantic disputes among hypocritical sects of purists. Why make these distinctions? Do they really matter? Is this not merely academic posing? But in fact these are empty objections: One needs in any field to determine what one is studying, and to outline at least in general those approaches to the subject that have been considered fruitful by those who have spent a considerable amount of time trying to understand the materials. One does not study medieval literature without first determining whether the literature in question is in fact medieval; one does not try to discuss poetry without first determining that the items under consideration are poems; one does not presume to discuss classical music without first determining the composer and date; and one may as well not begin talking about folklore unless there is the willingness to help establish what the ingredients of the field are, what the processes seem to be, and what the nature of the discussion should be. It is not purism but utility that leads to the discussion of what folklore is and what the focal areas are through which it may be examined. Liking the subject is only a prelude to talking about it. The old "heart-throb" school of literary criticism is gone (forever, one hopes), and we may similarly pray that the essentially elitist heart-throb school of folklore is gone forever; one does not study folklore by simply clutching a guitar and sighing, but by coming to grips with serious and difficult matters related to human expression and cultural dynamics.

It should be apparent by now that folklore is not a static field of inquiry. Not only are its approaches and methods subject to change as we sharpen our perceptions (as is true in any active inquiry), but the very content of the subject expands as our study shows us new kinships and forms. Other areas, such as medieval literature, have continually developed new approaches, but the materials studied have remained pretty much the same over the years. In folklore, by contrast, where a hundred years ago we were studying mainly tales, songs, and beliefs, we now include barns, quilts, chain letters, proxemics, games, and many other materials. The multiplicity of folklore genres and the diversity of critical approaches to them make for an extremely exciting field of study; they also inhibit the writing of textbooks on folklore, for one expert's favorite line of reasoning may be of only minimal use in the classroom of another. Yet it does seem to me that all these approaches are, or could be, complementary and that no single one needs to be championed as "the way" for which a given textbook must provide exclusive maps and charts.

This book is founded on the simple assumption that there must be some element all folklore has in common (else we could not lump it all together). No doubt an astute student could name several possible unifying characteristics, but I have chosen one: All folklore participates in a distinctive, dynamic process. Constant change, variation within a tradition, whether intentional or inadvertent, is viewed here simply as a central fact of life for folklore, and rather than presenting it in opposed terms of conscious artistic manipulation or forgetfulness, I have sought to accept it as a defining feature that grows out of context, performance, attitude, cultural tastes, and the like.

The various leading theories of folklore will be mentioned or implied in the text and will be noted in the bibliographical sections at the end of each chapter. The student should turn to these works for sound theoretical accounts of various particular problems in folklore; the present book, on the other hand, will provide examples of the dynamism in folklore, leaving readers (and teachers) free to follow particular theoretical interests on their own. To put it another way, the interdisciplinary nature of folklore, its professors, courses, majors, and orientations, calls for a book to describe the folklore without defining it so narrowly as to inhibit or denigrate particular theoretical interests.

Accordingly, this book will be highly anecdotal and suggestive, for it aims to help shape perspectives and to introduce the dynamics in a broad field. Examples come from my own field work, from collections done by my students, from friends, from fellow folklorists. Some of my examples, such as the urban legend of the girl with a bouffant hairdo who is found to have a nest of black widow spiders in her coiffure, may be as dated as the bouffant hairdo itself; others, like the "death car" for sale cheap in a local used car lot, may drift through our experience every couple of years. Both are examples of the continuing viability of folklore *and* its change-ability. The instructor and student will want to augment the examples given with their own repertoires of folklore. In any case, the book does not rest on antiquarian interests but on viability. If you haven't heard these urban legends, which ones have you heard?

Further, the anecdotal approach is founded in an intellectual view of education that I have come to share with a former colleague, Kenneth E. Eble, who made a survey of university teaching and came to the conclusion that the lecture is the least efficient way to pass on information to others. What the lecture can do is to excite, even inspire, and it can provide reasons, questions, approaches, and commitment to the subject (or, sadly, it can produce the reverse of all these). Information as such needs to be reflected upon and studied, and books are better for this purpose than lectures. I am convinced introductory textbooks are akin to lectures: The textbook (along with the lecture) should excite the student and provide reasons for reflection and study. The actual study should be carried out by the student in the usual tedious ways of scholarship, where the problem or the theory is worth constructing and coping with precisely because it relates to an exciting and important set of issues. Scholarship is pure drudgery only when it is empty of purpose. One aim of this book is to help provide some purposes.

I have wanted to avoid embarrassment for anyone whose folklore, originally delivered in its usual "home" context, is quoted here as vivid example. Some names are thus withheld or changed by request to insure privacy and to avoid making individuals into objects of scrutiny; this is especially a concern with Native American materials, particularly in those tribes where an individual may be perfectly willing to give his or her own opinion but cannot speak for the entire tribe. In addition, many of our Native American friends have been shocked at the way in which we so glibly throw their names around in our classes: Said a young Navajo woman at a recent meeting of scholars interested in working with American Indian narratives, "You people get *paid* to study us and to put our names in your books." I have made certain that the materials from Native

American backgrounds I have referred to here are acceptable for public scrutiny; at the same time, some of the performers do not wish to have their names brought forward as sources.

The reader hitherto unfamiliar with folklore must realize that many of the materials circulating in oral tradition among members of close groups might easily fall into the category of crude or obscene if they were quoted in a textbook. Some scholars even estimate that some 80 percent of orally transmitted material would be thought crude by someone if it were encountered out of context, especially on a printed page. Because the central interest of folklorists today is to deal with folklore as it actually is, I have made no attempt to expurgate the texts referred to here; rather, I have omitted some materials rather than change their essential nature by "cleaning them up."

This is not to champion "obscene" materials per se, but to point out that all folklore is phrased in terms appropriate to—and usually demanded by—the group in which it is performed. Often these particular manners of expression are registered as inappropriate when they are heard by outsiders, when they are presented out of their normal context, when their audience is expanded beyond the usual local group for which and in which the performance makes sense. For these reasons, the reader is urged to go beyond the antiseptic environment of the textbook page, beyond the restrictions of local views on propriety, and take a close look at the real folklore of real people for what it truly is. I hope this book will provide some helpful considerations for that quest.

# BIBLIOGRAPHICAL NOTES

The bibliographical supplements to the chapters in this book are meant to be selective, suggestive, and conversational, not exhaustive. The works cited are in many instances the sources or instigations for concepts advanced in the book; others are exemplary or typical of parallel or even contrasting ideas. Some will be repeated because of their application to different chapters. Most references to articles in periodicals are to work that has appeared since 1960, although there will be numerous exceptions to this rule where certain articles on particular subjects are too germane to omit.

I assume that the interested reader, and especially the beginning student of folklore, will become acquainted with some of the standard works in the field, chief among them the following: Stith Thompson, ed., *Motif-Index of Folk Literature* (Bloomington: Indiana University Press, 1955–1958), for the basic compendium of recurrent units in orally transmitted folklore; Antti Aarne and Stith Thompson, eds., *The Types of the Folktale*, 2nd rev., *Folklore Fellows*

*Communications*, no. 184 (1961), for the standard listing of recurrent narrative clusters in tale form; Maria Leach, ed., *Funk & Wagnalls Standard Dictionary of Folklore, Mythology, and Legend* (New York: Funk & Wagnalls, 1949), for a somewhat dated but encyclopedic view of folklore and its ingredients written by numerous folklorists of the day; Jan Harold Brunvand, *The Study of American Folklore: An Introduction*, rev. ed. (New York: Norton, 1978), for clear and brief delineations of the generic categories in folklore; Alan Dundes, ed., *The Study of Folklore* (Englewood Cliffs, N.J.: Prentice-Hall, 1965), for an anthology of important essays on folklore by a wide variety of scholars; and Richard M. Dorson, ed., *Folklore and Folklife: An Introduction* (Chicago: University of Chicago Press, 1972), for a modern invited symposium of professional folklorists on principal areas of interest to the serious student.

While this book will cite primarily the leading professional folklore journals, the reader, along with other serious folklorists, should make it a matter of obligation to follow up particular interests in other reputable anthropologically oriented publications as well as to check the smaller but important regional folklore journals and professional journals in geography, psychology, literature, linguistics, dialects, natural history, and history. Each of these latter fields, of course, has its own professional interests and demands, and it is well to remember that scholars in these areas do not always use the word (or the concept) *folklore* in the way professional folklorists might prefer. Thus, while the student should not hesitate to look into the recent journals and the contemporary standard texts of these fields for specific considerations on approach, theory, analytical models, and vocabulary, a good previous foundation in current folklore theory will be necessary to prevent disorientation and indigestion. Wherever possible, this book will call attention to some of the more helpful nonfolkloristic resources, and it will attempt to flag the topics on which specialists in the various fields may differ in their understanding (the concept of folk art, which will come up numerous times herein, is an example).

Richard M. Dorson, in *The British Folklorists: A History* (Chicago: University of Chicago Press, 1968) and in *Peasant Customs and Savage Myths: Selections from the British Folklorists*, 2 vols. (Chicago: University of Chicago Press, 1968), provides the most complete, and certainly the most readable, account of the exciting developments among English scholars during the emergence of the field we now call Folklore. Much of the theoretical orientation of modern British and American folklore scholarship has its origins in the arguments and discussions recorded in these books. Professor Dorson is well known internationally, not only for his historical perspectives in folklore study, but for his keen interest in the history of the field itself. For a comparison between the Anglo-American orientation in folklore and that found commonly in Latin America, see Américo Paredes, "Concepts about Folklore in Latin America and the United States," *Journal of the Folklore Institute*, 6 (1969), 20–38; also, note that since its inception *JFI* has provided a continuing account of folklore concepts and work in progress in a variety of countries.

*Historical:* Among Dorson's many works that deal with history and folklore, a good, brief sample would be "The Debate over the Trustworthiness of Oral Traditional History," in *Volksüberlieferung: Festschrift für Kurt Ranke zur Vollendung des 60. Lebensjahre* (Göttingen: O. Schwartz, 1968), 19–35.

*Anthropological:* An organic view of all connotative literature as folklore is given in an anthropological frame by Munro S. Edmonson in *Lore: An Introduction to the Science of Folklore and Literature* (New York: Holt, Rinehart and Winston, 1971); while very provocative, it pays little heed to the oral/nonoral distinction so basic to much of modern folklore theory.

*Literary:* Probably the classic work is Stith Thompson, *The Folktale* (1946; reprint ed., Berkeley: University of California Press, 1977); in it, the tale is discussed as a distinct literary genre that has been shaped by the processes of traditional transmission.

*Psychological:* Both Freud and Jung were extremely interested in folklore and mythology, although their theories have been beaten "to airy thinness" by their avid students. Freud believed that dreams are the less-developed materials of folklore, jokes, proverbs, and myths (see, among many others, Sigmund Freud, *The Interpretation of Dreams*, trans. A. M. O. Richards [New York: International Universities Press, 1958], and *Jokes and Their Relation to the Unconscious*, trans. James Strachey [London: Routledge and Paul, 1960]). Jung felt that the recurrent patternings in myth and folklore indicated an inherited fund of potential images shared by human beings generally, although he was more disposed than his disciples have been to the idea that local manifestations of these images might vary considerably. A helpful article is Carlos C. Drake, "Jungian Psychology and Its Uses in Folklore," *Journal of American Folklore*, 82 (1969), 122–131. Joseph Campbell, once almost exclusively a Jungian, has more recently combined Jung's theories with the resources of anthropology, archaeology, history, botany, and literature in his impressive four-volume work *The Masks of God: Primitive Mythology, Oriental Mythology, Occidental Mythology,* and *Creative Mythology* (New York: Viking Press, 1959–1968); although the examples he cites are partial to his particular viewpoint, the work, especially Volume I, is an exciting tour de force.

*Artistic and art-historical:* This is one of the unfortunate areas wherein trained experts in art and museology differ markedly from experts in folklore on the subject of folk art. For the former, it is usually seen as naive or untrained art, or as whatever is left over after one has exhausted the fine arts. Primitive art—that is, art produced by nontechnological peoples—is often given serious notice, as in Paul S. Wingert, *Primitive Art, Its Traditions and Styles* (New York: Oxford University Press, 1962), and in Ralph Linton, "Primitive Art," *Kenyon Review*, 3 (1941), 34–51; reprinted in *Every Man His Way: Readings in Cultural Anthropology*, ed. Alan Dundes (Englewood Cliffs, N.J.: Prentice-Hall, 1968), pp. 352–364. But folk art that lies outside the primitive category, while taken seriously by folklorists, occupies the stereotyped role of "quaint and folksy" among art historians. Munro Thomas, in *Evolution in the Arts*

(Cleveland: Cleveland Museum of Art, 1932), pp. 361–462, gives it fair but minuscule mention, while one of the standard art history textbooks, H. W. Janson's *History of Art: A Survey of Major Visual Arts from the Dawn of History to the Present Day* (Englewood Cliffs, N.J.: Prentice-Hall, 1962)—in spite of its omniscient-sounding title—overlooks folk arts altogether. One of the most informative pieces on folk art is the chapter so titled by Henry Glassie in Dorson, *Folklore and Folklife*, pp. 253–280.

*Language and Linguistics:* Of those whose work has aligned language study with the processes of tradition, the most prominent have been anthropologists seeking to understand better the relationship between culture and meaning. One should consult at least the following items. Dell H. Hymes, "The Contribution of Folklore to Sociolinguistic Research," *Journal of American Folklore,* 84 (1971), 42–50, as well as Dell H. Hymes, ed., *Language in Culture and Society: A Reader in Linguistics and Anthropology* (New York: Harper & Row, 1964), are samples of work by a dedicated and continually developing scholar in the field. One should review, as well, the work of Benjamin Lee Whorf, for example, his *Language, Thought and Reality* (Cambridge, Mass.: MIT Press, 1956); Harry Hoijer, ed., *Language in Culture* (Chicago: University of Chicago Press, 1954); John J. Gumperz and Dell H. Hymes, eds., *The Ethnography of Communication,* American Anthropological Association Special Publications, vol. 66 (Menasha, Wis.: American Anthropological Association, 1964); and, for a broader modern look at the whole live process of language, Peter Farb, *Word Play: What Happens When People Talk* (1974; reprint ed., New York: Bantam, 1975).

The antiquarians are often glibly dismissed for not knowing as much as we do today (may the charity of later generations be more generous when it comes to the scrutiny of present truths), but they and their works make some of the most fascinating reading in all folklore. The newcomer to folklore must be warned that an entry into John Brand's *Observations on Popular Antiquities: Chiefly Illustrating the Origin of Our Vulgar Customs, Ceremonies, and Superstitions,* 2 vols., arr. and rev. Henry Ellis (London: R. C. and J. Rivington, 1813), is an overwhelming and fascinating detour from which people seldom recover. Brand and other students of antique times were erudite and serious scholars, mostly, and were often the masters of several languages. They were among the central thinkers of their day, and they overlooked little in their searches through notebooks, country customs, and church and town records to find elements of thought and action that had flourished before the coming of Christianity. Brand lamented the way in which the Puritans and their successors had tried to obliterate the older customs (obviously his use of *vulgar* means "of the common people," and does not include the modern inference that *common* means "lowly"). Other representative antiquarians, often identifiable by the titles of their works, were Sabine Baring-Gould, *Curious Myths of the Middle Ages* (London: Rivingtons, 1866), among numerous works on songs and fairy tales; Henry Bourne, *Antiquitates Vulgares* (Newcastle: J. White, 1725);

Allen Cunningham, *Songs: Chiefly in the Rural Language of Scotland* (London: Smith and Davy, 1813) and *Traditional Tales of the English and Scottish Peasantry* (London: Taylor and Hessey, 1822); Francis Grose, *The Antiquities of England and Wales*, 6 vols. (London: S. Hooper, 1773–1787); Alfred Nutt, *Celtic and Mediaeval Romance* (London: D. Nutt, 1899); Thomas Percy, *Reliques of Ancient English Poetry*, 3 vols. (London: J. Dodsley, 1765); Walter Scott, *The Border Antiquities of England and Scotland*, 2 vols. (London: Longmann, Hurst, Rees, Orme, and Browne, 1814–1817); Thomas F. Thiselton-Dyer, *British Popular Customs* (London: G. Bells and Sons, 1871); William J. Thoms, *Anecdotes and Traditions* (London: Printed for the Camden Society by J. B. Nichols and Son, 1839); Edward B. Tylor, *Primitive Culture*, 2 vols. (London: J. Murray, 1871). Dorson gives a very full and fair account of them in *The British Folklorists*, mentioned earlier; more recently, Francis A. De Caro has related the antiquaries to our whole conception of how the field of folkloristics has developed in "Concepts of the Past in Folkloristics," *Western Folklore*, 35 (1976), 3–22.

No doubt the best-known German scholars of the early period were Wilhelm Mannhardt, whose *Germanische Mythen* (Berlin: F. Schneider, 1858) became the resource for many subsequent conjectural studies on the origins of medieval European symbols, and Jakob and Wilhelm Grimm, whose collection of *Kinder- und Hausmärchen*, 2 vols. (Berlin: Realschulbuchhandlung, 1812–1815), undertaken in part through their interest in the processes of language features, has been basic to all subsequent studies of European tales (and has made the name Grimm a household word throughout much of the world). Subsequently Johannes Bolte and George Polívka, in their monumental *Anmerkungen zu den Kinder- und Hausmärchen der Brüder Grimm*, 5 vols. (Leipzig: Dieterich'sche Verlagsbuchhandlung, 1913–1932), provided linguistic and cultural notes and explanations for the Grimms's collection, which made the materials even more rich and useful for folkloristic examination.

Alexander Haggerty Krappe, *The Science of Folklore* (1930; reprint ed., New York: Norton, 1964) shows the influence of the European scholarly-antiquarian stance at the turn of the century. Krappe, an American, was sure that folklore was essentially rural and antique, and it followed that progressive America would not provide much for the scholar. Statements like: "In every modern country the rural populations are still addicted to beliefs and practices long since given up by the bulk of the city people" (p. xvii) and "In the city proper, as is well known, the typical proletarian is the most traditionless creature imaginable" (p. xviii) give a typical picture of the state of mind of the well-educated scholar interested in folklore before the professional folklore explosion of the 1950s and 1960s. Even lately, some folklorists have felt the need to explain the importance of folklore in terms of what it could teach us about "high culture": see, for example, Francis Lee Utley, "Oral Genres as Bridge to Written Literature," in *Genre*, 2 (1969), 91–103, reprinted in *Folklore Genres*, ed. Dan Ben-Amos (Austin: University of Texas Press, 1976); the paper is of solid pedagogical value, for often students can see their own relationships to literature through comparison with traditions they already take part in, but most folklorists today feel that folklore need not be rationalized as a field whose primary function is to acquaint us more fully with elite culture.

The ballad wars cannot be quickly summed up, for they range from petty differences to substantial and creative scholarly arguments. The best single account is still D. K. Wilgus, *Anglo-American Folksong Scholarship since 1898* (New Brunswick, N.J.: Rutgers University Press, 1959), esp. chs. 1, 2. One should also consult Sigurd Bernhard Hustvedt, *Ballad Books and Ballad Men* (Cambridge, Mass.: Harvard University Press, 1930)—an unfortunate title, since one of the principal belligerents of the fray was Louise Pound, with her *Poetic Origins and the Ballad* (New York: Macmillan, 1921); Francis B. Gummere, another combatant, wrote *The Beginnings of Poetry* (New York: Macmillan, 1901), *The Popular Ballad* (Boston: Houghton Mifflin, 1907), and *Democracy and Poetry* (Boston: Houghton Mifflin, 1911); George Lyman Kittredge, a student of Francis James Child (the first principal American ballad anthologist and scholar) wrote an essay, "The Popular Ballad," in *Atlantic Monthly*, 101 (1908), 276 ff., and collaborated with Helen C. Sargent in the introduction to a one-volume abridgment of Child's great work, *The English and Scottish Popular Ballads* (Boston: Houghton Mifflin, 1882–1898). Although the flaming commitment to ballad studies characteristic of the old war seems to have waned, there are continuing attempts to assess and study this particular form of folk expression. Of several obligatory works, students should certainly consult Tristram P. Coffin, *The British Traditional Ballad in North America*, rev. ed. Roger deV. Renwick (Austin: University of Texas Press, 1977); David Buchan, *The Ballad and the Folk* (London: Routledge & Kegan Paul, 1972); Albert Friedman, *The Viking Book of Folk Ballads of the English Speaking World* (New York: Viking, 1956). Each of these will provide references to other important works in the field.

Some of Max Müller's theories are put forward in *Chips from a German Workshop*, 4 vols. (London: Longmans, Green, 1867–1875), *Natural Religion: The Gifford Lectures Delivered Before the University of Glasgow in 1888* (London: Longmans, Green, 1889), *Anthropological Religion* (London: Longmans, Green, 1892), and *Contributions to the Science of Mythology*, 2 vols. (London: Longmans, Green, 1887)—among many others. Reverend Littledales's refutation appeared in "The Oxford Solar Myth: A Contribution to Comparative Mythology," in *Echoes from Kottabos*, ed. R. Y. Tyrell and Sir Edward Sullivan (London: E. Grant Richards, 1906), 279–290. Richard Dorson gives a full account of the controversy in "The Eclipse of Solar Mythology," *Journal of American Folklore*, 68 (1955), 393–416, reprinted in Dundes, *The Study of Folklore*, pp. 57–83.

Raglan's statement on the hero is found in its fullest form in *The Hero: A Study in Tradition, Myth and Drama* (London: Methuen, 1936). Utley's witty and embarrassingly thorough rejoinder is *Lincoln Wasn't There, or, Lord*

*Raglan's Hero*, College English Association Chapbook (Washington, D.C.: College English Association, 1965). James G. Frazer, *The Golden Bough*, 3rd ed., 12 vols. (London: Macmillan, 1907–1915), is both a delight and a frustration; while the examples in it and the theories suggested are illuminating and thought provoking, the instances of folk custom outside Europe are often derived from the accounts of missionaries and other well-meaning tourists who had no professional training in how to observe people of other cultures with impartiality or clarity of vision. See Theodor H. Gaster's enviable abridgment of the work that gives modern evaluations of Frazer's theory and method: *The New Golden Bough* (New York: Criterion Books, 1959). George Laurence Gomme, in *Ethnology in Folklore* (London, K. Paul, Trench, Trübner, 1892), argued against the simple notion that folklore was made up of survivals from particular levels of human existence that could tell us, like tree rings do today, what things were like when our culture was at a particular stage. Gomme argued that much folklore in England was pre-Aryan, and had been retained and maintained precisely because of the pressure from newly arrived, intrusive, but stable "higher" civilizations. In this, he anticipated the modern notion that folklore is partly a function of internal group dynamics, of "esoteric" response, not to be easily explained only as leftovers from the past. The idea that folklore is always breaking down is discussed by Alan Dundes in "The Devolutionary Premise in Folklore Theory," *Journal of the Folklore Institute*, 6 (1969), 5–19; that it has had such a central role in folkloristics is challenged by Elliott Oring in "The Devolutionary Premise: A Definitional Delusion?" *Western Folklore*, 34 (1975), 36–44, and by William A. Wilson in "The Evolutionary Premise in Folklore and the 'Finnish Method,'" *Western Folklore*, 35 (1976), 241–249. A compelling and unstuffy account of the post-Dorson mavericks in folklore is given by Roger D. Abrahams in "Alan Dundes and the State of Our Discipline," *Folklore Forum*, 10:1 (Spring 1977), 31–34.

The standard single work on the "Finnish Method" is Kaarle Krohn, *Die folkloristische Arbeitsmethode* (Cambridge, Mass.: Harvard University Press, 1926); trans. Roger Welsch as *Folklore Methodology* (Austin: University of Texas Press, 1971). Typical examples of full attempts to study the variations in a particular folklore item are: Paul G. Brewster, "Some Notes on the Guessing Game, How Many Horns Has the Buck?" *Bealoideas: Journal of the Folklore of Ireland Society*, 12 (1942), 40–78, reprinted in Dundes, *The Study of Folklore*, pp. 338–368; Bertrand H. Bronson, *The Traditional Tunes of the Child Ballads*, 4 vols. (Princeton, N.J.: Princeton University Press, 1959–1972); Henry Glassie, "The Types of the Southern Mountain Cabin," Appendix C in Brunvand, *The Study of American Folklore*, pp. 338–370; Holger O. Nygard, *The Ballad of "Heer Halewijn," Its Forms and Variations in Western Europe: A Study of the History and Nature of a Ballad Tradition*, Folklore Fellows Communications no. 169 (Helsinki, 1958); Stith Thompson, "The Star Husband Tale," *Studia Septentrionalia*, 4 (1953), 93–163, reprinted in Dundes, *The Study of Folklore*, pp. 414–474. In his presidential address to the American Folklore Society, D. K. Wilgus made a special plea for the centrality of textual concern: see " 'The Text is the Thing,' " *Journal of American Folklore*, 86 (1973), 241–252.

The ethnological approach is used by far too many scholars to allow for a fair representation here. The following put forth the premise that traditional items in a culture cannot be studied except with direct reference to the cultural context from which they spring: Ruth Benedict, *Patterns of Culture* (Boston: Houghton Mifflin, 1934), and Bronislaw Malinowski, *Argonauts of the Western Pacific* (New York: E. P. Dutton, 1922), are classic. More recent studies by Clifford Geertz, such as "Ethos, World-view and the Analysis of Sacred Symbols," *The Antioch Review*, 17 (1957), 421–437, and *The Religion of Java* (Glencoe, Ill.: Free Press, 1960) show the continuing application of this culturally holistic approach. For a collection of essays by various specialists of this orientation, see Alan Dundes, ed., *Every Man His Way: Readings in Cultural Anthropology* (Englewood Cliffs, N.J.: Prentice-Hall, 1968).

Many folklorists are now focusing on performance and performance styles. For some solid perspectives see Roger D. Abrahams, *Deep Down in the Jungle: Negro Narrative Folklore from the Streets of Philadelphia*, rev. ed. (Chicago: Aldine, 1970), and its companion, *Positively Black* (Englewood Cliffs, N.J.: Prentice-Hall, 1970), in which Black toasts and dozens are discussed as performances (rather than as "texts"), and in which the whole dynamic of urban Black life, including economics and politics, is seen in terms of performance modes. For a more general statement on the subject, consult Richard Bauman, "Verbal Art as Performance," *American Anthropologist*, 77 (1975), 290–311. Michael Owen Jones makes it clear in *The Hand Made Object and Its Maker* (Berkeley: University of California Press, 1975) that the idea of performance is not to be limited to songs and stories, but must be extended to cover all kinds of expressive activities—including the production of material items—done for others.

One of the best-known essays on function in folklore is William R. Bascom, "Four Functions of Folklore," *Journal of American Folklore*, 67 (1954), 333–349, reprinted in Dundes, *The Study of Folklore*, pp. 279–298. A very brief and tightly focused study of function in a particular genre is provided by Bess Lomax Hawes, "Folksongs and Function: Some Thoughts on the American Lullaby," *Journal of American Folklore*, 87 (1974), 140–148. Elliott Oring takes up the nature of functional discussion in "Three Functions of Folklore: Traditional Functionalism as Explanation in Folkloristics," *Journal of American Folklore*, 89 (1976), 67–80.

As it will become clear from the rest of this book, context is one of the most important single considerations in folklore study today. Two clear statements on this are obligatory reading: Alan Dundes, "Texture, Text, and Context," *Southern Folklore Quarterly*, 28 (1964), 251–265; Dan Ben-Amos, "Toward a

Definition of Folklore in Context," *Journal of American Folklore*, 84 (1971), 5–15, reprinted in *Toward New Perspectives in Folklore*, ed. Américo Paredes and Richard Bauman (Austin: University of Texas Press, 1972), pp. 3–15.

An overview of the relationships between psychology and folklore is given in Ernest Jones, "Psychoanalysis and Folklore," *Jubilee Congress of the Folklore Society: Papers and Transactions* (London: The Folklore Society, 1930), pp. 220–237, reprinted in Dundes, *The Study of Folklore*, pp. 88–102. Roger D. Abrahams and Alan Dundes make a convincing statement on the aggressive function of elephant jokes, derived from contexts of ethnic tensions, in "On Elephantasy and Elephanticide," *The Psychoanalytic Review*, 56 (1969), 225–241; reprinted in Alan Dundes, *Analytic Essays in Folklore* (The Hague: Mouton, 1975), pp. 192–205. Dundes gives illuminating and helpful commentaries on psychological approaches to folklore in the notes to various essays in his *Study of Folklore*; see esp. pp. 88–89, 107–108, and 110. There Dundes provides both solid and ludicrous essays on the subject. Michael Owen Jones takes up both the psychological and immediate personal context in *The Hand Made Object and Its Maker*; Kay Cothran discusses the effect of immediate personal context (male narrator, female interviewer, wife of narrator sitting nearby) on anecdotal performance in "Talking Trash in the Okefenokee Swamp Rim, Georgia," *Journal of American Folklore*, 87 (1974), 340–356. For an excellent discussion of the effects of region on people and their folklore, see Suzi Jones, "Regionalization: A Rhetorical Strategy," *Journal of the Folklore Institute*, 13 (1976), 105–120. The dynamic relations among nature, geography, setting, and culture are brilliantly discussed by Yi Fu Tuan in *Topophilia* (Englewood Cliffs, N.J.: Prentice-Hall, 1974). The historical context of folklore is of course the foundation of Richard Dorson's standard, *American Folklore* (Chicago: University of Chicago Press, 1959). The early chapters of Lewis Mumford, *The City in History: Its Origins, Its Transformations, and Its Prospects* (New York: Harcourt, Brace and World, 1961) delineate a combination of geographical, historical, mythic, and folkloric forces that interplayed as a context for the earliest villages and towns; see esp. pp. 5–35.

Although heavily weighted toward psychological interests, Alan Dundes and Alessandro Falassi, *La Terra in Piazza* (Berkeley: University of California Press, 1975), is a model for modern folklore study, for it attempts to take all contextual features into consideration, ranging from the personal and psychological to the geographical, political, historical, and cultural (including the cultural-psychological).

Aesthetics in folklore will be taken up somewhat more fully in Chapter 5. For a central statement on the subject see Michael Owen Jones, "The Concept of 'Aesthetic' in the Traditional Arts," *Western Folklore*, 30 (1971), 77–104.

Anyone interested in teaching (either the doing of it or the receiving of it) should read Kenneth E. Eble, *The Craft of Teaching* (San Francisco: Jossey-Bass, 1976), especially Chapter 5, "The Lecture as Discourse."

Although "obscenity" is only one aspect of response to folklore out of its usual habitat, it is a matter the student should try to settle accounts with early. The *Journal of American Folklore* dedicated an entire issue to the subject (vol. 75, no. 297 [July–September 1962]). One might also consult G. Legman, *No Laughing Matter: Rationale of the Dirty Joke*, 2nd series (New York: Breaking Point, 1975); Vance Randolph, *Pissing in the Snow and Other Ozark Folktales*, ed. Rayna Green and Frank Hoffman (Urbana, Ill.: University of Illinois Press, 1976); Ed Cray, ed., *The Erotic Muse* (New York: Oak Publications, 1968).

# 1
## THE
## FOLKLORE
# PROCESS

**FOLKLORE COMES EARLY AND STAYS LATE IN THE LIVES OF ALL OF US. IN SPITE OF THE COMBINED FORCES OF TECHNOLOGY, SCIENCE, TELEVISION, RELIGION,** urbanization, and creeping literacy, we prefer our close personal associations as the basis for learning about life and transmitting important observations and expressions. From the childhood rhythms of "Patty Cake" to the joy of humorous graces ("Good bread, good meat, good God, let's eat") to the imagined sophistication of drinking games ("Cardinal Puff," "Fuzz-Buzz"); from courtship protocol to showers to wedding customs ("But you *can't* wear a red dress, dear; it's not *right!*") to birth cigars; from birthday spanks to hacks; from tree house clubs to stag and hen parties; from the Tooth Fairy to the Birthday Girl to Santa Claus; from Black dozens to Native American "forty-nine" songs to *curanderismo*; from Valentine's candy to Easter eggs to firecrackers to pumpkins to turkey to fruitcake to Tom-and-Jerries; from riddles to barroom jokes to epitaphs, death, and burial customs to placing flowers on a grave; from wart cures to waiting twenty minutes for a full professor; from cement-filled Cadillacs and girls with spiders in their hair to miraculous carburetors (kept off the market by the auto industry) and death cars for sale (cheap); from the pink and blue of the nursery through the white of the wedding to the black of the funeral, we continue to wend our traditional way through life.

To the surprise of those who thought (and perhaps hoped) that folklore was a part of the disappearing rural scene, city children seem to have more children's folklore than rural children do. The offspring of educated parents often are found to be more avid carriers of popular belief ("superstition") than others. Folklore is not dying out, nor is it to be found only in the Ozarks or among loggers. One ballad may go out of oral existence over here, but at the same time a hundred ethnic jokes spring up over there.

# ✍ THE EDUCATIVE MATRIX Clearly, folklore
is alive and well. It constitutes a basic and important educative and expressive setting in which individuals learn how to see, act, respond, and express themselves by the empirical observation of close human interactions and expressions in their immediate society (that is, the family, occupational group, ethnic community). Folklore structures the world view through which a person is educated into the language and logic system of this close society. It provides ready formulas for the expression of those cultural ideas in ways useful and pleasurable to us and to any group with which we share close and informal expressive interactions.

FOLK LANGUAGE AND LOGIC  Very early in life, long before we have come under the well-intentioned influence of professional teachers, we have learned the basic structure and meaning of an entire language. Past this point we refine it and add to its vocabulary. Before we are four years old, using rules we know mostly by inference, we create new sentences we have never before heard, continually guided by the recognition and responses of those around us whose very speech we have used as the pattern for our own learning. If we say something they do not understand, we try again or in another way. If we say something they like very much we are likely to keep it "on file" for further pleasurable use (we sometimes retain baby talk when encouraged by the laughter of our doting parents). We do not need language instruction, and except in those settings where the passing of grammar quizzes has become an important activity, we do not require any further training in the grammar we already know how to use. Language is a traditional frame for learning, a basis for human interaction, a form of practical or pleasurable expression, and a way of structuring and placing meaning on the myriad experiences coming at us from our world.

In addition to spoken language, we use gesture, facial expression, body position, tone of voice, proximity to others, and a large and complex vocabulary of options that tell us not only what to say on certain occasions but when not to say anything, or when it is necessary to change the "dialect" to something more appropriate (such as when Great Aunt Martha enters the room while we are telling a traveling salesman joke).

As we mature, we are taught several more formal or technical languages as the need arises. In addition to the gestures we have picked up by observation (for example, shrugging the shoulders in some cultures means "I don't know"), we also must learn a number of arbitrary and formal gestures (such as those we must know if we are to become ballet dancers, baseball umpires, opera singers, traffic police officers, basketball referees, or teachers of sign language to the deaf). The informal gestures learned from those close about are always open to continual modification according to their use and context at a particular moment, but the more formal gestures are less open to change, for they are parts of a language "dialect" used in dealing with outsiders. We use different words and gestures in a joke than in a graduation speech; we speak to friends in slang, but write for strangers in standard English. Deaf people who communicate by signing also have a vivid vocabulary of gestural slang learned from each other, not from instruction books.

FOLK LEARNING   In Western cultures children usually learn music harmony the same way they learn their early language: They pick it up. They come to know how to harmonize even though they cannot enunciate the technical rules in musicians' terms. Some never learn and are encouraged to keep quiet. But how does someone learn to harmonize? And why do we learn? And why is it pleasant for us to harmonize with others when they are singing? These questions make us consider what people learn in a close society, how they come to learn it, why, and from whom. The study of folklore leads us to recognize that there may be one kind of harmony in one culture, another kind in another culture, and none at all in still another. In fact, all forms of culture-based expression are likely to vary from one human communicative network to another. Most people growing up in a given culture will learn to harmonize, so to speak, on all levels of human interaction, and they will not require an anthropology text or a music teacher in order to do so. What is appropriate in the local tradition at the moment will determine the nature of the folk expression, and since the expression is thus culturally meaningful, we can say that doing it is a kind of performance for a discerning, close audience.

LEARNING STYLES AND CLUSTERS   In many cultures telling jokes is a prominent informal occurrence. We will return to it in another chapter, because joke telling represents a most important medium of learning and expression. At this point it is enough to use joke telling simply as a means of discovering some bases of our own expertise in folklore.

Anyone who has listened to jokes and has later told them knows that, generally speaking, we need to hear a joke only once in order to learn it. We do not memorize jokes verbatim, nor do we take lecture notes on them. In fact, if someone tells a joke as if it has been memorized word for word, it is often received badly. When we tell a joke, we are reshaping and recomposing clusters of ideas that we have heard expressed in a similar context at another time.

A learning process has taken place, and it is now followed by an expressive event, a performance, but only if we judge the context to be right. If the setting is appropriate, and if the joke performance is well done, the joke teller will be reinforced by noticing the pleasure of his companions. At this point, the joke telling has become another educative experience, and the joke has solidified itself into a cluster of potential ingredients in the mind of the teller; but no matter how many times the same person tells the same joke, it will almost never be performed exactly the same twice, for a dynamic process (depending on context, mood, intonation, and reason for telling) will be set in motion as that first event is continually reshaped, rephrased, and re-experienced in the mind and actions of the performer. Moreover, the performer will try to work always within that set of expectations that will be shared by the audience of the joke. All of these factors work simultaneously as a joke (or any other kind of folklore) is being heard, appreciated, learned, and, later, performed in another analogous setting.

This kind of learning comes through the process of what we call folklore; it is how we learn what a house is and how to find our way around in one (as well as how to tell a house from a home). It teaches us about time and its coordinates, and it allows us to learn and to become continually saturated with a total world view made up of those various networks of human interaction in which we participate. And some people are better at it than others.

Folklore functions in part as an informal system for learning the daily logic and worldview of the people around us. What we learn is more in the way of style and performance than specific content. We may say that folklore itself is characterized by (1) certain cultural rules that determine strongly what gets articulated and how and when, and (2) by a looseness, an informality, an inclination toward rephrasing and change, that will eventually result in an individuation on the surface of all articulations (*variants,* as they are called by folklorists). How does such a complex of rules and freedoms operate? How are their forms to be studied? Where to begin and how to define such a vast spectrum of human expression, complete with its cultural matrix?

## ✍ DESCRIBING FOLKLORE Since the time of the

Grimm brothers in Germany, scholars have sought out vernacular artists, studying their language, tales, customs, and beliefs, first in fear that the traditional world was disappearing (or becoming moribund), and more recently in the belief that only through a study of folk life can we ever understand the nature of human cultural expression. Some have concentrated on particular genres (forms) of folklore, some have concerned themselves with certain kinds of genres (for example, oral lore to the exclusion of material objects, or vice versa). Others of a more anthropological bent have centered their attention on traditional groupings of people (ethnic, religious, occupational) and have concentrated on the question of how the lore might show forth the dynamics of the group itself. All along, despite occasional huffiness between the humanists and the social scientists engaged in this broad venture, there has been the general recognition that our studies were all related somehow, that we have been engaged in a common venture even though we have approached our subject in fragmented and perhaps narrow ways.

Nonetheless, in spite of more than one hundred years of intensive study in Europe and America, folklorists have produced neither a satisfactory definition for that body of materials on which they fondly spend their scholarly lives nor an acceptable, consistent set of critical terms with which to discuss it. Certainly, one reason for these lacks is the almost startling variety and superficial dissimilarity of the materials themselves, ranging as they do from barns to ballads. The study of this vast body of cultural expression needs to be interdisciplinary in nature, and this has resulted in the amalgamation of a field that carries a sense of diffuseness, one that sometimes encourages scholars in other fields to disbelieve that folklorists know what they are doing or that they are doing anything at all. Another lamentable result is a lack of precision in scholarly conversation as folklorists attempt the theoretical study and discussion of a new, developing field.

THE TERM FOLKLORE   Still another problem, which seems at first more complicated than it really is, is that most folklorists today do not even feel that the word *folklore* itself adequately identifies or defines the area they are talking about. For one thing, they voice sincere doubts that there is any such static group as that usually implied by *the folk*. We know very well that most people in the world belong to several close groups, each based on different kinds of interactions, learning processes, and expressions. We are recognizing now, at least, that the idea of a single folk unit as a defining feature of the human context in which an individual grows up must probably be rejected.

Further, the word *lore*, even though it does indicate something about learning or knowledge, does not quite cover the wide range of communicative expression and experience and performance that now captures the focus of the professional folklorist.

William Thoms, who made up the term *folklore* in the nineteenth century, and many of those who first became involved in the study of what were then called *popular antiquities*, were not trained as professionals in this field nor could they have anticipated the development of their elite hobby into a demanding academic discipline. As a result, subsequent folklorists have had to create their own conceptions of a field of inquiry along the way, often using terms (and biases) drawn from their own academic specialties. Nonetheless, the word *folklore* is in widespread use and seems to be here to stay. And most scholars have at least some notion of the kind of thing they are talking about, even though its precise outlines and definitions are not easy to produce.

Actually, *folklore* is a word very much like *culture;* it represents a tremendous spectrum of human expression that can be studied in a number of ways and for a number of reasons. Its primary characteristic is that its ingredients seem to come directly from dynamic interactions among human beings in communal-traditional performance contexts rather than through the more rigid lines and fossilized structures of technical instruction or bureaucratized education, or through the relatively stable channels of the classical traditions.

NAMING OF PARTS   In the introductory comments to his anthology *The Study of Folklore,* Alan Dundes suggests it is inadvisable even to try to define *folklore*. Instead, he gives a long list of items and genres that have been interesting to folklorists over the years: In this view, folklore is as folklorists do. Each folklorist, of course, specializes in only a few of those items on any comprehensive list, but in spite of the varying interests and definitions urged by different folklorists, there should be in fact an area of general agreement among them from which a unified description of folklore dynamics may grow. It should be as applicable to string figures as to ballads, to barns as to oral epics.

Because a number of the genres in Dundes's list are simply not oral in nature, he rightly points out that an insistence on oral transmission can never be definitive, especially for those scholars who feel there is something folkloric about, say, graffiti, which is always encountered in its natural habitat in written form (although many people exchange recollections of a striking graffito in conversation, which very likely helps to spread particular items). Similarly, an insistence on a certain kind of content is unacceptable because of the great disparity between the genres, some of which—hand gestures, for example—may be said to be entirely lacking in content or to be entirely content, depending on one's viewpoint.

The simple list of traditional items (taken from those areas we have been interested in because they seem traditional) is also inadequate for definition, for if it remains open-ended, it will remain nondefinitive. If it is a closed list, it will represent only a parochial prescription and will be ignored or attacked by anyone who may want to expand or contract the list. Moreover, a list based on genre overlooks the fact known to any field researcher that folk expressions seldom occur in one genre at a time (the ballad text is related to its tune; the written graffito may have been learned in conversation; the carved "witching" stick or dowsing rod owes as much to popular belief as to the whittler's craft). We are obviously talking about a multidimensional set of occurrences and contexts. Single genre designations, while they may help us to think more clearly about the ingredients and forms of the folklore field, also help us to overlook the dynamics we seek to understand. Thus, for purposes of discussion, the dangers in the open-ended list are probably more acceptable for us to put up with as we scrutinize a field characterized by variety and dynamism.

Let us then assume that folklorists may be said to have some generally informed, if not precisely charted, notion that culture-oriented traditions exist, and that expressions made by an individual under the influences of culture-oriented traditions will share some characteristics that will argue for grouping them in a common field. Implicit in the study of folklore today, moreover, is the understanding that we may add to our list as the field becomes more clearly defined and as new cultural expressions are better understood. As with other disciplines (such as history, literature, music, mathematics), the term *folklore* will no doubt continue to be used in reference both to the content of the field (the material we collect and study) and to the discipline itself.

VARIETY AND VARIATION    What element or elements do the ballad and string figure have in common? On what grounds may one place *barn* and *folk song* on the same list? What similarities exist between a quilt and a Yugoslavian oral epic? How may we speak of latrinalia and folk dance as being in the same academic area? There may be in fact several elements shared by some of these items, but there is only one that works in them all. It has nothing to do directly with content or with genre, with method of transmission, with the definition of the group, or with level of literacy. The similarity lies in a common process. All these items have the common quality that as far as they continue to exist in their natural habitats, they are in continual and dynamic variation through space and time.

Since variety is not in any way limited to folklore, since all things in a culture change through time, how are the items on our list to be differentiated from other entities that vary: Shall we include automobiles, ladies' fashions, telephones? For several reasons, no. The items and events folklorists are interested in are recurrent forms of local, dynamic human expression—artifacts and performances created one at a time under particular circumstances. A quilt or a barn, as practical as its use may be, extends far beyond its mere thingness or its function. It is designed or phrased in such a way as to express and reflect the personal *and* cultural values in design and workmanship out of which the artisan works, and it is these designs and values, not the quilt or barn itself, that may be said to be dynamic, and thus to be folklore.

Moreover, the traditional artifact is not usually produced with the sharply varying demands of a vast, paying, consumer market in mind.

Traditional expressions, whether they be lingual, musical, gestural, or physical, reflect the notions of the practitioners in relation both to their own peculiar talents and aesthetics and to the tastes of the local network of people for whom they perform—the group whose members are familiar with their art: those from whom they have learned through traditional exchange.

TECHNOLOGY AND FORMALITY   This should not be construed as excluding folk crafts, in which certain technical demands are made on the artists for which they must be trained by their mentors. Any chair must have enough legs to stand, and any pot must be able to hold something. Different materials and aims require particular handling by the potter or weaver or carver, and these are usually transmitted to them by someone else so that they will not spend their early careers creating attractive blunders. We are, then, distinguishing between traditional ideas about pot-ness, say, and those technical devices through which the pot itself is produced.

To put it another way, the barn, pot, ballad, or tale as we find it in frozen, tangible form is a particular rendering of an older, pre-existing idea produced at a particularly appropriate time. The prototypes of barn-, pot-, ballad-, and tale-ness that circulate among members of a group are based on cultural attitudes and have comparatively little to do with technology. In these terms, our critical job is to present and study the processes of folklore that exist through time in a group of people by a comparative study of the items produced from the cultural premises of that group.

Thus, while certain technical competences often must come into play, the production of any traditional item is not chiefly related to professional training or to the external demands of technical or economic necessity. Of course some crafts become popular, and the artisan may make money. Some artisans are able to support themselves through their crafts. But their work has primarily local and cultural origins, and most often this is precisely why outsiders seek to buy it.

The process of folklore may be said in this sense to be local, communal, and informal. This does not argue that formal people have no folklore, or that folklore will not be passed among members of a highly trained profession. Rather, it suggests that even in the most formal groupings of any society, active traditions are passed not as a part of the formal training but as units of meaning interchanged commonly enough with other familiar people that a recognizable clustering of premises, formulas, and styles is built up and transmitted out of which the informal performer acts. Formal opera singing itself is not regarded as a part of folklore, for example, but opera singers may possess and transmit jokes, tales, beliefs, and customs ("break a leg") informally that particularly reflect the traditional values, beliefs, and attitudes of opera singers.

Similarly, nuclear physics would not ordinarily come under the scrutiny of folklorists, but there are numerous traditions passed among scientists (for example, legends of German rockets not lifting off properly until urinated upon); such traditions are clearly not connected so much to the formal aspects of physics and rocketry as they are to the shared experiences and anxieties of simply being a scientist. Generally speaking, the performers of traditional expressions do so because they want to or must, and usually their audience is made up of participating members of the same group in which the dynamic exchange of traditions through the years has formed the matrix out of which the performer operates.

For these reasons we might characterize or describe the materials of folklore as "tradition-based communicative units informally exchanged in dynamic variation through space and time." *Tradition* is here understood to mean not some static, immutable force from the past, but those pre-existing culture-specific materials and options that bear upon the performer more heavily than do his or her own personal tastes and talents. We recognize in the use of *tradition* that such matters as content and style have been for the most part passed on but not invented by the performer.

*Dynamic* recognizes, on the other hand, that in the processing of these contents and styles in performance, the artist's own unique talents of inventiveness *within* the tradition are highly valued and are expected to operate strongly. Time and space dimensions remind us that the resulting variations may spread geographically with great rapidity (as jokes do) as well as down through time (good luck beliefs). Folklore is made up of informal expressions passed around long enough to have become recurrent in form and content, but changeable in performance.

## ◤ MODE AND MOVEMENT IN FOLKLORE
It is important to note that there is a stress here on the mode of transmission rather than on the medium. The critical factor is not whether an item is found in oral circulation or in print (or on

a record), but whether it does or does not exhibit dynamic, substantive variation. However, we should not overlook the plain fact that the informal mode among humans is chiefly oral and gestural (we talk and gesture to each other more often than we build barns, for example). Folklorists are generally agreed that these informal expressions tend to become viable over a period of time or across a geographical area mostly among people who share some basis for informal communal contacts, some factor in common that makes it possible, or rewarding or meaningful, for them to exchange informal materials in a culturally significant way. Such human clusters have been called *folk groups* by many folklorists, but we should bear in mind that the grouping envisioned here is not static (as that term might imply) but is as dynamic as the materials it produces, for most people belong to several such groupings, and some (such as occupational) are subject to constant change.

It is particularly to the element of dynamic variation through space and time that this book directs its attention, for these coefficients provide a subject area on which virtually all folklorists are in tacit agreement, and for that reason it offers an acceptable set of premises that can be serviceable to all folklorists without the necessity of their abandoning or compromising previously held critical positions in the continuing debates on structure, texture, function, and definition in folklore.

Few folklorists would deny, for example, that folklore scholarship is based almost entirely on the study of variation. Nearly every scholar mentions the matter of variant study as basic to the critical examination of the materials. Weak folklore studies are more often than not the hasty output of writers who have failed to take into consideration a fair or representative sampling of variants. The most heavily used critical tools in folklore, the type and motif indexes, are founded on the proposition that no single item can be called *the* tale or song. It is axiomatic that folklorists need more than one instance of a tale or motif or ballad or popular belief even to know whether in fact they have before them an item from tradition. If fifty texts of one ballad were unearthed that were all alike in every detail, most folklorists would argue that they were not traditional. Structural and comparative studies are predicated entirely on the observation that certain units are continually recombined within the frame of a genre or type, and that an examination of such patterns as may be thus produced leads to valuable insights into the genres themselves and into the processes by which they are developed.

Not only must folklorists examine a maximum number of variants before making critical approaches to a particular item or genre, but many folklorists, in addition, see the process of variation as the very essence of their material. In the lingual, musical, and kinesic traditions the item *is* the performance, and the performance is nearly always a particular variation of a hypothetical prototype (one suspects Plato might have made a good folklorist).

In his recent study of traditional ballads, David Buchan declares that the story in a ballad is "a conceptual entity whose essence may be readily and accurately conveyed by different word groups." William R. Bascom, speaking of all forms of folklore, puts it this way: "Change occurs each time new variations are introduced and again these innovations are subject to acceptance or rejection. As this process continues, each new invention is adapted gradually to the needs of the society and to the pre-existing culture patterns, which may themselves be modified somewhat to conform to the new invention."

One photograph of a Pennsylvania Dutch hex sign, one plowshare supporting a mailbox, one tale, one quilt, one ballad, one graffito, can never be enough to establish the existence of a tradition. On the other hand, one hundred items alike in every detail establishes nothing but the fact of duplication. Variation in the particular appearance of one item is probably the most reliable hallmark of live folklore available to the student. It has nothing to do with purism; it has everything to do with the process of folklore.

THE TWIN LAWS   Variation, on the other hand, is not a random or a radical process. Balancing the dynamism of change in performance is the essentially conservative force of tradition itself. The weight of the familiar past continually exerts its subtle pressures on the bearers of these materials in at least two ways: the performers remember or adhere to some notions of the basic type (for example, in the use of their own language, or in the singing of a ballad like "Barbara Allen," in which a woman forsakes a man and the man dies), and they are sensitive to the reactions of the audience, most of whom speak the same language or subscribe to certain expectations about the ballad (or the quilt, barn, tale) in content, style, and occasion. These considerations will limit in varying degrees the freedom for variation felt by the performers. They may institute change, either consciously or inadvertently, but they will do so chiefly within the framework of the familiar and acceptable.

These two forces, or qualities—the one dynamic, the other conservative—are the twin coefficients of the particularized variation that finally does take place again and again in each traditional event—through space (geographical or human) and through time (moments or years). For simple reference, we may refer to these two forces descriptively as the twin laws of folklore process: Conservatism and dynamism will probably be the two most prominent characteristics in our perception of (and discussion of) any item tentatively classified as folklore. We will want to know what features of content and style have been carried through from earlier sources (conservatism). And we will need to know the extent to which the bearers of the materials, or the context in which they operate, have worked upon these materials in such a way as to change them (dynamism).

Conservatism refers to all those processes and forces that result in the retaining of certain information, beliefs, styles, customs, and the like, and the attempted passing of those materials, intact, through time and space in all the channels of traditional expression. Traditional matters related to religious belief, cultural mores, and culture-specific worldviews seem much less open to change than, say, the styles and attitudes relating to jokes. Myths (stories that relate or embody cosmic occurrences and experiences) are expressed in terms of a "time before time began," or in "collapsed time" or "distilled time," and are supported by a whole range of religious belief that conduces to a sense of ultimate truth. Although it can be easily demonstrated that myths do in fact change through time, the attempt on the part of the believer is to transmit them intact. They are not to be tampered with or rearranged, and often a special priesthood provides direct protective and conservative custody. Stylistic variation is suppressed or discouraged, for truth is not open to artistic manipulation. Even in some secular traditional forms, certain singers and storytellers sometimes do memorize their texts, or try to.

Dynamism, at the other extreme, comprises all those elements that function to change features, contents, meanings, styles, performance, and usage as a particular traditional event takes place repeatedly through space and time. Matters of taste, context, art, playfulness, change of function or meaning, forgetfulness, translation (language or dialect), shift of audience, age or sex of performer (and many more), all encourage continual change in the particular utterance or production or performance of traditional items, even when the bearer of the tradition tries to prevent it. The reasons for this will become more clear in later chapters. Here it is perhaps sufficient to note that when a singer says she is singing a ballad exactly as her father sang it, she may be referring to a fidelity to plot and symbol, not to an exact replication of a memorized text. In this sense, a person may indeed repeat a joke "exactly" without using the the same words.

In general, oral tradition itself is more variable than written tradition:

We are not surprised to find that orally transmitted jokes are less stable in form, style, and content than those myths that have been written down for a considerable period of time. In the same way, written language and spelling rules tend to slow down the natural changes that take place in the evolution of spoken language, and in some cases, as with English, spelling may lag conservatively two or three hundred years behind actual pronunciation.

THE SPECTRUM OF DYNAMISM   We must then envision a kind of spectrum, with conservatism on one end and dynamism on the other. All traditional materials will fit somewhere on this spectrum, some closer to one end than to the other. Myths, whose function in most cultures is to provide dramatic experiential models of protected truths and laws, which would otherwise be very abstract, are most likely to be closer to the conservative end of our spectrum. Jokes and other kinds of orally transmitted materials, whose function is largely fictional and pleasurable, are likely to be closer to the dynamic end.

The most typical relationship shown by these laws might be expressed: C/D, indicating that the conservative feature being passed along is subject to modification by dynamic processes (ballads and barns and folk tales are in this category). C/C might represent materials on one extreme end of the spectrum, in which both the item being transmitted as well as its performance or enunciation are under rigid control (such as might be noticed with some mythic materials). D/C would represent materials, such as jokes, that are almost entirely open to variations of style and form, but in which the modification is then brought about by the force of conservatism, for example, in the necessary retention of a punch line. D/D would represent the hypothetical condition in which entirely dynamic materials are passed along in entirely dynamic ways. This latter category is probably impossible to chart clearly in folklore because under these conditions there is very little chance for material to be retained long enough to be passed on, collected, and studied. Gossip, insofar as it may be considered pre-legend, might be an example here.

It is obvious that generic categories cannot be placed separately on this spectrum with any certainty because in each individual item or event or performance, depending on local circumstances in the total context of the utterance itself, conservatism or dynamism might play the larger role.

We can assume, however, that certain features of some genres tend to encourage conservatism while other features encourage dynamism. Any folk song or poem that depends for much of its effect on rhyme or rhythm will tend to change more slowly than such freer prose narratives as the joke or memorate. Within a tale or a song, certain striking phrases or recurrent, formulaic conventions are likely to be retained ("There was this traveling salesman" or "lily-white hand") while other features of the same text may be quite open to continual change. Proverbs, whose sense of truth is much distilled and in which the style and rhythm often become part of the meaning, change very slowly through time, if at all ("A stitch in time saves nine"). In fact, one favorite form of parody is to take a well-known proverb and change its meaning by overt manipulation ("Virtue is its own reward; but then, so is vice"). While one can make parodies of proverbs, one is not free to change the proverb itself substantially in meaning or tone: One may not say, for example, "A stitch in time saves seven," or "A stitch in time may prevent the necessity for even more work later," or "An airplane in time saves nine." This feeling that we are not entirely free to change the item by whim as it passes through our minds and lips is our reference point to the force of conservatism.

Obscene songs, many of which are entirely dependent for their effect on the clever use of obscene words, seem less open to change than other kinds of folk songs in which the words are not as centrally important as the "emotional core." In a typical joke, the punch line may be remembered exactly and passed on conservatively through considerable time and space while the "setup" may be reworded or reperformed in very different ways. Children's songs and rhymes, dependent on a kind of ritualism in rhythm and word magic, seem less open to change than other kinds of children's folklore. The following verse, for example, has been collected in nearly (but not exactly) identical texts in widely separated parts of the United States and in England:

> Quick, quick
> The cat's been sick.
> Where? Where?
> Under the chair.
> Hasten, hasten,
> Fetch the basin.
> Kate, Kate,
> You're far too late,
> The rug is in a dreadful state.

For all these reasons, our study of folklore process can hardly get us beyond superficial beginnings unless we are willing to cope with the multiple aspects of variation and the way they exhibit themselves within certain rather rigid cultural expectations.

We can probably say, then, that those artifact productions that remain traditional do so because they have retained their variability, have remained vital units of traditional exchange among participants in a close cultural set (they exhibit both conservatism and dynamism). We know that many of our urban legends (the cement-filled car, for one) have moved continually in and out of print, and we know that many of our most popular ballads have had as widespread a life on the page as in the mouth. Thus it would seem that, especially in our lettered society, duplication through print—in and of itself—is a matter of accident. It may or may not represent the fossilization that usually indicates nontraditional status (where dynamism of performance is lost and conservatism is maintained by technology).

A traditional item (whether oral or material or gestural or musical) is folklore only when it is actually used or performed in its indigenous set of live contexts. A ballad collected in the Ozarks and sung by a professor to a class in folklore may be said to be a traditional item which *was*—in its usual performance—a folk song. A Slavic dance taught by a returned student may be a traditional item which was—when danced in its regular habitat under traditional conditions—a folk dance. These intentional performances for outsiders (often for intellectual curiosity or amusement) are not in any way fake; but they *are* different, no matter how faithful to the original the intentional performer tries to be. In fact, in the very attempt to reproduce someone else's tradition "exactly as it was," one most likely insures that it has become a living fossil. This is no more lamentable than recognizing that any fossil is no longer a dynamic part of the process of life, but the distinction does need to be made. Nothing in this prevents the Ozark singer or the Slavic villagers from continuing the traditions of singing or dancing in their own contexts as long as they please. And nothing can prevent them from dropping certain songs and dances from the traditional repertoire when they please—even if it outrages the intellectual bystander who feels they should never lose their heritage. Life goes on, and so does folklore.

Just as the law of gravity does not itself cause an apple to fall from the tree, the twin laws do not obligate the bearers of tradition to perform in narrowly defined ways. Rather, by reference to them the study of complex and shifting interrelationships can be made more graspable, allowing us to narrow our discussion to some clearly functional minimal properties of folklore. These simply are described in terms of generalized laws concerning the "behavior" of our material.

## ◢ CULTURAL SELECTION AND CHANGE
Not all changes will strike the auditors or the performer as good. In terms of survival through time, however, we can assume that substantive mistakes will either be corrected or rationalized by subsequent performers or that a given traditional item will become so confused that it will cease to be viable. Of course, we are speaking in ideal terms of the good singer, dancer, midwife, raconteur. There will always be in an informal setting a number of people who remember parts of various traditions. These people seldom consider themselves proficient at the tradition even when they are active bearers ("I can't tell a joke right; ask Charlie to tell it"). Thus perhaps a garbled or confused item will not necessarily be corrected or discarded immediately, but generally people will not waste their time on the recitation or practice of traditions that mean nothing at all or have no function. Most people, and especially the competent bearers of tradition, want very much to express themselves and their lore in a communicative, satisfying way.

We can assume, then, that folklore lives through a generally selective process that insures, as time goes on, that traditions will demonstrate their viability, or change so that they can, or die off. If a former magical incantation has become now a nonsense refrain in a ballad, all we can say is that apparently the line has remained viable because it was usable as a refrain. We need not lament on that account the decline of magic or the stupidity of ballad singers.

Some students of history, even scholars of oral history, see variation as almost synonymous with error or degeneration. Actually, it is a matter of hypernaiveté for any student of tradition to expect generally exact duplication in tradition, much less to make value judgments on that basis, especially where there is no concept of a fixed text.

THE MEDIUM IS NOT THE MESSAGE  Because most informal expressions among human beings have been embodied in lingual, musical, and kinesic modes (since these are most direct, and the average person is more capable of reproducing them), it is likely that the study of folklore will always be heaviest in these areas. However, this condition must not be allowed to obscure the fact that the same kind of informality, expressiveness, and traditional dynamism may also occur when some visual or material mode is used that represents the same level of communication in the same cultural context of traditional exchange. While the written word is often a solidifier, a freezer of dynamism, it may sometimes be a vehicle for tradition when—as with chain letters, latrinalia, and ballad garlands —the conditions of informality, community exchange and taste, and anonymous tradition are present. When latrine poems exhibit centrally some of the same dynamic characteristics that we find in ballads, it would surely be poor scholarship to ignore them only because they are not sung or to reject them only because we feel that visible letters constitute a contaminant. The process, not the medium or the content, is central to our investigation.

It seems nonsense, then, to suggest, as some have, that folklore can exist only in a literate culture and in contradistinction to it, based on the argument that without written language one cannot speak of the category of oral expression. Oral literature came first, after all; it is written literature, its extension, that has developed into something else. Folklorists are dealing with a particular and well-established species of learning and expression by traditional codes and formulas: cultural communication interaction. It occurs with or without literacy. If there is no literacy, perhaps most of what happens in a culture might be included in the study of folklore. If there is literacy in a culture, it may very well take part in the dynamic interchange (as with the heavy use of printed broadside ballads in America). Print, for example, in newspaper squibs, in urban legends that appear in "Dear Abby," in items appearing in broadsides or popular publication, may take part in the dynamism of folklore as well as in its conservation.

Moreover, since the perimeters of the folk group will change with the focus of the investigation (remembering that a person may belong to several close groups), the matter of literacy hardly ever aligns directly with the lore being studied. For example, as citizens most loggers in Oregon are quite literate, yet as loggers their folklore is primarily oral and will very likely stay that way. Since in such cases the condition of literacy is really peripheral (if not entirely irrelevant) to the discussion, we might say that the bearers of folklore are *a*literate.

Conscious removals of traditional media from their original cultural matrices are familiar to us in all areas of folklore: the revival of folk songs on page and platter by professional entertainers, the mass production of folk toys, the publication of jokes in literate rather than in oral style, the sale of prefabricated log cabins and of corncob pipes made in Japan. What distinguishes these articles primarily is lack of traditional variation; the process has shifted from dynamism to duplication. As a corollary, those people involved in the process are no longer traditional cabin builders as such. They are instead producers and receivers who operate separately, who communicate and express not for each other but for outsiders (although, as coworkers, they may share other kinds of folklore).

THE EVOLUTIONARY MODEL   Because of the ongoing changes in folklore, it is illuminating to view a traditional item or event as if it were an animal in the evolutionary process. Just as there is no single cat that can be called *the* cat and no single dog that can be called *the* dog, there is no "Barbara Allen" that can be called *the* or *the original* ballad. In fact, when we say *cat*, we are really referring to a theoretical prototype, a biological mean that we conceptualize for our own convenience as constituting the most common recurrent elements to be found in the widest range of cats. And even if some cats and dogs look very much alike, we will find in the final analysis that the prototype in each case is clear enough for us to make a distinction between dogness and catness, or, even within dogness, between collie-ness and poodle-ness. And we would be upset if someone accused us of purism for making the distinction. Similarly, when we speak of "Barbara Allen," we are referring to our conception of a cluster of characteristics that seem to be connected with a particular narrative song (among other narrative songs), a cluster that gives us enough of a prototype for recognition so that we will not easily confuse it with others.

THE BIOLOGY OF FOLKLORE   In folklore as in the biological world, variation from a hypothetical norm is universal. No two individuals are exactly alike in every detail no matter how closely related. Variation affects every sort of characteristic, structural or functional, and occurs at every stage of life, in animal and plant life as in tradition. Members of any human family participate in the family appearance, but no one is more authentically a member of the family than any other. Indeed, in the biological sciences the very concept of species is based on our perception of the mean of the most frequently recurring characters, taking account of all variations from smallest to largest, and described by the scholar without value judgments. This is also what folklorists have done in the best of their work.

Moreover, where both geneticists and folklorists once stressed the importance of similarity in family traits, they now generally recognize that the very variety and richness of traits may allow for survival of the type.

In addition, the factors of traditional inheritance versus local adaptation, the possibility for individual items to lose their dynamism (to die) and exist only in recorded (fossilized) form, the occasional chance for a wide variation (mutation) to occur that will in turn die out or propagate a new line of dynamism, and geographical mobility, to mention only a few, all seem analogous to common considerations in the study of evolution and ecology.

These comparisons are of course only for clarification and suggest that the folklorist, like the biologist, must take a multidimensional view of the subject. Because folklore and life processes are not the same, and because folklore grows out of more conscious aesthetic manipulations than do biological developments, biological terms cannot be applied glibly to traditional phenomena. In other words, there is no inference here that a traditional item is in all respects like an animal; rather, the assumption is simply that in both the animal and traditional spheres the variations occurring constantly through space and time are far more diverse and complex than the word *variation* indicates, and that in both fields meaningful investigation must take such complexities into consideration. One can often speak of these complexities more accurately using terms developed by the scientific fields that have had experience dealing with the nature of variation without value judgment.

Folklore is ever-changing, always developing, on the move. The folklorist must keep pace, in field work, in theory, in vocabulary, if we are ever to understand fully and discuss accurately this dynamic area of human communication. Whoever approaches folklore for the first time might keep in mind, at least tentatively, the major premise of this book: Certain items and ideas have become folklore because they have entered into a common, dynamic process that affects them all similarly. The artifacts and the genres may be many, but the same processes have molded them all. The most rewarding focus of further folklore study would seem to be precisely on the process that binds all these various materials together into a single field of discussion.

We do well to bear in mind the words of old man Black Elk as he explained a certain feature of the Sun Dance to Joseph Epes Brown. The Sun dancer is pierced above both breasts and is attached to the center cottonwood tree by what appear to be two rawhide thongs. Black Elk stressed, however, that it was really one thong looped around the center pole, a symbol of unity within seeming diversity. "It is only the ignorant man," he said, "who sees the many where there is only the one."

# ✍ BIBLIOGRAPHICAL NOTES

The maintenance of older traditions in a modern, sometimes urban, environment, as well as the development of traditions distinctive to modern situations, are two processes now well recognized by folklorists and anthropologists. Américo Paredes and Ellen J. Stekert, eds., *The Urban Experience and Folk Tradition* (Austin: University of Texas Press, 1971), provide a symposium of scholars who have worked with old and new folklore in the city; Ari Kiev, *Curanderismo: Mexican-American Folk Psychiatry* (New York: Free Press, 1968), examines an older form of folk medicine that has continually reaffirmed its validity in modern times among members of a culture group who live in both rural and urban areas; Abrahams's *Deep Down in the Jungle* concerns the vital, ongoing oral tradition of young Black men in an inner-city setting; Iona and Peter Opie, *The Lore and Language of Schoolchildren* (Oxford: Clarendon Press, 1959), and Mary and Herbert Knapp, *One Potato, Two Potato: The Secret Education of American Children* (New York: Norton, 1976), both deal with oral materials that have been maintained by children, mainly of urban backgrounds, in some cases for over three hundred years—and with keen modern oral parodies of the most up-to-date sort—demonstrating a combined propensity to conserve and an inclination to create; Robert S. McCarl's "Smoke-jumper Initiation: Ritualized Communication in a Modern Occupation," *Journal of American Folklore*, 89 (1976), 49–66, shows the retention of ancient ritual techniques in a modern, practical setting, while James P. Leary, "Fists and Foul Mouths: Fights and Fight Stories in Contemporary Rural Bars," *Journal of American Folklore*, 89 (1976), 27–39, discusses how daily activity of the most common sort develops traditional modes and structures that are reflected in both narrative and human action; James P. Spradley and David W. McCurdy, *The Cultural Experience: Ethnography in a Complex Society* (Chicago: Science Research Associates, 1972), examines a number of common human groupings in the urban environment, showing their customary systems of organization and expression. Although the data on which it is based are now some fifteen years old, my essay on college folklore, "The Folklore of Academe," Appendix B in Jan Harold Brunvand, *The Study of American Folklore*, gives some idea of the vitality of oral and customary tradition in an environment whose sophistication many would have thought hostile to folklore. Brunvand's chapter on superstition (pp. 178–196) mentions several university-level experiments with urban and well-educated people.

The details of language acquisition and the extent of the relationship between worldview and language are still very much under discussion. It is my feeling, based on work with the Navajo and Sioux languages, that language and worldview are inextricably bound, although I do not accept the notion of Whorf that language imprisons us in a single (or simple) ideational set. Here we should recall Whorf's basic work in *Language, Thought and Reality*, as well as Edward T. Hall's practical application and extension of it in *The Silent Language* (Garden City, N.Y.: Doubleday, 1959) and *The Hidden Dimension* (Garden City, N.Y.: Doubleday, 1966). In the latter book, Hall discusses the traditional uses of space and proxemics in various cultures, touching in part on the corresponding changes in language. Peter Farb takes up a number of Whorf's ideas in fascinating detail in *Word Play;* see especially Chapter 8, "Man at the Mercy of Language," and for language as a setting that educates us, see Chapter 1, "The Ecology of Language." A better understanding of the pervasiveness of early traditional worldview training can be gained from Erik H. Erikson, *Childhood and Society*, 2nd ed. (New York: Norton, 1963). A valuable set of essays on communication seen in its cultural setting is provided in Alfred Smith, ed., *Communication and Culture: Readings in the Codes of Human Interaction* (New York: Holt, Rinehart and Winston, 1966), especially Chapter 5, "Signals: Verbal and Nonverbal," Chapter 10, "Code and Culture," and Chapter 13, "Intercultural Communication." Ray L. Birdwhistell examines unspoken gestural body-language in *Kinesics and Context: Essays on Body Motion and Communication* (Philadelphia: University of Pennsylvania Press, 1970). Alan Dundes shows how fully our daily metaphors, proverbs, slogans, and sayings reflect a rather consistent general worldview in "Thinking Ahead: A Folkloristic Reflection on the Future Orientation in American Worldview," *Anthropological Quarterly*, 42 (1969), 53–72, and in "Folk Ideas as Units of World View," in *Toward New Perspectives in Folklore*, ed. Américo Paredes and Richard Bauman (Austin: University of Texas Press, 1972), pp. 93–103.

John Wilson Foster, "The Plight of Current Folklore Theory," *Southern Folklore Quarterly*, 32 (1968), 237–248, suggests that the lack of unanimity among folklore scholars arises because they have concentrated on approaches that have seemed very different while the materials they have studied, seemingly chaotic, "share a common mode of existence governed by their tendency to persist and their tendency to transform. Each instance of folkloristic expression, in fact, is a product of the twin forces of conservation and dynamics" (p. 247). I am indebted to Professor Foster for the lengthy discussions that led both to his article and to the basic theoretical position of this book.

William J. Thoms, writing under the pseudonym Ambrose Merton, sought to provide a solid English term for what had been called antiquities. His suggestion of *folk-lore* caught on rapidly, and was in wide use among writers within a few years. The original letter appeared in *The Athenaeum*, no. 982 (August 22, 1846), 862–863. Alan Dundes, *The Study of Folklore*, "What is Folklore?" pp. 1–3, although it declines to define folklore, provides a succinct picture of the field of inquiry today.

We will find in many cases that the production of traditional objects for the consumption of outsiders may in time become influenced by the particular kinds of traditional items the outsider most wants to buy, such as has happened with Navajo rugs. The tradition thus becomes skewed toward exoteric ideas about what the tradition should be like. But, as Kate Peck Kent demonstrates in "Pueblo and Navajo Weaving Traditions and the Western World," (in *Ethnic and Tourist Arts: Cultural Expressions from the Fourth World*, ed. Nelson H. H. Graburn, [Berkeley: University of California Press, 1976], pp. 85–101), a native tradition may still preside over the process, conception, and mode of presentation, as well as remain associated through custom and popular belief. Graburn's book gives similar examples from Eskimo, Haida, Laguna, Seri, Cuna, Shipibo, Ainu, Sepik, Benin, Lega, and other peoples.

Eleanor Long's fine monograph *"The Maid" and "The Hangman": Myth and Tradition in a Popular Ballad*, University of California Folklore Studies No. 21 (Berkeley: University of California Press, 1971), was able to show by a close study of many variants that the speaker in the ballad called by Child "The Maid Freed from the Gallows" (Child #95), assumed by ballad scholars to be a woman, was generally thought by traditional ballad singers to be a man. At first this might seem to be a petty detail, but it causes a complete revision in our concept of what the ballad is about and how it achieves its dramatic impact; it also shows what we miss if we consult only a few variants that may not be representative of the type. At the other extreme, William H. Desmonde's article "Jack and the Beanstalk," *American Imago*, 8 (1951), 287–288, reprinted in Dundes, *The Study of Folklore*, pp. 108–109, based on only one version of the story—and a literary one at that—shows us nothing. For other examples of the amassing of variants for profitable explorations, see Jan Harold Brunvand, "The Folktale Origin of *The Taming of the Shrew*," *Shakespeare Quarterly*, 17 (1966), 345–359; Bronson's *Traditional Tunes of the Child Ballads*; Nygard's *The Ballad of "Heer Halewijn"*; and Hector Lee's *The Three Nephites: The Substance and Significance of the Legend in Folklore*, University of New Mexico Publications in Language and Literature, no. 2 (Albuquerque: University of New Mexico Press, 1949).

David Buchan, *The Ballad and the Folk* (London: Routledge & Kegan Paul, 1972) is one of the most highly regarded books on the subject to be written in recent years. See pp. 158 and 163 especially for the idea of a ballad as a *concept* with variable wording. Bascom's statement on continual change in folklore comes from his essay "Folklore and Anthropology," *Journal of American Folklore*, 46 (1953), 283–290. My first exposition of the "Twin Laws" was in an article composed jointly with John Wilson Foster, "A Descriptive Nomenclature for the Study of Folklore: Part I, The Process of Tradition [Toelken]; Part II, The Evolutionary Model [Foster]," *Western Folklore*, 28 (1969), 91–111.

I am deeply indebted to Ed Cray for insisting on bringing the high level of conservatism in children's lore and in obscene songs to my attention when I was obstinately fixed on seeing only the dynamic element in folklore. The term *emotional core* was put forward by Tristram P. Coffin in reference to that basic central idea of a ballad whose text is otherwise in flux. The full argument can be found in "Mary Hamilton and the Anglo-American Ballad as an Art Form," *Journal of American Folklore*, 70 (1957), 208–214, reprinted in *The Critics and the Ballad*, ed. MacEdward Leach and Tristram P. Coffin (Carbondale: Southern Illinois University Press, 1961), pp. 245–256; Coffin's comments on emotional core begin on p. 246 of the latter. I think the term can safely be applied to the performer's awareness of the traditionally important prototype in *any* performance of folklore.

For some very pointed discussion of ballads going in and out of popular print, see Vivian de Sola Pinto and Allan E. Rodway, *The Common Muse* (New York: Philosophical Library, 1957), especially the introduction, pp. 1–29. Urban legends are very susceptible to movement in and out of print. Among many others, see Louie Attebery's account of the cement-filled Cadillac story, "It Was a De Soto," *Journal of American Folklore*, 83 (1970), 452–457. See also Florence H. Ridley, "A Tale Told Too Often," *Western Folklore*, 26 (1967), 153–156, which concerns the recurrent story of the castrated boy, to be discussed herein in a later chapter.

Jan Vansina, *Oral History: A Study in Historical Methodology*, trans. H. M. Wright (Chicago: Aldine, 1965), sees variation as almost synonymous with error and degeneration, but he bases his remarks on the oral traditions of a very formal African system in which accuracy and fact are high priorities. It seems to me that, even when content accuracy is a chief consideration, exact duplication of wording is relatively rare in orally transmitted materials. For a more moderate view of the matter, see Richard M. Dorson, "Oral Tradition and Written History: The Case for the United States," *Journal of the Folklore Institute*, 1 (1964), 220–234. Ed Cray has given a solid account of the role of printed versions in the development of traditional ballads in America in " 'Barbara Allen': Cheap Print and Reprint," in *Folklore International: Essays in Traditional Literature, Belief, and Custom in Honor of Wayland Debs Hand*, ed. D. K. Wilgus (Hatboro, Pa.: Folklore Associates, 1967), pp. 41–50.

The application of biological terms to folklore is not new: C. W. von Sydow, a Swedish folklorist, had proposed the term *oicotype* in 1945 to refer to the process of local adaptation in an item of tradition. His essay, translated and published in *Selected Papers on Folklore*, ed. Laurits Bødker (Copenhagen: Rosenkilde and Bagger, 1948), is reprinted in Dundes, *The Study of Folklore*, pp. 219–242. For other suggested terms (usable only as analogies to traditional processes, not as definitions or measurements), see "Descriptive Nomenclature," mentioned earlier, Part 2.

Black Elk's striking account of the Sun Dance is given in Joseph Epes Brown, *The Sacred Pipe* (1953; reprint ed., Baltimore: Penguin Books, 1971); pp. 94–95 give his warning on faulty seeing.

# 2

# DYNAMICS
## OF THE
# FOLK
# GROUP

**DYNAMICS MAY BE VIEWED**
SIMPLY, FOR OUR PURPOSES, AS THE
NATURE OF ACTIVE TRADITIONAL MOMENTS
THAT OCCUR BETWEEN AND AMONG PEOPLE. WHAT
motivates customary human interactions? How do they start? When do
they cease? How are they received and responded to? Human society is
obviously defined by its dynamics. Of interest to the folklorist and
anthropologist are those special dynamics that are known most fully and
participated in most actively by members of such groupings as ethnic,
regional, occupational, clan, and family clusters.

**THE LIVE CONTEXT** Every examination of folk-
lore, every approach to the study of folklore, must take into consideration the multiple and complex interactions that occur among members
of a close group whenever a traditional performance of any kind takes
place, from a single slang term in its live context to a whole fiesta in its

live context. For example, when someone tells a joke, it is almost never done on the spur of the moment, nor is it told in a vacuum, alone to the picture on the wall. Usually there will be a group of people, often closely related by occupation or family ties, who have for various reasons developed a particular shared mood. Something reminds someone of an anecdote and he tells it, feeling the group will appreciate the application. This will remind someone else of a joke she heard from someone at the office, and that in turn will remind another person in the group of some related joke. The kind of jokes, the vocabulary used, the topics, the volume of voices, the length of time devoted to the session, and the protocol of alternating jokes from one teller to another will be determined by unspoken but recognizable attitudes shared or developed by the group. These in turn may be affected by the weather, the time of year, recent historical events (an election, the Arab-Israeli War) or a feeling the group may share about those who are unlike themselves (Polacks, summer folks, Aggies, Newfies, Texans). All these elements will have something to do with the particular "joke texts" one might hear told on a particular occasion; consequently, no text can be fully understood without considerable reference to the dynamics of context, the total live situation, in which it came forth.

What makes the study of context more complex than it may initially seem is that several kinds of simultaneous surroundings may affect the interactions among the members of a folk group: a particular place, a particular time (of day, month, year), a certain group of people present, an esoteric language being used, a particular shared culture or tradition, a particular activity taking place, and so on. The jokes and stories told by an exclusively female group while quilting may thus be quite different from the jokes told by some of the same women when at a Grange supper or rodeo breakfast. Certain stories told in some Native American tribal settings are related only when a whole family has gathered and only at certain times of the year, while traveling salesman stories are more often told by European American men outside their families when "the boys" are gathered together at any time of year.

It should be clear, then, that the word *context* may not fully suggest the varying dynamic environments of folklore, especially those provided by the participants themselves, the folk group. Since most people are members of more than one such group, and since people do not always do the same things when they come together, it becomes necessary for the student of folklore to make (or to have available) close observations of that particular group in which a traditional performance takes place, preferably focusing on the dynamics of the performance itself, whatever they may be.

In doing so, however, it is well to remember the Heisenberg principle, the fact recognized by scientists that the very presence of an observer is bound to have some effect on the phenomenon under scrutiny. In folklore fieldwork, this may produce negative results when the observer impedes the process under study, confusing results when the process takes place only because the observer is present, or positive results when the observer is able—as an outsider—to ask about things or observe matters that would be difficult or impossible for an insider to deal with.

THE FOLK GROUP: ENVIRONMENT FOR ESOTERIC DYNAMICS  Chapter 1 suggested that a folk group can be described as any group of people who share informal communal contacts that become the basis for expressive, culture-based communications. In addition to these observations, we would expect to find that the group will have maintained itself through its dynamics for a considerable time and that the expressive communications have thus become the educative matrix in which children of the group—or newcomers to it—are brought up.

"A considerable time" defies a pat definition; how much time is considerable? We want to be able to exclude ephemeral informal groups who share dynamic communal experiences (on a hayride, a picnic at the beach) that have not been extensive enough to have produced a traditional system of communication directly related to the group. On the other hand, some of the examples that follow will indicate that antiquity is not a necessity, either.

One of the key features of a folk group will always be the extent to which its own dynamics continue to inform and educate its members and stabilize the group. Because the members share so much information and attitude, folk groups are what Edward T. Hall would call *high context groups:* For them, meaning and action are more directly related to context than to the simple denotations of words themselves. In some cultures, people share a tremendous amount of context with everyone; the Navajos and the Japanese, for example, are high context groups whose members all see themselves as parts of a single community that "knows." Nonetheless, even these large high context cultures are observed to have smaller localized folk groups based on village affiliation, clan membership, occupation, and so forth.

In America, Hall would say that on the whole the larger society is *low context,* preferring to get meaning from information, data, and the formal content of language itself. However, we know that within the larger culture there are many folk groups that do provide high context dynamic systems for their members. What are these high context groups like? What is it that their members share? How do the people relate to each other and to the traditions passed along by such a group? In what ways do the traditions bear upon the lives of the members when they are in the group and when they are elsewhere? These are only a few of the questions to be asked about the folk group and its dynamics. *Folk group* is therefore not a static label to be applied simply where people are observed to be loggers, quilters, Ozarkers, or Russian Old Believers; rather, the term should indicate a dynamic system of human interchange where the members of any group interrelate on a high context level of attitude, reference, connotation, sense of meaning, and customary behavior, precisely as members, and to be members, of that group.

Loggers, for example, are not a folk group simply because they are all engaged in the timber industry; we notice by observation that there is a way of being a logger that each person learns from the others. In terms of the formal designation, or denotation, one may be called a logger by cutting trees for a living. But one becomes a logger on the folk group level only by participating in the dynamics of loggerdom, being absorbed by the live context, being taken in as "one of the boys" often after a long period of insults, teasing, pranks, and customary tests. Loggers themselves see their group as an esoteric system with its own attitudes and rules. Without acknowledging the power and wisdom of the group a person can hardly expect to join the ranks as a full participant; for one thing, such a person would be a hazard to others in the woods, for he does not have time to learn all the hard rules of survival and cooperation by experience. He must go with the group, for his benefit and theirs. At the same time, there is a certain sense of personal independence called for in logger custom that elevates the value of the individual and encourages him not to knuckle under to the group. If we look for both of these ingredients in logger folklore, we shall not be disappointed.

ESOTERIC RECOGNITION OF DYNAMICS   One way to get a sense of the group's own concept of itself is to ask its members what they recognize as important tokens of membership. In the case of loggers: How do you recognize another logger on the street? What kind of words are used by loggers among themselves? What kinds of songs and stories do you tell? What do you do to greenhorns? What are the important things to watch for on a logging crew? And so forth.

Some aspects of logger folklore are regional. Anyone from the eastern part of America will probably wonder why the word *lumberjack* is not used here instead of *logger*, for example. The reader from the Northwest will have seen lumberjack mostly in print, and it will seem elitist. Ask a Pacific Northwest woodsman, and you might hear that " 'lumberjack' is what city folks call a logger" or "a lumberjack is a guy who stacks lumber in a mill; they're all pantywaists—don't call *me* one of them" or "a lumberjack is a guy who steals wood."

On the other hand, some logger terms and customs are nationwide, *stagged britches* (pants cut off with a knife at the cuff and left ragged so they rip easily and the logger will not be tripped by brush snags getting caught in the material) being one of the most common both in customary dress and terminology. Thus there are both local and universal aspects to logger lore and to the loggers' concept of the group's dynamics. The best approach might be to focus on a particular area and see what the loggers in that setting think about their own traditional characteristics, remembering that scholarly descriptive words like *folklore, traditional, customary,* and so on are not likely to be in the everyday vocabulary of those interviewed.

In the Pacific Northwest one often hears that a logger can be recognized by "his tin hat, hickory shirt, tin pants, and cork boots." This is obviously a high context statement, for the hat is not really of tin but is the usual workman's hard hat; the shirt's appellation is based on a trademark; the pants are made of heavy canvas or rubber (to ward off the water in the soggy Northwest forests); and the boots are not of cork but are caulked, and fitted with sharp hobnails for increased stability and traction in the woods. Beyond this, one may note that most loggers feel they are above wearing tin pants, and thus the description is meant to be confusing to the outsider, both through content, which may not be totally true, and by word play on *tin, hickory,* and *cork*. The fact remains that a typical logger in the Northwest wears calf-length laced boots with a high heel, stagged black pants (cut about eight to ten inches above the ground), a gray-striped workshirt, red Logger's World suspenders, and a hard hat. Only the last is a requirement brought in recently by law; the rest of the uniform constitutes a folk costume by means of which loggers belong and recognize each other. Yet obviously anyone could dress up in such an outfit and—at least momentarily—look like a logger.

More active and dynamic than costume in the workings of a folk group are the kinds of verbal interaction that take place among and between members. But a researcher would certainly be in the way if he tried to collect logger folklore on the job; and if he tried to do it by joining a crew, he would have to write down his recollections later, after the work was done. In an attempt to sidestep this problem for the purposes of illustration here, I asked several loggers to share with me the topics, words, and stories they felt were closest to their notion of what loggers are and how they relate to each other. The following is a partial inventory, based on a list of "favorite logger topics" given to me by logger Bill Hamilton: hard work, humor, independence, boasts, pranks, names, camp life, sex, and customs. First, so the subsequent stories and descriptions can be better understood, here is a brief glossary of common terms used by loggers in the Northwest woods.

## ESOTERIC VOCABULARY

*apple-knocker*   a part-time logger.

*barber chair*   a tree that starts to split and fall before the cut is finished; it breaks off high, kicks out, and sometimes kills.

*bucker*   a sawyer whose principal job is to cut up fallen trees into standard-sized logs.

*bull*   (adj.) main, principal. Usually refers to the most important item or person among several, as in bull-block, bull-cook, bull-buck. Sometimes used in a noun phrase like bull-of-the-woods, usually a reference to the toughest man in the vicinity, sometimes to a woods boss. "There is no such thing as a bull-hooker, bull-faller, or bull-climber; each one of these is unique, and one is not more important than another."

*chaser*   a man who kicks chokers off logs being drawn in from where they have been bucked; his job is to detach the logs from the line at the cold deck (the stack from which logs are then reloaded onto logging trucks for the trip to the mill).

*choker*   a heavy cable that acts as an adjustable clamp or noose with which logs are pulled up from the hillside to the central area of a logging operation by means of high lead rigging, a system of cables, blocks, and pulleys powered by a donkey (a powerful engine).

*choker-setter*   the worker who places the cable around the log so it can be pulled in to the cold deck. This job is seen as the basic unit of the actual logging team and constitutes generally the first rung of the logger's hierarchy in the woods. It is also considered one of the most dangerous jobs because logs often roll or pitch end-for-end when the slack is taken up on the main cable.

*climber*   sometimes called a high-climber, the man who climbs a tree and cuts the top off so the tree can be used as a central spar pole for a high lead logging operation. This kind of logging is done today primarily with a mobile mechanical spar pole, so the climber is increasingly a rarity in the woods. Since a tree can split when its top comes off, the climber was considered to have one of the most hazardous jobs, and the employment often attracted those who needed to demonstrate their bravery. A common custom of climbers was to climb on top of the still-swaying spar pole and, either standing or sitting, roll a cigarette and smoke it with studied nonchalance.

*Coos Bay splice*   a splice in a steel cable apparently made by someone more accustomed to splicing rope (Coos Bay is a prominent fishing and seaport town on the Oregon Coast); hence, derogatory.

*corks*   heavy logger boots with sharp hobnails. Although spelled *caulked* boots, both the boots and the nails are referred to as corks.

*crummy*   the crew van or truck that carries loggers back and forth to their jobs, probably so named after the earlier crew car on logging railroads. "Where that term came from? That ought to be obvious; everybody's got a lip full of snoose, boots full of mud, and britches full of splinters." Often the crummy is hosed out at the end of its homeward run by a junior man on the crew.

*faller*   the mainstay of a logging crew, the man who actually cuts the trees down.

*gut hammer*   in a logging camp, the dinner bell or triangle.

*gypo*   (adj.) most often used in connection with the word *outfit* to mean a small, private, independent logging company, often run by a single family or small group of friends.

*haulback*   the smaller cable used to haul the main line back out to the woods where the choker-setters are working.

*haywire*   a small-gauge wire used to set up and extend the first lines of a high lead operation. Since the main cables are too heavy to be dragged around the entire perimeter of the operation, the haywire is used first, and then by means of it the main cables are drawn around and tightened.

*haywire outfit*   any logging operation that uses lighter-gauge cable than the job demands; therefore used in a derogatory sense to indicate a company so parsimonious that it is willing to endanger the lives of its men.

*hooker*   also *hook tender;* the boss of a given logging operation. The name is based on an obsolete item of logging paraphernalia; nowadays no hook is used, but often the greenhorn is sent to "get the hook for the boss."

*knot bummer*   a man whose job is to knock the limbs and any large protruding knots from the logs, usually with an ax.

*Mormon silk*   baling wire (based on the Mormons' high reputation for farming).

*misery whip*   a two-man cross-cut saw; also known as the *Swedish fiddle*.

*nosebag*   usually a lunch box, but applied to any container used for bringing food into the woods. Named after the horse's feed nosebag in recognition of the hard work done by a logger in the woods.

*prunepicker*   a farmer, hence someone unused to hard logger work (many of the inland valleys of the Northwest contain extensive fruit orchards).

*show*   the general area where a particular company is engaged in logging; the logging show may be made up of several *sides*, although a clear distinction between these two terms is not always made.

*side*   a particular area where logging is going on; a logging company may have several sides operating at the same time.

*skidroad*   a roadbed made up of logs placed side by side crosswise to the direction of traffic over which logs were hauled in earlier times into the mills over swampy or spongy terrain. In logging towns, various service businesses grew up along the skidroad, and it became known as the low district of town. Many western loggers feel that Easterners have mistakenly derived the term *skid row* from *skidroad* by an effete parallel to such terms as Millionaire's Row.

*slickshod*   wearing boots without corks, therefore being in the woods without proper traction, a danger to oneself and, potentially, to others.

*snoose*   in the Northwest woods, a moist snuff, especially Copenhagen, for dipping (carrying a small pinch usually behind the lower lip) while working in the woods, since smoking is often prohibited, especially during dry season.

*springboard*   a board inserted in a small cut in the side of a tree. Northwest fallers stood on it while falling a tree; it kept them above the brush and allowed them to cut above pockets of pitch often encountered low on big trees.

*whistlepunk*   often the youngest man on the crew, who relays the signals of the choker-setters to the man running the donkey engine, which supplies power to pull the logs into the cold deck.

*widowmaker*   a heavy broken branch so caught in the other branches of a tree that it may be dislodged by a wind or by the tree being cut, thus providing an unseen hazard for the loggers below.

HARD WORK Part of a logger's sense of his occupation becomes evident in his grudging pride for the excessively hard work demanded of him. Sometimes this comes out in jokes that refer to other occupations as easy or uninteresting because the labor is not so difficult, and sometimes it comes out in the high praise of those who have been able to labor heavily and patiently as loggers without complaint. In the former category, often it is the farmer, the sailor, or the millworker who is singled out for ridicule; in the latter, it is often the Swede who emerges as the epitome of the long-suffering, hard-working logger. Sometimes, in a wry, humorous inversion, it is the logger himself who is described as being so simple and stupid as to labor hard and long at an occupation that can only lose him money or his life. In one logger narrative common in the Northwest, an unemployed logger gets a temporary job on a nearby farm. He milks the cows, plows the fields, milks the cows again, feeds the stock, plows in the late evening until it is too dark to see. The next morning he is up at 4:00 A.M. and comes to the breakfast table with all his gear packed, ready to leave. The farmer says to him, "I thought you were looking for steady work." "I was," he says, "but there's about four hours at night I don't get nothing done but sleep around here."

Two Swedes, fallers, come to work for a local company and cut trees quietly and diligently in the woods for ten years. Another man is hired at that time who follows behind them, bucking the trees up into logs for six years. One day the bucker quits. One old Swede says to the other, "When that young feller came, I knew he wouldn't stay."

Although the Swedes are often dealt with satirically in logger stories and yarns, the image of the much-admired hard worker comes through solidly. As well, stories are told extolling the ability of Swedes to drink more, lift more weight, and dip more snoose than others on their crews. One old logger told me with a straight face that in the old days, when any unidentified man on the crew was killed during the day, the first step in finding his identity was to pull his lower lip out; if there was a hole the size of a quarter burned inside it (from a life of snoose use), the conclusion was that he was a Swede. The story is told that during the Depression an old Swede was working with a gypo outfit, setting chokers. The crew hadn't been paid for three months and everyone was complaining all day long as they worked. Finally, during lunch, the Swede took issue with his fellow workers: "What are you guys complaining for? I know there ain't no money, but we sure got a gude yob."

It is said by loggers that a wealthy man once went into the streets of Portland, Oregon, to see if he could find a likely recipient for some charitable assistance. He stopped people randomly on the street, asking them what they would do if he were to give them a million dollars. He stopped one young man who said, "Wow, if I had a million dollars, I'd buy myself a big house, some fancy cars, and I'd be able to get married and live in high style." This didn't satisfy the charitable intentions of the millionaire, so he looked further, and asked a second man, who responded, "Well, if I had a million dollars, I'd invest it in a chain of cheap, fast food stores, and I'd make even more than a million dollars in profit right off." The wealthy man thought this was on the selfish side, and he looked further, stopping a logger to ask the same question. "What would I do with a million dollars? Well, I guess I'd just keep on logging till it was all gone."

HUMOR IN A DANGEROUS SETTING In many dangerous occupations humor provides, at least in part, a means of mitigating the daily fears and anxieties that beset the people who share the same concerns but who are hesitant to articulate their fears. Often loggers will describe a terribly dangerous job with hilarity; in the midst of terrible pressure and anxiety, when a job has been done in spite of insurmountable difficulties or odds, someone will speak of himself with hyperbolic modesty; on other occasions when anxiety threatens, someone will break the tension with an unconscionable string of braggart's lies. In the examples that follow, one sees the delicacy of a "macho" humor that stretches a thin protective layer over an abyss of fear and concern.

The lead horse on a horse logging crew gets spooked and begins prancing and kicking in thick brush, sending men and clods of dirt flying in all directions and endangering the lives of the driver and helper, who are trying to attach the drawbar to a chain around a precariously lodged log. After fighting the horse, slapping with the reins, yelling at the top of his lungs, and narrowly escaping being kicked several times, the "skinner" drops the reins, goes limp, turns to his companions, and says, in the mildest of voices, "I do believe this horse used to be in show business, don't you?"

> There's this one old bucker, working out on the end of this big log stuck way out over the canyon. He gets way out near the end of this log and starts his cut, but he loses his balance, and falls way down into the canyon. Well, those boys was really concerned about him and they watched for a long time and finally they see him come crawling up through the brush. He dusts himself off, and just climbs

back up on the log and says, "Lucky I was catty on my feet, or I mighta killed myself."

Well you know how them old toppers are—when they've been on the job for a few years they get started thinking that pretty soon their number is going to be up. They think maybe it's the next tree that'll split and kill them off. Lots of those guys get to be alcoholics and have to be taken off the job because they start getting careless. One thing and another, you know, and pretty soon, sure enough, they just get killed on the job. There was this one old topper we had working with us one time, and he was getting pretty old, but as toppers go, you know, he must have been feeling really old, 'cause he had been at it a long time. Well, we tried to get it out of him, how old he was, and finally he says, "Well, boys, you remember when Jesus walked on the water?" he says, "Well, I was right behind him on a spruce top."

When I was a choker-setter, we used to use up a pair of work gloves pretty quick. You have to have pretty heavy work gloves on in order to keep from getting all them metal jaggers from the cable into your hand. Well, just about the time you'd get one pair of gloves broke in, if you left them sitting around someplace, somebody would come along and run off with them. So we got in this big argument among a bunch of us choker-setters about who it was was stealing our gloves. And one day we were arguing about it while we were eating lunch and one old faller came walking by and says to us, "I don't know what you guys are moaning about; I've wore out more cork boots than all of you have gloves."

One time I was working on this side, and one of the fallers just got started into his cut with his power saw really wound up, and he stepped up on some brush, some loose brush near the tree where he was trying to make a stand, and he tripped and fell in toward the saw. Couple of us ran up to see if he was okay, and we yelled at him, "Did you hurt yourself?" But he came back, "No—I fell, but luckily it was toward my work."

Once we had this big old log snagged up there and the

old hooker was down trying to help us fight that hang-up out of there, and we just couldn't get the log out any which way. While we was standing around, finally, a woodpecker come along and lit right on the log. The hooker says, "Well, go ahead and eat it up, I can't do anything with it." Boy, we finally just had to leave that log in there; that country was so steep it'd wear the hairs off the bottom of a chipmunk's tail.

WALKAWAY: THE INDEPENDENT LOGGER   Complementary to the logger's close group interaction in a dangerous occupation is his insistence on independence. This is manifested in logger stories and custom, especially in the days of the logging camp, by the ease with which a worker might quit his job and go on down the road to another logging show. In the early 1900s, loggers often went more by their nicknames than by their legal names, sometimes in order to stay clear of the law. Some of the common nicknames are listed later in this chapter, but one particular character who shows up time and time again in logger legend is a man known only as Walkaway. According to the usual story, someone named Walkaway comes into camp, asks for a job, and is usually put to work driving a team or doing some kind of labor in conjunction with the younger crew members. Eventually, curiosity gets the best of a young man, and he begins pestering Walkaway about his real name. Walkaway refuses to talk about it. The young man then insists on knowing how he got the name Walkaway, at which point Walkaway hands him the reins to the team and walks into the woods. An hour or so later, when the foreman checks to see why the load has not come in yet, he finds the young man standing on the skidroad with the team and a load of logs. "Where's Walkaway?" the foreman demands. "I don't know," the young man replies. "I just asked him how he got his name, and he walked off into the woods." "My God, he's done it again!"

There was lots of guys who used to work in the logging shows up in Alaska who used to have a kind of calendar they used so they'd know when to move on: They'd keep this beer bottle next to their bed, see, and fill it up with cigarette butts, and when it got full, then they'd just move out. I heard there was this one guy called Down-the-Road Dugan; he kept a pair of corks in two different crummies so that no matter which one went down off the side first he could go with it. He was famous for walking off the job, and once he seen one of the fallers heading down the road to get his nosebag, you know, at lunchtime, and Dugan thought the guy was quitting the job and yelled, "Wait up, I'll go along with ya." Then he found out the guy was just going to lunch, but the foreman had already heard him and he yells down the road, "That's okay, Dugan, just keep on a-goin'!" And there was these old guys from the old days that would sit around at night and just brag about how much wandering around they'd done. There was this one old guy we had, and every once in a while he'd throw his head back and say, "Oh, I've dangled afar with a big stick and a small bundle." And there was this other old guy who'd get mad and fed up with the job after a couple of weeks, but he wouldn't be able to quit, you know, because he needed the dough, see, so he'd just yell out every time when he fell into the sack at night, "Oh God, come down in the shape of a wild goose, and carry me off to hell!" There was another old-timer I knew, and if you just went up and asked him "What state are you from?" he'd get all huffy and make believe he was mad, and he'd say, "I'm from all forty-seven and I'll be from this one if you'll just turn me loose until sundown."

There was this faller working in Washington some years ago and he gets this idea in his mind to quit early, see, so he just comes in from the woods and the foreman docks him five dollars for not bringing in his ax and springboard. Well, about eight years after that he comes back to the same camp as a hooker. Well, he works there for a while, then finally he gets fed up and decides to quit again, so this time he hauls in all the lines and the blocks from the woods, all the tree blocks, you know, guylines and all the gear, and loads all this gear and everything, even the donkey sled, on the flatcar and here he comes pulling into camp with the whole crew and gear riding the car. The boss threw a fit about it because they just got that one side set up, but the hooker says to him, says, "Last time I come through this camp I got docked five dollars for not bringing in my tools, so I don't want to lose anything when I quit this time."

PRANKS: INDUCTING THE GREENHORN Pranks, often aimed at the new man on the crew, are among the most commonly encountered interactions in the woods. If one of the crew is newly married, some men will be willing to lose a considerable amount of pay during the day to gather all the insects they can cram into his lunch bucket after the noon break so that when he takes it home and his wife opens it, the house will be full of grasshoppers, bees, spiders, and butterflies. Someone with mechanical ability on the crew will spend his spare time running a hot line from the electrical system of the crummy to the seat that will be occupied by the new man on the crew. The greenhorn will be sent to find a cable stretcher, a left-handed wrench, a sky hook, spark plugs for a diesel tractor, all of which are, of course, impossibilities; on the other hand, he may be sent to find any number of obscene-sounding objects that actually do exist, although he may assume from the term that they do not. In the one case, he will get in trouble with the foreman or hooker for wasting his time on a fool's errand, and in the other he will be in trouble for not bringing back the needed implement. Since anyone is fair game for a prank, loggers learn to be very wary of each other, especially during the brief lull toward the end of lunchtime, when it is common for friends and colleagues to set fire to the fringed pants of a dozing crew member, hide his gloves, or place unmentionable substances in his hat. Of course the pranks played upon the newcomer are a means of incorporating him into the camaraderie of the logger society; they are not expected to engender fights, although it is assumed that the butt of any prank will properly become incensed. Perhaps the most delicious pranks of all are those that can be played on senior members of the crew, who should know better than to be caught. It seems to be their prerogative to catch and thrash anyone associated with such a prank.

One typical trick played on newcomers to a logging crew in the Northwest is the test of accuracy, or the axmanship test. The older men on the crew will gather around a stump and become very busy vying with each other and arguing about who can strike the ax a certain number of times in the same cut. The new man on the crew is asked, when he comes up to investigate, whether he thinks he can strike three or four ax blows into the same crack. He of course is interested in demonstrating his accuracy and usually agrees to try. Then he is told that the rules of the game require that he be blindfolded. It is clearly too late for him to back out now, so he agrees to try his accuracy without being able to see. After the blindfold is put on, he is placed in front of the stump and given an ax; he brings the ax down sharply on the stump to whistles of amazement and general congratulations from the crew. Then he is told to do it a second

THE DYNAMICS OF FOLKLORE

time, and the comments of the crew make it clear that he must have hit the same spot with accuracy. When he raises his ax for the third blow, however, his gloves or his lunch box will be placed on the stump to be neatly dissected by his own unerring blow. People who cannot take pranks of this sort are sometimes ostracized, but perhaps more often they leave the crew for better pastures. What remains is a group that continually reaffim their total dependence on each other by being able to joke and play pranks upon each other that would certainly be considered outrageous and disastrous if applied to someone outside the group.

We had this one trick we used to play on guys in the logging camp. We had these showers outside the bunkhouse, and everybody had to use them to get cleaned up before going into town for a good Saturday night, you know. The problem is that these showers had the taps for hot and cold water outside the stall, so a guy had to turn the water on and get it adjusted the way he liked it, and then climb in and take your shower. What we used to do was hide around the corner and wait until some guy got in and started lathering up in the shower and then we'd barricade him in there, turn off the hot water, and turn the cold water on full. Used to just leave him there to find his own way out, while the rest of us would go on down to town.

Up in Washington when they used to ride to work on the logging trains, sometimes it would be a long while before you'd get into the side, so you would just doze for most of the trip until you got up to work. Well, if you were riding in on a rainy morning, everybody would have slickers on, sort of like ponchos, see? Well, when some green man would start nodding off pretty well, the guys would nail down his slicker to the bed of the car, then pour kerosene down the back of it and light it on fire. Soon as the guy started getting warm, he'd wake up and see that his coat was on fire. But when he tried to jump up, see, his coat wouldn't move, because it's all nailed down. So the only way out was to rip off all the snaps, and by this time the guy was usually moving so fast he'd jump right off the train. Then of course he'd have to walk to work in the rain.

You know a steam donkey [engine] had a hose coming out of the boiler so it could be used for cleaning off the engine.

Sometimes the guy around the landing would put mud in that hose and blow a load of it at some passing logger. One chaser loaded it up one day and let it go at the old wood buck who was carrying wood to fire up the donkey. A rock about the size of a marble hit the old wood buck right between the eyes. He dropped that wood and chased that chaser about four miles back to camp, then thrashed him so solid he couldn't work for two days.

NAMES AND EXPRESSIONS: FOLK POETRY IN THE WOODS Although many loggers may feel themselves immune to or disinterested in the kind of poetry encountered in a school setting, nevertheless vivid expression confers a high status upon the user within the loggers' folk group. One seldom describes a person or a job without colorful and hyperbolic language. The following examples are only a few of the poetic expressions one might hear in the woods. Indeed, they are among the paler examples available.

From part of a logger's account of his unfruitful interactions with a company representative:

Well, the problem with him is, he's a push-a-pen; he only works from the ears up. When I went in to see him about my problem, and I told him everything that I thought he ought to know, why, his heart swelled up just as big as a raisin. . . . Anyway, he's so dumb he couldn't feed guts to a Hudson Bay hound. I don't know why I expected anything out of him, because you could see right away he was dumb. His wife was the ugliest woman I ever saw—she was so buck-toothed she could eat apple pie out of a jug.

Well, I won't say I'm very smart, but I've been able to stay on my feet and alive in the woods for many a year. Probably I got some good advice early on, because when I left home Daddy said, "Don't walk under any boxcars or haul-backs if they are moving." But I know some guys who are really dumb in the woods, and I suppose they won't be around long unless they get into the management and save their lives that way. We got one guy in our company who's so dumb he don't know if he was punched or bored. He don't even know if Christ was crucified or killed with a marlin spike.

Two loggers, comparing the severity of work in steep country: "Why, down in the Rogue country, you know, that country is as steep as a cow's face." "That's nothing, I was working up in Alaska, one place, the side we had to work on for three months was as steep as the back of God's head."

Of course we had lots of good names for people back then. The boss, you know, was sometimes the Commander, or Nuts of the Outfit, or My Strength and Redeemer, of course not to his face. Some of the guys even had names for Jesus Christ, like Nazareth Blacky or Jerusalem Slim, and I remember a lot of the old-timers had nicknames like Pasco Slim, Ashland Ole; there was a couple of foremen called Roughhouse Pete and Panicky Bill. We had one climber called Billy the Monk, and there was rigging men like Brooklyn Joe, and of course Down-the-Road Dugan; and everybody knew about characters like Walkaway. And there was this one character everybody knew as Three-Day Jake—he never worked more than three days at any one location, but he just kept circulating from one camp to another. They always gave him some kind of job around the kitchen so they wouldn't have to keep training somebody.

Now there's one thing that I do know, and that is, the best logger is a cross between a gorilla and a mountain goat. Now you think about that.

Did I ever hear of anybody named "Down-the-Road Dugan"? What do you mean? *I'm* Down-the-Road Dugan!

RESPONSES TO LIFE IN CAMP   Logging camps are an increasing rarity in all parts of the country, but they remain a very strong feature of logger folklore, especially when older loggers reminisce about "the days when logging was tough" to their friends over lunch or over drinks on weekends. Somehow the logging camp has remained an essential part of logger lore long after it has ceased to be a functional part of the actual logger setting. Probably because it was a time when men were gathered together for mutual living experiences over a considerable period of time, the camp functions in the folklore as a kind of symbol for the fraternity. However, it is not fashionable to be pleasantly nostalgic about the camps, for they were notorious in their inhospitability to human life: There were often vermin in the beds, outrageous smells in the bunkhouse, unpalatable (sometimes unrecognizable) food in the kitchen, and—the bane of all masculine society—there was always a dearth of women. The stories about camp life, then, feature the privations that once functioned, along with the hazards of the job, to weld loggers into a close society.

That was what they called a "fast camp"; they only had two signals—go ahead, and stop. There was three meals in that camp: cornmeal, oatmeal, and miss-a-meal.

Well, in a lot of these old camps, you know, they had this custom where guys would take turns doing the cooking. Of course, some camps had regular cooks in there, if there was a lot of guys and the company could afford to bring somebody in to do nothing but cook. But in some of the smaller camps, and on them gypo crews, why, the guys would just take turns doing the cooking. And sometimes they got this bargain going where each guy would cook until somebody complained about it, and then the guy that did the complaining would have to be the next cook. In a situation like that, see, nobody's any better cook than anybody else, so if one guy's going along okay, everybody would just go along with that, no matter how bad it was, because usually nobody wanted to get stuck with all that kitchen work. So there was this one guy who got cookin' in the camp for quite a while. Nobody liked the stuff he put on the table, but anyway they got used to it and they didn't complain, so he got stuck with it for quite a while. So he got real sick of that kitchen, and he got to looking for ways to make somebody complain about the food he set out. Well he tried everything he could think of—put Tabasco into the dessert, put salt in the coffee, burned the meat, and did whatever he could to make somebody complain, but they wouldn't have no part of it. So he got real frustrated about it, and when he was out in the woods one day trying to hunt up some fresh camp meat, some "side-hill salmon," you know, he come on to this big pile of fresh moose pellets. A real stack of mountain muffins, you know? So he says to himself, "By God, them guys would complain if I fed 'em that for supper." So he scoops all these pellets up into his knapsack and hauls them off to the cook shack and he whups up this tremendous supper before the guys get there and trims it off with this big fine pie made out of them moose pellets. Well, that night all those guys came in, sat down, and gritted their teeth and waited for the garbage. But then they got this big meal which was better than anything they ever had while he had been cookin'. And then to top it off, he brought out that big pie and laid it on the middle of the table and told them guys to dig in. So of course they did and they laid into that pie like it was going out of style. Course, they all starts gagging, spitting, and turning green, and one guy keeled over right off the bench, and just before he passed out he yelled, "My God! Moose turd pie!—*good*, though!"

I worked one time in a camp where nobody knew what was happenin'; as far as I was concerned, that camp was a home for the old and a school for the young. They didn't know nothin' there, and I wasn't in any position to teach them. All they knew how to do was eat, and they ate so fast that no matter how close you came to the head of the chow line, there'd always be somebody coming out belching.

SEX  Although loggers seem to agree that sex is one of the favorite topics of conversation and joking among loggers, they are extremely hesitant about expressing their thoughts on the matter outside the confines of the esoteric group. One elderly logger, for example, was willing to allow his repertoire of songs to be recorded and placed in an archive only with the stipulation that it would never be played for a woman under twenty-one, because he was afraid some of his own grandchildren might discover his relationship to songs he had carefully sheltered them from during his life. While sex is a common topic among many loggers, it is a considerable impropriety to talk about it in mixed company or in print. Typically, loggers will adopt a polite, almost hyperliterary style when talking about sex, or else they will attempt to avoid the subject altogether when talking with outsiders. Said one logger to me recently, "Sex? I leave it alone: Why, some women will get pregnant if their husband goes by the bedpost on a motorcycle with his coveralls on." Another logger recalls how delicately a Black hook tender he had known revealed the nature of his ethnic background: "Well, you know I'm really an Indian. My grandma was ice-fishing and a Black man come out there on the ice to see what she was doing. Well, she had moccasins on, and he had corks, and my old man was the result of their conversation."

It would be interesting to speculate on the motivations behind logger diffidence on the matter of sex when they are speaking to people outside their own group. No doubt the subject can be approached fruitfully from a psychological perspective as well as from the sociological observation that many loggers also are members of a larger cultural group with northern European, perhaps Puritan, backgrounds that still urge a conservative attitude on the propriety of such topics in mixed company. For loggers, there is an intensification of the distinction made between propriety on the job and propriety in town because many operations and items in the woods are referred to by sexual and anatomical names and because, while the men are trading stories and jokes among themselves, sex is a very prominent topic. The completely different dialect used when loggers come home is, for our purposes at least, indicative of their own awareness of an internal dynamic system shared without question by loggers, but a system of expression so special and vivid as to require innocent outsiders to be shielded from it.

Of course, in recent times women have been entering many traditionally male occupations, and they have found, generally, that they are subject to the same rules of conduct and vocabulary. That is, a woman must become a logger in loggers' terms in order to be accepted. A woman I know recently got a job in the woods. Her letter shows the obligation she felt to make it in the woods, her sensitivity to the importance of logger lore, and her awareness of how her sex had an effect upon her relationship to the crew:

> I have now spent six months with loggers. It was tough, but of course they are my kind of people, and in retrospect, I can see I loved it. I took copious notes, although they seemed superficial, juvenile. For example, I noted in January that the hairs in my nose froze every day, and I was literally constipated by fear (they drive like madmen). Loggers don't use Saran Wrap on their sandwiches—they use wax paper so they can grill them in the warming fires. I took a bad fall while scaling one day in snow and ice—slipped in a clear cut of piss fir and fell 30 feet. One of the fallers, Shitty Pants by name, called out to me, and the energy to yell, the strength required for me to yell back, "I'm FINE!" was beyond belief, as I was hurt so bad. Once I realized the ribs weren't broken, and got the blood stopped, I buried myself in the branches and cried. I quit taking a bath after work because I was so offended by the ring around the tub. I ruined one pair of suspenders from peeing on them. The

men like to say SHIT and get it over with. Some of them need for me to say SHIT, too. Sometimes I say PISSED, because I'm so conscious of SHIT. Today a few FUCKS flew around the crew bus, and everyone watched me very closely. . . .

From a folklore point, the work is fascinating. I'm avidly collecting hand signals. I tend to spend a lot of time with the old-timers, and as always, they love to talk to an interested woman. There are some decided advantages to my sex. One of my favorite stories is told by an old faller, who describes being chased by a bull, across a large meadow, without a tree in sight. He ran and ran, and could see the bull was gaining on him. His fear grew, and no matter how fast he ran, the bull got closer until he could finally feel hot breath behind him. With his last bit of strength, the faller scrambled up a tree. At this point I cried, "But you said there were no trees!" "Well, there had to be!" he roared.

POPULAR BELIEF AND CUSTOM   Much of this folklore implies that loggers participate in a chiefly male, occupationally oriented group only. Especially the exclusiveness of sexual topics in their folklore might indicate that they share very little of their own ideas and worldview with their family or other members of their community. But the folklorist must look at the total context in which a logger lives to determine the extent to which the logger also participates in a somewhat larger folk grouping, that of a community of individuals related to the logging industry. Loggers' picnics, loggers' carnivals (in which loggers—and sometimes their wives—participate in competitive games based on occupational skills), various kinds of social fraternities that include entire families and towns, should be taken as evidence that the loggers' sense of themselves is not limited strictly to the inner circle of the occupation itself. If the folklorist, for example, interviews the wives and families of loggers, a larger and richer picture of logger folklore dynamics will emerge. For example, many women who raised their families in the logging towns of the Northwest during the 1920s recall the very tight and cheerful community support for almost any individual in trouble, any family in crisis, any young couple at their wedding. Mrs. Vintie Holt recalls that when a marriage occurred in an Oregon logging community in the 1920s, the people of the town would usually circle the newlyweds' house, everyone holding hands, and serenade them far into the night.

On some occasions, of course, a shivaree was held: Friends, both male and female, would descend on the newlyweds' home, abduct them both, and place them in a wheelbarrow and parade them through the camp to the accompaniment of singing and laughter. Thus, even though the newlywed husband might expect pranks to be played on him in the woods by his male colleagues, the community as a whole played a supportive role. The loggers in the community, of course, took part in both sides of these activities. It would be unfair to draw even the barest delineations of logger folk dynamics without taking the specific and larger dimensions of life in logging communities into consideration.

Out in the woods among the loggers, of course, there were the usual popular beliefs about bad luck, forebodings of disaster, means of avoiding accident and misfortune, and the like. Loggers had a widespread belief that if a man couldn't sleep at night, and if he had cold hands or cold feet, it meant he would have an accident at work. If a logger had one of these presentiments, it would be common for him not to go to work the next day and everyone would understand. If a wife knew of her husband's hunch, she would encourage him to stay home from work on such a day. Thus, the belief had two sides—the aspect experienced by the worker in the woods, and the response recognized and encouraged by the members of his immediate community at home.

A related popular belief among loggers in the Northwest is that accidents, especially deadly accidents, are most likely to occur during the last few days—and most likely on the very last day—of a man's employment. This kind of belief, experienced by the men in the woods, occasioned a considerable amount of anxiety during a man's last days of employment; apprehension under these circumstances was recognized by other loggers not as a sign of fear, but as a functional, normal aspect of finishing a life in the woods. Obviously there is a comment here on the assumptions made by loggers on the probabilities of a man being able to finish his employment in the woods without dying prematurely. The community side of this belief is reflected in the custom among many logging foremen of firing a man before his appointed termination day and paying him up through the day he would normally have quit. This allows a man to forgo the apprehension and the psychological danger of the last day at work. Mrs. Vintie Holt pointed out to a folklore fieldworker that her husband had had cold hands and sleepless nights two days before he was killed—on what was to have been his last day of work in the woods. It is certainly not far-fetched to suggest that any anxiety generated by these beliefs may actually contribute to enough malaise during the last days on the job virtually to insure that a person might make a fatal mistake during a delicate maneuver. Be that as it may, the logger, in male company—perhaps over a drink—would characteristically pass it off as a macabre joke: "Did I ever hear of getting killed on the last day of work? Well, I guess if you got killed, it *would* be your last day of work, wouldn't it? [Laughs.] Anyhow, you know, no matter whether you're injured or killed, they leave you there by the cold deck and take you in with the last load of the day, so you won't lose out on the day's pay. And no matter what, a day's pay is a day's pay."

In these examples of logger folklore, the actual dynamics are not spelled out. Rather, they are to be inferred from the topics, styles, language, and attitudes expressed in the lore itself. The examples follow the lines suggested by loggers themselves, grouped together by topic rather than genre, and with a considerable overlap in intent and meaning. It is only proper that this should be so, for real dynamics operate as interactions among people, not as categories invented by the observer. Even so, the dynamic system suggested in these examples needs to be augmented by the reader through further reading and field research; the dynamics themselves will change somewhat according to the age of the loggers one interviews, the particular kind of trees they cut, the part of the country, the methods of logging used, and so on. What is given here, then, is only a start: a clear indication that loggers as a group do conceive of themselves as a group, and largely through the live folklore they share with each other within the immediate circumstances of their job.

Loggers may be as well members of other close folk groups whose contexts will act similarly upon the members under those other unique situations shared. For one, the logger will no doubt participate in family folklore; he may also share ethnic folklore, if he is, say, of Swedish descent and still participates in Swedish traditions; he might also be a Mormon, and on that basis share with other Mormons such lore as J. Golden Kimball stories, Nephite legends, esoteric stories of marvels, providences, revelations, and the like; if he is a lifelong resident of Oregon, he may furthermore share in the regional suspicion of people from out of state (especially from California), and may use a whole battery of regionalisms—such as *webfoot* to denote someone who lives in the rainy part of the state west of the Cascade Mountains. Each of these groupings provides a relatively high context situation in which group members recognize each other and talk to each other by using that special cultural dialect that binds them together. Folk groups may be exclusive, but they are not mutually exclusive.

# ◤ THE MULTIPLICITY OF TRADITION

The probability that most people belong to more than one folk group is a consideration that must remain central in the study of folklore dynamics; it requires us to recognize that a given person may have a wide repertoire of potential traditional dynamic interactions, each of which is set in motion by certain particular live contexts. The logger folk group as perceived and participated in by the loggers themselves is primarily occupational in its live setting. The insider recognizes and performs for other insiders a certain variety of jokes, pranks, speech customs, and so on. It is these live, traditional interactions and not the cutting of trees per se that defines the logger as a member of a folk group.

We must make the same kind of inquiry when we look at other folk groups suggested by other than occupational factors. In other words, we will want to recognize that it is not theology that makes a Mormon a member of a folk group, it is the dynamic traditional interactions a Mormon shares with other members of the same faith (customs, proverbs, jokes, slang terms), factors distinctive to a sense of "us." Similarly, in the case of ethnic groups, the question of whether the group is a folk group will rest not on surnames or skin color or genetics but on the existence of a network of dynamic traditional interactions. A Black American who does not participate in any Black traditional systems is not a functioning member of any Black folk group. A white American who does participate fully (language, custom, dance, food, etc.) in an American Indian tribe may be said to be a member of that folk group—whether or not his grandmother was a Cherokee princess, while someone who is genetically 100 percent Native American may not be a member of that folk group if he does not participate in the folk customs. Thus we must look at the nature of the dynamic interaction, not at superficial details. How is a person said to be a member of a Yugoslav-American folk group: by having a Yugoslav name and learning to dance the *kolo* in college or by participating in the traditions of an American Yugoslav community? Obviously, the latter.

Just as obviously, participating in these ethnic traditions is not in the same dimension as participating in the loggers' occupation. Some Yugoslavs may work on different jobs and wear different clothes than other Yugoslavs. Where can we look, then, to find in the ethnic group the dynamic equivalent of occupational lore? What is it that they do together that is traditionally distinctive enough to provide a basic recognition of an "us"?

DYNAMICS OF ETHNICITY   One of the best areas of focus is traditional food lore, partly because people change their inherited tastes in food very slowly, partly because when people eat at home, they are with a close group whose members share a high family or ethnic context. Especially in the case of immigrant groups—who are well known for their tendency to maintain traditions even after they may have changed or disappeared in the original home country—family meals and meals shared with other immigrants become celebrations of ethnicity, assertions of a continuation of an "us." Watch the ethnic foods that come forth at a Scandinavian or a Greek wedding, at a Portuguese fishing celebration on a saint's day, at a Japanese funeral, at a New England Thanksgiving. Ask what recipes are passed along family or ethnic lines. What foods do you connect with your ancestry? Why? And when? It is no accident that many multicultural communities have found the local cookbook one of the only satisfactory ways to describe and celebrate the reality of local culture variation. For example, as a Bicentennial project the Butte Silver-Bow Bicentennial Commission in Montana issued *Butte's Heritage Cookbook*, a rich compilation of ethnic recipes along with stories about their national origins and about the people who brought them to Butte, a mining town of incredibly varied cultural backgrounds.

I have suggested that one of the best ways to detect and experience folk group dynamics is to observe how and why the members of a given group recognize each other. What cues tell one insider he is dealing with another insider as an insider? What cues tell an outsider he is operating in a different set of assumptions than his own? If we take folk foods as a point of focus, how can we be sure that we are dealing with real traditional dynamics as compared to commercial interests or the perfunctory enjoyment of ethnic foods by hobbyists? After all, not everyone who eats *chow yuk* is Chinese; not everyone who eats matzoh-ball soup is Jewish; not everyone who eats *teriyaki* chicken is Japanese. The dynamics tell us the difference.

ESOTERIC EATING: JAPANESE-AMERICANS   One possible start is to observe a picnic where most participants are members of the same ethnic group. What do they do and what do they bring that one might not see if the occasion were a mixed group where others' tastes are central? At first, one might notice the usual hot dogs, hamburgers, and soft drinks; then, as focus improves, one might be puzzled by some unknown substances: What are those things wrapped up in grape leaves? What holds those balls of rice together? Those things look like chicken, but they're dark brown. What's that yellow stuff the old-timers are drinking? And after the questions, the tasting, which in the case of ethnic foods is far more complicated than the chemical action of food on the taste buds. If one suggests eating raw fish to a group made up of Japanese-Americans and European-Americans, half the room will smile and the other half will look sick. What accounts for this?

I once watched an artist trying to explain to an audience of teachers what he felt art should "do" to the viewer. His effort was received with polite boredom until he brought out a fresh lemon, cut it, and began sucking one half with considerable relish. The audience's immediate response was to pucker, squint, grimace, and shudder—obviously because they recognized the taste and the visual stimulation of seeing someone else having the experience was enough to cause them to have it, or at least to have an appropriate, real response to it. Ethnic foods—their appearance, smell, and taste, as well as their customary construction and deployment—create a similar response of recognition, and in addition to personal tastes there is the further dimension of the experience of belonging to a close group with whose members one has shared and enjoyed the same responses many times before. This experience is strong evidence of the continued vitality of folk dynamics.

INGREDIENTS AND TERMINOLOGY   What might we find at an ethnic picnic that triggers such cultural reflexes in the insider but inspires only questions in the outsider? A close look at the typical foods taken to a Japanese-American picnic will indicate the extent to which occasional recreational foods may lead us to more general observations about the relations between food and folk dynamics. The most distinctive items at a Japanese-American picnic fall into a few particular categories: *gohan* (cooked rice; uncooked short-grained rice is called *okome*), *otsukemono* (pickled vegetables), *sushi* (various finger-foods made with rice seasoned with vinegar), and *teriyaki* (various meats baked, barbecued, or broiled in soy sauce).Of these, *gohan* is easily the most important, not only because many of the picnic foods are made with cooked short-grained rice, but because it is usually served with all other foods as well. Its important position in Japanese foodlore is apparent in the use of the word *gohan* to mean food in general; if someone calls "Gohan!" it is the equivalent of the American "Soup's on!" At a picnic, the rice is seldom eaten in a bowl; rather, it is made into round or triangular balls, usually with a salted item in the center (such as *umeboshi*, a pickled plum). Rice in this form is referred to as *onigiri*.

*Sushi* uses *gohan* as its primary ingredient, but it stands in Japanese-American folk tradition as a separate category because of the distinctive way in which the rice is mixed with other items. One of the most popular forms of *sushi* is *norimaki*. *Nori* is a kind of processed sea-lettuce that is bought in sheets; vinegar-soaked rice is laid out across the sheet in a small mound, other colored ingredients are added (usually in uneven numbers), and the whole item is rolled into a cylinder about one and one-half or two inches in diameter. The roll is cut into cross sections about one inch thick, which are then stacked on a plate. Looking at the cross section of *norimaki*, one sees first the dark green "seaweed" sheet on the outside, then a white circular rice filling in the middle of which are usually three or five colored ingredients. Another kind of *sushi* features a small, hand-sized pocket of fried bean curd (*age*) into which the rice has been packed. Since this kind of *sushi* was offered to the fox deity (Kitsune) in Japan for prosperity in business, some older Issei still refer to it as *kitsunezushi*; usually in America the term is *agezushi*. Balls made of this specially cooked rice are referred to as *nigirizushi*, from the verb *nigiri*, to grasp. Still another kind, which features other chopped-up items mixed in with the rice, is referred to as *chirashizushi* ("*sushi* made of mixed separate items").

An extensive use of meat in Japan is fairly recent due to the early Buddhist influence, which recommended against using animal substances in human food. Japanese-Americans, however, seem to have adopted the American propensity for meat-eating, but in their own traditional way they have maintained distinctive Japanese methodologies for producing the appropriate taste. One of these is the process called *yaki*, literally "roasting, baking, broiling." If vegetables and meat are slowly stir-cooked together in a large heated pan, the term used is *sukiyaki*; because this dish requires elaborate preparation and careful cooking, it is seldom taken on picnics, but it is commonly used in the home when special guests visit. Pieces of any meat may be chopped into sizes easily handled with chopsticks or the fingers and cooked separately in a thick mixture of soy sauce, sugar, and other flavorings; this process is known as *teriyaki*, and is a typical way of fixing meats for picnics.

Of extreme interest and importance to the folklorist is that Japanese-Americans of the second and third generations, most of whom consider themselves far more American than Japanese, seldom use the Japanese language as a means of communication. Of course, some second-generation people who grew up speaking Japanese at home use it when talking to their parents, but for the most part, the Japanese language is not in everyday use among members of the Japanese-American folk group. Nonetheless, almost all members of this group, regardless of generation, recognize and use all the Japanese words for folk foods, for items and implements used in their preparation, and for attitudes concerning their arrangement and seasonal use.

For example, Japanese-Americans use the honorific prefix *o-* for many of the foods, some even attaching the form to *gohan*, unaware that *go-* is already an honorific. *O-gohan*, while technically nonstandard Japanese, reveals an ongoing concern for propriety in traditional foods. Another similar element is the use of traditional Japanese phrases before and after eating, usually spoken with head bowed quickly, palms together: *itadakimasu*, indicating the intention of accepting food, and *gochiso sama*, literally "honorable feast," a compliment to the cook and a recognition of respect for food generally. This is another key indication that for this group of people foods are indeed a cultural link as well as a method of survival.

It is important to note that the foods one might find at a Japanese-American picnic are also used centrally at all occasions of import to the community: weddings, funerals, holidays (*obon*, *hanamatsuri*, New Year's) and at any celebration or special event where visitors or dignitaries may be present. Thus we may say that the very presence of these foods indicates that a dynamic folk interaction is taking place. Of course, an insider (a Japanese-American) would note further the qualities of the foods and the traditional aspects of their preparation and appearance. Just as the loggers' recognition of each other is based not simply on recognizing the clothes but how they're worn, the Japanese-American recognition of folk food in a live, dynamic context is not based exclusively on the foods themselves but on how they are done (that is, whether it is obvious they were produced properly and appropriately by traditional standards). Asked what she considers really distinctive about Japanese-American traditional food, a Nisei grandmother from Ogden, Utah, Mrs. Chiyoe Kubota, answered that the most important elements would be (1) the foods and ingredients themselves, (2) the flavor, (3) the arrangement, (4) *tsukurikata*, how the food is made, and (5) *kirikata*, how the food is cut. The matter of flavor is distinctive, of course, because of the various spices and materials used, many of which are indeed imported from Japan even today: *shoyu* (soy sauce), *ajinomoto* (monosodium glutamate), *shoga* (ginger), *mirin* (sweet cooking sake), *sake* (fortified rice wine), *miso* (fermented bean paste, either white or red). Not only do these distinctive seasonings provide particular flavors not found in other ethnic foods, but their precise applications to different kinds of foods can be learned only by lengthy practice and association with traditional cooks who have themselves learned the process usually in their own families. Thus Mrs. Kubota can say that the taste, methods, and arrangements are distinctive aspects of Japanese-American folk foods; she does mention that the recognition of ingredients is basic, but she insists that their preparation and especially their looks are the keys to the recognition of ethnic dynamics.

Still other foods should be mentioned here as distinctively used by Japanese-Americans in traditional foodways. There is a widespread use of Japanese green tea (*ocha*), a preference for short-grained rice (partly because it is more glutinous and sticks together better than long-grained rice, which may be puzzling to those European-Americans who have been led to believe that rice should be dry and flaky). Japanese-Americans enjoy *umani* (vegetables seasoned and cooked together in a stew), *sashimi* (sliced raw fish, usually sea bass or tuna, served with hot mustard or horseradish), octopus either raw or cooked, squid either raw or cooked, *manju* (a sweet bean paste bun), *yokan* (hardened sweet bean paste or jelly made into solid rectangles, or sliced and eaten with tea), *tofu* (soy bean curd, often cut up into small squares and used as an ingredient in everything from soup to sukiyaki), and *omochi* (a rather dense rice cake made from pounded, cooked sweet rice).

FOOD AND COMMUNITY *Omochi* is certainly one of the more interesting folk foods from the standpoint of the esoteric scholar, for it is made of a special kind of rice and is produced in a communal manner as follows: A large mortar (*usu*) made of stone, wood, or concrete is filled with steamed sweet rice. It is then pounded with large wooden hammers (*kine*). Two or sometimes three people take turns hammering the rice with these large mallets, timing their actions to the rhythms of a song sung by all present. At a certain beat in each measure, a woman reaches into the mortar and moves the glob of rice so it will not stick. Each movement must be timed carefully or the woman's hands would easily be crushed by the mallets; she wets her hands on one beat, reaches in and moves the rice on another, and each person wielding a wooden hammer strikes on a certain beat. People in the community take turns at all these jobs, although usually the most knowledgeable and agile woman is allowed to retain the job of turning the rice. Some communities have begun to use a mochi-machine more recently, but the communal, celebrative element is still retained even so. When the *omochi* has been sufficiently pounded to a consistent rubbery pulp, it is formed into small, flat rice cakes ranging from about four inches in diameter down to two inches.

These cakes are sold to be given away to friends and relatives at New Year's time; they are placed in a small stack on the family altar or before pictures of the family ancestors, and one small mochi cake is put into the bottom of each bowl of the special soup *(ozoni)* eaten on New Year's morning. In this kind of custom, the dynamics of the folk group can be seen vividly. Not only does the sweet rice function as a means of feeding the community on a larger level, but it is used symbolically to feed the spirits of the ancestors of the family. In addition, it is the occasion for a communal gathering, and it is the larger symbol of the community's own recognition of its long-term kinship with rice and all the seasonal and religious observances connected with it.

A number of cooking implements have retained their Japanese names in America. Commonly known are such terms as: *shamoji,* a wooden spatula for serving rice; *hashi,* chopsticks; *sudare,* a bamboo mat used for rolling the *norimaki; suribachi,* a grooved ceramic mortar for grinding sesame seeds, and the like; *handai,* a round wooden tray with a three- or four-inch vertical edge used for mixing and seasoning *gohan* for *sushi.*

CUSTOM AND NUMBER   Foodlore of course goes much deeper into the culture than simply the culinary techniques of presenting familiar ethnic tastes. Custom and cultural aesthetics also play a large role in how foods are produced. In the case of Japanese-Americans, one very strong cultural element brought from Japan dictates that in arrangements of things such as flowers and foods, any individual but related components should be presented in uneven numbers. Typically, the numbers three, five, and seven are stressed. In the case of *norimaki,* the seasoned rice that is rolled up in a sheet of sea-lettuce with several colored ingredients at the core, the usual family variety has three colored segments, while festive occasions call for five and very special occasions require seven. The colors themselves originally had particular meanings, but the one that remains in Japanese-American folklore is red, which connotes prosperity and good luck. The red ingredient in *norimaki* is usually made with shredded shrimp dyed red. When such food is served at a funeral, however, four central ingredients are used because the word for four, *shi,* sounds exactly like the word for death, *shi* (although of course their characters are quite different). The use of four central ingredients in *norimaki* is considered appropriate, therefore, at funerals, while it is considered inappropriate and perhaps even insulting or shocking at another time: One would never serve *norimaki* with four central colored ingredients at a picnic, for example.

The number four, in fact, is avoided whenever there is a reference to such human matters as birthdays or anniversaries; many Japanese-Americans, following the older Japanese tradition, either downplay or omit fourth birthdays, fourth anniversaries, and fortieth birthdays. Similarly, in counting the generations of Japanese-Americans, one might normally use the regular Japanese words *ichi* (one), *ni* (two), *san* (three), *shi* (four), but the very fact one is counting human generations requires a shift from *shi* to *yon*. Thus the first generation, the immigrants from Japan, is called *issei* (literally, "first people," or "first generation"), the second generation *nisei*, the third generation *sansei*, and the fourth, *yonsei*. The customary attitudes toward the number four are thus reflected not only in the production of Japanese folk foods, but throughout the culture generally. This further demonstrates the deep connection between foods and other worldview aspects of an entire culture.

A YEAR OF FOOD    Another example of dynamic vitality in Japanese-American food folklore is the existence of a traditional food calendar, which allows us to see the importance of the traditional foods not only in and of themselves, as just described, but as they fit into the larger customary observances during the year. This is a common phenomenon in all cultures, of course; for example, most Americans find it at least familiar to think of turkey in connection with Thanksgiving. Turkey may be eaten at any other time, but turkey with all the trimmings is by tradition more appropriate for some families on Thanksgiving Day than any other food. There are great differences among American sub-cultures as to what foods are appropriate on which holidays; even the concept of the kinds of foods appropriate at certain times of the day will vary considerably. For some rural New Englanders, for example, apple pie is a common breakfast food, while for most other Americans it is a dessert. In the case of the Japanese-American food calendar, we will expect to find particular foods associated with certain holidays, and we will not be surprised to find a substantially different attitude toward the foods that are eaten at certain times of day within those holidays.

One of the sharpest examples of this is the New Year's Day custom of eating *ozoni* soup with one's family the very first thing in the morning. This soup is made of a fish stock and contains some green vegetables (such as Chinese cabbage or spinach), *kamaboko* (a fish cake, sliced), and at the bottom a soft, dense cake of *mochi*. For those European-Americans who spend New Year's Eve drinking heavily, this would be a very strange if not dubious treat for New Year's morning. For the Japanese-American, however, it sets the stage within the close family group for an entire day of eating traditional foods, many of which feature the color red, which is appropriate to ideas of good fortune associated by the Japanese with the New Year. An inventory of the entire day's activities will appear in Chapter 4, but here we should note that New Year's Day for Japanese-Americans is a kaleidoscope of those same traditional foods that they might find in use sporadically throughout the year. It is as if New Year's Day is a conscious celebration of ethnicity through food, of shared traditionality through the dynamics of group members sitting down to eat continuously for the entire day as they visit from house to house. This conscious use of traditional foods as a means of maintaining and strengthening cultural interactions among members of a folk group certainly indicates not only the group's vitality, but the position of food traditions in the study of its folklore.

DYNAMICS AND IDENTITY    As we would no doubt find in the case of most immigrant groups in America, there must be a number of reasons for maintaining food customs, but the case of the Japanese-Americans in particular illustrates a set of dynamics that seems to reach beyond mere sociological observations about group identity. In fact, we might have expected the extinction of many of these food customs because of the very scarcity of several of the ingredients, especially during the Second World War, when relationships with Japan were fractured. Moreover, the Japanese-Americans, especially in the second and third generations, have been extremely eager to prove themselves Americans without substantial foreign attachments. Many of the foods discussed here are so exotic as to call attention to themselves as foreign, a possible negative factor for those Japanese-Americans who wished to become quickly Americanized. What can account, then, for the maintenance of strong Japanese food customs among people who themselves sought to strengthen their American identity? Why didn't they give it all up and adopt the generalized American food system? Surely the dynamics of folklore give us one of the best answers for these questions.

For one thing, it is important to note that in Japanese custom the family, not the individual, is the basic unit of society. The earliest creation myths are founded upon family relationships, the early feudal governments of Japan were based on family systems, and indeed, in Japan today the family is still often seen as a microcosm of the country and of the universe. The most central single family custom is sitting down to eat together: In addition to an ethnocentric attitude about themselves and their customs, the concept of the family as the central unit of stability and normalcy has led to a very strong set of traditions within which the Japanese learns what is right and what is wrong both as an individual and as a member of a culture. Eating traditional foods together with other Japanese people is one very powerful way of reaffirming one's position within the total family system. No wonder, then, that among the very earliest Japanese immigrants to America were many farmers who immediately set about growing Japanese vegetables and producing Japanese condiments for the other Japanese in America. Apparently these earliest immigrants stuck together very tightly as a community, and most of them, at least by their own admission, were planning to make money and eventually return with it to Japan. Of course, as time went on, many decided to settle in the United States and get married; many of these people sent for brides from Japan, so that as nuclear families began to be established on the West Coast, the parent, or *issei*, generation was pretty solidly Japanese in its orientation and food customs.

As the *nisei* generation came along, in accordance with Japanese family custom, the children spent a good deal of time at home, usually speaking Japanese with their parents and speaking English only in school. And even now, in the third and fourth generations, it is customary for Japanese-Americans to live rather close to their *issei* parents and grandparents. Thus they maintain a close family system in which the sharing of traditional foods is one of the few strong ties between the immigrant generation and the present Americans of Japanese descent. Further, not many generations have passed in this immigrant group when compared to the generations of European groups who settled the eastern seacoast two and three hundred years ago. Even in those older groups ethnic foods are still culturally functional, and we would expect them to be even more so in the case of more recent immigration, especially among people with such strong and continuing family ties.

For many Japanese-Americans, Buddhism has further encouraged the generations to live together rather than separately and has stressed filial piety as the basic means of maintaining stability and security in the world. This has strengthened still further the tendency of the younger generation to follow the older ways, and in a culture where traditional cooking is so central to cultural recognition, we would expect this force to have had a considerable impact on maintaining food traditions as well.

Certainly, as Marvin Opler and others have pointed out, there must have been an intensification of Japanese folklore during the internment years of the Second World War, when most Japanese-American citizens and their resident alien parents were placed in civilian concentration camps, mostly in the American West. Opler studied the conditions in the Tule Lake internment center and concluded that Japanese folklore had experienced a strong revival because of the tensions and anxieties of internment; after the war, he contended, Japanese-Americans went their own way and dropped a good many if not most of these strongly Japanese traditions. But we should note that the Tule Lake camp was the one camp where Japanese nationals were segregated for their return to their home country, as well as where Japanese-Americans who openly favored the Japanese cause in the war were sent. Under these circumstances, we might expect nationalistic Japanese tradition to have run strong.

But the case is even more complicated, for what Opler and others unwittingly encountered is that we knew little of Japanese-American folklore before the Second World War, largely because the Japanese and Japanese-Americans reserved most of their folk traditions for use at home and at special celebrations, hence they were not easily or multiformly seen. During the camp experience, however, they were under heavy observation, for the government had hired teams of anthropological and sociological investigators to record the reactions of people to internment. During these years, the Japanese-Americans probably had as many anthropologists following them around as had the Indians. After the war, when interest in the Japanese-Americans as objects of scrutiny waned, their use of folklore returned to the family setting and to those customary celebrations (*obon*, etc.), where they now reside solidly as they did before. Japanese-American family folklore continues to be, sometimes along with Buddhism, the central dynamic feature of Japanese-American cultural awareness. I hope it is evident from these few examples that this is not simply because "Japanese women so love to cook" but because methods of food preparation and consumption in a family setting are powerful symbols of participation in the group's dynamics.

## DYNAMICS OF FAMILY FOLKLORE

IMMEDIATE FAMILY  In some cultures (like those of northern Europe, the United States, and Canada), the individual, not the family, is considered the basic, indivisible unit of society. Nonetheless, family folklore may be said to be the first and basic dynamic traditional system encountered by most people the world over. In the family setting, as observed in Chapter 1, we learn our language, dialect, and elemental worldview all from hearing and observing others' speech and action. It is in this setting that we note, and participate in, certain traditional roles. And it is within these growing dynamic interactions that we develop a strong sense of an "us." As we grow older, we are made aware of still larger implications and meanings for the family "us": For instance, we can distinguish between our own immediate family (with its dinner table customs, baby teeth disposal practices, family words) and that larger group of cousins, uncles, and grandmothers who gather at family reunions or in smaller groups at Christmas or Seder. This larger family may also have customs, and they may or may not coincide with those of the smaller family. For example, Christmas in my own family meant opening one small gift on Christmas Eve, then waiting until my parents were up Christmas morning to open the rest. No particular custom dictated the order or frequency of opening presents. Christmas dinner required no blessing beforehand, but the meal itself was festive, with the special extra items usually reserved for Sunday dinners.

HORIZONTAL FAMILY   Christmas with my larger family, however, had other contours. Dinner was central, and came before the opening of gifts. The preparation was done entirely by the women, who filled the kitchen of whichever house (we never knew the mechanism for this delicate choice) while "the menfolk"—including the young boys—gathered in another room where jokes were told, cigars were smoked, and an occasional drink was shared. Dinner always began with a blessing, given impromptu by one of the youngest present at the request of the aunt or grandmother who had presided over the preparations. Of course the youngsters had all been coached by uncles to substitute a parody (like "Good bread, good meat; Good God, let's eat!"); sometimes, to everyone's amazement, a child would actually give the parody, receive an appropriate scowl from a mother, and begin again.

Presents were passed out one at a time by one of the children, who was designated Santa for the purpose. The entire room watched as the person opened the gift. Other nostalgic details could be added here, but you will be able to supply better ones from personal experience with the family "us" and the Family "us."

VERTICAL FAMILY   Beyond this larger frame, still another family eventually emerges: the family tree "us"—the vertical family as we recognize its existence in time, often through family scrapbooks, genealogies, diaries, and the anecdotes of grandparents. This still larger family enters into the traditional dynamics chiefly through inherited items and family custom. We see it in comments like, "Oh, our family has *always* done it this way." On our Christmas tree were several "really old" decorations handed down from my great-grandmother's time. On one bed was an old friendship crazy quilt, with pieces of fabric from dresses and ties still recognizable to the old-timers in the family. There were areas and farms still called by the names of family members long dead.

There were annual visits to relatives we knew only from their gravestones and from what we took to be their sentiments, expressed in rhymes or aphorisms we assumed they or their closest kin had made up themselves:

*Man goeth to his long home.*

*Peace to thy dust,*
*dear friend farewell.*

*Remember me as you pass by,*
*For as you are so once was I.*
*As I am now you soon must be.*
*Prepare for Death and follow me.*

*Boast not thyself of tomorrow*
[on a grave of three small children]

*The grave is near the cradle seen*
*And swift the moments pass between*
              [girl, age 3]

*Parents and Friends adieu:*
*Here in this Earth I wait for you.*

*I have come to my grave in a full age*
*as a shock of corn fully ripe.*
              [woman, age 87]

*My time was short.*
*What age are you?*
              [boy, age 7]

These engraved messages mean something different to members of the family than they do to outsiders. They seem to represent serious communicative relationships with our family tree; on the other hand, we are quite conscious that other families' tombstones can be appreciated for other reasons. In Knights' Corner Cemetery, near Pelham, Massachusetts, we often stopped just to read the gravestone of a man allegedly poisoned by his wife. Since it did not concern our family, we considered it humorous:

Warren Gibbs
died by arsenic poison
Mar. 23, 1860
AE. 36 yrs. 5 mos.
23 dys.

*Think my friends when this you see*
*How my wife hath dealt by me*
*She in some oysters did prepare*
*Some poison for my lot and share*
*Then of the same I did partake*
*And nature yielded to its fate*
*Before she my wife became*
*Mary Felton was her name.*

Erected by his Brother
WM. GIBBS

This tombstone was a continuing and vital part of Gibbs and Felton lore, for the families had been feuding for years. The murder charge was never proven, but the stone remains to proclaim the Gibbs version of the story. It has been toppled, defaced, and stolen numerous times, and is now protected, it is said, by the curse of William Gibbs. Here an inanimate object continues to maintain an important role—perhaps a central one—in the dynamics of one family's history and tradition. For them it was serious; for us it was funny.

In studies of graveyards and epitaphs, researchers have noted a continuing relationship between elements of cultures and the specifics of cemetery structure and meaning. In "Social Commentary from the Cemetery," Edwin S. Dethlefsen and Kenneth Jensen observe: "The community cemetery is an entity of the past. As families have lost their geographic cohesiveness, modern gravestones have lost much of their individuality."

In Norwegian, the three recognizable dynamic sets for the family are called *familie, slekt,* and *aett,* an indication that the distinctions are important enough to the Norwegians to warrant particularizing terms. The *familie* is the familiar, immediate, so-called nuclear grouping at home.

The *slekt* is a particular generation of related people: A family reunion would bring the *slekt* together. *Aett* refers mainly to one's lineage, descent, the family line through time. Other cultures have still more distinctions: The Navajo clan is made up of one's mother's relatives, while the Japanese clan is based on the father's relatives and on regional origin.

THE ETHNIC FAMILY    The next larger dynamic unit along these lines would seem to be a nation or a people, the ethnic group in which the various family sets operate. When a Jewish family sits down to a Seder, they know that other Jews are also doing it the world over. In some cases, such as that of the United States, the nation is a political, not a cultural, reality, and there may be little congruency between what happens on the national level and what happens in the family. In countries like Japan there may be a powerful congruency among traditional dynamic systems, where the family and its lore are the core of cultural existence. In Austria, at Christmastime, when one family is preparing its daily traditional supper according to particular dates, when one family gathers about the tree on Christmas Eve (after Christkindl has erected it secretly and rung a silver bell), the participants have the substantial and powerful awareness that almost everyone in the entire country is doing exactly the same thing. This kind of cultural congruency between the dynamics of family and nation is understandably difficult to part with, and when an Austrian or Japanese family emigrates to another place, the immediate family level of this dynamic system will be the only cultural support left. It would be a wonder, under these circumstances, if family folklore among immigrants did not become more intense than it was in the home country.

We have ample proofs from sociologists, of course, that all families do not act exactly alike, and we are now aware that the very term *family* must be defined according to the way a family actually takes shape within varying ethnic and economic situations. For many urban Black people, *family* can include a dynamic, extended system of unrelated "brothers" and "sisters" in the street, and it can also mean a mother and those of her children living at home. For these reasons, the word *family* is only an initial indicator of some particular set of dynamic interactions based primarily on kinship. The "us" referred to in any particular instance must be defined by those aspects of kinship that determine what relationships are in fact stressed and what performances will properly take place.

Our awareness that we function in such sets as *familie*, *slekt*, and *aett*, even when we do not necessarily use separate words for them in English, should indicate to us that these are real groupings of traditional dynamics and not just convenient categories for the scholar. In fact, since they are not precise terms, they are not very convenient for the scholar—another good reason for us to pay attention to them here, for they reveal the categories and arenas of traditional actions of the people themselves.

# ✍ BIBLIOGRAPHICAL NOTES

The folk group, regardless of its size or basis of organization, is the primary live context for any folk performance. For more specific discussions of group dynamics, the ways groups are known to pass on information, their tendency to persist through time as well as to change dynamically, and their importance as the matrix for traditional expressions, you should consult the following important works. Homer Barnett, in his *Innovation: The Basis of Cultural Change* (New York: McGraw-Hill, 1953), addresses a number of larger issues in cultural dynamism that also apply to our understanding of the dynamics of the close groups in which folklore is performed. Erving Goffman's *Interaction Ritual* (New York: Doubleday, 1967) and *Frame Analysis: An Essay on the Organization of Experience* (New York: Harper & Row, 1974) are only two of his works on group dynamics; see his bibliographies for other important references in this area. *The Sociology of Small Groups* (Englewood Cliffs, N.J.: Prentice-Hall, 1967), by Theodore M. Mills, has some interesting observations that may be applied to folk groups by adding the dimension of cultural tradition to his "levels of group process" (pp. 57–59); since not all folk groups can be classified easily as small, however, Mills's findings will not apply in all instances of folklore study. The role of the folk group in continually reshaping the original performances of a creative individual were stressed heavily at the beginning of the twentieth century by Phillips Barry, a passionate scholar of the traditional ballad. His "Folk-Music in America," *Journal of American Folklore*, 22 (1909), 76; "Native American Balladry in America," *Journal of American Folklore*, 22 (1909), 365; "Communal Re-Creation," *Bulletin of the Folk-Song Society of the North-East*, 5 (1933), 4–6, all support his concept of "communal re-creation," in which he held that songs originally composed by one artist were continually re-created by the community. Probably today's folklorists would feel that the entire community is not actively involved in such a process, for not all people in the community are singers and not all singers perform the same repertoires. At the same time, the idea is an attractive one if we extend it to account for all those continual reperformances and reshapings of folk expression by any members of a folk group.

Most folklorists today deal with live context as a matter of course. Probably the two most important articles addressed directly to the importance of this consideration are Alan Dundes, "Texture, Text, and Context," *Southern Folklore Quarterly*, 28 (1964), 251–265, and Dan Ben-Amos, "Toward a Definition of

Folklore in Context," *Journal of American Folklore*, 84 (1971), 3–15 (also in *Toward New Perspectives in Folklore*, ed. Américo Paredes and Richard Bauman [Austin: University of Texas Press, 1971]). Ben-Amos suggests that folklore as a live process "can be considered a sphere of interaction in its own right" (p. 15). Some suggestions for analytical considerations of live context are provided by Roger D. Abrahams in "Folklore in Culture: Notes Toward an Analytic Method," *Texas Studies in Language and Literature*, 5 (1963), 98–110.

The basic statement on the function of in-group folklore is by William Hugh Jansen in "The Esoteric-Exoteric Factor," *Fabula: Journal of Folktale Studies*, 2 (1959), 205–211, reprinted in Dundes, *The Study of Folklore*, pp. 43–51. More detailed explorations into the kinds of tension and misunderstanding that regularly occur between members of various in-groups are to be found in Edward T. Hall, *The Silent Language* (Garden City, N.Y.: Doubleday, 1959), *The Hidden Dimension* (Garden City, N.Y.: Doubleday, 1966), and *Beyond Culture* (Garden City, N.Y.: Doubleday, 1977). Although these books are written for the general reader, they are treasuries of illustrations for the esoteric-exoteric factor. Hall, the originator of the term *proxemics*, discusses high and low context groups in the last-named work.

In most occupational groups with a considerable hazard on the job, the survival of the individual is closely allied to the survival and success of the entire group. At sea or in the woods, a new man on the crew needs to know far more than he can learn rationally on the job. Inducting the greenhorn is thus more than a spare-time exercise in fun and games. See the remarks of Horace Beck in "Sea Lore," *Northwest Folklore*, 2 (1967), 1–13, as well as Robert S. McCarl, Jr., "Smokejumper Initiation: Ritualized Communication in a Modern Occupation," *Journal of American Folklore*, 89 (1976), 49–66.

A more extensive glossary of loggers' terms, especially those used on the West Coast, can be found in Walter F. McCulloch, *Woods Words: A Comprehensive Dictionary of Logger's Terms* (Portland: Oregon Historical Society, 1963), although McCulloch, formerly dean of the Forestry School at Oregon State University, deferred to the tastes of the general public enough to leave out many of the more vivid examples. Another list is given by Wilbur A. Davis in "Logger and Splinter-Picker Talk," *Western Folklore*, 9 (1950), 111–123. An Oregon version of the Walkaway story, with some brief remarks on its background, is given by Rod Collins in an article of the same name in *Northwest Folklore*, 2 (1967), 18. I would like to thank the following people for sharing the logging stories and comments I have used in this chapter: Bill Hamilton, Ernie Sanford, Joseph Hannon, Greg Hamilton, John Urquhart, Vintie Holt, Leo Bishop, Ray Scofield, Tom McBride, and George Wasson. Because some of the stories were collected in the woods, without the benefit of tape recorder, I have retold them here in a somewhat literary style to set them off from the verbatim texts transcribed in the loggers' own words, which are shown in quotes. Most of the narratives were recorded in local taverns and in loggers' homes.

It is abundantly clear that there are almost unlimited bases for calling a group a folk group: religious affinity, regional identity, occupational definition, ethnic awareness, and so on. For a few revealing discussions of these matters, one might consult Bruce E. Nickerson, "Is There a Folk in the Factory?" *Journal of American Folklore*, 87 (1974), 133–139; William A. Wilson, "The Paradox of Mormon Folklore," *Brigham Young University Studies*, 17 (1976), 40–58; Suzi Jones, *Oregon Folklore* (Eugene: University of Oregon, 1977).

I am indebted to several Japanese and Japanese-American acquaintances for their perspectives on ethnic aspects of their foods. Particularly helpful have been Mrs. Chiyoe Kubota and Mrs. Asako Marumoto of Ogden, Utah; Mrs. Mary Joo of Caldwell, Idaho; Mrs. Ayako Kawai of Nampa, Idaho; Mrs. Seiko Kikuta of San Jose, California; Mrs. Yachi Shiotani of San Diego, California; Ms. Donna Misao Joo and Mrs. Yoko McLain of Eugene, Oregon; Ms. Nancy Nakata of Portland, Oregon; Mrs. Harumi Taniguchi and Mrs. Itsuko Asada of Seabrook, New Jersey; Mrs. Tomiko Shibaoka of Tokyo and Mrs. Shingo Kawaguchi of Shimizu, Japan; and Mrs. Miiko Kubota Toelken, my wife. Important discussions of Japanese culture in America are to be found in John De Francis, *Things Japanese in Hawaii* (Honolulu: University of Hawaii Press, 1973); Fumi Kawamoto, "Folk Beliefs among Japanese in the Los Angeles Area," *Western Folklore*, 21 (1962), 13–26 (esp. pp. 23–24, "Food Superstition," in which, among other things, there is listed a belief in the avoidance of three slices of anything on the grounds that the Japanese term for it, *mikiri*, means "to cut one's flesh"). Harry H. L. Kitano, *Japanese Americans* (Englewood Cliffs, N.J.: Prentice-Hall, 1969) mentions a widespread consciousness among Japanese that the attraction of cultural pluralism is precisely that a foreigner can keep some cultural elements and discard others (pp. 144–145). Marvin K. Opler, in "Japanese Folk Beliefs and Practices, Tule Lake, California," *Journal of American Folklore*, 63 (1950), 385–397, discusses what he considered to be a revival of older Japanese custom in the so-called relocation camps in which Japanese-Americans were interned during the Second World War; Rosalie H. Wax, in *Doing Fieldwork: Warnings and Advice* (Chicago: University of Chicago Press, 1971), discusses the Japanese at Tule Lake and her anthropological work among them on pp. 59–174.

Joseph Campbell, in *The Masks of God: Oriental Mythology* (New York: Viking, 1962), discusses the Japanese concept of the mythic past as based solidly on the model of family relations (pp. 465–474). Especially interesting are his summary and comments on the *Kojiki*, one of the principal mythic texts of ancient Japan, in which it is made clear that in Japanese thought there are concentric areas of concern in what he calls the religious "cults": There is first a concentration on the domestic, then the community, then the generalized craft or occupational, then the national, scene. Each of these is seen as congruent with the rest; hence anything that threatens one of these threatens the stability of the others. See also Richard M. Dorson, ed., *Studies in Japanese Folklore*, Indiana University Folklore Series, no. 17 (Bloomington: Indiana University Press, 1963), for a number of interesting studies of Japanese traditions, many of which may be traced further into the American context, as we will discuss in Chapter 4.

*Over Their Dead Bodies: Yankee Epitaphs in History,* by Thomas C. Mann and Janet Greene (Brattleboro, Vt.: Stephen Greene Press, 1962), is not a complete or particularly scholarly book, but it is full of excellent examples of the traditional contents of New England gravestones when it was still fashionable to provide extensive commentary on the stone. More germane to this chapter is Edwin S. Dethlefsen and Kenneth Jensen, "Social Commentary from the Cemetery," *Natural History,* 86:6 (June–July 1877), 32–38. The Gibbs gravestone in Knights' Corner graveyard, near Pelham, Massachusetts, was written up in the *Springfield Union* as "Pelham Epitaph Carries Feud Beyond Grave," by Neil L. Perry, Wednesday, August 20, 1969, p. 23; I mention it here because such articles are often extremely valuable sources of folklore. Feature articles such as this one, column fillers, articles on local elderly people, and the like must not be overlooked for the perspectives and leads they can supply the folklorist interested in relating folk ideas and performances to the live society.

For bringing the Norwegian terms *familie, slekt,* and *aett* to my attention, I am much indebted to Knut Djupedal, a graduate student in the History Department at the University of Oregon, 1976–1978. Some interesting perspectives on the dynamics of the family can be gained from William J. Goode, *The Family* (Englewood Cliffs, N.J.: Prentice-Hall, 1964), but a really good definitive work on family folklore has yet to appear. The Smithsonian Institution has been developing a program that not only studies family folklore but encourages families to share records of their own lore with the public (providing, for example, for the archiving of family albums, home movies, and encouraging the collection of family-oriented oral histories—including the prominent "crossing over" stories, which detail the adventures of the first immigrant ancestors of a family). A particularly interesting program sponsored in 1976–1977 by the Smithsonian took folklorists Amy Kotkin and Steve Zeitlin to selected cities around the United States, where they gave presentations and displays of family folklore to interested parties and solicited their oral histories in return. The Archive of Folk Song in the Library of Congress has issued one solid family collection: See the entry on the Hammons family in the bibliography for Chapter 3.

Because interest in our own ethnicity has become more acceptable since the demise of the melting pot concept, and because scholarly investigation of ethnic groups has concurrently been freed of the specter of racism (once based, I suppose, on the vague feeling that if we paid attention to someone's ethnic background it could only be in scorn), we can now find many more treatments of ethnic folklore than would have been possible twenty years ago. For a work concerning a people with a solid sense of their own ethnic identity, one might consult Asen Balikci, *The Netsilik Eskimo* (New York: Natural History Press, 1970); especially helpful is Rosan A. Jordan, "Ethnic Identity and the Lore of the Supernatural," *Journal of American Folklore*, 88 (1975), 370–382. *Western Folklore*, 36:1 (January 1977), presents an entire special issue on ethnicity in folklore edited by Larry Danielson; see especially Yvonne Lockwood, "The Sauna: An Expression of Finnish-American Identity," pp. 71–83, and Stephen Sterne, "Ethnic Folklore and the Folklore of Ethnic Identity," pp. 7–32.

# 3

## THE

# FOLK

## PERFORMANCE

**IT IS DIFFICULT, IF NOT IM-** **POSSIBLE, TO DESCRIBE THE DYNAMICS** OF A FOLK GROUP WITHOUT REFERRING TO A TRADITIONAL EVENT OR PERFORMANCE, SOMETHING expressive that has taken place among members of a high context group. Just as the dynamics discussed in Chapter 2 mean little if nothing happens, so a traditional performance or event means little if it does not occur in a traditional framework. This chapter focuses on the performance as a particularized aspect of dynamics by showing some details of traditional expressive interaction.

**PERFORMANCE IN SITU** The following anecdote of a Navajo storytelling event concentrates on the people and how they did what they did, their ideas concerning what happened, their reasons, how they got into the event, and how the whole interaction was seen by three non-Navajo visitors. A later chapter focuses on the inventory of ingredients for events themselves; obviously, in reality, events as dynamic performances and people as dynamic participants cannot be separated.

CONTEXT Background: Three folklorists (Barre Toelken, Jan Brunvand, John Wilson Foster) have arrived at a Navajo home after a long drive. Toelken is already known to the family; the other two are interested observers.

Setting: A small frame house in a desert town in southern Utah, just north of the Navajo reservation. The inhabitants of the house are Navajo and have moved off the reservation because of hard times. The children go to public school but their parents try to keep home life traditional. Everyone speaks Navajo at home; the parents speak only a few words of English.

Time: About 9:30 P.M. in late December; there is snow on the ground, and it is very cold. This is the time of year when Coyote stories can (and should) be told. And this is the only season when string figures can be made.

Situation: The father sits in a chair, dozing; small children are playing on the floor. The mother weaves on a loom on the far side of the room. The folklorists sit quietly, talking occasionally in low tones. In white American terms, nothing is happening, although in Navajo custom this is a common way of enjoying someone's company. One hour passes in this manner. The teen-age children of the family come in suddenly, accompanied by a Mormon missionary. The missionary wakes up the father, reminds him that the children should be in church this coming Sunday, then notices the white visitors. "You fellows with the Bureau of Indian Affairs?" "No, just friends, visiting." There is a puzzled look from the missionary; he departs. The teen-agers say hello and sit down quietly; the father returns to a half-doze. After about fifteen minutes he says sleepily, in Navajo, "Perhaps these visitors are Mormons, too?" "No," I reply, "this one is from back East originally; he likes to study old stories, as I do. This other one is from Ireland."

This translates in Navajo as "He comes from beyond the ocean," and the mother turns suddenly from her loom, grins, and holding her hands as if using a machine gun, makes a whispered t-t-t-t-t sound. "What does she mean?" asks Foster. "She thinks you're from Vietnam; that's also called 'beyond the ocean.'" Foster replies, "Tell her Vietnam is a vicarage tea party compared to Northern Ireland." The translation suffers. There is some puzzlement, but general cheer ensues because the visitors are not Mormons. "Now let's have some coffee," the father says.

THE PERFORMANCE   Everyone converges on the kitchen. While coffee is being prepared, Brunvand asks for a piece of string; he has a game he wants to show the children, and he pretends not to know the Navajos' great interest in string games. He makes a simple cat's cradle and shows it to a nearby child of about ten. "Could you do that?" The boy asks him innocently to do it again, slowly. Then, with mock care and deliberation, the boy reproduces the same figure perfectly, holds it up briefly, and then starts quickly on a more complicated one. He asks Brunvand with a grin, "Could you do that one?" Brunvand acts stumped. The boy produces another and another. The string passes to others in the family, and in rapid succession we see a Navajo rug, a bolt of lightning, arrowheads that race away from each other, a bat, and a worm that crawls over and under two parallel strings.

"Where did you learn those designs?" we ask. The children confer with their father for a while, then answer, "I don't know. I guess it's all from Spider Woman. They say if you fall into Spider Woman's den she won't let you out unless you can do all these. And then if you do these in the summer you won't get out at all anyway."

"Why is that?"

"Well, we're only supposed to do it in the winter when the spiders are hibernating, because it's really their kind of custom to do things with string." During this conversation, the mother has gone back to weaving momentarily, and the other children are still doing string figures.

"The Spider Woman taught us all these designs as a way of helping us think. You learn to think when you make these. And she taught us about weaving, too," a teen-age daughter puts in.

"If you can think well," the first boy adds, "you won't get into trouble or get lost. Anyway, that's what our father says."

Toelken: "But Spider Woman didn't teach *you* these things, right? Where did *you* learn them?"

"Well, we probably picked them up from each other and from our father, but they were already around, you know. All the people know about them. Spider Woman taught us."

The father speaks now for the first time and, taking the string, makes a tight design. "Do you know what that is?" he asks us. We do not. He shows his children and they all respond: "Sǫ' Tsó" (Big Star). He nods with satisfaction and makes another figure; he holds it up to us, and we shake our heads. He holds it up to the children, and they respond, "Dilyéhé." Since I have never heard the term I ask one of the children to translate it; everyone looks blank. "That's the only word there is for it."

Suddenly, in an attempt to explain, the father motions us all outside. There, shivering in the night wind, we watch him carefully hold the string figure above his head and point beyond it with pursed lips to the Pleiades.

Back inside, the father helps cover our embarrassment at not knowing our astronomy by making string figure caricatures of those present: a face with vague glasses to represent Brunvand, another with a loop hanging down for Foster's beard, another with a piece of string trailing down to depict the power cord on Toelken's tape recorder.

Finally, the father puts the string down and says seriously, "These are all matters we need to know. It's too easy to become sick, because there are always things happening to confuse our minds. We need to have ways of thinking, of keeping things stable, healthy, beautiful. We try for a long life, but lots of things can happen to us. So we keep our thinking in order by these figures and we keep our lives in order with the stories. We have to relate our lives to the stars and the sun, the animals, and to all of nature or else we will go crazy, or get sick."

Now a silence of about ten minutes occurs, but no one moves away from the table. There is an air of expectancy. The mother comes in and pours more coffee for everyone. We start the tape recorder. The father clears his throat and begins speaking slowly:

Ma'i [Coyote] was walking
    along over by Kayenta, up by     *children exchange quick glances,*
    those cliffs.     *smiling broadly*
He was hunting for something
    to eat but he wasn't having
    any luck.
He got very hungry, going along
    there,
And his stomach was making     *one girl giggles, quietly*
    noises.     (Navajos generally do not
He couldn't take it.     complain about hunger.)
He was almost crying, he was     *smiles, heavy expelling of breath*
    so hungry.

      •     [pause: four seconds]

Ma'i was going along and he
    met Golízhí [Skunk].     *narrator smiles; audience smiles*
He said, "Come along with me     (Golízhí, literally "one with
    and we'll hunt together.     stinking urine," is often the

Maybe we'll find some prairie
  dogs and cook them up."
"I'm not a hunter," Golízhí said
  to him.
"I won't be any help.
The prairie dogs will smell me
  and run into their houses.
You should get someone else."

     .

"There isn't anyone else
  around."
Ma'i was starting to get angry.
He was so hungry he could eat
  a skunk
If he could find some way not to
  get urinated on.
"Come along anyway.
We'll find something."
Ma'i asked him that four times,

So Golízhí went along with him.

     .

They went along together but
  they didn't find anything to
  eat.
It was getting dark
And Ma'i was so worried about
  being hungry that he could
  hardly walk.

     .

"Let's stop and make camp here,
  Shiłna'ash," Ma'i said.
"We'll build a fire and play
  some games."

     .

butt of Ma'i's attempts to
  manipulate others.)

[pause: three seconds]

*laughter* (Ma'i is too anxious to
  get food.)

(Ma'i is trying hard to get a
  recognizably poor hunting
  companion.)
(Four requests usually create an
  obligation to respond.)
*smiles, expelling of air*

[pause: four seconds]

*laughter, including narrator*

[pause: four seconds]

(Shiłna'ash, literally "one who
  travels with me," is a term
  used for close friends and
  relatives.)

[pause: two seconds]

"I don't know about that;
I don't know any games,"
   Golízhí said.

      ·

[pause: two seconds]

"Well, I'll teach you a game I
   learned from the birds.
We'll take our eyes out and
   throw them up into the air.
Then we'll catch them in our
   eyesockets," Ma'i said.

(In another story Ma'i has lost
   his eyes by throwing them in
   the air as the birds do.)

*one boy looks up at the ceiling;
   others giggle; narrator smiles*

[pause: two seconds]

      ·

"I don't know that game."

      ·

[pause: two seconds]

"It's a good game," Ma'i said.
"You can see for a long distance
   when your eyes are up in the
   air."

*everyone laughs*

[pause: two seconds]

      ·

"I don't know how to play it;
You go first."

      ·

[pause: four seconds]

Ma'i pulled out his eyes and
   threw them up in the air.
He said, "Come back to my
   sockets!
Come back to my sockets!
Come back to my sockets!
Come back to my sockets!"
Ma'i said.

      ·

[pause: two seconds]

They came back to his sockets.

*expelling of air; smiles*

      ·

[pause: two seconds]

Then he did it again, and he
   threw them higher.

"Come back to my sockets!
Come back to my sockets!
Come back to my sockets!
Come back to my sockets!"

*much giggling* (Ma'i is carrying his example to excess.)

[pause: two seconds]

·

And they came back to his
    sockets.

[pause: four seconds]

·

He did it again.
He threw them way up.
He could see all around the
    countryside while they were
    up there.
He said, "Come back to my
    sockets!
Come back to my sockets!
Come back to my sockets!
Come back to my sockets!"
Ma'i said.

*narrator slows down, sounds nasal and almost tired* (Ma'i has "committed himself" to the usual fourfold pattern, totally ignoring Golízhí, totally carried away by his own pleasure.)

[pause: two seconds]

·

They came down and got caught
    around the branches of a tree.

*extended laughter, lasting seven seconds*

·

Everything got dark for him.
He couldn't see.
He groped around all over and
    finally found the tree.
It was an old tree with pitchballs
    all over it.
He could feel them with his
    hands.
He pulled two of them off and
    put them in his eye sockets.

*narrator laughs so hard that these lines are distorted*

*laughter*

[pause: two seconds]

·

He couldn't see very well with
    them,

So he got too close to the fire.
All that pitch melted down into
   the corners of his eyes.                    *laughter*

                                    [pause: two seconds]

That's how coyotes got all that
   brown stuff in the corners of
   their eyes.

                                      [pause: five seconds]

That's what they say.           *audience looking at floor,*
                                      *general smiling, expelling of*
                                      *air*

                                      [pause: ten seconds]

Now let's hear that back.        *narrator looks at visitors for the*
                                      *first time and acknowledges*
                                      *the tape recorder*

INFORMANT'S COMMENTARY  After a replaying of the tape, general conversation ensues, and we ask if he knows the other story where Coyote does the same things with the exception of the ending: "That's how coyotes got those yellow [amber] eyes." I ask which is the final story: Do coyotes have pitchballs for eyes, as in the one story, or has the pitch melted, as in the one just told? And in either case, how can coyotes see?

The narrator answers, "Coyotes can see. Everyone knows that. Just watch them. Why do you ask?"

"Do you believe these stories?" we ask.

"Of course. That other one is where Ma'i learned about throwing up his eyes from the birds. Birds are *supposed* to see up in the air."

"Then do you believe a person can see with pitchballs for eyes?"

"No. This is Ma'i. He can do anything he wants. But anyway the story isn't about eyes, it's about what Ma'i is doing. He cries about being hungry, he chooses a poor hunter for a partner, then he calls Golízhí shiłna'ash even though he might eat him. Maybe he shouldn't see those things. It's not right to fool around with our bodies that way. It can make you sick. That's how eye diseases came to be. That's the important thing. That's what the story is about. If my children hear these stories they'll grow up to be good people. They won't play around with their bodies and they won't try to see things they shouldn't. You people are teachers, but I think you don't know these things."

One day Ma'i was walking
   along out in the desert where
   there used to be trees.

(Here another narration takes
   place.)

CONTENT AND MEANING   A careful observer will notice several important aspects of this performance. First and most evident is that the various observed events were very much conditioned by the presence of outsiders. How can we be sure that what we saw was in fact traditional if we recognize that much of it was brought about by our presence? What would have happened had we not been there? Here is a puzzle in the same category as the tree falling in the forest where no one can hear it (does it make a noise?)—with a major exception. Assuming our informants are not kidding us, we have their word that these things happen in the winter anyway. Indeed, from the testimony of the father of the family, these performances are not only appropriate, they are almost obligatory. Thus, while the particular event may have been sparked by a certain set of circumstances that included our visit, we are justified in believing that some other set of esoteric conditions would have brought about a similar performance at another time.

But our presence apparently did relate to another important aspect of this performance: the content. Take a closer look at the sequence listed above, and note that from the very first the traditional behavior throughout is related to the presence of guests:

1. A period of friendly silence occurs while the guests and hosts enjoy each other's proximity.
2. An interruption brings the family's new religious orientation to the attention of visitors, followed by a careful ascertaining of the visitors' religion so that they would not be offended by being offered coffee—a Navajo staple but a stimulant discouraged by Mormons.
3. Coffee is offered, and the visitors can now be brought even closer to a Navajo traditional family setting—one in which winter tales may normally occur.
4. String figures are begun innocently but end in the pointed demonstration that the visitors, for all their interest, are ignorant of important ways of avoiding confusion, getting lost, and sickness.
5. A Coyote story is told that dramatizes the foolish and competitive ways we may mistreat our bodies (which continues the topic of health brought up in the string figures and continues the thread of outsiders' ignorance).
6. A recognition of the tape recorder is made and an overt expression

of concern is voiced on the subject of teachers not knowing what is important.

One need not read very deeply to see the delicate irony of this performance situation, in which a father uses traditional modes of expression to show his children what they know in comparison to their potential teachers. Yet the subject is handled gently and covertly, showing respect and warmth for the guests while giving a tremendous boost of morale to the children.

Another important and obvious aspect of that rather full Navajo evening is the fact that for the Navajos it was a *high context* event—to use Hall's term—and not a series of separated genres, as a European-American scholar might set them down. By the scholar, the genres or forms of folklore might be listed as follows: greeting customs, weaving, foodways, games, folk astronomy, storytelling, folk philosophy. While the Navajo would certainly recognize these differences in behavior, it is likely that they would see no situational reason to separate them out; rather, they all fall into a more important category: those things performed between the first killing frost and the first thunderstorm—that is, in winter, as winter is defined by nature. The category foremost in the Navajo concern, then, is not "what kinds of traditions people practice," but "what traditional practices bind us to nature."

We can appreciate easily how much of the evening was based on the shared context of Navajo life, categories, and custom. The family literally flooded into the kitchen for coffee, obviously knowing what was to come. They already knew the string figures, and the star constellations and animals they represent (some Navajos still navigate at night by patterns so learned). They had already heard so many Coyote stories that they knew what was coming in this one, what Coyote's weaknesses are, and how those weaknesses represent ludicrous behavior or attitude for the Navajo (thus they knew when and why to laugh). They knew that what their mother was doing on her loom was directly related to what they were doing in their string games. And they knew, further, that all these matters related to rituals and dances that also are unavoidably a part of the winter season. In this context, the whole evening was a performance. Some of these ideas, fortunately, came forth in conversation, but one suspects that we visitors were only able to scratch the surface.

There are enough studies of separated folklore genres to make us aware that we sometimes amputate rather than dissect when we study traditional events. We become painfully aware of it when, as with a complex culture like that of the Navajo, a hundred years of anthropological and folkloristic study seem to have brought us very little closer to understanding. We need to guard against similar fragmentations when we study our own folklore or that of groups more closely related to us. Basically, we can say that a clear delineation of genre or structure of a folk item is only one small part of understanding a folk performance. Without the whole live context and the comment of the performers, it is unlikely that we will ever get very close to understanding—or even seeing—the dynamics that underlie the traditional process.

## ≝ TINA'S PROVERB

CONTEXT AND PERFORMANCE    I attended a party one evening at the home of a senior professor who had recently remarried. His new wife, a well-educated and elegant person fluent in several languages, was busy producing hors d'oeuvres in their tiny kitchen while he played the witty host to a group of his colleagues. However, the host soon became afraid his wife would never be able to leave the kitchen, so he stepped through the doorway to offer his help. All at once we saw him propelled back into our midst accompanied by a sharply spoken phrase from the kitchen in what sounded like Slavic.

"What did she say?" we asked. "I don't know, but whatever it was, she really meant it." He was cheerful but visibly puzzled. Naturally, when later in the party she joined us in an obviously good mood, we pressed her for an explanation of her magical phrase, for we had never witnessed our colleague—himself a forceful and charismatic person—so deftly put in his place. "No, no, I could never tell you," she said. "It's a very crude Polish proverb I heard my mother use occasionally. I could never repeat it to you in English. It's too crude. I'm sorry—it just slipped out before I could think, because of the circumstances, and I didn't even realize I was saying it." Several of us pursued the question off and on during the evening, but to no avail. It was not until the waning moments of the party, when only a few close friends remained, that the proverb finally came forth: "Well, essentially it says, 'A husband in the house is like a pimple on the ass.' "

MEANING    Here the performance of the proverb and the final perception of its meaning by the audience were separated by about three hours, which would not have been the case, presumably, had we been

Poles in Poland. Clearly, however, the performance itself was of great importance to the performer, who needed a culturally sanctioned way to eject an alien from a context that was culturally hers. Though in fact they both owned the kitchen, her cultural background had trained her to have control there. She did not want to reject her husband's help or to suggest anything personal about what was happening (if so, she could have said, "Out of the kitchen, you incompetent oaf!"). Indeed, the man was a rather good cook and used the kitchen, solo, on many occasions. Here, the dilemma was a cultural one (how to entertain guests properly after a marriage), and it was solved—at least for the performer—in a culturally generated manner: "The way we Poles see it, a man gets in the way."

STYLE AND OCCASION   Other aspects of the performance were equally interesting and important. Sudden response, sharp vocal tones, loud volume, and physical action (shoving) made a certain amount of the message clear long before the words themselves were translated. The proverb text, then, was only part of a larger set; shall we not call it a *proverbial performance?* This is another instance of the necessity for contextual observations. Proverbs seldom, if ever, occur at random. People usually do not just sit around "telling proverbs" (even in that case, there would be a context). Nor do we walk up to a stranger and say, "Hi there. A bird in the hand is worth two in the bush!" Proverbs normally come forth in response to a situation in which a person feels called upon to offer culturally appropriate advice to another person (in Europe and America, usually a friend or a relative).

Another aspect of performance may be seen in the meaning and the poetic style of the proverb itself. While the actual performer has chief control over the dynamics and the stylistic devices mentioned above (volume, action, and so on), the structure and wording of the proverb are the conservative features and are really the extended performance styles of the culture itself. We ask here not "How did Tina say the proverb in a certain context?" but "How have the Poles phrased an attitude about a man's place in the kitchen?" While there are many ways to approach this question, perhaps the literary method allows the quickest route. The simile suggests some kind of equation between "a husband in the house" and "a pimple on the ass": x is like y. The nature of the equation comes from the imagery of the pimple applied as a value judgment to the man. One easily thinks of such a pimple as, perhaps first, objectionable. Then, in no particular order: out of place, undesirable, potentially dangerous, dirty, painful. Then, by extension: something that gets in the way of important, obligatory work, something that cannot be ignored, something that must be gotten rid of at all costs.

INTERPRETATION Admittedly, these are *assumptions* about the value judgments suggested by the pimple image. They are founded on the idea that such a pimple would be seen as unpleasant by Poles and that the negative attitudes cited help us to understand the proverb's meaning. If ethnographic evidence were to show that posterior pimples were highly prized among Slavic peoples, we would be forced to reinterpret the performance above: perhaps seeing the performer as one who remembered the proverbial text but had forgotten its real meaning so that she had misapplied it. In this case, the dynamic part of the performance would emerge as the most important and effective (for the husband was in fact ejected from the kitchen), and the conservative aspect—the continuity of culture-based attitude—would be seen as eroded. Since such new ethnographic evidence is not likely to appear on this subject, the possibility of misinterpretation is hypothetical, but nevertheless the performance and its live context are only the beginning of a full study of folkloric meaning.

There are proverbs of all sorts, offering what might at first appear to be conflicting advice ("Look before you leap"; "He who hesitates is lost"). Arguing that proverbs thus advise expediency rather misses the point: It is always the situation that brings up the context for what advice seems to be needed, and situations in life differ considerably, as we know. We might advise one person here to leap and another person there to hesitate. But since the proverb allows phrasing the advice in a culturally recognized form, it comes out not as our own personal opinion (which might be thought intrusive anyway) but as a cultural norm, with all the authority, antiquity, and stability of that category of thought.

The performance and perception of proverbs allow both speaker and audience to exercise culturally acceptable philosophies, and to demonstrate in so doing their own hold on tradition, their membership in the group. So important is this function of proverbs in Nigeria that tribal courts are more likely to rule favorably for the person who knows and uses proverbs most correctly regardless of other evidence brought forward in a case. Here, the performance of traditional philosophy and the recognition of its stabilizing influence in the culture are more important in and of themselves than the relatively superficial question of who stole a chicken, or who's in the kitchen.

# ▨ AUDIENCE

Speaking of verbal folklore, William Hugh Jansen insists that performance implies not only a speaker but an audience (the same concept, of course, is implicit in Roger D. Abrahams's work on rhetoric in folklore): "The speaker, or the reciter of a bit of folklore steps outside himself as an individual and assumes a pose toward his audience, however small, that differs from his everyday . . . relationship to that same audience." The matter of pose, of self-conscious movement into another role, varies considerably according to the genre of folklore and particular contextual settings—especially as we try to apply the idea to nonverbal folklore. But even in the verbal category we would note that some sea songs were sung routinely as a way of timing and pacing the actions of men during daily work aboard ship, while other songs were sung chiefly ashore—perhaps in dockside taverns and pubs— where someone would step forward and consciously sing a lead part. Applied to material culture, we would observe that a Japanese woman cooking traditional daily food for her family is not setting the pose for her audience which might be inevitable if she were producing traditional food for a Japanese banquet. These variations in self-consciousness and pose must be held in mind as we discuss the following general situations.

The main effort here is to stress the importance of an audience as the responsive part of a folk performance. As William Wilson says of the function of audience in Mormon folklore, "If the story is to live, [the storytellers] cannot, in the telling of it, depart too far from the value center of the audience whose approval they seek." I think Wilson's term *value center* is a good one, for it represents in the folk group a clustering of concern and attitude shared by enough people that it can be transmitted through time as a philosophical reality. It is the human counterpart to Coffin's term *emotional core* in ballads, that central clustering of actions and concerns that characterizes the main idea of the ballad. Perhaps we might suggest the term *ideational core* for the same quality in all items being performed (since emotion may not always be the defining feature). There is a something being done, performed, by someone who has done it before, for an audience of people who already know it. Their reason for doing and experiencing the performance time and time again is of course that—beyond the pleasure of entertainment—such familiar performances help to reinforce and maintain the central ideas of the group (their value centers), help to induct newcomers (children, greenhorns), into the group, and help to define outsiders and strangers.

An accurate perception of a traditional performer-audience relationship must rest on each instance of expression taken separately. For example, a traditional singer might sing an old sailing song for a group of fellow seamen who already know the song, though perhaps each might sing it in a somewhat different way. The same singer might sing the song at a festival for people who have never heard it or who know it only from records. Or it might be sung for other family members at home. In each case, even though there is an audience, the dynamics of aesthetic and cultural interaction will be different. If there are suggestive or obscene verses, the singer would be more likely to use them in the first instance, leave them out in the second, and perhaps use some of the least suggestive in the third, all because of the singer's perception of the audience in each case. On the other hand, the performer can get away with greater modifications in length or phrasing for the second, comparatively unknowing audience than with the first or third.

FORMATIVE INFLUENCES   In one New England family where sea songs are sung around the Thanksgiving dinner table, there are family proprieties about some verses that would be totally meaningless aboard ship. The chorus of the old song "Rolling Home," sung as a memorial to family members who did not come home from the sea, can have a metaphorical, almost religious, feeling:

> Rolling home, rolling home, rolling home across the sea,
> Rolling home to old New England, rolling home, dear land,
>    to thee.

On shipboard the anticipation of getting home and the nostalgia of leaving behind the girls of the port can be re-experienced in the verses:

> Good-bye you fair Hawaiian ladies, we must bid you all
>    adieu—
> We'll recall those pleasant hours that we often spent with
>    you.
> We will leave you our best wishes as we leave your rocky
>    shore—
> We are sailing home for Rockport; you won't see us
>    anymore.

But those verses, sung at the Thanksgiving table, tend to reduce the chances of the chorus having a religious connotation of "rolling home" to heaven; they are likely to give aunts and grandmothers indigestion by reminding them of the human inclinations of their forebears. The singers need to know this if they want to avoid causing family malaise at a festive, semireligious occasion. Such a consideration on board ship, however, would seem laughable and overscrupulous.

Among seafarers, moreover, the singer may easily substitute "Mexican," "Australian," "Japanese," or any other seaport nationality for "Hawaiian," while among family singers (not seated at the Thanksgiving table) the allowable substitutions are set by those ports and nations actually known to have been visited by ancestor sailors. Particular words within the song may be changed, then, or held fast to directly because of the audience present at a given performance. When "Rolling Home" was sung by a member of that family in a film about the Oregon coast, the words "rolling home to misty Oregon" were substituted for "rolling home to old New England"; a single older member of the family watched the film to that point and then stalked out because he considered the change totally illegitimate (although he felt easy with other typical changes mentioned above). If the performance had been live, this one member of the larger audience would have constituted a negative traditional audience, which very likely would have impeded the singer's willingness to make that particular change (or at least to repeat it in the same company).

CENTRAL AUDIENCE  We may say, then, that the central audience of a folk performance can be defined as any person or persons present who know the tradition well enough to exert influence on the nature of the performance. The audience includes the performer, and may indeed be limited to the performer on some occasions where the performance is done in private.

BYSTANDER AUDIENCE  There may be other audiences as well—for example, bystanders, tourists, paying customers—and they may in fact be most enthusiastic about those aspects of performance style that match their own stereotypical expectations. These people may also affect the nature of the performance, but the influence may lie along the lines of outsiders' taste. So, for example, when a traditional singer is asked to perform a few songs for a local public school, pieces may be chosen according to what the singer feels local folks ought to know and enjoy; if the audience is a group of college professors, the singer is more likely to sing the kinds of songs most easily shared with outsiders. Thus, the researcher in folklore needs to re-create a sense of familiarity and trust in order to elicit the fuller repertoire.

**OUTSIDER AUDIENCE** In some cases, the singer's perception of audience variation is so strong that he or she will not sing for outsiders at all. I tried to collect songs from an old Utahn who was a central figure at all local weddings and celebrations. His response to me was a deep chuckle, and then, "Aw, I'm no singer; you don't want to hear those old songs I sing." And he stayed cheerfully adamant about it for a full day. A woman in Oregon sang innumerable "heart songs" from the turn of the century, but steadfastly refused to sing the old mountain songs she knew from her grandfather: "Oh, you college folks don't really know how crude and rough those mountain songs are. No, you don't want to hear *them*." These are not mere expressions of modesty or embarrassment; they are acknowledgments of an inappropriate or "foreign" audience.

**CULTURAL AUDIENCE** In addition to highly varied immediate audiences for folk performances, there is a more general implied cultural audience that either approves or disapproves of the tradition itself. Consider the old man who told me, about a kind of basket he had learned to make when young, "Oh, no, I don't do it much anymore; nobody cares about it. Nobody will learn it. What's the use, anyhow? Nobody cares about this kind of thing anymore." Compare that with the quilter who said, "My quilts are on my family's beds all over this country [meaning locale]; people like my quilts, and when I give one away it's like knowing a part of me is being appreciated by someone, even if I die." Our awareness of this larger implied audience helps us see how nonentertainment folklore may be approached, for we can observe that people are not always performing for a physically present audience.

**SOME AUDIENCES CONSIDERED** This is an important subject for us, for singing, the telling of a story in its traditional context, and the speaking of a proverb in an appropriate situation are easily understood as performances, because they seem very much like the self-conscious performances we see and hear on stage, screen, radio, and television. Other kinds of folk expressions as performances may be a bit more complicated; we need to ask what sort of performance can be said to take place when someone is quilting? What does a dowser perform, and for whom? When a Ukrainian-American cymbaly (hammered dulcimer) player plays his instrument for a Ukrainian wedding reception, it is easy to see who is performing and for whom; but for whom did the dulcimer-*maker* perform when crafting the instrument, working alone for many nights? And in all cases, since we are trying to see simultaneously the dynamism and the conservatism in a folk expression, to what extent did the tastes and demands of these presumed audiences modify or encourage certain elements of the performance or occasion the whole performance itself?

QUILTS For most quilters, the central audience, the one that may impose the greatest influence on the performance, is made up of other quilters. Their practiced eyes not only see the final quilt and its colorful design but notice the piecework, the sewing articulation and fineness of stitch, as well as the finesse of the quilting, the attachment of the backing and filling for the more prominent top pattern. From this observation we should recognize the existence of a dynamic folk group called *quilters*, made up of performers and audiences, which exists as a viable entity in addition to its members belonging to other folk groups as well.

There are other valid audiences for the quilter. The family, who do of course pick up at least some of the ways of judging a quilt, apply some of the beliefs about quilt meaning and usage. For example, in some families it is considered good luck for a newly married couple to receive a Double Wedding Ring quilt; in other families it is felt inauspicious to give a married couple the Wandering Foot quilt, for the subtle influence of its design might cause the husband (not the wife?) to "wander." Since these beliefs are not shared by all quilters and their audiences, they seem to be related as much to family folklore as to quilting per se.

The buying public, which may range from tourists looking for something folksy to take home from the Ozarks to art experts buying quilts for a museum show, also exerts an influence on the quilter, but it is less immediate in time and less considerate of insider lore. Very possibly, these broad categories could be subdivided: Isn't the art specialist—well schooled in folk art—more discerning and demanding than the tourist? Only a specific instance would show us. However we demarcate the varying levels of audience participation in the aesthetics or structure of the final traditional performance, we will probably always notice two general kinds of audiences: insiders and outsiders. And the outsider audience can be divided into (1) local people, who know the tradition but are not skilled in it, and (2) strangers, who don't know the tradition at all or who know of it only intellectually.

HAMMERED DULCIMERS Although he is not a musician, John Palanuk of Springfield, Oregon, is a maker of Ukrainian-style hammered dulcimers. He does not play them, and until recently no one in his immediate family did, either. Who is his audience then? Whose tastes and demands does he satisfy by producing these traditional instruments? For whom is he performing when he builds an instrument? First of all, unlike some craftspeople, he does not make dulcimers to sell to strangers, so the "tourist art" category does not fit his case at all. Rather, as he explains, he makes dulcimers because the local Ukrainians use them on festive occasions; they are needed by the people he identifies with, and there is no one else to make them. Palanuk himself was not brought up making traditional instruments; he has been a farmer and a mechanic and is considered very talented with his hands. In the same shop where he fixes his lawn mower he occasionally builds a dulcimer, making all the parts, wooden and metal, out of pieces he has saved. If he had learned to make dulcimers from other traditional instrument makers, we could have said that he is his own central or immediate audience, judging his "performance" by reference to an inherited system of culture-based knowledge of wood resonance, color, design, and so on.

Instead, however, John Palanuk has figured out how to make dulcimers just by being around them all his life. The design, the sound, the usage, are all dictated for him by the way dulcimers have always looked in the various Ukrainian communities of which he has been a member. For example, he carefully includes an extra small hole on each instrument "because you have to put money into the instrument to pay the boy who plays it." But the internal structure, the composition of such things as bridges and tuning devices, he had to learn by himself using good mechanical sense and woodworking talents. So in the case of John Palanuk, we can suggest that the Ukrainian community as a whole is his audience for the performance of dulcimer-making, while in terms of general mechanical traditions (making do with pre-existing pieces of metal) Palanuk (and other shop workers) are potentially the central audience. These simultaneous audiences are discernible because we can see at least these two sets of interactions helping to dictate and channel what Palanuk does when he makes a dulcimer.

In the Ukrainian community, of course, are people who play the dulcimer. Viewed from the maker's standpoint, these are the "local outsiders"; they belong to the larger community but are not themselves engaged in making dulcimers. They are part of the community audience for Palanuk. They need not be present while he works. From the standpoint of musical tradition, however, these dulcimer players—who come forth at weddings and baptisms to play in small bands (usually: hammered dulcimer, accordian, drums, and violin)—are "inside" performers, while John Palanuk is a part of their audience as a "local outsider" who knows the songs and dances but does not play the instruments. None of these components operates very well without the others; John Palanuk and his community are a striking example of the interdependence, the symbiotic relationship, that sustains tradition in a dynamic community.

TALL TALES  The same two kinds of audiences (insiders and outsiders) can be seen in other kinds of folk performances as well. Take the telling of tall tales: Some people—Len Henry, Hathaway Jones, B. F. ("Huckleberry") Finn, to name three prominent Munchausens of the Northwest—tell tall stories, or "windies," as a regular habit. Their immediate central audience are those other raconteurs with whom they swap stories and the usual group of local admirers—"the boys down at the store"—who know the stories but do not consider themselves to be "characters" enough to tell them. The outsiders may be local but not so knowledgeable, such as the youngster down the street who still hasn't figured out which are the true stories but knows that something funny is going on (partly at his or her expense), or strangers who have no way of knowing what is going on. The first audience may listen to a tall tale with quiet amusement and nodding of heads; the "local outsider" (who might be in fact a "young insider" still wet behind the ears) may laugh openly, as if at a joke. The stranger, irked at being told a falsehood and having no basis on which to share the joke with the others, may respond, "Aw, I don't believe such a thing," or may just leave in a huff. I saw an exasperated eastern tourist in a desert town in southern Utah trying to interest a service station mechanic in fixing an overheated car. "Does it always get this hot around here?" he demanded, mopping his face. The mechanic responded, with a straight face, "Well, when it *really* gets hot in these parts the farmers start feeding cracked ice to the chickens to keep 'em from laying hard-boiled eggs." Another attendant added, "Couple of years ago the ice machine broke down and every café in town had specials on boiled eggs for three weeks." The tourist didn't laugh, but two teen-agers leaning against the wall did, and had to turn away. "Wait till summertime sets in, you'll see some *real* heat," the first mechanic said. The tourist had no time to wait, and drew the conversation back to the car, which was eventually attended to. This is as good an example as any of two insiders performing to themselves and to two outside audiences at once. Probably without the stranger the performance would not have occurred, so we cannot dismiss the outsider as unimportant in the total event. The understanding and style used by the two mechanics as tall-tale performers and the responses of the two locals were of different sorts, both more knowledgeable than that of the tourist, yet different in quality from each other.

RIDDLES   The same kinds of levels occur in a traditional rendering of a European or American riddle: There is the performer who remembers the riddles, their phrasing, and their answers. There is perhaps the central audience of others who also know the riddles and their answers. These are insiders, and they can—and do—correct each other's phrasing or solutions. The local outsiders in riddling, as with tall tales, are often the neophytes of the family or community; they have heard the riddles but do not know them very well. As they learn them, of course, they become —as riddlers—insiders. The strangers are those who don't know the riddles or who, because of different backgrounds, have no way of perceiving the key metaphor or image that gives the riddle its core meaning. Insiders eventually learn the riddles by heart so that for them performance and reception involve a pleasant and poetic word game the knowledge of which provides a constant demonstration of membership in the group and its traditions. Strangers, even intelligent ones who know other riddles, are often at a loss to answer correctly or to begin figuring out even a plausible answer. Alan Jabbour gives an account of a riddling session that occurred when he and others were recording the traditions of the Hammons family in West Virginia. Several riddles had been recited, some of which Jabbour had recognized; then Burl Hammons said, "And what is that one about

> Crooked as a rainbow and teeth like a cat,
> You can guess all night but you can't guess that.

His sister, Maggie, said, "Yes, yes—

> As crooked as a rainbow and has teeth like a cat,
> You can guess all night but you can't guess that.

Jabbour tried to figure it out and asked help from a friend; then Maggie, in slight exasperation, repeated it again. At the phrase *you can't guess that*, Jabbour responded, "I think you're right," immediately followed by Maggie saying, "Well, now, that's a greenbrier." "What, a green——" "Yes sir, that's a greenbrier."

It's not hard to imagine that a young person growing up in a tightly knit community would learn riddles such as these—as well as a lot of other traditional expressions—and become a full-fledged insider as soon as possible. The term *local outsider* thus represents a potentially ephemeral position, depending on the tradition being discussed. A Ukrainian in a

Ukrainian community might never learn to play the dulcimer, and in that area he would remain a local outsider to the tradition; but he might have learned hundreds of riddles before he was twenty years old and thus would have become, in that traditional setting, an insider. Jabbour suggests in his notes to the Hammons family record that all traditions were learned by the Hammonses as they participated first as a family audience for their father and other relatives (who instructed by giving "model" performances, not by overt teaching) and then by becoming performers themselves, following their own personal predilections for instrumental music, singing, or story-telling. This is the typical folk learning situation.

PRANKS   Outside the family audience context, we may refer for another parallel set of audiences to the loggers' initiation of the greenhorn, the hazing of the newcomer. Again there are the insiders who perform, the strangers who know little or nothing, and the local outsiders, the new workers, who—by means of the pranks—become insiders. Each of these audiences is essential: The very fact that the stranger knows nothing about the process helps to strengthen the esoteric sense of heightened participation in a special group. And the victim, to cease being a victim, must try to move as quickly from the outside audience category to the inside audience, there to become a performer to other fresh audiences.

DOWSING   Dowsing is a way of detecting water, oil, or minerals by the use of a divining rod—often a forked twig cut from a live tree, but sometimes a steel rod, crowbar, welding rod, wire, spring, or chain. The process is nearly always passed on by personal example and oral tradition by one considered adept at it to someone who "has the feel for it" but has not yet learned a technique. There is a sense of exclusiveness about dowsing because, in the words of one dowser, "you either have it or you don't. When I found out I could find water, I was really surprised, but you know, a lot of people can't do it, even if you put them right over a vein."

Dowsers, or "water witches," therefore have for their most central audience the community of dowsers. They can discuss knowledgeably and can correct each other. The local outsiders in the audience believe in dowsing and want to have it done but don't know how to do it. In fact, some people have it done even though they don't believe in it. One Utah rancher told me, "It's a lot of foolishness. I don't believe in it at all. But I wouldn't for my life drill a well without it was witched first." The strangers are entirely skeptical and have nothing to do with dowsing functionally—although they might be willing to drive to Danville, Vermont, and witness the annual convention of dowsers, just for curiosity's sake.

SIGNING    Deaf people who have learned how to sign their communications spend a good deal of time signing with others who share the experience of impaired hearing. Their sign language is, basically, as formal as any standard language, and it is formally taught. But among users of sign language there has developed a folk speech, perhaps more properly a folk sign, a kind of visual/gestural slang. Insiders know and use it. Local outsiders (who can hear, but because of their job or their relation to someone deaf have learned formal signing) see it but often do not catch the meaning. Strangers, who know and use no signs more complicated than shrugging for "I don't know," are unaware that there is such a folk communication, even though they may actually witness it happening.

THE AUDIENCE AS FOLK GROUP    Members of religious groups may also experience these levels of performance and audience when they share the oral traditions that have grown out of their common experiences. The Amish have their German proverbs and planting customs; Catholics trade stories of adventures in parochial school (unwittingly repeating stories and motifs heard around the country); Jews tell stories of Elijah coming in disguise to someone's Seder and jokes about Jewish mothers and chicken soup; Mormons tell three Nephite legends and J. Golden Kimball stories. In each instance, the central audience is made up of insiders who share enough experience and attitude so that connotation runs high (Hall's high context situation), and the value center, as Wilson calls it, is recognized by most if not all participants.

It is extremely important to note that this works in one direction but not in the other. That is, we can say that Mormons tell three Nephite stories, that most Mormons know what those stories are, that most Mormons derive more live meaning from them than do total outsiders (who are inclined to scoff at the legends). But we may not say that every Mormon tells them or believes them. In other words, our recognition of an inside audience is not the equivalent of a stereotype and it does not suggest that all members are alike in any way. It does suggest that one group of people may be more likely than another group to maintain certain traditions.

Similarly, the toasts, rhymed narratives recited by many Black men, are not known to all Blacks in the United States. Like the dozens (continually escalating formularized insults exchanged by men), they feature language that does not match the demands of polite society. Women, especially older women, and men who wish to be more genteel are less inclined to learn the toasts and may in fact never put themselves in a context where they may be heard. Nonetheless, we are still justified in saying that present research indicates we are more likely to find the toasts recited by Blacks than by anyone else. And for those Blacks who do share them we can see that the dynamic interaction between performer and audience is closely related to other cohesive factors in the group and is parallel in style to other kinds of performance (chiefly, in this instance, seen in the antiphonal, or call-and-response, relation between performer and audience). In such a case, we expect Blacks to get a deeper meaning and a fuller experience out of a toast than outsiders might—even though Black mothers might well be shocked if they heard their own sons reciting one.

William Wilson provides an excellent example of the kind of connotative knowledge shared by an inside, central audience: Mormons listening to J. Golden Kimball stories. Kimball was a lesser authority in the Church of Jesus Christ of Latter-Day Saints (commonly called Mormon), but he had been a rancher and a cattle driver, and he had a vivid vocabulary as well as a quick wit and puckish sense of humor. He loved to puncture those whose pomposity got the better of them. The church authorities were so worried about his potential for swearing in public that on one occasion the president of the church, Heber Grant, wrote out a speech for Kimball to deliver at the annual conference, which was being broadcast live from Temple Square in Salt Lake City. Before the hushed crowd, Kimball squinted at the speech Grant had handed him and then screeched over the microphone in his well-known high voice, "Good hell, Hebe, I can't read a damn word of this!"

The stranger listening to this—as no doubt many did over the radio—would certainly see the unexpected humor of a crusty old man swearing in church and on the radio at that. The local outsiders—perhaps, say, non-Mormons who nonetheless had heard some J. Golden Kimball stories before—would fit the incident into a still larger picture of the beloved, feisty, but now untrusted old man giving some superior his just desserts. But the insiders, the Mormons (those present on the occasion and those who still today form the primary audience for the Kimball stories), catch a sharper and more ironic humor from the daring deed performed by their favorite trickster figure. In the words of Wilson: "The real laughter is evoked by the word 'Hebe.' Prophet, seer, and revelator—yes. But never Hebe. Therein lies the sacrilege." Wilson goes so far as to suggest that the Kimball stories are not really about Kimball but about Mormons, for they embody all those tensions that inevitably arise when people's own inclinations must be subordinated to authority.

It is this sense of a "we" that unifies the folk audience, and it is exactly that which allows us to speak of such an entity as a folk group. The folk group, then, is not a stereotype but a community of audience in which traditional performances take place and have meaning. The folklorist watches for those expressions—like the Black dozens or the J. Golden Kimball stories—that are seen in the informal performance repertoires of any close group. Rather than using another group's folklore as a basis for value judgment, rather than defining a group (or each member of it) by its own folklore, we seek to find out how the people in that group communicate with each other using what may well be a distinctive insiders' code.

## ✎ BIBLIOGRAPHICAL NOTES

The Coyote story performance is given line by line (as closely as my translation permits) from the tape. The recorder was turned on just at the outset of the narrative by permission gained during our conversation upon arrival. The text and the comments try to convey the pacing and style of the performance as well as the responses of the audience. Although I have not been able to correlate volume and tone with the performance as it is represented here in print, the mode of my presentation is obviously much indebted to Dennis Tedlock's impressive *Finding the Center* (New York: Dial, 1972). Explanatory cultural footnotes are in parentheses; timing details in narration are in brackets; the actions of audience and narrator are noted in italics; distinct pauses of more than a second are shown by a heavy dot in the text. See also Tedlock, "On the Translation of Style in Oral Narrative," in *Toward New Perspectives in Folklore*, ed. Américo Paredes and Richard Bauman (Austin: University of Texas Press, 1971), pp. 114–133.

For another, fuller discussion of Navajo Coyote tales and their function, see Barre Toelken, "The 'Pretty Languages' of Yellowman: Genre, Mode, and Texture in Navajo Coyote Narratives," *Genre*, 2 (1969), 211–235; reprinted in *Folklore Genres*, ed. Dan Ben-Amos (Austin: University of Texas Press, 1976), pp. 145–170. Lee Haring discusses critical aspects in the presence of an outside observer during a traditional performance in "Performing for the Interviewer: A Study of the Structure of Context," *Southern Folklore Quarterly*, 36 (1972), 383–398. He suggests that the performance is valid even if the interviewer is a total stranger, because even then the outsider has become a part of the human context and fills a certain social role, often, as in the instance described in this chapter, providing the central reason for at least part of the traditional performance itself. Jansen's remark is found on pp. 112–113 in his "Classifying Performance in the Study of Verbal Folklore," in *Studies in Folklore*, ed. W. Edson Richmond, Indiana University Folklore Series no. 9 (Bloomington: Indiana University Press, 1957), pp. 110–118. Roger D. Abrahams sees the folk performance as having an essentially rhetorical nature, in the classical sense of that word. See "Introductory Remarks to a Rhetorical Theory of Folklore," *Journal of American Folklore*, 81 (1968), 143–158. William A. Wilson uses the term *value center* on p. 46 of an extremely provocative essay, written from an insider's point of view, "The Paradox of Mormon Folklore," *Brigham Young University Studies*, 17 (1976), 40–58. Tristram P. Coffin proposed the term *emotional core* in "Mary Hamilton and the Anglo-American Ballad as an Art Form," *Journal of American Folklore*, 70 (1957), 208–214; reprinted in *The Critics and the Ballad*, ed. MacEdward Leach and Tristram P. Coffin (Carbondale: Southern Illinois University Press, 1961), pp. 245–256; the term itself is discussed on pp. 246–247.

Tall tales abound throughout Europe and America: One thinks most easily of the "Baron Munchausen" stories as well as of the regional hyperbolic tales found in virtually every rural part of America. One of the best regional collections is Vance Randolph, *We Always Lie to Strangers: Tall Tales from the Ozarks* (New York: Columbia University Press, 1951). Representing a rich Northwest tall-tale tradition are Susan Mullin, "Oregon's Huckleberry Finn: A Münchausen Enters Tradition," *Northwest Folklore* 2:1 (Summer 1967), 19–25; Jan Harold Brunvand, "Len Henry: North Idaho Münchausen," *Northwest Folklore* 1:1 (Summer 1965), 11–19. In *Tall Tales from Rogue River: The Yarns of Hathaway Jones* (Bloomington: Indiana University Press, 1974), Stephen Dow Beckham provides a book-length collection of fancy lies by and about a real local character who carried mail along the primitive Rogue River around the turn of the century. Hathaway Jones had a harelip and a cleft palate, and stories about him that still circulate in oral tradition feature this peculiarity of speech in the punch lines. Concerned with tall tales in the Midwest is Roger Welsch, *Shingling the Fog and Other Plains Lies: Tall Tales of the Great Plains* (Chicago: Swallow Press, 1972). The far Midwest is treated by Erik Wahlgren in "Scandinavian Folklore and Folk Culture in the Trans-Mississippi West," *Northwest Folklore*, 3:1 (Summer 1969), 1–16. An extremely helpful essay on the nature of tall tales is Gustav Henningsen, "The Art of Perpendicular Lying—Concerning a Commercial Collecting of Norwegian Sailors' Tall Tales," *Journal of the Folklore Institute*, 2 (1965), 180–219.

A great number of works have been issued on riddles and riddling. Standard is Archer Taylor, *English Riddles from Oral Tradition* (Berkeley: University of California Press, 1951). Brunvand has an interesting chapter on riddling in *The Study of American Folklore* and adds a useful basic bibliography. The *Journal of American Folklore* produced a special issue on riddles and riddling in 1976 (89:352), edited by Elli Köngäs Maranda. On the dynamics of riddling, Lee Haring insists, in "On Knowing the Answer," *Journal of American Folklore*, 87 (1974), 197–207, that in the case of African riddles there may be several possible answers, the particular one being brought forward by the context at hand. His argument is answered by Lyndon Harries in "Semantic Fit in Riddles," *Journal of American Folklore*, 89 (1976), 319–325. The riddles from the Hammons family are found on pp. 31–32 in Alan Jabbour and Carl Fleischhauer, eds., *The Hammons Family: A Study of a West Virginia Family's Traditions* (Washington, D.C.: Library of Congress, 1973). This combination of two long-play records and an extensively researched booklet, issued by the Archive of Folk Song in the Library of Congress, has established itself as a standard for the recorded presentation of family songs and traditions.

For a critical discussion of proverbs in their live setting, see E. Ojo Arewa and Alan Dundes, "Proverbs and the Ethnography of Speaking Folklore," *American Anthropologist*, 66 (1964), 70–85. Another engaging article is "The Role of Proverbs in a Nigerian Judicial System," by John C. Messenger, Jr., in *Southwestern Journal of Anthropology*, 15 (1959), 64–73; reprinted in Alan Dundes's *Study of Folklore*, 299–307. Neither of these pieces concerns Polish proverbs, but both indicate the extent to which facility in proverbial expression helps to mark one's traditional position within a community. In the case of the Nigerian use of proverbs in tribal court proceedings, it is clear that the person who knows the most appropriate proverbs is usually the one who wins the case. In this demand for close involvement with the high context group, the most traditional person is the one retained and encouraged by the society. For many people, as with Tina, the proverb may represent the principal link to one's cultural sense of propriety.

Stories of the three Nephites are most easily found in Austin and Alta Fife, *Saints of Sage and Saddle* (Bloomington: Indiana University Press, 1956), and Hector Lee, *The Three Nephites: The Substance and Significance of the Legend in Folklore* (Albuquerque: University of New Mexico Press, 1949).

For an extensive discussion of dowsing (water-witching), see Evon A. Vogt and Ray Hyman, *Water Witching U.S.A.* (Chicago: University of Chicago Press, 1958). A widely used book on signing, *A Basic Course in Manual Communication*, ed. Terrence J. O'Rourke (Silver Spring, Md.: National Association of the Deaf, 1973), gives extensive diagrams for signs, even the most complicated, that have become standard, but it addresses no attention to the subject of slang or folk signing.

Roger D. Abrahams has stressed for some years now the central element of performance in much of Black folklore; especially important are his two related books: *Deep Down in the Jungle: Negro Narrative Folklore from the Streets of Philadelphia* (1963, 1970) and *Positively Black* (1970), both cited fully in the introduction. William Wilson's comment on the J. Golden Kimball stories is on p. 55 of "The Paradox of Mormon Folklore." A tremendously interesting compendium of "J. Golden Stories" is provided by Thomas E. Cheney, *The*

*Golden Legacy: A Folk History of J. Golden Kimball* (Salt Lake City: Peregrine Smith, 1974).

A few more important studies of performance in folklore are listed here, but remember that these are only a scattered few, and, in the main, recent ones at that. Each provides footnotes and bibliographical references to be used in sharpening and extending any serious investigation of traditional performance. Melville Jacobs was one of the very first folklorists to insist on the essentially dramatic nature of oral performances. His works stressed the idea that a narrator, reciting stories to the people around him, was in effect creating a mental drama for them, one in which visible furniture was not necessary but where descriptions and culturally important references could eventually crowd the "stage" with meaningful personages and symbols. His works are of basic importance to our considerations here: *The Content and Style of an Oral Literature* (New York: Wenner-Gren Foundation, 1959) and *The People Are Coming Soon* (Seattle: University of Washington Press, 1960).

Beyond Jacobs, see the following: Roger D. Abrahams, "A Performance-Centered Approach to Gossip," *Man*, 5 (1970), 290–301; Richard Bauman, "Towards a Behavioral Theory of Folklore," *Journal of American Folklore*, 82 (1969), 167–170, which insists that folklore is not made up of things or materials but is constituted in a "communicative process"; Bauman, "Verbal Art as Performance," *American Anthropologist*, 77 (1975), 290–311; Kay L. Cothran, "Talking Trash in the Okefenokee Swamp Rim, Georgia," *Journal of American Folklore*, 87 (1974), 340–356; Henry Glassie, *Pattern in the Material Folk Culture of the Eastern United States* (Philadelphia: University of Pennsylvania Press, 1968), for material aspects of performance; John J. Gumperz and Dell Hymes, eds., *The Ethnography of Communication* (Washington, D.C.: American Anthropological Association, 1964); Dell Hymes, "Breakthrough into Performance," in *Folklore: Performance and Communication*, ed. Dan Ben-Amos and Kenneth S. Goldstein (The Hague: Mouton, 1975), 11–74; Hymes, "Discovering Oral Performance and Measured Verse in American Indian Narrative," *New Literary History*, 8 (1976–77), 431–457; Heda Jason, "A Multidimensional Approach to Oral Literature," *Current Anthropology*, 10 (1969), 413–420 (which focuses on models relating to narratives as items. See Roger D. Abrahams's comments on performance in his rejoinder, *Current Anthropology*, 12 [1971], 391). James H. Jones, "Commonplace and Memorization in the Oral Tradition of the English and Scottish Popular Ballads," *Journal of American Folklore*, 74 (1961), 97–112, tries to apply the Parry-Lord oral-formulaic theory of composition in performance to the English ballads; Albert Friedman (pp. 113–114 in the same issue) argues stoutly against certain faults in the reasoning of Jones's article, but the basic point remains valid and has not been adequately pursued since. Charles W. Joyner, "A Model for the Analysis of Folklore Performance in Historical Context," *Journal of American Folklore*, 88 (1975), 254–265, gives a complicated but convincing visual model for variables that affect any folklore performance, including tradition itself, community structure, a performer's individual characteristics, family and significant others, the performer's individual perception, and the immediate context in which all of these forces are brought to bear on each other in the actual folklore performance. Barbara Kirshenblatt-Gimblett, "A Parable in Context: A Social Interactional Analysis of Storytelling Performance," in Ben-Amos and Goldstein, *Folklore: Performance and Communication*, pp. 105–130; James Porter, "Jeannie Robertson's 'My Son David': A Conceptual Performance Model," *Journal of American Folklore*, 89 (1976), 7–26, suggests a circular chart for demonstrating the relationship between the forces bearing upon the performer and the attitudes of the performer herself. Jarold Ramsey, *Coyote Was Going There: Indian Literature of the Oregon Country* (Seattle: University of Washington Press, 1977), insists that the entire range of Native American oral literature cannot be considered unless the reader is willing to try reconstructing the actual performance situation in which those stories and tales were originally carried out. Bruce A. Rosenberg, *The Art of the American Folk Preacher* (New York: Oxford University Press, 1970), studies the oral-formulaic composition of folk preachers in the performance situation of church services where variation on standard themes is *de rigueur*.

For important observations on everyday aspects of performance styles, see Erving Goffman, *The Presentation of Self in Everyday Life* (Garden City, N.Y.: Doubleday, 1959), pp. 17–76, and Michael J. Bell, "Tending Bar at Brown's: Occupational Role as Artistic Performance," *Western Folklore*, 35 (1976), 93–107.

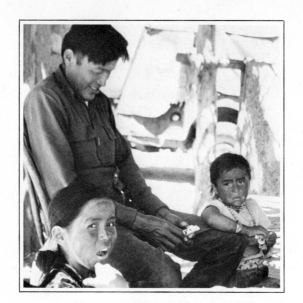

# 4

# DIMENSIONS

# OF THE

# FOLK EVENT

IN CHAPTER 3, "THE FOLK PERFORMANCE," WE CONCENTRATED ON THAT IDENTIFIABLE, OFTEN CAREFULLY DEVELOPED, POSE THAT RELATES A PERFORMER TO AN audience when a traditional expression takes place. Now we move to focus on the event itself: When did it start? How and why did it come about? What were its principal parts? And when did it end? Essentially, the study of a traditional event requires noting a discrete set of actions and expressions that are motivated and directed more by group taste and demand than by the idiosyncrasies of an individual. Life is full of events; some of them are folk performances.

Anthropologists are inclined to study all recurrent events in a culture (religious holidays, quilting bees, football games) because they all provide valuable data about the culture, its workings, and its tastes. Folklorists, on the other hand, are likely to concentrate on those events relatable to smaller, more cohesive groups within the larger society in which some aspect of performance (or at least some conscious transmission of culturally important ideas) is at the heart of the occurrence.

**⧉ INVENTORY** One way to deal with the make-up of any event is to inventory its principal parts in a sequential array from the beginning ("at what point did we notice that something else was starting to happen?") to the end ("at which point did we notice that something else was starting to happen?"). This method provides an observer's list of ingredients and may be helpful in breaking down a complex event into units discussable at a later time. However, this method has several problems: The inventory does not necessarily provide the inside view of the event or when it started or what parts are considered principal by those involved. It assumes that things happen one at a time; and it relies on a sequential time reference as the only connection between the principal parts.

As we shall see, these are fascinating problems, and they need not cause scholarly panic or despair. They do suggest, though, that we must develop a fuller way of seeing events so that we are able to perceive their variable dimensions.

What would be a good way of noting and studying the Navajo storytelling performance described in Chapter 3? Was it one event or several? Was the performance of Tina's proverb really an event or was it only one small part of a larger folk event, the party? Has the performance now assumed the feel of an event because it was singled out for discussion (both then and now)? To approach these questions, we need first to relax and to observe that the word *event* can cover anything from a phenomenon visible only through a microscope to an occurrence involving all of humanity. The range in folk events is hardly that great, of course, but there is the similar possibility of simultaneity and the probability of sharply varying dimensions. If we use for a working definition of a folk event "any actual occurrence or performance of a traditional expression" (keeping in mind all we have said previously about tradition), we will be focusing properly on those aspects of the tradition that are *done,* and not on comparatively superficial considerations of genre or chronology. The singing of a ballad, not the remembering of it, would be the event; the communal building of a barn, not the memory of it, would be the event— though the narrative retelling of the memory might be seen as another kind of event. The observance of a custom, the use of a proverb, the employment of an ethnic recipe—these are fully understandable only when we can see them done in their home contexts. How to see the event, then, is our first concern: What happened, and how do we know it?

A NAVAJO INVENTORY  A sequential inventory of identifiable

"happenings" at the time the Navajo story was told (recounted in Chapter 3) might look something like this:

1. Opening of the occasion: Their own arrival begins, for the visitors, a sequence of observable events. Something was happening before they arrived, and they have now become a part of it, but as far as their ability to observe is concerned, the sequential list must begin here.
2. General framework: observable folk events in progress as scrutiny begins.
   a. Children are playing.
   b. Mother is weaving.
3. Subsequent "discrete" events:
   a. A round of string figure performances
   b. An offering of legendary and belief-oriented explanations.
   c. A string figure/folk astronomy performance
   d. A string figure/caricature performance
   e. A folktale narration
   f. A discussion of traditional elements in the tale (metafolklore)
   g. A folktale narration (artificially cut off for the sake of discussion in the chapter)

As we admitted in Chapter 3, the Navajos involved in this sequence did not abstract out each kind of performance from the others. For them, the evening itself was a single experience, perhaps enlivened by visitors but dictated by seasonal customs in the aggregate. As far as the naturalness of this family setting is concerned, a person may well hesitate to dissect into antiseptic pieces an obviously holistic phenomenon. Yet it is often only through such dissection that we can understand the full nature of what we have observed. Thus, along with the student of anatomy, we do not seek by dissecting to ruin our appreciation of the animal, but to increase our ability to know it more fully the next time we see it in the live state.

One thing we can clarify for ourselves in setting out a sequence of folk events like this is the extent to which our own predilections lead us to stress certain elements. For example, in describing these events within the Navajo family situation, I have shown them in such a light as to suggest that they led up to, or at least provided the context for, the storytelling performance. The assumption in such an approach is that I had gone there to collect some Coyote stories, and so I was naturally looking forward to those events that most closely approximated that genre. Thus, although perhaps the weaving was of greater economic importance to the family at that moment, although the string figures were perhaps more centrally important to the children at that moment, although perhaps the Navajo philosophy was closest to the father's interest at that particular moment because of his concern for his children's education, the quarry, from my point of view, was the folktale, and all other items were subordinated to it. A weaving specialist in the same group might have placed such emphasis on watching the mother weave that we might never have moved to the kitchen for storytelling. A scholar interested in string figures might have focused such attention on those expressive events that even if all the other kinds of expression had taken place they might have seemed peripheral to that activity. Since we did not try to push the evening's activities in any particular direction, we can be relatively sure that what we witnessed was a natural set of occurrences; just as obviously, my description of them reflects my own scholarly interests.

INVENTORY "ON FILM"  There is no point in hoping that a folklorist—or anyone else, for that matter—should be able to see and appreciate all phenomena simultaneously with equal clarity. We will always be interested in one kind of event more than another. Yet in order to understand even one small part of a folk event, we will want to understand its relationship to the other elements of the whole situation. How can we approach this problem, at least hypothetically, in order to train ourselves for such a demanding task? One method might be to imagine filming the entire event: Where would we place our cameras? How many cameras would we need? When would we begin filming? What would we need to film so that the eventual viewer might understand the event and what led up to it, how it came about, how it related to other contextual elements, and how it ended? The benefit of carrying out this exercise hypothetically, of course, is that we can use more imaginary cameras than we could ever hope to in real life; moreover, with an imaginary camera we do not run the risk of entirely changing the family's pattern of life while we set up lights, sound systems, and other equipment to record what might by that time become a very self-conscious performance. (Jorge Preloran and John Marshall have succeeded elegantly in making unobtrusive movies of folk events, so I do not mean to suggest that it is impossible.) For purposes of discussion, how would we want to film the situations described on this one evening with a Navajo family?

Ideally, we would want a camera fixed into the ceiling of each room so that an objective record could be made of all activities and movements simultaneously. We would also want to have a camera operating before the visitors arrived so the effect of their entry upon the normal events of the evening could be noted (this is an unsolvable dilemma in real life, since the very presence of a camera would have constituted an intrusion already). Other obvious positions would be a fixed camera on the mother while she weaves, augmented by close-up shots of her technique and pattern. At least two cameras would be needed to film the children's string games activities: one to pick up the entire group as the string is passed from person to person so that the interaction among the participants can be noted; another to move in close to the string figures themselves in order to see how they were made and to provide a record that could be compared with other string figures in other cultures. We would want to have at least one camera that could sweep across all these activities to show where the focus of the group's attention might shift from one moment to another. At least one camera would have to be mobile to follow us all out into the kitchen while we prepared to hear stories. Perhaps the same camera could also follow us outdoors and show the alignment of the one string figure with the Pleiades (since we are using imaginary cameras, there will be no problem of light source on this shot). During the tale-telling activities one camera would be needed to hold on the narrator to record not only the story but his style and mannerisms in telling it, while another camera would focus on the entire group to show their responses.

Now in reality, a filmmaker, even if he had all these cameras at his disposal, would want to consolidate some of the shots and some of the work: At what point could he use one of these cameras for another shot? The technical question is a good one to ask for our hypothetical purposes, for it requires us to consider when certain actions stopped, if indeed they did. Did the mother continue weaving at her loom intermittently while the tales were being told or not? If so, a camera would be needed to register that ongoing event, even though the immediate audience was in the kitchen listening to a story. Since all the children moved into the kitchen with their father, we could assume that we would no longer need the cameras originally used for their play and for the string figures.

UNDERSTANDING THE INVENTORY: FROM WITHIN AND WITHOUT   With all this imaginary footage on hand, we would need to decide how we might best show the films. We can assume, I think, that we would show them all uncut so that we would not miss any detail of the events. But we would need to devise some way of showing which events overlapped with each other; perhaps a split screen or multiple projections would work. We would still be left with the dilemma of whether we had in fact captured the events in such a way as to lead efficiently to an understanding of them. We will wonder, for example, if the Navajos would have filmed these events in the same way, whether they would have focused on the same items, and whether they would have handled them the same way. It is too easy to say that an event is an event, and that anyone present would see it in the same manner. Sol Worth and John Adair brought forth some striking examples of this in their experimental work with Navajo filmmakers. One twenty-minute film made by Susie Benally, *A Navajo Weaver*, showed only about four and a half minutes of weaving, and most of that is at the very end of the film. Only two or three inches of a fairly large rug are shown being woven at that. There are several extremely brief shots of the weaver holding up different completed rugs, but the main interest in the film seems to be in people moving over the landscape herding sheep, gathering the various plants to be used for washing and dyeing the wool, preparing the wool by carding, dyeing, and spinning. We may well wonder why a Navajo making a film of a Navajo weaver would show only a few minutes of weaving and instead focus about three-quarters of the entire film on other activities. By asking Navajos about it, we would learn that the live processes involved in the weaving are of the greatest traditional interest to the Navajos, while the final product, the finished rug, is an item usually traded for food or cash. From a Navajo point of view the rug and its physical pattern are not of great importance; the interaction with animals, landscape, plants, the mastery of preparation procedures, the knowledge of dyes, and the creative imagination that brings forth the patterning are the central elements.

Going back to our hypothetical film, we may guess in retrospect that the part we filmed of the mother weaving at her loom, holding the camera there as long as she was weaving, might have been thought highly unusual by the Navajos present, because it would seem to focus on only one element of a much larger event, and perhaps one of the least meaningful elements at that. What can we say, then, about the rest of our filming? Are the other events open to the same kind of esoteric correction? We should always hold out this possibility, for the observer, even armed with a hundred cameras, will not be able to get the full view of a folk event without the help and direction of the participants themselves.


Margaret Mead has called attention to the preference shown by folklorists and anthropologists for verbal materials—both for texts to study and for ways to describe the items under scrutiny. She suggests that this

THE DYNAMICS OF FOLKLORE

has blinded us to other kinds of expression and communication and has encouraged us to overlook, or subordinate, other kinds of description such as those that might be afforded us by photography, either still or movie. In this discussion of hypothetical filming, I have not given proper exposure to the real technicalities and promises of the cinematic instrumentation, which is surely, as Mead and others have eloquently shown, an indispensable means of observation in folklore and anthropology. I have introduced the idea of hypothetical filming only to suggest a set of considerations that must be kept in mind as we seek to register a folk event fully. Imagining that filming is going on encourages us to see our subject matter in a richer way than a mere lineal sequence would suggest. It is said that good and bad movies are made in the editing, in the cutting room; the same thing may be said of scholarly articles and books on folklore and anthropology, for one always wonders how much was left on the cutting room floor and how much even the most well-intentioned editing and analysis alters our perception of what actually happened.

# ⚠ STUDYING THE EVENT

A CHECK LIST: APPARENT AND ESOTERIC DIMENSIONS
Considerations such as those just cited should encourage the student of folklore to keep in mind the following topics when studying a folk event:

1. Context and occasion
2. Framework
   a. Apparent beginning and end
   b. Esoteric beginning and end
3. Participants and their roles
4. Sequence (the normal or typical order of events)
   a. Apparent sequence
   b. Esoteric sequence
5. Simultaneous or overlapped elements, and intersections with other events
6. Weight and dimensions of components in the event
   a. Apparent inventory
   b. Esoteric inventory, including value judgment and rationale

This check list cannot be followed serially, but must be adjusted to each particular event. It simply asks us what items we might have forgotten to consider. Most important, its topics recognize that there may be at least two strands of any observation of a folk event. There will be those occurrences that are apparent and obvious to any onlooker, and there will be those that are noticed and valued variously by the insiders. Both elements are needed for a full understanding of an event, for the insiders, even though they may have complicated rationales for what has happened, may overlook similarities between their customs and those of others, while the outsider, lacking the system of values of the insider, may fail to appreciate—or even to see—important details of the event. The apparent inventory of items and actions in a folk event may therefore be far longer than the esoteric inventory, for the insider may see only a few of the actions as centrally related to the event while the outsider has no way of knowing which actions or items are typical or obligatory.

For an example, take any well-known folk event and imagine how an outsider might approach it, then how an insider might clarify the ingredients. A commonly celebrated holiday like Thanksgiving provides a good place to start. We might easily agree that the central part of Thanksgiving as an event is the usual turkey dinner "with all the trimmings." We might decide in advance to set up our hypothetical cameras just before a Thanksgiving dinner takes place and then note how it starts, who comes to it, how the participants comport themselves, what they do while they're at the table, and whether other things are going on in the house that seem directly related, and we would want to focus on those items that seem to be centrally involved. If we did so, however, without asking the advice of the insiders in the family under scrutiny, we might find later that we had not been able to film the entire event.

The women in the family who prepared the meal might insist that Thanksgiving had actually started early in the morning with the preparation of the food. At the turn of the century, and up through the 1930s, when it was typical for many families to provide their own meat and poultry, we might find someone insisting that Thanksgiving had begun the previous day with the killing of the bird. In other words, by focusing only on the most obvious aspect of the event, that element most recognizable to everyone, we would be dealing only with the apparent framework and the apparent inventory, not with the full dimensions of the event as seen by those who carry it out.

Moreover, if we set our imaginary cameras over the table and recorded all the items that were there on that occasion without asking the participants to identify them and their relation to the event, we might have no way of determining which of the foods and utensils related to the event of Thanksgiving alone and which ones related to the daily event of eating. Thus, while our film might be full of colorful items and actions, it would not necessarily be full of meaning; perhaps, more accurately, it might be full of meaning that was generally unavailable to us because of our lack of a system by which to focus on the primary elements of the event.

COMPARATIVE INVENTORIES   I asked the members of two families in widely separated parts of the United States to describe what they considered the obligatory elements in their celebration of Thanksgiving in terms of the topics listed earlier. Although each family considered its Thanksgiving customs to be unique for various historical and geographical reasons, I found them very similar in many respects. The Kimball, Damon, and Howland families, related by marriage, are primarily rural people in central Massachusetts. The Wodtli and Tabler families, related by marriage, live in Foster, Oregon, in the foothills of the Cascade Mountains. Their recollection and current celebration of Thanksgiving are essentially rural in character; for example, they recall Thanksgiving as a harvest holiday that separates the active outdoor work of the year from the indoor winter maintenance and restricted dairying of the winter.

THE KIMBALL THANKSGIVING   The apparent framework of Thanksgiving for these New England families would be Thanksgiving Day itself, most obviously the dinner at which members of these and other families related by marriage gather. However, the members of this family said that Thanksgiving actually began for them at least a week before the actual date, when in school they were obliged to write essays on why they were thankful. On the surface, this might seem to be an essentially nontraditional aspect of the event, but it is so solidly a part of the participants' concept of Thanksgiving that it cannot be overlooked. Among other things, it testifies that Thanksgiving, for all its traditional elements, is also a part of the formal calendar of holidays in the United States and is therefore to be encountered in formal as well as informal settings.

The participants in the Kimball family Thanksgiving are family members and their spouses and children; rarely is someone outside the immediate family ever invited to Thanksgiving dinner, although such is the practice at other times of the year. Central areas of focus during the actual development of events during Thanksgiving Day are the kitchen, where most of the women prepare the food, and the den, where the men gather for conversation and sometimes a smoke. The central person in the kitchen is the woman whose house is being used for the dinner; the same woman presides over the table during the meal itself and usually requests someone else present to say grace, most often a younger person. Since there are two particular areas of activity, the kitchen and the den, two entirely separate kinds of conversation have developed by the time dinner is served. These conversations are brought as far as the table, but dropped there in favor of a generalized set of recollections, mainly of family and regional history.

Our hypothetical camera over the table would reveal at a Kimball family Thanksgiving dinner of today a large turkey, various kinds of vegetables and condiments, and, eventually, a number of pies served with coffee and tea. Conversation with family members indicates, however, that the turkey is a recent arrival; up until the mid-1940s, the family usually enjoyed a chicken or capon, sometimes a duck. The turkey, thought to be so traditional at Thanksgiving, was not an obligatory tradition for this family until the last twenty-five years. Having some kind of bird on the table is the obligation. Of the vegetables that appear, only some are traditional: Sweet potatoes must be present (in more recent years, yams have been added, but they are considered a modern frill), small stewed onions, squash and usually peas. Two kinds of cranberry sauce are necessary, fine and chunky. Regular potatoes may or may not be present, other vegetables may or may not be present, pickles of any variety may be present, and usually there is at least one kind of salad. Gravy is obligatory. The stuffing used to fill the bird when it was cooking is excavated and placed on a separate dish, and all are expected to take some whether or not they like it.

The "oysters," two small hollows of tender meat along the back of the bird, are always given to the senior people present (in a smaller Thanksgiving event in an immediate family, they always go to the parents). Everyone around the table usually takes a small helping of each kind of food offered, and each makes a request for light or dark meat. In earlier years, this helped to avoid references to embarrassing parts like breast, thigh, and leg. Usually the legs, the drumsticks, go to the children—to the fussiest ones if there are more than two present.

Dessert is served after the dishes of the main meal are cleared away. Four kinds of pies are obligatory: mince, pumpkin, squash, and apple. Other kinds of pie may also be offered as long as those four are present. After the meal, the women return to the kitchen and wash dishes and divide up the leftovers to be taken to the various homes. The men return to the den or the living room for further conversation and napping. From this point on, as families begin to leave for their separate homes, Thanksgiving itself is considered over. The turkey and some of the other foods may survive a day or two in the form of sandwiches and leftovers, but they are no longer considered directly to be aspects of Thanksgiving.

Clearly, for this family, the Thanksgiving event centers on the gathering of family members around a traditional meal. The event is separated in some of its aspects into the same sex roles found prominently across America at the turn of the century. The communal performance of the event, then, is at least in large part a symbolic re-enactment of those factors that the family sees as part of its history: clearly divided sex roles, traditional handling of food, discussion of family history, invocation of a religious perspective at the beginning of the meal, hierarchies of relationships in the parceling out of the food supply. It is doubtful, however, that particular members of the family would describe Thanksgiving in these terms. Rather, they would insist that they continue to celebrate Thanksgiving in large part as a memorial to their cultural heritage: Since both the Howland and the Kimball families descend from *Mayflower* pilgrims (Howland and White), the re-enactment of Thanksgiving is also a family reassertion of lineage.

Moreover, in the 1930s the families were removed from Quabbin Valley in central Massachusetts, where five towns were obliterated to make way for the reservoir that now helps supply Boston with drinking water. The sense of having been dispossessed of the rural basis of its heritage is also evident at the Kimball family gatherings, where stories of "the Valley" and of people prominent in the family's past are brought forward as central topics that accompany the actual eating of the traditional foods, binding the family together in a communion with its past. Members of the family believe that theirs is a "good old-fashioned New England Thanksgiving," and that people in other parts of the United States probably do not celebrate the event in a similar way. Said one family member, "Well, sure, they probably all eat turkey these days, just like we do, but they probably wouldn't make much sense out of the rest of what we do when we get together for Thanksgiving."

The folklorist is in a position to follow up on such surmises by taking his imaginary movie cameras to another location and researching the same event with another family in another part of the country. What differences will we find? To what extent will we be dependent upon the insider again for pointed evaluation of obligatory items in the traditional performance?

THE WODTLI THANKSGIVING  The Wodtli and Tabler families are of Swiss and German background. Thanksgiving is for them also preceded by official notice of it in school. In the early 1900s, for example, the children always dressed up at school as Pilgrims and Indians and put on a public program. Thus, as with the New England Kimballs, official occasion ushered in the observance of the traditional event as celebrated within the home.

Thanksgiving Day itself begins early in the morning with the stuffing of the chicken. The stuffing, always a celery and onion mix, never varies; the chicken is stuffed on the same day it is cooked because it might spoil if it were prepared earlier. The typical bird is chicken or duck, although the family occasionally has had roast pork. In more recent times the family has used turkey because they are given away by the local logging companies to their men. Participants in the Thanksgiving Day event are principally family members, with a focus on the older people; Grandmother Wodtli always has to have a nice clean apron, Grandfather Wodtli always says grace, in German, in about the same words each year.

The apparent inventory of foods on the table is, as in the New England instance, larger than the obligatory, esoteric list: The family always has sweet potatoes, never yams ("the people around here were not yam people"), canned vegetables (the family did not have a refrigerator until the late 1930s), pickled crabapples, homemade pickles, hot rolls. In earlier years, there was no cranberry sauce ("we didn't even know about cranberries"), and liquor was not allowed ("wine and whiskey were medicine"). For dessert, homegrown pumpkin pie and mincemeat are mandatory, although recently chocolate and cream pies have been added.

Thanksgiving dinner is usually held at the home of someone on the maternal side of the family (at a Wodtli home rather than a Tabler). The women gather in the kitchen to prepare the food while the men move to the living room for conversation. Although alcohol is frowned upon, uncles occasionally gather outside on the porch for a couple of quiet drinks. Both sexes gather together at dinner, and the conversation turns primarily to family anecdotes.

After dinner, the women go again to the kitchen to wash dishes and divide the leftovers while the men return to the living room for more talking and smoking. During the Thanksgiving dinner itself, children usually receive the drumsticks, and people around the table are expected to state their preferences for light or dark meat, which is served from a central platter. Thanksgiving as an event is considered ended when the people leave, taking the divided leftovers with them.

The family relates the holiday primarily to the harvest season, but sees the celebration of it as primarily an American event. Both Grandmother and Grandfather Wodtli were immigrants to America (from Germany and Switzerland respectively), and the family today believes that the holiday is in part a confirmation of their conversion to the American culture as well as a partial recollection of their own rural past.

THE BEGINNINGS OF QUESTIONS (A SUMMARY)  There are some distinct differences between the two Thanksgiving events discussed sketchily above, but it is also evident that these two families, although at opposite ends of the United States and from different national backgrounds, celebrate the holiday in very similar ways that they themselves are unaware of. If we were to discuss in depth only one of the similarities, we would notice that our understanding of it would depend both on internal evidence from the participants themselves as well as observations only an outsider would be inclined to make. For example, in both families, the sex roles during the Thanksgiving event are clearly delineated: the women are in the kitchen, the men are in the living room, each group engaged in what would be called women's talk and men's talk. When the sexes merge over dinner, the conversation turns to more general family affairs; then the sexes separate again when the dinner is over. Is this a pattern we might find across the country at Thanksgiving time? Is it a pattern we might find in rural communities generally at any family gathering? Is it an event motif that indicates a deep conservatism about sex roles that can be celebrated openly or perceived during festive occasions? Is it perhaps a female-centered holiday, coming as it does at the end of the harvest, which has featured essentially male labor? Is it thus a threshold festival, marking the transition of the agricultural year from the outdoor, male-dominated arena of work to the indoor, feminine domain? These and other questions naturally arise in the mind of the researcher when confronted with comparative evidence such as presented here. Yet, these questions cannot be answered without considerable fieldwork among diverse families celebrating the same event across the country. Here, the researcher as an outsider develops questions and hypotheses for further pursuit that lie beyond the interests and inclinations of a particular family eating its Thanksgiving dinner. Without the aid of the insider's view, however, the researcher has only a generalized mass of evidence: a mixed batch of family members gathered together, a table loaded with food, various arenas of conversation. What do the women talk about in the kitchen while dinner is being prepared? What kinds of conversation are taking place among the men? Are the participants themselves aware of the propriety involved: Would a man feel at ease moving into the kitchen on such an occasion and taking part in the food preparation? Would it be likely for a woman in the family to slip quietly into the living room and participate in the men's conversations? In either case, would topics and vocabulary change abruptly? One suspects that these boundaries are not made of concrete, but that they are seldom crossed; such a conclusion cannot be stated firmly, however, until the event is studied further in all its multiform appearances across the country.

I cite the Thanksgiving holiday here because on the surface it seems to be a simple example of a traditional event. People do not regard it with the same deep religious involvement inherent in some other holidays, and many who celebrate Thanksgiving shrug off questions with quick answers such as, "Well, of course we have Thanksgiving, and I suppose we always have a turkey just like everyone else, but all the other things we do are just things that the family has done over the years." In other words, people are aware that they share certain customs with others around the country, and they are aware that their own particular families have certain traditions that may or may not be shared by others. But no one is particularly inclined to make a deep-level study of it to see the extent to which these traditions are tied in with larger processes and ideas within the culture as a whole, or within a region, or among members of similar ethnic backgrounds. By asking only a few questions of inside participants, we quickly notice that Thanksgiving as an event has both official (national) and local family dimensions. For the family, Thanksgiving specifically begins with the preparation of food for the Thanksgiving dinner itself, and ends, at least in the case of these two widely separated families, when the participants leave the scene and begin their trip home. The event, in other words, is not strictly limited by the calendar, but its dimensions are seen in terms of the gathering of family members itself. It thus has its own inner dynamics as far as the participants are concerned, and while its celebration is occasioned by a certain calendar holiday, its active parts are decided not by time constraints but by the internal scheme of the event itself.

AN ETHNIC EVENT: THE JAPANESE NEW YEAR   The celebration of the New Year by Japanese-Americans seems on the surface to be very much like that of Thanksgiving: A nationally recognized, official holiday is the scene for a special meal to which family members and friends are invited. A visitor to a Japanese-American home on the afternoon of New Year's Day would notice, of course, the distinctly ethnic character of the food, but might be inclined to classify this event alongside Thanksgiving as one in which a meal allows or encourages people to experience a sense of togetherness and thanksgiving. By asking questions, of course, we can try to determine whether indeed the meal is central to the event; by asking the hypothetical questions about the placement for our imaginary cameras in order to film the entire event, we can uncover information leading us to a clearer understanding of the event's dimensions.

CONTEXT AND OCCASION  While the occasion for this event in America is the transition from one year to another, in Japan this was a midwinter festival concerned with fertility. Great stress was laid on the delicacy of the earth at a time when rice was not yet growing, and great concern was shown for the spirits and memories of departed family members and ancestors. In previous times, the New Year festival in Japan was celebrated at the same or nearly the same time as the Chinese New Year. Japanese people today generally celebrate New Year's with the rest of the Western world, and Japanese-Americans in particular see this holiday as distinctly a New Year holiday, not an agricultural event. Nonetheless, it becomes evident in a close study of the inventory of the important items and actions of this event that there has been a strong carryover of concern for the relationships among family members, food, and community. Thus, while the occasion itself is recognized and celebrated by most Americans of Japanese descent, the particular meanings of the event follow an older, traditional Japanese set of assumptions. Part of the event focuses on the individual and his or her orientation to the larger family, represented by ancestors. Other elements celebrate the individual's relation to the immediate family, and the family's relationship to the community around it. Through all of these areas of focus runs the constant theme of sharing food, basically a ritual form of rice, the small cakes of *mochi* mentioned in Chapter 2.

FRAMEWORK OF ACTIVITY  The frame for the event would seem to be New Year's Day itself, apparently beginning—as we found with Thanksgiving—with the preparation of food, following through its consumption by visitors, and ending with the disappearance of the last guests. The esoteric framework, however, forces us to begin our consideration of the Japanese-American New Year several days before January 1 and extend it in some cases for several days beyond. Typically, the community awareness that New Year's is starting comes almost immediately after Christmas, when people begin to discuss the making of *mochi*. In some communities, the *mochi* is now produced by machine; in others it is still produced in the old way, using large wooden mallets that pound the sweet rice into a rubbery pulp, as described in Chapter 2. In either case, whether a group of families gather to make *mochi* for themselves (each bringing a quantity of rice and taking home *mochi* cakes in proportion) or whether a Buddhist church group makes it for sale among community members, this opening of the New Year's event is essentially a festive, community-oriented foodway custom. The *mochi* will be eaten, not only by family members on New Year's Day, but will be given as gifts to others, will be offered as part of the food for visitors, and will be offered to ancestors symbolically at the family altar.

The *mochi* cake is made by turning the small ball of rice dough around and around in the hands until it is smooth and almost flat, but without edges. It symbolizes harmony, happiness, and peace. In the local Buddhist church, two large *mochi* are placed on the altar. Called *kagami mochi* ("mirror *mochi*"), they signify a reflection of brightness, good fortune, and happiness. During the days before January 1, while the *mochi* is being prepared throughout the community, women are also doing extensive shopping for the particular foods required on New Year's Day, and many families are shopping for "dress up" clothing, especially for children. In the same period of time a thorough housecleaning is undertaken, going far beyond the usual compulsion for cleanliness and order.

PARTICIPANTS AND SEQUENCE   On New Year's Eve, the women of the family begin the extensive food preparation for the following day, an inventory of which follows. The preparation of food may take almost all night, and so it is rare for families celebrating the Japanese New Year to be free on New Year's Eve for the revelry that characterizes other Americans' celebration. Sometimes the men of the family will participate in the New Year's Eve parties of other American friends. During New Year's Eve the women of the house may make an offering of *mochi*, usually two or three cakes placed on top of each other and topped with a tangerine (including stem and leaves), at the family altar to the spirits of any family members who have died.

New Year's Day itself begins at breakfast, with the family gathering to eat *ozoni*, a soup made of fish stock that has a glutinous *mochi* cake in the bottom. Parents pay respects to the deceased of the immediate family by lighting incense and bowing at the family altar, which may be decorated with the written names of recently departed relatives. All dress in their Sunday best, children are alerted to be on their best behavior throughout the day, everyone is reminded that it is improper to become irritated for any reason during the day, and food preparation and final arrangements for serving the food are carried out.

Beginning in the early afternoon of New Year's Day, some members of each family will begin circulating to other homes in the Japanese-American community, stopping off to visit, sharing some of the traditional foods, and wishing friends and relatives a happy New Year. Usually the women in each family stay home to continue offering hospitality to others in the community making their rounds; children and older males do most of the visiting. Among Japanese immigrants who take part in this custom, a typical New Year's greeting would be *"Akemashite omedeto gozaimasu!"* ("Congratulations on the opening of the New Year"), followed by *"Honen mo dozo yoroshiku onegai shimasu"* ("Please take care of me this year as you have done during the past year"). Other simpler greetings, such as "Happy New Year," both in Japanese and English are used, but it is clear that the sense of the event is a renewal of reciprocal relations among members of the community, not simply a matter of making a social call.

DIMENSIONS AND ESOTERIC VALUE    The foods offered to visitors at this time are primarily the typical festive foods one might find at a Japanese picnic: various kinds of *sushi*, teriyaki chicken, deep-fried shrimp, and so on. There may also be raw fish and a number of different condiments. Alcohol is usually available in abundance, primarily in the form of warmed *sake*, and typically a variety of beers is offered, sometimes including Japanese brands. The drinking of hard liquor is rare, but a bottle of whiskey may be brought out at the arrival of a Caucasian visitor. The outsider, then, would notice a table absolutely groaning with a wide variety of identifiably ethnic Japanese foods but might not be aware that only some of these are obligatory on this occasion: Somewhere near the center of the table will be either a *tai* fish (a rather large reddish-colored fish cooked so that the fins and tail are raised upward as if the fish is swimming), or perhaps a lobster, and certain other foods that feature the colors red and white. These colors indicate good luck and prosperity—hence the central focus on these foods—and their use at this season corresponds to a wish that anything done on this day will presage the nature of things to come in the ensuing year. In addition, many of the foods are seafoods, which are strongly connected to the concept of fertility in Japanese folklore. These foods, in conjunction with the rice that is the staple of Japanese food custom, bring together the main concerns for a bountiful food supply during the coming year and for prosperity and good fortune in the community.

As the menfolk circulate from one home to another on New Year's Day, they may pay off personal debts; some prefer not to do this on New Year's

Day but to handle it over the next day or so after the holiday. In Japanese custom, usually seven full days are required for the celebration of the New Year, each day given over to some particular custom such as the paying of private debts. The precision of this seven-day event has generally faded in America, with much of the observation and celebration being focused on New Year's Day itself and the preceding days of preparation.

It is important for us to ponder whether the previous days of preparation are to be indeed included as part of the event in our use of that term: Are these important aspects of the event itself, or are they only aspects of getting ready for the event? We need to know what the event is and what it means before we can answer this question, for if we answer it from the outside, we are likely to view these elements sequentially as items leading up to an event largely because that particular observance we can most fully identify as an event, the New Year's Day dinner, is that part of the observation most open to our scrutiny (as outsiders) and most familiar to us (because it resembles our own traditions). We may therefore incline, unintentionally, to subordinate other aspects of this celebration to the one feature we think is central. If we are going to take our human subjects seriously, we need to listen when they say "oh, of course New Year's begins with the making of *mochi,* and with house-cleaning." And we need then to find out what making *mochi* and housecleaning have to do with the central aspects of a celebrative event.

One approach in this case may be for us to take a close look at the Japanese word for New Year: *shogatsu.* This word is usually translated "New Year's" or "January." The word *gatsu* means "month"; the first part of the word, *sho,* can mean "just," "punctual," "right," "righteous-ness," "justice," "redress," "straighten," "amend," "correctly," "surely," "proper," "natural," "lawful," "healthy," "moral," "straight," "straight-forward," "perfect." Thus, while *shogatsu* means on one level a simple reference to the beginning of the year, all of its connotative meanings suggest bringing things to a recognized norm, celebrating things that are natural and just and proper, in other words, setting things straight for the New Year.

Everything done at the time of the New Year is done with the intent of realigning the individual and the family to the requirements of the normal community design. This is obviously more than just the occasion for merriment that another year has passed or another has begun; it is a sense of personal and communal commitment to maintain the reciprocal interactions necessary to the continuation of one's family and culture over the coming year.

It features, basically, a very private personal and familial kind of preparation for straightening things out and making the world regular: the extra housecleaning, the intensive efforts to dress up and behave correctly, the personal rededication to act properly in one's family context. The responsible older members of the family are expected to rededicate themselves to their family lineage at this time, which is done privately and out of the sight of visitors at the family shrine. The family gathers for a specific, symbolic, traditional meal as the very first family action of the first day of the New Year, and for many Japanese-Americans this observance is the central feature of the whole event.

The afternoon of New Year's Day opens out this tight concern with propriety and familial obligations into its application to the community at large, the larger family with whom Japenese-Americans must relate during the public parts of their lives. This part of the day is less intense and somewhat more social in nature. The outsider might conceive of it simply as an ethnic holiday and entirely miss its larger relationship to the specific and very intense breakfast that was shared earlier, out of sight of the observer. To treat this event accurately with our imaginary movie cameras, we would want to understand the communal preparation of the *mochi* and the private preparation of home and person as the opening coefficients of a very complex cultural observance. They start the sequential framework from the insider's point of view; from this joint concern with the individual and his community the event then moves to a focus in the privacy of the family late New Year's Eve and early New Year's Day morning, then widens out again to community participation later that afternoon.

The Japanese-American New Year might be diagrammed as an hourglass with community and personal concerns at each end and the focus on the nuclear family at the center. Obviously, any one aspect of this event would be difficult to understand apart from the others. Yet, as outsiders, we would be most likely to have noticed and to have been able to film only one end of the hourglass had we not asked for the help of insiders in guiding us to the full sequence of events, which, taken together, allow us to discover a cultural meaning in the continuation of an important ethnic custom.

INDUCED OR RECALLED EVENTS: MRS. JUDKINS'S *CANTE-FABLE*  One particular kind of folk event recurs continually in the study of folklore, yet it is one of the most difficult to deal with. When a collector of folklore goes into the field and elicits performances from a chairmaker, a barnbuilder, a ballad singer, a storyteller, and others, the researcher is trying as far as possible to bring forth a normal traditional event that can be studied as a text of a particular performance. Modern folklorists always try to collect tales and ballads and barn raisings in their home contexts so that all the details will be reliable in the tradition and not simply brought forth because of the presence of the collector. Nonetheless, it is inevitable that the presence of the collector, which is often limited by time and money, is a certain urgent factor in many performances, and hence a force in any related folk event. Observations thus generated should not be discredited for this reason, but they need to be carefully scrutinized for exactly what they can and cannot tell us about the traditions observed.

On the positive side, as we have already noticed, it may always be true that the researcher will be able to bring to the experience comparative knowledge of other folk performances that will allow for a fuller perspective on an event than might be provided by the single event itself. This is particularly the case when the performer does not (or cannot) do a proficient job. On the negative side, it may place unfair stress on some traditions over others (folklorists have numerous stories of field collectors who went after one kind of folklore in areas where others abounded or where others were actually more typical of local traditions), and it may also elicit poor texts from a performer who might have been a fine resource some years earlier but whose repertoire has remained in hibernation long enough to make awkward an event that otherwise could have been carried forward with alacrity and articulation. Since these dilemmas cannot be predicted in advance, the folklorist must always be ready to sense in any fieldwork situation the limitations and the promises presented in each event/performance.

Mrs. Clarice Mae Judkins was said to be at one time the leading traditional singer in Lane County, Oregon. Her family was among the pioneers to the area, and she herself had married the son of one of the more prominent local pioneer families. Her repertoire was estimated to be in excess of 250 songs, which included old traditional ballads, folk songs of the westward movement, Civil War songs, and popular songs of the late 1800s and early 1900s. She was often invited to sing at the meetings of pioneer societies, clubs of old-timers, and at family picnics. In her elderly years, she was visited by a number of local folk-song collectors who found her an inexhaustible source; invariably on second, third, and fourth visits she would bring forth songs she had not remembered earlier. I am certain that no one ever heard her entire repertoire. In her eighties she was still being invited to parties and old folks' homes to entertain, so when I visited her on numerous occasions to get her to sing for the tape recorder, although we lacked numbers in the audience, I sensed that I was not getting essentially different texts than might have been heard had she been singing for a large audience of friends or family. Nonetheless, eventually I realized that she was trying to recall those songs that had not been in the the most active part of her repertoire. On one occasion she began singing snatches of a song I had never heard before interspersed with spoken narration. Since this was one of her ways of recalling the words of a song she had not often sung, I thought nothing of it at first and simply requested that she try to recall what the song was in its entirety so we could tape it. (Under these circumstances I usually start the tape recorder and leave it on so the mechanical manipulations do not in and of themselves become part of the opening and closing reference points for performance events.) A transcript of the tape reveals the following interchange between us, in which she tried to recall how another traditional singer she had heard in her youth had performed the song. In her estimation, the earlier singer had not known the song very well, for he could only sing parts of it. The induced event, in the case of this one fragmentary text, went as follows:

TOELKEN:   Can you remember how that one, that one you were just singing, goes all the way through?

MRS. JUDKINS:   I don't think I've ever heard it all the way through. I think that he would say that this man lost his horse and somebody'd stolen his mare and they didn't want to give him any information about it, so they told him, "Yes, I saw your mare, she went wavering through the air." So the fella finally became convinced that that was where his horse was. They kept telling him, "In yonder cloud I see thy mare—she goes wavering through the air."

TOELKEN:   Finally convinced him.

MRS. JUDKINS:   Finally convinced him. He'd asked a shepherd, and he'd asked a farmer, and everyone would tell him the same thing. They didn't want him looking for a mare. He, probably someone, had stolen it, but they didn't want to give him any information. They got tired of his questions so they told him that the mare was up in the clouds, which is another way of telling him they didn't know.

TOELKEN:    Well, how did the tune go again?

MRS. JUDKINS:    Oh, let's see. This man would tell the first of it—tell the incident, so apparently he didn't know all the song, uh, the words. And, uh, so but every now and then he burst out singing it, and then everybody'd look disgusted and say, "There's that man with the old gray mare going wavering through the air." But the first he sung and all the others he just talked about. [She sings:]

> Oh tell me, shepherd, tell me truly,
> Have you seen a man a-riding?
> A man and a mare with coal black hair,
> Methinks he is not far behind me.
>
> Oh naddle doodle dow ridden, naddle doodle day,
> Oh naddle doodle dow ridden, naddle doodle day.
>
> Oh yes kind sir to my surprise,
> A man and a mare went into the skies.
> A man and a mare with coal black hair,
> I can see him yet, I can see him yet.
>
> Oh naddle doodle dow ridden, naddle doodle day,
> Oh naddle doodle dow ridden, naddle doodle day.

[Speaks:] And then the other man was so convinced that he began saying,

> [Sings:]
> In yonder cloud I see my mare,
> As she goes wavering through the air.

[Speaks:] And that seems to be about all of it.

TOELKEN:    And then the man would go on once more telling parts of the story?

MRS. JUDKINS:    Yes, telling part of the story, and then stopped for the chorus. So all the music part of it was that, and the other people would say, "Well there goes that old gray mare, wavering through the air again." That was an old song, and that was all he knew of it.

What Mrs. Judkins didn't realize—and what I didn't realize until much later, listening to the tape again—was that the event she and I had shared was an attempted recounting of a curious performance she had heard many years before of a genre folklorists call *cante-fable*, a narrative that alternates a spoken story with a verse or chorus sung to a tune. Since Mrs. Judkins did not understand that it was a particular kind of performance, she had assumed that the man did not know all the song, that he sang only the part he remembered. But her constant reference to a repetitious chorus with highly formularized wording and tune, and to what seems to have been a repetitious and perhaps rambling story told in prose, indicates pretty clearly that the real event, which took place long ago, was a performance of a well-known genre of folklore that may have been recognizable to others in the audience but apparently not to young Clarice Mae.

In this case, it seems that the event witnessed by the folklorist, induced by the attempt to research and recover old songs, was really in the category of an anecdote, a memorate, or to some extent a recitation of oral history; and yet within that somewhat codified event lay the remnants of another event that could lead eventually to some research on the *cante-fable* there suggested through partial recollection. Here the role of the researcher, the outsider, has become almost more important in the generating of meaning than was that of the insider whose familiarity with the material was not conducive to a full sense of the traditional meaning. Hypothetically, it will be possible for a researcher eventually to come up with a more complete text than Mrs. Judkins was able to do.

There is also ample evidence of overwhelming awareness and articulation in events induced by a folklorist. For example, Charles Cultee, almost the last of his people—the Kathlamet Chinook—narrated several striking and powerful myth texts to Franz Boas at the turn of the century. Boas took the texts down phonetically and then, interrogating Cultee in the Chinook jargon, provided an interlinear translation that can still be used by students today as a means of getting back to original elements of style and structure and meaning in the storytelling event, as Dell Hymes has brilliantly shown in his reconstruction of the full text of the Sun Myth. Even so, such a text cannot reveal to us all the details we need in order to understand a folk event fully and therefore to discover in it the actual meaning of a performance. Even the best of these texts remain powerful fossils of an even more powerful occurrence.

## ✍ FOLK EVENTS: AN OVERVIEW It should

be clear by now that folk events are not all the same "size," that they may occur simultaneously with other folk events, and that some folk events may consist of smaller components that themselves may be dealt with as events. If we return now to the question posed earlier in this chapter about Tina's proverb—was it a folk event or does it take on the look of a folk event because of the attention we give it?—we can probably say that because the occurrence is extractable and discussable as a separate entity, yes, it can be dealt with as an event, and in so doing we are not denying that it was also one of several components of a larger folk event called a party. Setting up our imaginary camera equipment under those circumstances, then, we would envision at least one roving camera taking in the small groups of people at the party as they told jokes and anecdotes, another camera in the kitchen focusing on the kinds of food considered appropriate on that occasion, another camera taking in the entire sets of components, and one at the ready (because hindsight is cheap and we might as well use it) to zoom in on the particularized event in which a proverb was "done." Usually proverbs are not aimless observations on philosophical matters of general interest; rather, they are pointed applications of well-known, culture-oriented attitudes under conditions in which perhaps tension, indecision, or some other similar frustration has entered a human interaction, and in which specific personal advice might be embarrassing or intrusive. The fullest and most impressive account of such an event is given by Barbara Kirshenblatt-Gimblett. In her study of a parable in context, the entire situation in which the event took place is detailed, both by the collector and by the main participant, the teller of the parable. In many respects, a parable is a narrative proverb: Both try to represent in formularized ways the wisdom of the community as applied to a particular instance in which easily recognized philosophy can solve a dilemma when personal intrusion would be doomed to failure.

Whether the event is a proverb that takes ten seconds to recite, a parable that takes somewhat less than a minute to tell, a folk tale that takes fifteen or twenty minutes to relate, an epic poem that takes a day and a half to be sung, a holiday that takes a week to celebrate, or a barn that takes a week to build, each will have some identifiable markers, some framework within which the occurrence is recognized by performer and audience as a communicative event. In each case we find our attention focused on the particularized articulation of all those possibilities that lie dormant in the mind of a tradition-bearer at any particular moment. Even the custom of throwing spilled salt over the shoulder is only a potentiality until it is actually done by someone; when it is done, there will be some reason for it, which will often be stated in a phrase as the action takes place. There will be a beginning and an end to the action, and some framework within which it can be understood. Not all who know of the belief of throwing salt over the shoulder actually perform the custom when salt is spilled; therefore, we are distinguishing between beliefs and actions when we discuss folk events. For every traditional event, there may be any number of possible events that never take place; these may be discovered through discussions with members of inside groups, who can very often give us the typical dimensions of possible traditional acts, but it is only when the traditional act is made manifest within a natural context that we can actually study it as a folk event.

# ✍ BIBLIOGRAPHICAL NOTES

If the active part of folklore can be called *performance*, then the actual total occurrence of that performance, including performer, audience, and context in a time-frame, can be called *the event*. Most of the references in the previous chapter thus apply inferentially here. This chapter parallels many of the considerations offered by Dell Hymes and others in the study of sociolinguistics: Hymes's division of topics into speech community, speech situation, speech event, speech act, and speech styles, is an attempt to focus on the actuality of speaking in live context, not on the language, word, or grammar as abstracted phenomena. See Hymes, "Models of the Interaction of Language and Social Life," in *Directions in Sociolinguistics*, ed. John J. Gumperz and Dell Hymes (New York: Holt, Rinehart and Winston, 1972), pp. 35–71; nearly every essay is parallel to, or directly involved with, the dynamics of folklore discussed in the present book.

*Metafolklore* is Alan Dundes's term for (among other things) the commentaries and remarks made by tradition-bearers about their own traditions, that is, folklore about folklore. See his "Metafolklore and Oral Literary Criticism," *The Monist*, 50 (1966), 505–516. In "Toward a Definition of Folklore in Context," *Journal of American Folklore*, 84 (1971), 3–15, Dan Ben-Amos asserts that "in the real habitat of all folklore forms, there is no dichotomy between processes and products. The telling is the tale; therefore the narrator, his story, and his audience are all related to each other as components of a single continuum, which is the communicative event" (p. 10). Robert A. Georges, "Toward an Understanding of Storytelling Events," *Journal of American Folklore*, 82 (1969), 313–328, suggests that storytelling must be seen "holistically rather than atomistically"—that is, as a total event (or series of events), not as a simple text. Folklore lies in the doing, according to Georges, in the performance-event, not in the artifact as a structural entity. The present chapter is obviously aligned with these sentiments.

Paul Hockings, ed., *Principles of Visual Anthropology* (The Hague: Mouton, 1975), presents a fascinating array of essays, several of which lend themselves to the filming situations hypothesized in this chapter. See especially J. Marshall and Emilie de Brigard, "Idea and Event in Urban Film," pp. 133–145, and E. R. Sorensen and Allison Jablonko, "Research Filming of Naturally Occurring Phenomena: Basic Strategies," pp. 151–163. The work of Sol Worth and John Adair is presented in *Through Navajo Eyes: An Exploration in Film Communication and Anthropology* (Bloomington: Indiana University Press, 1972); a brief synopsis of Susie Benally's film *A Navajo Weaver* appears on pp. 267–268. Of a more practical bent, but still of value to our imaginary filmmaking, is John Collier, Jr., *Visual Anthropology: Photography as a Research Method* (New York: Holt, Rinehart and Winston, 1967). Margaret Mead's comments about the importance of film can be found in "Visual Anthropology in a Discipline of Words," in Hockings, *Principles of Visual Anthropology*, pp. 3–10.

For their willingness to share their family traditions with me for this book, I am deeply indebted to Mr. and Mrs. William Tabler and their daughter, Twilo Scofield. Even more profoundly am I obliged to my own Massachusetts relatives, Leslie and Virginia Howland (Granby), Alice Kimball and Ada Collis (Pelham Hill), Kenneth and Alyce Damon (West Springfield), Leila and Homer Damon (Belchertown)—all formerly of Enfield, before Quabbin Reservoir—for passing the traditions of Thanksgiving on through me.

The Japanese and Japanese-American people listed in the notes to Chapter 2 are my sources here as well; my special thanks go to Mrs. Chiyoe Kubota, an excellent cook, a serious conservator of family tradition, and an indefatigable source of cultural information. Further cultural backgrounds on rice and its relation to the New Year may be found in Toshijiro Hirayama, "Seasonal Rituals Connected with Rice Culture," in *Studies in Japanese Folklore*, ed. Richard M. Dorson (Bloomington: Indiana University Press, 1963), pp. 57–75, esp. pp. 73–74, and Ichiro Hori, "Mysterious Visitors from the Harvest to the New Year," also in Dorson, pp. 76–103, esp. pp. 83–88 and 97–98.

An article focusing on Mrs. Judkins's songs is Russell M. Harrison, "Folksongs from Oregon," *Western Folklore*, 11 (1952), 174–184. The full text and commentary on the Sun Myth is in Dell Hymes, "Folklore's Nature and the Sun's Myth," *Journal of American Folklore*, 88 (1975), 345–369.

Many folklore studies have indeed centered their attention on the event rather than on the artifact. Three studies of differing dimensions may provide some idea of the possibilities in focus for such work. James P. Leary, "Fists and Foul Mouths: Fights and Fight Stories in Contemporary Rural American Bars," *Journal of American Folklore*, 89 (1976), 27–39, shows the striking correspondence between the structure of fight stories told in bars and the structure of the actual fight events. Instead of the story being treated merely as a text, or the fight dealt with as a mere chance occurrence, the two are seen as interrelated traditional structures, each deriving meaning from the other, which can be understood only by scrutinizing the entire traditional performance event. Richard Bauman, "The La Have Island General Store: Sociability and Verbal Art in a Nova Scotia Community," *Journal of American Folklore*, 85 (1972), 330–343, rests its evidence on the continual series of evening sessions of traditional conversation events at a local community store. Seen as events, these culturally structured conversations reveal much of the local aesthetic sense. Alan Dundes and Alessandro Falassi, *La Terra in Piazza* (Berkeley: University of California Press, 1975), is a study of an event that captivates the lives and emotions of an entire city, Siena, Italy, as its annual horse-racing and related activities interweave in the most intricate system of event frames imaginable.

# 5

# COMMUNITY
# TASTE

The Mixed Repertoire, Decorum,
and Traditional Aesthetics

BASIC TO MOST FOLKLORISTIC STUDY IS THE CONCEPT OF GENRE AND GENRE DIFFERENTIATION. REGARDLESS OF OUR ULTIMATE THEORETICAL INTERESTS (STRUCTURAL, psychological, social, linguistic, stylistic), we must know the various forms that folk expressions commonly take. Of course, these forms are of differing dimensions, and generic theories in folklore have consequently never been very specific. Nonetheless, just as doctors do not talk about the body without knowing all the principal parts, just as a linguist cannot talk about language without a vocabulary of terms that describe words, sounds, and meaning, so the folklorist hesitates to discuss folklore without a sound knowledge of its elements. And just as some doctors specialize in ears, bellies, feet, or in single processes like childbirth, and as linguists specialize in verbs, sounds, or whole languages, so do folklorists specialize—in tales, songs, or in the traditions of a whole group of people. Without a generic terminology, we would have little hope of understanding each other, especially when, just like doctors, we try to see how the arm or leg, tale or belief, functions as part of the whole live phenomenon.

Unlike the human body, however, folklore—as a creature—may not always have the same structure on each occasion. The motifs and ideas of a particular item or performance of folklore are always changing (while humans usually continue to appear with one head, two arms, and two legs). That is to say, folklore is not limited by genre or by the repertoire of one person. Folk ideas and expressions have a way of appearing in several genres, and people in a close group are likely to know many genres and perform in more than one of them.

One result is that we may find the same idea or motif here in a tale, there in a legend, here in a ballad, there in a news item. Another is that we discover the woman we sought out for her quiltmaking is also a great storyteller and a specialist in local foodlore, the man we started to collect ballads from is an even better whittler and blacksmith, while another person we gathered jokes from turns out to have nothing else to offer (from tradition) besides jokes. Cecil Sharp and Maud Karpeles, the British folk song scholars, made three extensive and intensive trips into the Appalachians of the United States; they collected many hundreds of folk song texts in an area that we today realize is also one of the richest places for folk tale tradition in the country. Take any one of their informants: Were the songs actually the central or most important part of that person's traditional repertoire? Were the motifs or the stories in the songs and ballads also found in local folk tales? Was the song tradition in those areas actually more active than other kinds of folk tradition? Answers to such questions are difficult if not impossible to come by now, years later; in their understandable zeal for collecting folk songs, Sharp and Karpeles overlooked perhaps dozens of other related kinds of folk expression that might have afforded us the full view of folk experience and expression in those areas not long after the turn of the century. Since the character of that region is now vastly changed, it is impossible for us to recover those perspectives that could have been easily noted and studied by scholars who were actually there. This is not merely an antiquarian quibble, for the same myopia is possible for any folklore fieldworker, whatever the date.

## ✒ GENRE AND FOCUS The generic approach to folklore is of basic importance, but it is equally clear that we cannot let generic boundaries become ideational restrictions, especially when we

seek to understand the live processes behind the descriptive categories of folk structures. The choices open to a traditional performer at any time will be encouraged or restricted by the traditional context of the event. On the immediate level, the community's taste in such matters as language, topic, propriety, and decorum, will help to determine how a particular song or tale or barn will take shape. Over the long haul, community taste will help to condition the choices on larger matters, such as the forms a given idea may most likely take. These choices may come to our attention most clearly in generic terms, as when someone says, "That song you just sang is a story I used to hear from my father." But the deciding factors are not generic details; they are instead those dynamic and constantly shifting canons of traditional taste that continually recombine to influence (and even to cause) any particular folk performance. In this chapter, then, I propose to discuss some aspects of folklore dynamism that seem unrestricted by generic categories: repertoires of traditional performers in which the same folk item may fall into different categories depending on function and context; folk ideas found in a number of genres without appreciable apparent difference in meaning; matters of community taste, aesthetics, and decorum that help to decide who does what, when, and with what import for the close group. This chapter does not suggest, however, that genre is a useless term; to the contrary, genre allows us to group similar items together for purposes of analysis and discussion. But generic distinctions in and of themselves seldom lead us to clear understanding of traditional processes.

MULTIFORM REPERTOIRES "Chris" Christensen, a retired teacher in Oakridge, Oregon, is known as a whittler. He carves fans, balls in cages, and chains; most of the traditional items of the whittler's craft are found in his work. Probably in generic terms a folklorist's category for Mr. Christensen's work would be *craft: whittling (wood)*. Yet, when Mr. Christensen talks about how and where he learned whittling, we find out that he picked it up from other commercial fishermen years ago: It was customary to whittle when work fell off and the men were bored. Now, is his whittling a craft or a custom? Obviously both, and this can be accommodated (in an archive collection) by crossreferencing. But what the cross-reference does not indicate is the relative importance of the genres mentioned. Seen as only one small part of a fisherman's repertoire of folklore (folk speech, popular belief, occupational custom, song, story, gesture), whittling is an insignificant—or at least a subordinated—activity ("we used to just throw them away, back then"). Seen as a craft now practiced quite often by Mr. Christensen, who is no longer a fisherman, it appears central. It relates him to neighbors and friends to whom he gives (never sells) the carved items. Moreover, his own dedication to the aesthetic and personal details of whittling, though modestly understated, are strong: He is very careful to choose the right wood (Alaska cedar, when possible) and to treat it properly by soaking it in water before beginning his work. Usually he has a few pieces asoak for those moments "when I feel the whittlin' comin' on." We might suggest, then, that even though the whittling has remained an interest for Mr. Christensen, its generic focus has changed in weight: Had we "collected him" years ago we might have called his whittling a custom, while now we might call it a craft since it has been singled out by him, excerpted, so to speak, as something he particularly likes to do. In this case, since the tradition-bearer himself has done the excerpting, the theoretical problems are comparatively few.

All too often, however, it is the folklorist who unwittingly does the excerpting and presents a vivid record of what is thought to be a genre without providing a sense of where it stands in the traditional repertoire of the informant. An example of such an omission is provided earlier in this book: the case of the New England family that sings "Rolling Home" at Thanksgiving. I did not supply the observation that for only a few people in that whole family is it part of a repertoire of songs. For the others it is a custom, performed on a particular date because "we've always done it." Most people in the family remember only the chorus, and they do not sing it at other times of the year. Without this information, we might easily suppose that the family is one with a rich song repertoire, so active that they even sing at the table. Then is "Rolling Home" not to be placed in the genre *folk song?* Of course it is a folk song, when considered separately and when seen in terms of its own form, transmission, development, and variation in oral tradition. But the situation is more complex when we consider where and how the song lies in the particular repertoires of its various singers. An item once a part of a song repertoire passed on by sailors and fishermen for use at times appropriate to their traditions has become an occasional item within another context. In both instances, custom plays a role, of course, but in the case of the New England family, custom seems to have the upper hand. It is evident that judgments about whether a given folk expression can be called a tale, a song, or a custom must be based as much on its function in the live process as on its appearance when written out on a page.

Hugh Yellowman is a Navajo living in a small town in southern Utah, just north of the Navajo reservation. He is known locally as a moccasin maker of great talent; the people of his town bring him their deer hides and commission him to make Navajo-style moccasins for their families. Proprietors of nearby tourist shops and trading posts sell his moccasins when they can get them. His wife, Helen, is a well-known weaver who sells her rugs through a local trading post. Both of these activities would no doubt be classified as folk crafts by most folklorists, for the kinds of performance under scrutiny here require manual formations of culturally recognizable items, in culturally transmitted ways, from material goods. Yet, as we shall see in Chapter 6, the weaving of a Navajo rug is only part of a larger set of culturally important actions: herding sheep (animal lore, folk science, custom, belief), gathering plants and herbs for washing and dyeing (plant lore, belief, folk medicine), and spinning (craft, belief). And Yellowman's moccasins entail a set of hunting beliefs and rituals that go far beyond the manual dexterity required to produce the actual items: Proper hunting and skinning of the animals must be in congruence with the annual round of ceremonies, with the mental and physical preparation of the hunter, with the stories told each day in the hunting camp, and so on. If the rug is the least important aspect of the process that produces it, if the moccasin is only symbolic of a larger set of relationships, are we not warping Navajo reality if we focus chiefly on the structure of items in determining genre? Do we not miss a great deal of meaning when we apply our generic concepts to performances of other cultures? The answer to both is yes.

On the other hand, how are we to understand anything unless we try to see clearly in the codes we already know? This may seem at first to be a dilemma sufficient to discourage anyone from studying folklore further, but it can be solved by admitting that genre designations are devices for clarity, not natural definitions in and of themselves. Genre may indicate something to us of structure and substance, as well as of import, meaning, and function. Since we can articulate generic distinctions and hold several of them in mind at one time, we should be able to approach even more fairly those traditional expressions that might otherwise puzzle us or evade our understanding.

THE BASKET AS FOLK SONG  Suppose we hear an Indian woman from northern California say that we cannot learn to make baskets until we learn all the proper songs. We are told that the materials for the baskets must be softened and shaped with the lips and teeth, and that without the songs the baskets will be meaningless. We infer as the conversation develops that a basket seems to be in the same category as a song, perhaps because they both come from the mouth, perhaps because they both use the same or similar kinds of images. The basket seems to fit into a genre other than the one we might have assigned it had we not asked into the matter. Suddenly, we think, They must believe the basket is a visible song! and we ask the old woman, who smiles back as if to say, "What *else* could it be, after all?" Note that we have made the discovery and have been able to articulate it because we could hold two generic concepts in mind simultaneously and recognize that for this culture they are apparently registered as one. In a parallel instance, N. Scott Momaday shows that an arrow is an aspect of both language and communication for his tribe: A brief description of how Kiowa arrows are made with toothmarks on them is superimposed on a story of an arrow-maker who recognizes the presence of an enemy (and shoots him with a newly made arrow, right through the buffalo hide tipi) because the unseen person cannot answer in the Kiowa language. In such discussions, we must have our generic concepts straight or we will not be able to articulate the wide variations in function, value, focus, and process that lurk behind all live performances of folklore. Holding two (or ten) genres in mind is confusing only if we make the mistake of thinking that they are, or should be, mutually exclusive.

One could go to Yellowman and make a documentary film of his work in producing a pair of moccasins. The film might even show the hunting scene preceding the skinning, which would precede the tanning, which would precede the moccasin-making. But even so, the filmmaker might leave town totally unaware of Yellowman's ability to make silver and turquoise jewelry, his extraordinary talents at storytelling, his singing and dancing in the very important *yei-bi-chei* ceremony, his making and use of bows and arrows, his extensive knowledge of plants, astronomy, medicine, mythic lore, and so on. Notice that it is not the live context that would be missing from such a documentary (for there might be plenty of contextual material), but the esoteric idea-context would be fragmented; thus the Navajo idea of what a moccasin is would disappear, leaving an image of what *we* think a moccasin is. In practice, genres are difficult to separate, and this should be approached as a positive matter for speculation.


Rather than focus, then, on a single presumed genre, we need to ask— at least to begin with—what is the range of folk performance in this person? In this group? On this occasion? In this medium? Are there elements of meaning, style, or structure that strike us as belonging to more than one generic category? We might, later on, excerpt the songs, say, for special focus, but we will not then have overlooked the other expressions and their relationships to the songs. Thus we will not have missed the real place of songs in the total fabric of this person's (or group's or region's) normal traditions.

## ◤ MULTILATERAL LEARNING Another important aspect of traditional repertoires is that each item or genre or idea may come from a different source within the folk group. A person may have learned how to whittle from his grandfather, how to make willow whistles from an uncle, how to play the guitar from another uncle, how to sing songs from an aunt, how to know the traditions of crossing the equator from his later buddies in the coast guard. For this reason, each tradition-bearer is a unique combination of folk expression. Equally, we cannot conclude that because one person has only a partial recollection of a tradition that the tradition itself is dying out. Mrs. Mary ("Grandma") Spivey of Buckeye Cove, North Carolina, was the matriarch of a large traditional mountain family when I visited her in 1952. She was a walking treasure of mountain wit, traditional cooking lore, herbalism, folk medicine, stories and legends, beliefs, and folk songs. Even so, her fourteen-year-old granddaughter, Carolyn, had a far larger repertoire of songs and ballads—numbering in the hundreds. Clearly, Carolyn was the current carrier of ballads in the family, and she had learned them from everyone else (most of her relatives sang at least a few songs), including a now-deceased grandfather. Considering the frequency with which this kind of situation is met, we would surely be hasty to assume that all members of the community should know the same genres in the same quantities or that older tradition-bearers should normally "have" more folklore than younger ones.

The tendency toward multiple repertoire assures that the total quantity of folklore in a particular person's repertoire will be highly variable, as will be the kinds of folklore in each repertoire; these variations will be as much a function of the person's own tastes as they are of differences in the people from whom the traditions were learned and the ages at which they were picked up. This condition is obviously an important component of the concept of dynamic variation brought up in Chapter 1: Not only is each item of folklore subject to variation at every remove in tradition, but the traditions themselves and their role in the lives of each folk performer are in continual flux.

TRADITIONAL DEFERENCE   In addition to such encouragements to generic variation as creativity, contextual constraints, memory lapse, source, and age, many folk groups feel a delicacy about intruding into any field of expression associated with a particular person. Thus, people in a family may all know of a certain tradition, but one particular person performs it for the rest. Grandma's reputation for a special pie usually insures that others will not offer their versions of it while she is present unless some conversational arrangement has been made previously. Indeed, in some families, no one else will make that pie at all according to her special recipe until Grandma is deceased; at that juncture, someone else may step forward to fill the traditional slot. In the Spivey family of North Carolina, Carolyn was the acknowledged singer, although others also sang; earlier, Carolyn's grandfather had been the family singer. Bess Hockema, a grandmother living in Pistol River, Oregon, makes afghans for her grandchildren as her own mother once did for hers. Others in these families know the same traditions and perhaps can perform them as well, but the actual centrality of the performance focuses on a particular person because of age, talent, interest, or because of simple family custom. As one tradition-bearer dies or retires, several others are available to take that place in the generic spotlight.

One hears people say, "Oh, don't ask me to tell a joke; ask George over there, he's a scream." On logging crews, often one member is the chief trickster, is acknowledged so by his buddies, and relishes his position. On Indian reservations, we are directed to "the last basket-maker in this tribe"; some years later, when she dies, another person (who was there all along) becomes "the last basket-maker in this tribe." I have heard a quilter (a man) say, "Well, you know, I never did mean to become a quilter, but when there weren't any others left in the family it just didn't seem right to let it drop, so I just started doing what Mom did." Such attitudes testify to a kind of deference to recognized traditional performers on the part of those in the close group who know the traditions. In turn, this widespread deference—in the ways we actually encounter it in conversation—indicates an awareness of genre ("Oh, yes, he's the best storyteller in these parts") and of a set of shared aesthetics. The aesthetics we will take up later in this chapter, but here it is important to realize that deference to tradition-bearers helps to determine who will perform in certain genres, and at what intervals in time. Keeping in mind that some traditions are more prominent in childhood while others blossom when we are older, that some traditions seem to skip generations in the family, that many traditions are learned from peers not necessarily older than ourselves, we see that almost any member of a close group is a potential performer in a great number of genres at different times and for different reasons. Meanwhile, as we will see more fully later in this chapter, many folk ideas can be and are expressed in any of several genres, and with varying focuses within genres. All of these possibilities make up the ideational context from which arises any particular formulation or performance of a tradition, and they inform the way in which the formulation is made, by whom, and when.

Such a range of variables can be better understood if we refer to a particular person and see how real situations actually bring forth the choices and performances that demonstrate the conservation of traditions in dynamically responsive ways. Even so, we should not allow ourselves to hope that in any one person, family, or ethnic, regional, or occupational group we will see all the possible permutations of genre, motif, style, and performance. Rather, one clear set of examples can give us some insight into the tremendous richness of tradition in everyday life, a demonstration that for the tradition-bearers in a close group there exists a constellation of potential folk expressions that are not limited by generic differentiation and that seldom exist alone, even though they may be described separately for convenience in discussion.

THE INTEGRATION OF GENRES IN A TRADITIONAL REPERTOIRE Bess Hockema of Pistol River, Oregon, is a striking example of the multiple repertoire in action. As a farmwoman, she performs daily in a wide variety of genres, most of them closely interrelated. Complicating the picture, however, is that the traditional performances were learned from different people (chiefly from her father and mother), who came from another part of the country. More complicated still is that her performances are geared to a sense of local and family decorum and deference so that they are shared with others in the family under rather solidly recognizable rules.

First, some background on this richly traditional family: Bess Hockema was born Bess Finley, daughter of Ed Finley from Tennessee and Genarah Beckham of Arkansas. In 1923 she married George B. Wasson, son of George R. Wasson (from Nova Scotia) and Adulsah, daughter of Gishgiu and Kits-un-jin-jn (of the Coos tribe, southwestern Oregon). Their five children (Wilfred, Susan, Bette, George, and John) are thus the inheritors of a richly mixed set of traditions. After the death of George Wasson, Bess married Paul ("Dutch") Hockema, whose son, Earl, subsequently married her daughter Bette. Four of Bess's children have children of their own, so she now enjoys the role of matriarch in a close-knit family group whose traditions, though they come from sharply varied sources, act as a unifying force. The family gathers for special holidays like Thanksgiving and Christmas, for shared outings like hunting, fishing, picnicking and camping, and for any other event that provides an excuse. On these occasions stories are told, songs are sung, and memorates and anecdotes about family history are shared among members of all ages.

The whole family possesses, and is the context for, traditions too complex to assign to one person. Yet if we look at where Bess Hockema stands in this traditional world—and how she performs in it—we will have at least one clear cross section of folklore dynamism. If we focus on any other person in her family (and we shall, briefly), we will find another kind of cross section, equally vivid, equally valid. In both cases we will find that some of the folklore in Bess's family is shared and performed by everyone, while other expressions are attached chiefly to one specific person, even though others in the family know the tradition and could probably perform it themselves.

In the case of Bess Hockema in particular, what are the genres through which she shares tradition with her family, and how do these categories relate or overlap? She and her family consider the following to be her chief areas of tradition. In discussion, they do fall into generally recognizable generic categories: planting and harvest customs, folk foods, animal husbandry, folk medicine, crafts, folk song, proverb, memorate and family history. In practice, however, they interpenetrate so fully that generic boundaries seem almost unimportant.

PUTTING IN A GARDEN AND GARDENING Bess is the primary family gardener, and although everyone who happens to be at home when the gardening is done is expected to help out, she directs the planting and decides the relationships and order of plants within the garden. The cornfield, a separate garden plot, is the full responsibility of Dutch. During his illness and inability to plant corn, his own son, Earl, performed that duty in his father's behalf when Dutch determined the time was right. Bess's gardening traditions come chiefly from her father (i.e., from Tennessee); she plants marigolds by the pole beans to keep aphids away, garlic next to other vegetables to discourage cutworms. Interestingly, even though Bess plants a good deal of garlic for this purpose, she does not use it in cooking, even in the smallest amounts—though her mother was so fond of it that she ate it raw. This is a good example of how a traditional performer is not constrained to follow all aspects of custom; personal taste—in this case, Bess's distaste for the smell of garlic—plays a strong role in determining the precise details with which a tradition is or is not performed. Zinnias and other such flowers are placed strategically in Bess's garden to repel some insects and attract others. A typical city gardener, used to keeping vegetables and flowers separate, might look at Bess's garden with puzzlement; although the plants are all presented in neat rows, they appear to the outsider an odd combination. But here, surely, is where tradition exerts its influence, for Bess's garden is not primarily for show but for function, and a customary function at that, connected with old family practices. Within that function, the garden is of course expected to look neat and beautiful. While there is a central practical motivation for placing the vegetables and flowers, then, the traditions that dictate their placement are cognizant of culturally recognized aesthetic features. Clearly, these are not the high art aesthetics of formal gardeners.

FOOD PRESERVATION During the summer and fall, as vegetables, berries, and fruits ripen, Bess begins the canning procedures she learned from her mother (from Arkansas). Here again, although she performs in the tradition, she elects to make certain changes of her own. For one, she cans her string beans whole, even though her mother had always "snapped" hers. In fact, Bess pays heavy attention to beans, both string beans and dry beans (which others call "Bess's beans"); a common family joke is her intense interest in beans. In addition, of course, she cans other vegetables and fruits as well as meats such as beef, venison, tuna, and chicken. She makes the usual jams and jellies from local berries as well as other kinds of preserves from beets and other vegetables, using crabapple and quince for pectin. She is famous in the family for her pickles and relishes, nearly all of them produced from recipes and traditions handed down to her from her mother's side of the family.

ANIMAL HUSBANDRY Although Bess does not do the heavy work with the animals on her farm, she is considered the best milker in the family, and she also owns the milk cow. She delights in her ability to wean calves and teach them to drink from a bucket, and she presides over lambing even in the most inclement weather. It is her traditional duty to select those calves that will be allowed to mature into bulls. Although her own busy schedule seldom permits her to work more directly with the animals (in such matters as health care for livestock, paring horses' hooves, and so on) she is a fund of opinion and advice to her husband.

BUTCHERING Bess knows how to do the killing of animals (*butchering*, it is called by the family), but usually defers to the men in these matters. She enjoys skinning an animal, and is considered very adept at it; when time and occasion permit she fills this traditional role with acknowledged talent. Her butchering, meatcutting, and animal husbandry were learned from her father, while her ways of drawing chickens came from her mother.

FOLK COOKING  Since Bess is the principal cook of the family and spends much of her time cooking (quite in addition to that done under the particular traditions of food preservation), the breadth and depth of her lore in this category is far too extensive to .treat fairly here. In this family, as we shall see, some of the recipes prepared traditionally by Bess have been taken over by various of her children. There is now a traditional assignment of certain dishes to certain ,family members. Of those that Bess always prepares, and that therefore others would not think of preparing, are corn bread, sour cream biscuits, applesauce cake, and an ad hoc cake made from whatever ingredients may be available that is called simply *cake* by the family. "Mom's cake" is an inside family joke, for outsiders always ask, "What kind of cake is it?" The family members reply, "Just cake." Bess's talents are such that she can simply lay hands on enough varied ingredients to come up with a fine cake under any circumstances. While perhaps other members of the family could also do the trick, no one would be so intrusive as to offer to do so. Bess does not consider herself a good cook, however, and claims her expertise is only the result of necessity.

FOLK MEDICINE  Bess of course knows the various local herbs and teas that can be used for minor specific ailments. More particularly, in years past she was known as a local diagnostician for baby illnesses. Families who had already taken their babies to a doctor would come to Bess and ask what she thought. Bess would look the infant over, make some kind of deliberation and statement on what she felt the ailment might be, and then suggest the parents take the baby to a doctor. On at least one occasion the parents replied, "Well, we already have, but we wanted to check with you to see if the doctor was right." While not functioning specifically as a midwife, Bess has served informally in this capacity on a number of occasions in the various rural areas where she has lived.

KNITTING AND CROCHETING  These particular crafts are saved for the long and dark winter months, and Bess learned the traditions from her mother. As I mentioned previously, the crocheting of afghans for grandchildren was a tradition carried on throughout her life by Genarah

Finley. After her death, Bess moved into this role and now supplies the expected afghans for her own children and grandchildren.

QUILTING AND NEEDLEWORK These crafts were also learned by Bess from her mother, but more important than the craft itself in this case is the manner in which it is carried out. Grandma Finley had made numerous quilt tops in her spare time throughout her life. The tops were put away, and when people in the family got married, they were given a quilt. Many of these quilt tops are still in the family, and even today, when someone gets married, his or her top is quilted and given; the family gathers, as is traditional, and puts in stitches as the quilting is done. Thus, each quilt represents the handiwork of all family members. Here is a solid example of a case in which the craft in its manual aspects, or the item in its physical existence, comes nowhere near the connotative power that inheres in the quilt for the members of this close group.

FOLK NARRATIVES Although her children perform extensive reper- toires of folk tales, most of Bess's narratives would be classified as memorates, family legends, anecdotes, and oral history. One of her favorite stories concerns an adventure she had as a young girl growing up in Texas. Early one morning, when she went out to get the cows, she heard some thrashing around in the dry slashing above the road and concluded that one of her cows had gotten entangled in the dried brush. She tried and tried to call it out, but every time she stopped to hear where the cow was, the cow would stop moving so she couldn't hear it. After a while she gave up and went to get the rest of her cows and found to her surprise that they were all there. When she got home she told the details to her parents, especially how the cows had raised their tails and had run wide around that place. Someone went back out and found cougar tracks all along the road where she had passed. This personal anecdote comes forth whenever there is a low drift of early morning fog hanging close to the ground on the farm; at times like these, undecipherable noises can be heard in the forest, and the stage is set for her recitation of the story. As with other personal accounts of this sort, the content of the story is recalled history, not transmitted lore; but the choice of what makes a good anecdote, the continued telling of a given story in a close group, the style, structure, wording, and context, are all solidly traditional, and thus such stories cannot be dismissed by the serious folklorist.

Bess also tells in a similar fashion her impressions on coming to Oregon by steamer from San Francisco in the early 1900s. Again, all the details of the trip are not mentioned; only those high points that relate to her tastes and attitudes and that respond to the demands of the close group receive special focus. She also recounts stories of humorous happenings in her family: A family favorite recalls the time Grandma Finley tried to administer a dose of Epsom salts to her daughter Verna, promising it would make her feel better. Verna steadfastly refused, an argument ensued, and Grandma got so angry that she took the dose of salts herself so as not to waste the proven remedy. Other stories are memorates she recalls having heard from older family members who had lived back east: encounters with ghosts, meetings with strange creatures in the woods, stories told by her mother, are all parts of her narrative repertoire. A few folk tales are there, of course, but they are a small part of the whole. One favorite of the family today is the tarbaby story, one of several Bess tells that feature Bur Rabbit.

Not confined to anecdotes from her own side of the family, Bess enjoys passing on stories that concern the Indians and the Scots in her first husband's family. There are memorates about her husband's relatives being able to foretell deaths in the family; a recurrent story held in high regard by all members of the family tells of Great-grandmother Gishgiu's escape from the soldiers. The army had rounded up members of the small southwestern Oregon bands and tribes and had moved them at gunpoint up the Oregon coast, first to a spot near present-day Reedsport, then to Yachats. There the Coos among others were confined on a small promontory jutting out into the sea while a tiny reservation was being defined inland for some of the others who had treaties (the Siletz Reservation, in later years "terminated" by the government). The people on the promontory were close to starvation, and they could barely gather enough shellfish to stay alive; some drowned in the rough surf while gathering mussels on the rocks. Gishgiu would not put up with this degradation any further, and she dove into the ocean, heading south for home. She made her way down the coast, moving along the beaches at night, hiding by day in the dense undergrowth of the forest, and swimming out around the precipitous headlands to avoid meeting soldiers and other whites who might be using the narrow trail above. She eventually made her way back to the South Slough country on Coos Bay, living for some time in a hollow cedar tree in the forest near the home of her daughter. Here she remained undetected by the soldiers but in contact with her daughter's family at night. Finally, when she felt secure enough to move into the house, she resumed the duties of clothing-mender even though totally blind by this time.

Somewhat later, an alarm was received that the soldiers were on their way to get Grandmother and return her to Yachats. There was a great commotion to hide her tiny frame under the bottom stair step by shoving boxes and sea trunks underneath the stairway behind her. An older child was sent to the woods where her son-in-law was logging with an ox team while the two soldiers ransacked the house, ignoring the youngest children who, unable to keep the secret, kept saying "Gekka, gekka" (Coos for "grandmother") while pointing to the stairs. George R. Wasson, a man of large stature, burst into the house, grabbed a soldier in each hand by the back of the neck, and heaved them into the front yard with instructions never to return. Gishgiu was able to live out her life close to the people and the land she loved. For her descendants, the story is not simply an account of Great-grandmother's bravery, but an ironic and poignant re-experiencing of the perils and frustrations that beset many of the families in the Oregon Country who intermarried with Indians (a practice more common than is realized today).

PROVERBS Proverbs are used by nearly all the members of Bess's family, a clear indication of their involvement with traditional modes of advice. In addition, proverbs and proverbial phrases are often accompanied by a tag line identifying someone from a previous generation in the family who had been well known for using the particular saying. Having not seen one of her sons for a considerable period of time, she told him over the phone, "When you come home for Thanksgiving we'll put the big pot in the little pot and make soup out of the dishrag; [pause] that's what I remember Grandma used to say."

FOLK SONG Both of Bess's parents were quite musical; her mother played a concertina and her father a fiddle. Her father, however, would not play for dances or even for play-parties for religious reasons. Her mother, Genarah Beckham, sang a good deal, and many of her songs are still in the active repertoire Bess uses on those rare occasions when she has time to sit down among family members and sing. There are strong traditions surrounding two particular songs that are well worth mention here. For over fifty years the Finley family had the tradition in the town of Coquille of going Christmas caroling after midnight on Christmas Eve. Their distinctive song on this occasion was "Song of the Angels," which people in the family had learned in full four-part harmony out of a very old book. In this case the song itself was not for them a folk song, but the custom with which the song was employed was squarely in the folk tradition. The tradition itself still survives, though Bess now lives on a farm so isolated from the rest of the community that the family does not ordinarily go singing Christmas carols to neighbors. In earlier years, when they lived in town, it was a standard occasion for the Finley family to go caroling at the houses of neighbors and relatives starting at about two in the morning, when everyone was sure to be in bed, and continuing until daylight. Those who were normally visited often lay awake, sometimes with their windows open for the special treat. This custom is so central to the family's sense of itself that it conjures up strong memories of family ties and of deceased relatives—so much so, that the family today can seldom finish singing the song without several people in tears.

Another folk song that has become central in the ongoing traditions of Bess's family is "Old Mister Fox," which Bess's mother sang to the accompaniment of her concertina. Although no one in the family now uses the concertina, the song is still sung with a pause at the end of one line where Grandmother had to stop and draw air into the bellows of her instrument. On almost any occasion when a considerable number of the family have gathered, if there is a chance for people to sit around and relax, this song is sure to come forth. Everyone in the family knows it, and all the verses are sung in unison by everyone:

> 1. Old Mister Fox on a moonshiny night,
>    Stood on his hind legs just about right; [pause]
>    I'll have some meat for my supper tonight
>    Before I leave this town-e-o,
>    Before I leave this town-e-o.
>
> 2. He marched up to the farmer's gate,
>    There he spied an old black drake; [pause]
>    "Mister Drake, Mister Drake come and go with me—
>    You're the finest old fellow in this town-e-o,
>    The finest old fellow in this town-e-o."
>
> 3. Mister Drake stood still and he replied,
>    "No, Mister Fox, I will not go; [pause]
>    If you never eat meat 'til you eat me, oh,
>    You'll never eat meat in this town-e-o,
>    Never eat meat in this town-e-o."
>
> 4. Old Mister Fox he took his track back,
>    Grabbed up the gray goose by her back; [pause]
>    Her wings went flip flop over his back
>    And her legs hung dingle dingle down-e-o,
>    Her legs hung dingle dingle down-e-o.

THE DYNAMICS OF FOLKLORE

5. *Old Mrs. Flip Flop lyin' in the bed*
   *Raised up the window and poked out her head; [pause]*
   *"Old man, old man, the gray goose is gone,*
   *For don't you hear her goin' crank crank-e-o?*
   *Don't you hear her goin' crank crank-e-o?"*

6. *Old man raised up in a mighty, mighty rage,*
   *Wiped out his mouth and it full of sage, [pause]*
   *"Old woman, old woman, just let them go*
   *I'll make mighty music come-a-hime-e-o*
   *Make mighty music come-a-hime-e-o."*

7. *He marched on 'til he came to his den;*
   *There were the young ones, nine or ten, [pause]*
   *The old ones eating up all the meat*
   *And the young ones gnawing on the bone-e-os,*
   *The young ones gnawing on the bone-e-os.*

8. *"Daddy, oh daddy, when you goin' back agin?"*
   *"Hope to the dingle dingle never to go agin" ("Why?")*
        *[in falsetto by youngsters]*
   *"Oh, don't you hear the music come-a-hime-e-o?*
   *Don't you hear the music come-a-hime-e-o?*
   *Don't you hear the music come-a-hime-e-o?"*

GENERATIONS AND GENRES  Even though Bess Hockema remains proud of her first husband's dedication to his Native American traditions, it is obvious that she herself has continued to live in an essentially white American tradition. She illustrates as well as anyone the survival and maintenance of traditions that are shared with other people of the same ethnic background throughout the United States. If we close our account of Bess's traditions, however, without regarding those of the rest of her family, we will be forced to overlook some of the most interesting dynamic qualities of folklore being exercised around her, for her children have not simply accepted the traditions of their mother as is. For one thing, three of them (Wilfred, Susan, and George) are avid tellers of the Coyote stories they learned from their father and from his Indian relatives. Even though Bess does not tell these stories, they have nonetheless become a standard part of family interaction, and they condition to a large extent the interactions that take place at any traditional family occurrence. Thus, if we look only at Bess's traditions, we will fail to see the extent to which they affect and are affected by the Native American traditions once represented by her husband and now carried on by her children. Moreover, the family members are so imbued with a sense of deference toward each other that they take quite seriously the roles into which they have moved in the family network. George was singled out by his father and other Indian relatives to be the special receiver and bearer of the Indian traditions in the family. Although his father died before George was able to assume this task fully, he takes the role with utmost seriousness and sees his position in part as an important aspect of tradition maintenance. Moreover, so sensitive are the members of this family to each other's roles that the three who tell Coyote stories do not usually tell each other's favorites; each has a subrepertoire of stories known to them all but thought of as more or less under the proprietorship of one person.

Some members of the family specialize in certain foods: Bette is the one who makes lemon meringue pies, Susan makes mince pies and all the wedding cakes, and George makes the fresh apple cake. When I asked George if he would ever make lemon meringue pies for a family gathering, he responded, "No, Bette makes lemon meringue pies." When I asked if he would ever make lemon meringue pie for himself at his own home, he responded with the same answer. When the family gathers for a salmon bake, it is usually George who is considered the salmon baker, and using his father's recipe he directs the preparation of the fish and determines when it is done. Wilfred, however, is the one who digs the pit and prepares the fire. All the people in the family with the possible exception of the youngest children, are brought up knowing all these traditions; they are also brought up with a sense of propriety and decorum that dictates that it is appropriate for some members of the family to specialize in certain genres. Under these circumstances, it would be difficult indeed to go back over the separate genres and excerpt them from their total family context, for just as some of them are based on manual production of craft items (such as quilts), they are also founded upon a rich background of custom and belief.

OLD MISTER FOX AND OLD MAN COYOTE The Coyote stories told by these people, taken by themselves, would undoubtedly fall into our genre of folk tale; at the same time, the customs that dictate the use of Coyote stories by the Wassons/Hockemas and the beliefs and attitudes that lie behind the Coyote tales among the Coos and related tribes are so strong that the story as a narrative stands only as a tangible marker of cultural details far more complex than any single story itself could possibly show. The stories feature Old Man Coyote, a personage of extreme selfishness on the one hand and brilliant creativity on the other who is depicted as gluttonous, underfed, oversexed, overinquisitive, cruel, benevolent, witty, playful, and lazy. A good many of the stories have such a strong sexual component that early white people in the area were repulsed by them; the tales and their tellers were branded as pagan and evil. At the same time, the stories are excruciatingly funny, and many have lasted. People delight in telling them and in hearing them, but, especially with the older generations, there is a kind of apologetic embarrassment about their content. Thus, while they have survived, they have developed a certain kind of feel that can be handled only through a considerable exercise of decorum. If one announces that Coyote stories are about to be told, there is a ripple of excitement and smiling among the family. Nonetheless, the custom is never to tell Coyote stories in the house, and they are not told before the youngest of the children for fear that they will not be able to cope well with the content. There is an attempt in general to tell the stories only at the proper time of year (in the winter) and in circumstances that approximate their earlier natural environment: while camping "up river," or while hunting. Whenever possible, a further restriction is noted: The old Coos custom was that no one person could tell the same tale more than once during the same season. This insured that other people in the tribe had constant practice in telling the various stories. Among the Wassons and Hockemas this has led to a minor problem, for while people would prefer to pass the stories around, some stories have become associated rather solidly with particular narrators.

On the other hand, "Old Mister Fox" may be sung at any time of the year, in the house or outside, and it is palatable in front of the youngest of children. It is not restricted in any way as to who its singers may be, and it comes of course from the white American background of the family. At the same time, Old Mister Fox in the ballad is, like Old Man Coyote, witty, crafty, and desirous of food. It is tempting to think that in this family of mixed heritage Old Mister Fox and Old Man Coyote exist in complementary fashion, each one representing a certain key part of the family's valuable traditional backgrounds. This might explain why, of all the songs sung by Bess's parents and relatives, it is "Old Mister Fox" that exists today among her children and grandchildren as the family song. Her children, participants in both cultural worlds, have perhaps sensed the kinship between the two characters as well as the cultural distinctions.

I think we can see how hazardous it would be to take any one of these genres or items out of its rich family context; we can sense how much would be lost in meaning. It is precisely this hesitation that the folklorist must develop into a kind of healthy cynicism about generic categories.

The categories must never be allowed to seem more important or more solid than the live people and processes that produce them. We must note as well that although the Wasson-Hockema family has rather centered its attention on "Old Mister Fox" as a song, this does not indicate that singing or song traditions are dying out for them. Neither can we assume that Bess Hockema, being older, knows more folklore than her children; neither can we assume because her children do not practice all the genres she knows, or all the items within each genre, that her folklore is dying out in the next generation. Rather, I think we see a rather typical gravitation of people in a close group into certain traditional roles that satisfy them in relation to each other.

Bess Hockema's family is not unique; no doubt all our families and all our folk groups experience the idea of special roles or slots in tradition. If farm families seem to be more vivid examples of this phenomenon, it is most likely because they feature a necessary cooperation among members of a close group toward common goals. In the cities today, and among the members of that group often referred to as the middle class, individuation, individuality, independence, and competition have been stressed over cooperation with the *close* group, while allegiances to the larger national or corporate groups have been encouraged. In addition, the rural life has become almost a mythic stereotype of the good old days for many Americans, and its images seem heightened in meaning when we encounter them. Nonetheless, we find many groups of people in the city and elsewhere that for various reasons have encouraged or thrived upon group interests rather than individual strivings; many ethnic groups and nationalities in America, many religious groups, many occupational groups, have stressed the individual's strong ties to the close group as a central issue in survival. Among these groups (among which we may number Blacks, Italians, Mormons, smokejumpers, and students) we will expect to find the kinds of traditional dynamics suggested here. Because a farm features such a close interaction of those traditions that have to do with getting, preserving, and preparing food, as well as those crafts and customs that totally relate to personal and cultural survival, the term *folklife* has come into wide use among scholars in referring to the total rural life tradition. We should not forget that we may find this dynamic interactive fabric of traditional performances in the settings of many groups not necessarily rural in nature.

# MULTIFORM FOLK IDEAS Stith Thompson's

*Motif-Index* is founded upon the observation that some ideas have been so recurrent in tradition that we may encounter and recognize them in any number of situations. This is as good an indication as any that folk performers are not bound entirely by generic distinctions as they help to conserve certain ideas that have become important to them or expressively useful to the close group. Just as a ballad story or a folk tale may be recounted in innumerable ways within the same genre (the ballad or the story core being conserved while the manner of singing or telling is dynamic), so may an idea be conserved through expression in several different genres. Moreover, the same story can have a number of meanings.

MIRACULOUS FIRE DELIVERANCES   Some years ago, when I was working for the U.S. Forest Service, I was taken off my normal work on the trail to help fight a fire. During one rest period, as we tried to ignore our fatigue and sore muscles, a companion began telling a story about a friend of his who had been on a fire crew somewhere in the Pacific Northwest on "one of the biggest fires of the century." Working nearby had been a small squad of Zuni tribesmen, firefighting specialists who had been brought in by the Forest Service to help on the fire line. The fire had suddenly raced toward them at a terrible speed, and most of the firefighters felt lucky to be able to make their way quickly to a nearby stream and find potholes where they could submerge themselves at the moment the fire would pass over. Once assured of safety, they looked to see the Zunis moving calmly from tree to tree in a small perimeter around the area carving curious marks into the bark. "The fire swooped down on 'em, but it split and went around, and never touched anything inside that circle of trees the Zunis had put their marks on." Our companion went on to insist that this adventure proved that the American Indian had greater than normal abilities to deal with natural phenomena. The whites on the crew, who may have been somewhat disdainful of their Indian colleagues, were saved by them because they had magical help that the whites, even with their technological know-how, could not match.

The story is told in many parts of the United States, from New England to the West Coast, that a small busload of tourists, including three nuns, was once trapped by an advancing forest fire. While most of the tourists screamed and panicked and ran in circles, the nuns calmly knelt to pray, and the bus and its passengers were spared as the flames swept around them. In some versions of the story a practical tour member who had run off for help or to find a phone was the only one killed, while those who fell under the protection of the praying nuns were saved. The nuns in this story are akin to the Zunis in the previous legend: They represent contact with unseen powers that, although perhaps not believed in by onlookers, may be invoked in an emergency to indicate the relative weakness of the technical system in times of all-out panic and to illustrate that there is, after all, "something beyond."

In the northwestern United States, especially in Oregon, a story circulates about another forest fire, "the Tillamook Burn," a gigantic fire that swept through the coastal range west of Portland and east of the coastal town of Tillamook in the 1930s. A group of visiting dignitaries from Washington were being shown through one part of the forest by a young ranger named John Pulaski. They were taken by surprise when the forest fire advanced toward them, and they were saved only by the ranger's superior knowledge of the surrounding terrain: He herded them quickly to a small cave he knew about from which issued a cold stream of air, presumably from a deep underground cavern. Cramming his charges in ahead of him, Pulaski protected them with his body, and all escaped unscathed, except for Pulaski, who suffered fierce burns on his back. In recognition of his bravery, the Forest Service later named a special firefighting tool after him. In this recounting of the motif, it is not magic or divine intervention that saves people's lives, but thorough knowledge of the terrain. The first story was told by someone who was a great admirer of American Indians; the second story was told to me at first by a devout Roman Catholic (but I have heard it from believers of other faiths); and the last was told in a Forest Service meeting by a ranger trying to illustrate the necessity for a thorough knowledge of the countryside in which one worked. It would be beside the point to observe that no doubt the dates of the first two occurrences have never been established and that the Pulaski was not named in such a way. What we notice, rather, is that the same motif has been used in three legends but for somewhat different purposes and with different shades of meaning in each case. The motif is recognizable, the genre remains the same (assuming that by *legend* we mean the recounting of an occurrence that is believed by the teller to have happened); it is the context, the dynamic live situation in which each legend was told, that determines the real meaning in these cases.

The same motif, sometimes even with specific words related to it, may appear in numerous situations over a wide geographical area and have much the same meaning as well. Stories of Bigfoot, or Sasquatch, in the Northwest seem to be very similar to the motifs found in the eastern United States in such stories as "Yoho Cove," collected by Richard Dorson in Maine, and the story of the Yeahoh collected by Leonard Roberts in the mountains of Kentucky. Further, there seems to be a kinship of motif between all of these and the figure of Grendel in the old English epic *Beowulf* as well as the wild man of the forest featured in those widespread and curious woodcuts from the Middle Ages. It is impossible to say that all these appearances of this motif have the same meaning; on the other hand, they all seem to appear in contexts that demonstrate or probe the fear people have of wild, unrestrained nature along a frontier or in the deep forest.

WHO WILL GLOVE YOUR HAND? Some years ago, in the mountains of western North Carolina, Clif Bushnell taught me a deceptively simple song:

> *Who's gonna shoe your pretty little foot?*
> *Who's gonna glove your hand?*
> *Who's gonna kiss your ruby red lips?*
> *Who's gonna be your man?*

> *Who's gonna be your man?*
> *Who's gonna be your man?*
> *Who's gonna kiss your ruby red lips*
> *Who's gonna be your man?*

> *Papa's gonna shoe my pretty little foot,*
> *Mama's gonna glove my hand,*
> *Sister's gonna kiss my ruby red lips,*
> *And I don't need no man.*

> *I don't need no man,*
> *I don't need no man,*
> *Sister's gonna kiss my ruby red lips,*
> *And I don't need no man.*

In these sparse words a man seems to be inquiring of a girl whether she is being properly cared for in life, and she is responding that her family is doing just fine at the job. For years I assumed this song featured a young man suggesting that he might become the one who would take care of the girl, with the girl replying that she was not interested. On one occasion, however, when I was singing with friends who were about to leave the country, it suddenly occurred to me that the song could have an entirely different meaning: A young man leaving his sweetheart for a considerable length of time might inquire, in effect, "Who's going to take care of you while I'm gone?" to which she might respond reassuringly, "Don't worry about a thing, dear, my family will do just fine, and I will not require the company of any man while you are gone." As with so many items in folklore, it is impossible for us to revisit the originator of these verses to find out if indeed either of these interpretations comes close to what the creator had in mind. But it is interesting to note in passing that the same words can have such different meanings depending on the implications brought forth by certain contexts in which the song may be sung and certain attitudes on the part of the singers or the audiences. In addition, these same verses, with some small differences, are the opening stanzas of one of the best-known Scottish ballads, "The Lass of Roch Royal," Child #76. Version E in Child's collection, written down from the singing or recitation of the famous Mrs. Brown in 1800, offers the following stanzas:

> 1. *O wha will shoe my fu fair foot?*
> *And wha will glove my hand?*
> *And wha will lace my middle jimp,*
> *Wi the new made London band?*

> 2. *And wha will kaim my yellow hair,*
> *Wi the new made silver kaim?*
> *And wha will father my young son,*
> *Till Love Gregor come hame?*

> 3. *Your father will shoe your fu fair foot,*
> *Your mother will glove your hand;*
> *Your sister will lace your middle jimp*
> *Wi the new made London band.*

> 4. *Your brother will kaim your yellow hair,*
> *Wi the new made silver kaim;*
> *And the king of heaven will father your bairn,*
> *Till Love Gregor come haim.*

Here essentially the same words have a very distinctive meaning, for Annie of Roch Royal is lamenting that her lover is not there to care for her now that she has a baby. Someone, obviously a member of her family, offers help and protection until her love should come home, pointing out

THE DYNAMICS OF FOLKLORE

that God will protect her child. As the ballad progresses, however, she sets out to sea to find her lover, and when she arrives at his gate in the midst of a storm, she is not admitted by Gregor's mother, who manages to keep her outside until she and the babe in her arms die in the storm. The next morning the evil deed is discovered by Gregor, and he ends the ballad with a curse upon his cruel mother. It would be too easy to argue that these verses represent a mere commonplace that can be used whenever there is a concern about someone's proper care. Some might suggest that the version I learned from Clif Bushnell is one of those many examples of an "emotional core" to which a longer ballad had eventually distilled itself (or, as some might feel, degenerated). Both of these arguments would overlook that for whatever reasons we may assign to the case, the version I learned in North Carolina is a distinctly adequate little lyric that can stand by itself and can carry at least two fully acceptable poetic meanings. It would be difficult to believe such a neat coincidence to be the background for a mere floating cliché.

Further, the way these verses are used in "The Lass of Roch Royal" indicates that the singers of this ballad have been aware of how it effectively poses the question of family protection for a girl in such a way as to juxtapose very cleverly the warm concern of her own family to the cruel rejection of her potential mother-in-law. The effects are too considerable to be shrugged off as coincidental or as the surprisingly fortunate effect of a cliché. The fact that these stanzas can exist by themselves as a lyric *and* be used as a strongly integrated part of a longer dramatic ballad indicates the extent to which this particular folk idea is not limited by generic categories. It is worth mentioning that the same stanzas were used by Huddie ("Leadbelly") Ledbetter in one of his several versions of "John Henry." After the death of John Henry, others on the crew are interested in finding out who will have the enviable task of taking care of John Henry's girlfriend:

> Now who's gonna shoe your pretty little foot?
> Who's gonna glove your hand?
> Who's gonna kiss them red ruby lips
> After that steel-drivin' man, oh Lord,
> After that steel-drivin' man?
>
> Papa's gonna shoe my pretty little foot,
> Mama's gonna glove my hand,
> Sister's gonna kiss my red ruby lips,
> And I can't use no man, Lord, Lord,
> Not after that steel-drivin' man.

Here the stanzas function in the way I had originally assumed Clif Bushnell's song did: A man applies to watch out for a girl, and she refuses his advances. In this case the refusal is couched in some of the terms used in the song itself, and within those terms is the connotation of sexual vigor and potency as well as the general strength and ability admired on the work crew. Admittedly, the migration of this particular cluster of folk ideas must have been facilitated by the fact that these are, after all, songs. Similarly, the three stories of miraculous escapes from fires are all legends. But we will want to remember that stories about the wild man of the woods often appear in legends on the one hand, origin stories on another, and, at least in the case of *Beowulf*, in a sung epic—that is, in forms generically quite dissimilar from each other.

SIR HUGH AND THE INTERNATIONAL MINORITY CON-SPIRACY  An outstanding example of the way in which a folk idea may be performed in a number of different genres is the widespread story whose principal ingredients seem to be the following: A young boy about ten or twelve years old (that is, presexual in terms of experience, and therefore "innocent") is attacked and mutilated by thugs belonging to the local feared minority group. There are some variations in this cluster, but this is the most typical combination. Indeed, as several scholars have shown, it is quite an ancient story, and it has kept cropping up in cultures where minority groups of one sort or another have posed a threat to the security of the majority group. There is sketchy evidence that the story circulated in Greece with the culprits being members of the various secret mystery cults; it was said they required the blood of innocent young boys for the proper observance of their rituals. In somewhat later times it appears to have been used by the Romans concerning the Christians, who were famous for requiring the blood of an innocent lamb as a sacrifice, a central aspect of their religious ritual. In medieval Europe, the culprits were usually the Jews, who were believed to require the body and blood of an innocent young child, usually a boy, for their paschal ceremonies. We know from the medieval writings of Matthew Paris and others that the story must have had wide circulation in Europe as a legend, for nearly everywhere it is recorded, local names and dates and the testimonies of good citizens are provided. Chaucer used the story as a central aspect of his Prioress's Tale, and the same cluster of ideas was used in song form (there are over twenty versions of the ballad "Sir Hugh, or, The Jew's Daughter," Child #155, collected from Scotland, England, and America).

The other side of this idea comes forward in family histories, especially where immigrants to America use the story as a testimony of their family's escape from oppression. During the Easter season of 1977, the *Eugene Register-Guard* ran some interviews with local Jews in which one young woman noted that when her grandparents were still living in Russia they would cross the street when passing a Christian church. "In 1913, the Russians were still accusing Jews of murdering young Christian boys and using their blood for Passover," she lamented. It was clear that her family had suffered the persecution that resulted from such attitudes as that encapsulated and symbolized by this widespread idea. As abhorrent as the idea itself is, one cannot help note its vitality and its geographical spread. While it may not represent the typical intellectual attitudes of people in the various places it has been found, it must certainly represent the inner, in-group feelings and tastes of many, or it could not possibly have survived in so many versions and in several genres. We can call such an idea *multivalent*, for like some elements or chemical compounds, it has the power to combine itself with other ideas in order to express powerfully a local, deep fear of minority outsiders.

Within the legend versions of this story there is considerable variation, especially in details of time, place, and victim. In the dramatic ballad, there is much more attention to colorful detail and less to factual material. The young boy is usually lured into the garden of a Jew by the Jew's attractive daughter; he is led into the castle or down into the cellar and there killed, usually with a knife. In some American versions, the Jews have been replaced by a jeweler, and in one version sung for me by an Ozark friend, "The Fatal Flower Garden," the boy is lured into a garden by flowers, which then kill him.

My initial firsthand acquaintance with modern versions of this legend occurred when I had stopped to spend the night with friends in Boise, Idaho, and the town was all aflutter because of an outrage that had occurred the previous night in a local drive-in theater. A young boy of ten was at the drive-in with his parents and left them to visit the restroom. When he did not return, an older brother went to check on him and found him bleeding profusely, having been castrated by a group of teenage Indians. The evening I arrived, vigilante committees of parents were patrolling some of the drive-ins with baseball bats looking for suspicious characters lurking in the dark. When I arrived in Salt Lake City a day later, my friends welcomed me, and the woman, a dietician in a hospital, burst forth with the news that a terrible thing had happened there just the evening before. A young boy of about ten had been castrated by Mexicans in a local drive-in and was now at death's door in the hospital. She had heard her colleagues talking about it, and everyone in town was quite sure that it presaged a long-awaited racial conflict. On a hunch, I called the hospital where the young boy was said to be a patient; the woman at the information desk immediately recognized the case and referred me to another hospital. I called every hospital in town, in each case talking to someone who knew of the occurrence but who was abso-lutely certain that the boy was at another hospital. When I had contacted all the hospitals, I called the police to find out the details and was told that the incident had actually not taken place in Salt Lake City: "It happened down in Reno two weeks ago." Inquiries among friends since have convinced me that the story is a continually recurring rumor that breaks quickly into legend and can be easily adapted to almost any locale where there is friction between a majority and a minority group.

Friends of mine went to a baseball game in Philadelphia a few years ago and heard the rumor that at the very game they were attending a young white boy of ten or twelve had been castrated in a restroom by a gang of Black thugs. My students have reported the same story as having been told in Los Angeles about "Pachucos," in various cities about Indians, and especially in the East with reference to Blacks. More recently, a student of mine collected in Portland the "true story" of a young boy, about ten, who had been castrated by hippies and left to die in an elevator in one of the downtown department stores. Still more recently, students from Salt Lake City, Portland, and Seattle have re-ported hearing accounts of girls disappearing while shopping who were later found drugged, being carried out of the store in the arms of counter-culture druggies.

The element of castration will be brought back for discussion in Chapter 8; it seems to parallel a number of similar themes in which the threat posed by minority groups is interpreted and responded to with sexual symbolism. Here it is sufficient to point out that the idea in this traditional cluster has remained the same, very likely because it provides a succinct and usable traditional experience for any majority group that wants to rationalize and vivify its symbolic fears of the minority group: In each case the person being attacked is young and innocent, usually a male (a potential leader in the culture), and he is attacked while doing something normal by somewhat older thugs who in effect take away the power of the majority by emasculation, slitting the throat, or drugging. This is not a common idea among minority groups; rather, it seems to be a kind of cultural paranoia among the majority, as if to say: "Watch out for those people, they're out to get us and they'll be likely to attack us in the most vulnerable places and most objectionable ways." The appearance of this idea as an active rumor, as a traditional legend,

1. "Climber" topping a tree to make a spar pole, Oregon, ca. 1900. (Courtesy Special Collections Section, University of Oregon Library)

2. "Climber" waving from a tree just topped, Oregon, ca. 1900. (Courtesy Special Collections Section, University of Oregon Library)

3. Fallers on springboards, Oregon, ca. 1900. (Courtesy Special Collections Section, University of Oregon Library)

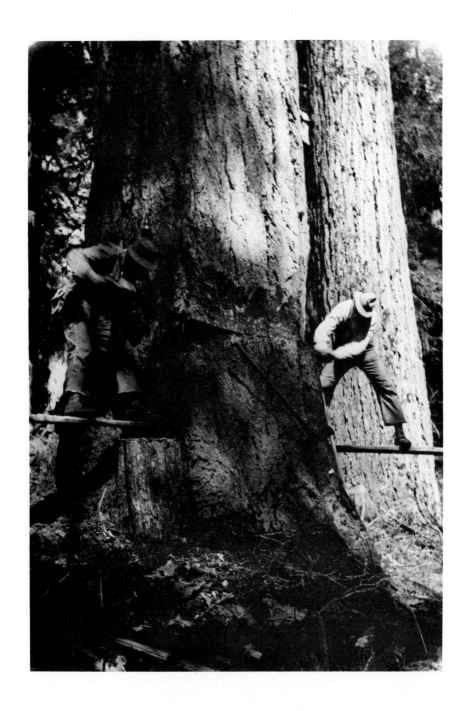

4. Fallers on springboards, Oregon, 1930s. (Photo by logger William Tabler)

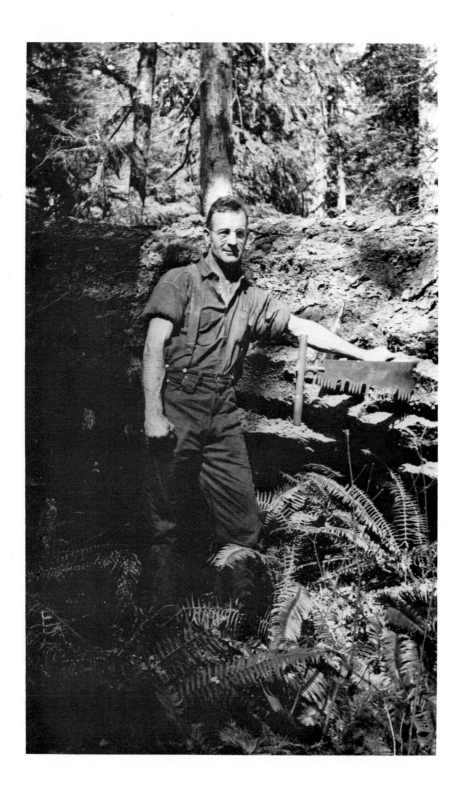

5. Bucker, cutting tree into standard logs, Oregon, ca. 1930s. (Photo by logger William Tabler)

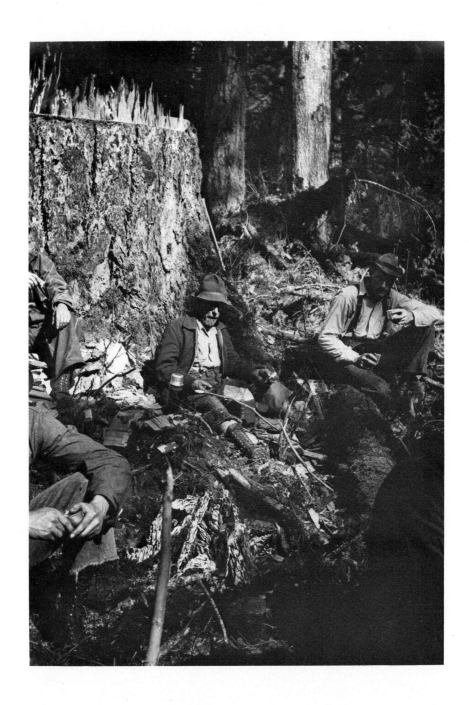

6. Loggers at lunchtime, Oregon, 1930s. Note staged pants, "cork" (nailed) boots. (Photo by logger William Tabler)

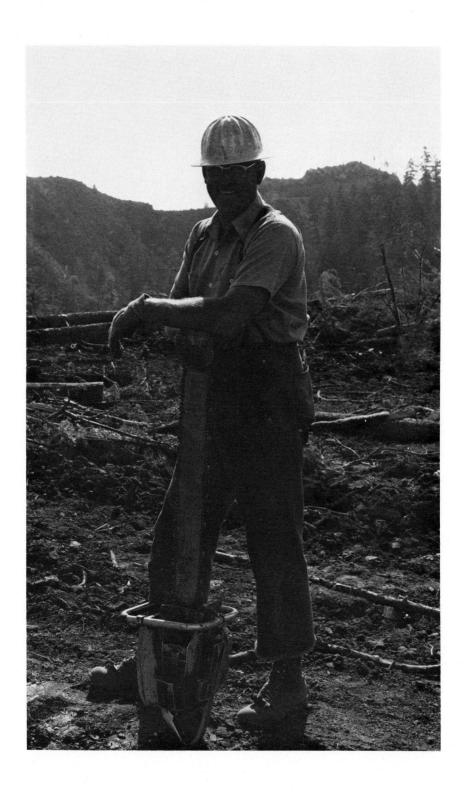

7. Modern logger, a foreman, rests at day's end, Oregon. (Photo by Suzi Jones)

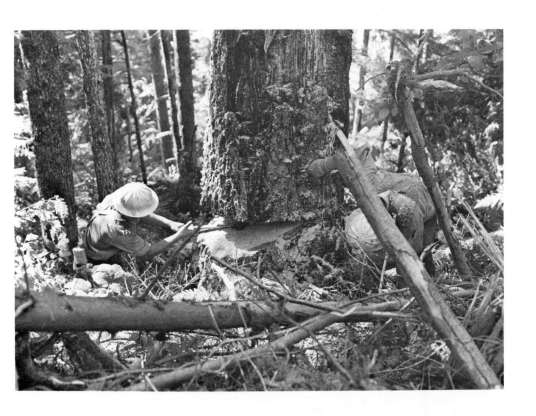

8. Modern fallers, Oregon. (Photo by Suzi Jones)

9. *Sushi:* the equipment, consisting of *shamoji* (paddle), *handai* (bucket), *sudare* (bamboo placemat). (Photo by Barre Toelken)

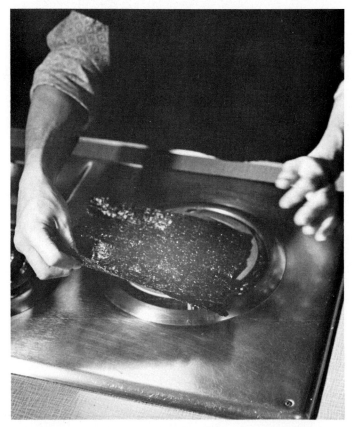

10. *Sushi:* toasting the sheet of dried seaweed over electric stove. (Photo by Barre Toelken)

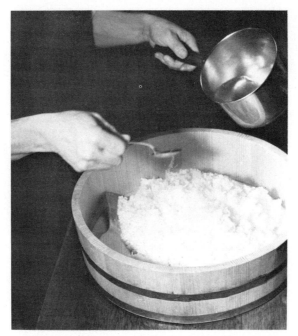

11. *Sushi:* solution of rice vinegar and sugar is poured over rice. (Photo by Barre Toelken)

12. *Sushi:* cooling the seasoned rice so it will not get sticky. (Photo by Barre Toelken)

13. *Sushi:* a layer of rice is placed on seaweed sheet; in a small depression are placed the three, five, or seven center ingredients. (Photo by Barre Toelken)

14. *Sushi:* beginning the roll. (Photo by Barre Toelken)

15. *Sushi:* the roll. (Photo by Barre Toelken)

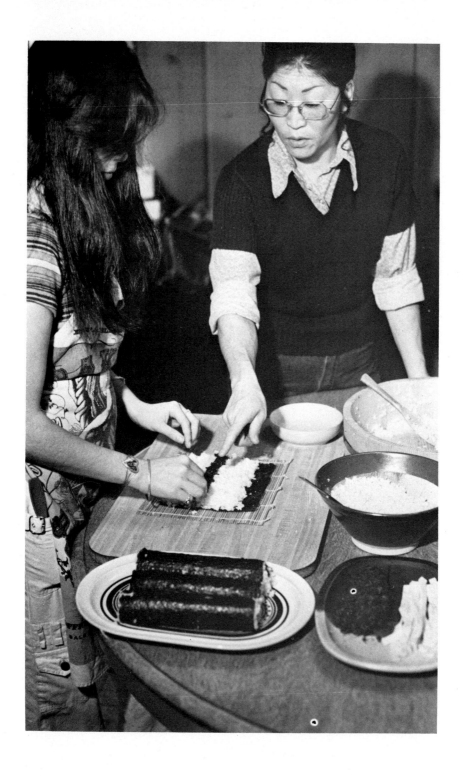

16. *Sushi:* a Japanese-American mother explains the meaning of the ingredients and shows her daughter proper placement. (Photo by Barre Toelken)

17. *Sushi:* a Japanese-American mother shows her daughter the rolling technique (don't get the bamboo caught in the seaweed). (Photo by Barre Toelken)

18. *Sushi:* proper cutting and placement on dish; end pieces and non-standard slices are discarded (rear) and eaten by cook. (Photo by Barre Toelken)

19. Bess Hockema working on white afghan for her son George. (Photo by Suzi Jones)

20. Bess Hockema in her pantry, surrounded by home-grown, home-canned goods. (Photo by Suzi Jones)

21. Clarice Mae Judkins, traditional singer. (Photo courtesy of Mrs. Chandler Stevens)

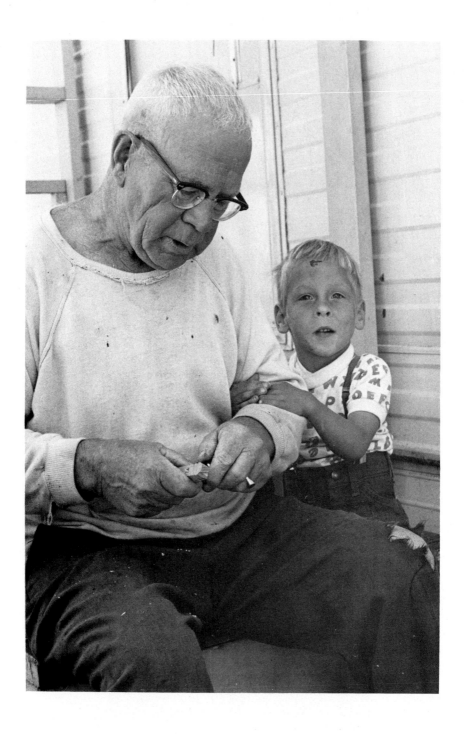

22. "Chris" Christensen whittles for a neighbor. (Photo by Suzi Jones)

23. "Chris" Christensen splits wood for fan. (Photo by Suzi Jones)

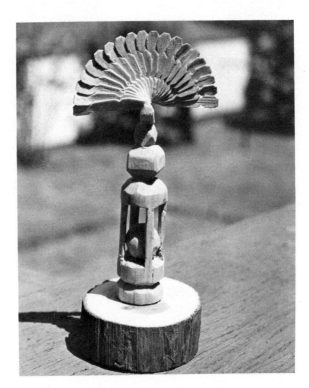

24. Ball-and-fan whittled by "Chris" Christensen. (Photo by Suzi Jones)

25. Ida Moffet applies beeswax to an egg with an electric "writer." (Photo by Suzi Jones)

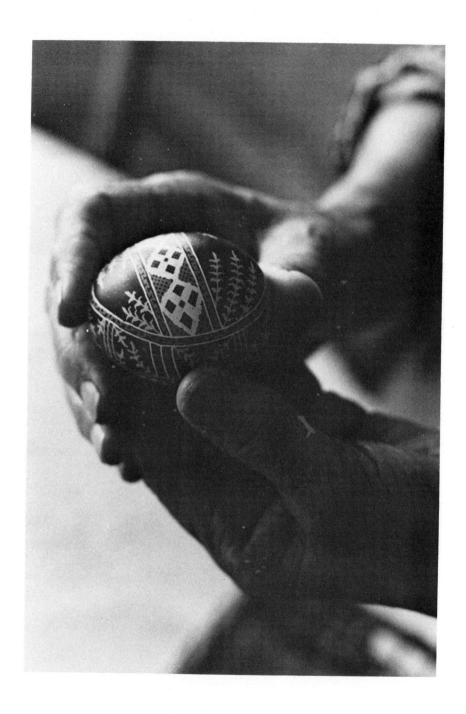

26. Ida Moffet holds Ukrainian Easter egg with wheat design. (Photo by Suzi Jones)

27. John Palanuk working on Ukrainian hammered dulcimer. (Photo by Barre Toelken)

28. John Palanuk's room full of Ukrainian hammered dulcimers. (Photo by Barre Toelken)

29. Navajo string figure: "Navajo rug." (Photo by Barre Toelken)

30. Navajo string figure: "Dilyéhé" (The Pleiades). (Photo by Barre Toelken)

31. Navajo string figure: "Sǫ' Tsó" (Big Star). (Photo by Barre Toelken)

32. Navajo string figure: "Two coyotes running away from each other," step 1. (Photo by Barre Toelken)

33. Navajo string figure: "Two coyotes running away from each other," step 2. (Photo by Barre Toelken)

34. Navajo string figure: "Two coyotes running away from each other," step 3. (Photo by Barre Toelken)

35. Navajo string figure: "Two coyotes running away from each other," step 4. (Photo by Barre Toelken)

36. Navajo string figure: "Two coyotes running away from each other," step 5. (Photo by Barre Toelken)

37. Medallion necklace of juniper seeds (Navajo). (Photo by Barre Toelken)

38. Navajo rug by Helen Yellowman showing *yei* (sacred spirits) representing health and longevity; dyes made from medicinal plants. (Photo by Barre Toelken)

39. Navajo moccasins made by Yellowman from sacred deerhide. (Photo by Barre Toelken)

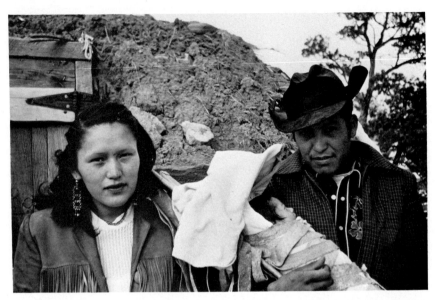

40. Modern Navajo couple in "Anglo" clothing, baby in cradleboard surrounded by sacred deerhide, traditional hogan in background. (Photo by Barre Toelken)

41. Grandma Johnson (Navajo) spinning yarn sunwise. (Photo by Barre Toelken)

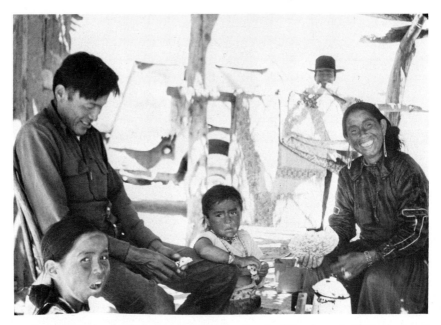

42. Yellowman family, Navajo reservation, eating traditional meal of Navajo bread and coffee (1955). (Photo by Barre Toelken)

43. Helen Yellowman, after moving into town, still grinds berries and prepares foods in traditional manner (1968). (Photo by Barre Toelken)

44. Grandma Johnson (Navajo) and her hogan, facing east. (Photo by Barre Toelken)

45. Barre Toelken and Grandma Johnson joking. (Photo by Van E. Porter)

46. Mrs. Sophie Sandberg, Finnish immigrant to Astoria, Oregon, makes fir-root baskets by softening materials in her mouth. (Photo by Suzi Jones)

47. Mrs. Sophie Sandberg's bone tool for making fir-root baskets. (Photo by Suzi Jones)

48. Mrs. Sophie Sandberg using bone tool to weave fir-root basket. (Photo by Suzi Jones)

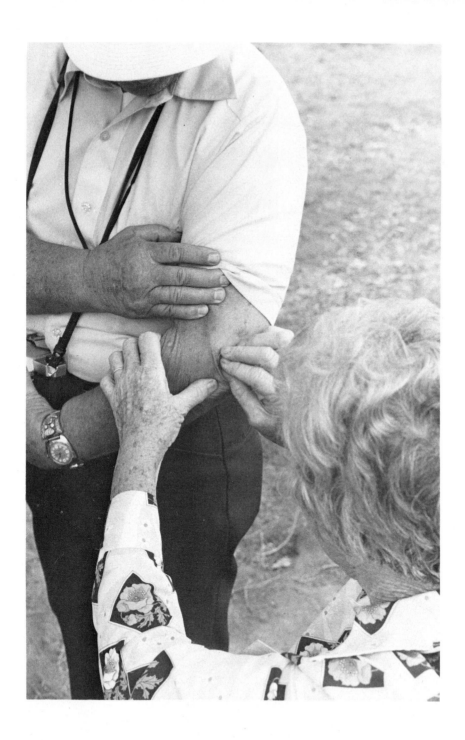

49. Wart charmer Onie Ruesch rubs nickel on a wart. (Photo by Barre Toelken)

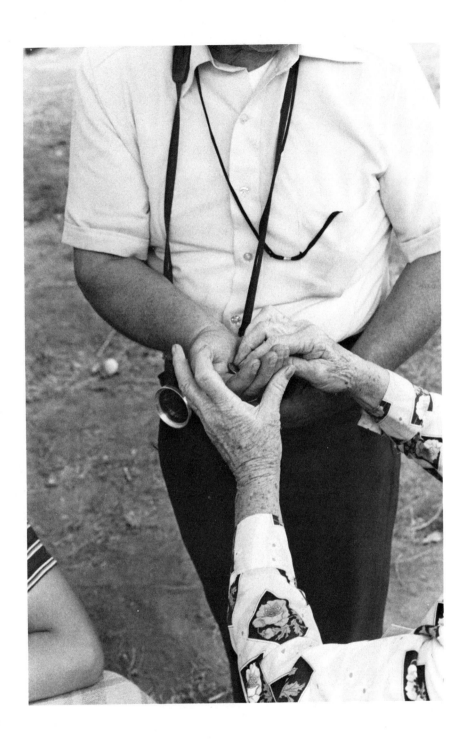

50. Wart charmer Onie Ruesch gives nickel to patient, thus "buying the wart." (Photo by Barre Toelken)

51. Water dowser Eldon McArthur gives instructions in "water witching" to spectators at the Southern Utah Folklife Festival, 1977. (Photo by Barre Toelken)

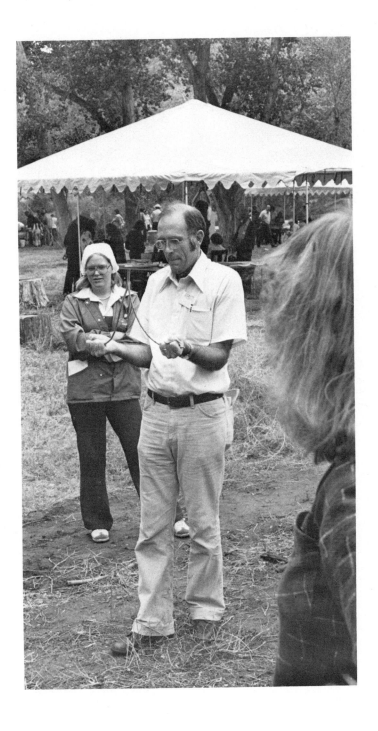

52-54. Folklorist William A. Wilson tries out the dowser's wand at the Southern Utah Folklife Festival. (Photos by Barre Toelken)

55. Apology offered for "capping" an adversary in "playing the dozens"; apology, in the form of "two fives," is reluctantly accepted. (Photo by Edwin L. Coleman, II)

56. Mollified, loser in "the dozens" begins to offer "five" back again; everything is now okay. (Photo by Edwin L. Coleman, II)

57. Reciting a "toast," storyteller incorporates a girl walking by: "She looked exactly like that!" (Photo by Edwin L. Coleman, II)

58. A gesture of solidarity or agreement; in this case, "That chick was really fine!"
(Photo by Edwin L. Coleman, II)

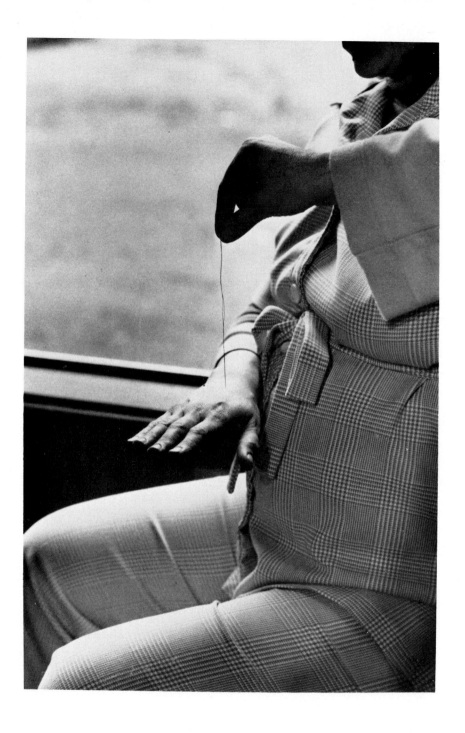

59. Divining sex of unborn child, step 1: needle pricks back of hand seven times.
(Photo by Barre Toelken)

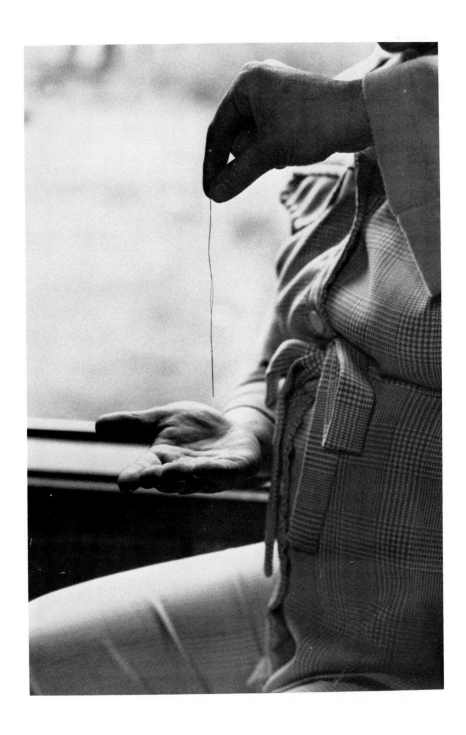

60. Divining sex of unborn child, step 2: pregnant woman's palm is turned upward, needle circles for a girl, swings back and forth for a boy. In this case, prediction is for a girl. (Photo by Barre Toelken)

61. Standard lineal placement of graves in European-American cemetery intensified, perhaps, by military theme. (Photo by Barre Toelken)

62. Native American cemetery (Nespelem, Washington) showing "random" placement of traditional graves, lineal placement of Christianized Indians in background. (Photo by Barre Toelken)

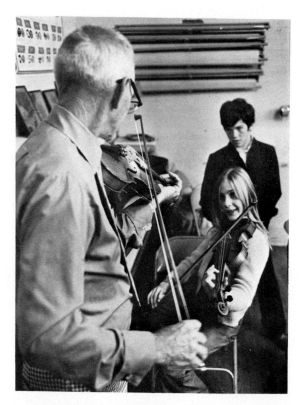

63. Younger fiddler getting traditional pointers from
senior fiddler at a local fiddlers' meet in Mississippi.
(Photo by Carl Fleischhauer)

64. Folklorist Mick Moloney, right, visits Irish musicians Mary McDonagh and
Terry Teahan during the American Folklife Center's 1977 field project in Chicago.
(Photo by Jonas Donydenas, courtesy of American Folklife Center)

65. Maria Lecas and Theodora Siakotas demonstrate cup and palm reading for folklorist Peter Bartis during American Folklife Center's 1977 field project in Chicago. (Photo by Jonas Donydenas, courtesy of American Folklife Center)

66. Folklorist Alan Jabbour plays back tapes to members of the Hammons family, Marlinton, West Virginia. (Photo by Carl Fleischhauer)

67. Folklorist Alan Jabbour records songs and stories from Maggie Hammons Parker in Marlinton, West Virginia. (Photo by Carl Fleischhauer)

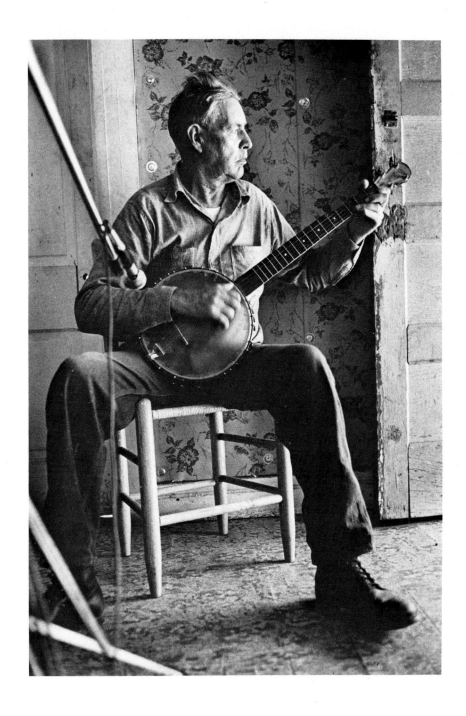

68. Burl Hammons, Marlinton, West Virginia, playing for field recorders Alan Jabbour and Carl Fleischhauer. (Photo by Carl Fleischhauer)

69. Branding at the L S Ranch, Post, Oregon. Calf held at end of rope is simultaneously branded, earmarked, castrated, and vaccinated by neighbors of rancher, all of whom have learned the procedure traditionally. (Photo by Ellen Waterston Bartow)

70. Branding at the Rafter Q Cattle Company Ranch, Paulina, Oregon. Two separate irons are applied simultaneously while calf is held by one of crew. (Photo by Ellen Waterston Bartow)

71. Branding at the Rafter Q Cattle Company Ranch, Paulina, Oregon. Entire families of neighboring ranches help at each branding; women help both with the branding and with supplying food for the communal feed that follows. Here, Sandra Reed and son Russ, of Prineville, Oregon, prepare a calf for branding. (Photo by Ellen Waterston Bartow)

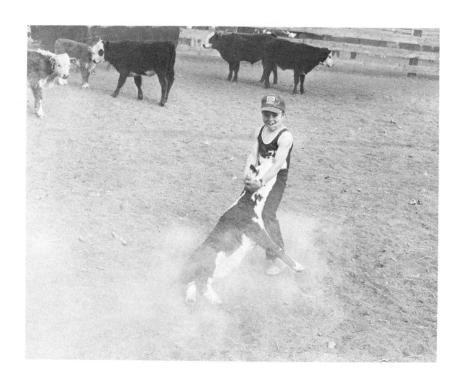

72. Branding at the L S Ranch, Post, Oregon. Tobacco-chewing eleven-year-old Travis Severance has pounced on a calf and is dragging his reluctant captive toward the branding irons. (Photo by Ellen Waterston Bartow)

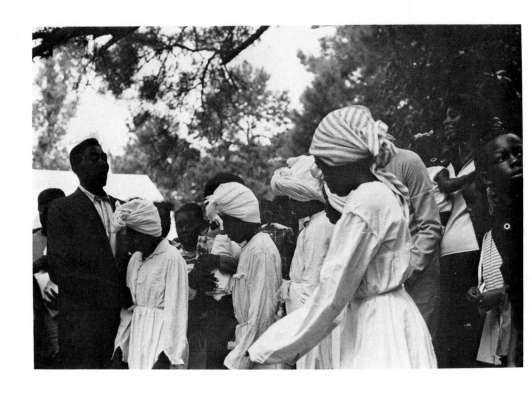

73. Prayer before river baptism in Alabama; note local traditions of dress for this otherwise nonfolkloric event. (Photo by Lucinda Mason)

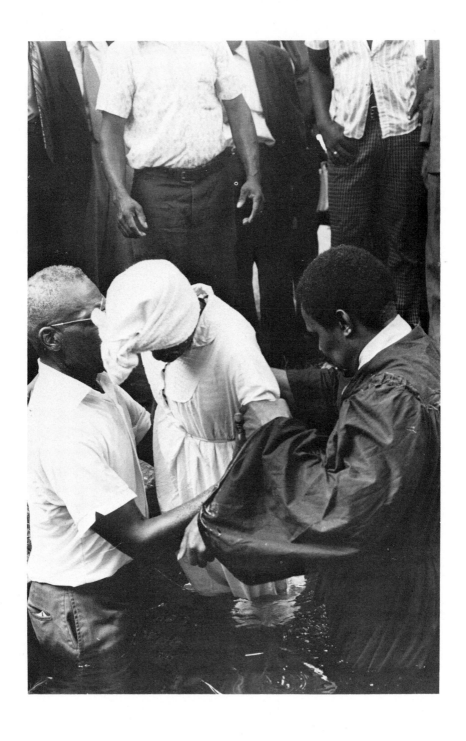

74. Minister and deacon help baptismal candidate into river. (Photo by Lucinda Mason)

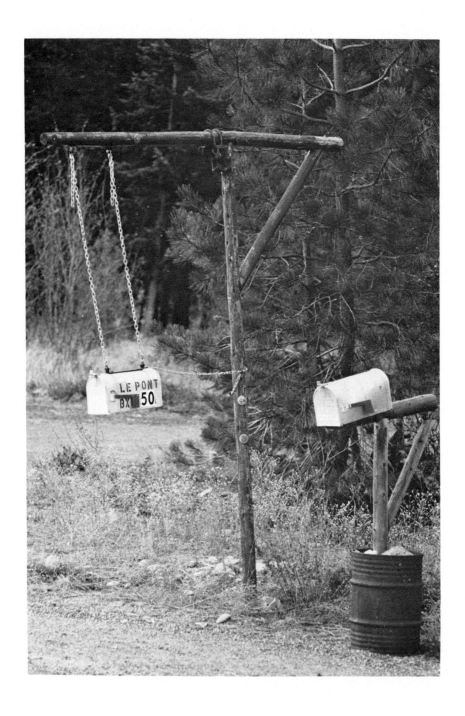

75. Hanging mailboxes near Mazama, Washington. In an area of heavy snowfall, this allows roads to be plowed and mailboxes approached with ease; each property owner, however, creates a personal variation of the basic idea. (Photo by Barre Toelken)

76. Hanging mailboxes near Mazama, Washington. (Photo by Barre Toelken)

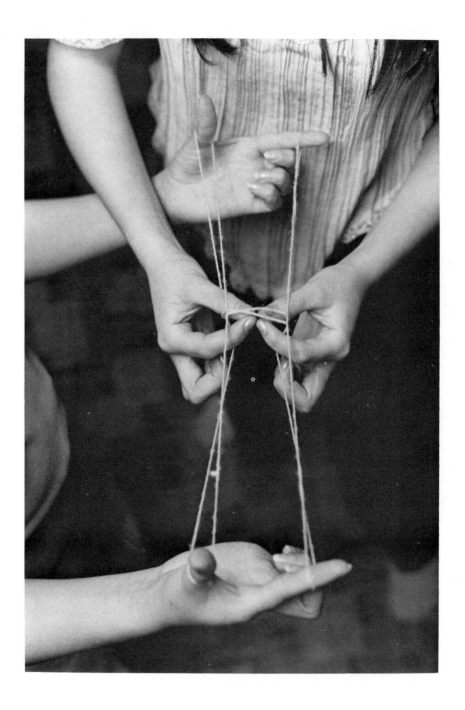

77-82. "Cat's cradle" played by two teenage girls. (Photos by Barre Toelken)

78.

79.

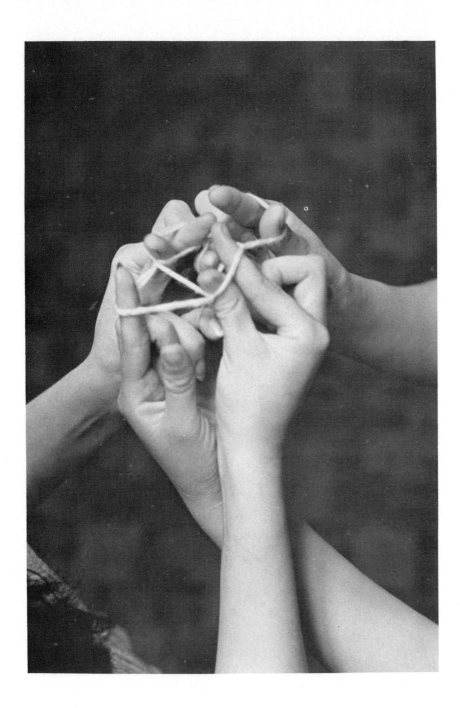

as a ballad, as an ingredient in a modern novel (Bernard Malamud in *The Fixer* uses it prominently), and in memorates and family anecdotes testifies to its viability and its capability of combining with other factors of expression to provide an important clustering of culture-specific ideas, performed in what can only be called a culturally pleasing way.

GOOD, THOUGH!   Another example of multiformity, one in quite a different humor and key, is a song I collected in Wild River, Maine, in the summer of 1954. It is easily recognizable as a folk song version of the moose pie story given in Chapter 2. The song features not only the well-known idea of the inedible pie used as an excuse for the current cook to get out of his chores, but it places that story within a local context that mentions a local character, Jigger Jones, apparently a logger who in his later years manned a lookout tower for the U.S. Forest Service. It is said that when he was a logging foreman, he would not allow anyone to join his crew who could not kick the knots off a frozen hemlock log with his bare feet. The song places this tough character in a situation where he has obviously been victimized by the custom of alternating the cooking chores by having complained previously about someone's unacceptable products. He at first seems to have found the answer to his dilemma, but even then he is outwitted by the fast-thinking comrade who gasps a compliment on his way to the floor:

> Chorus: *Oh, the Wild River crew is a rough old crew,*
> *And I'll tell you the reason why:*
> *We live on brew and cat-liver stew,*
> *And a daily piece of moose-turd pie.*

> 1. *Old Jigger Jones kicked the knots off logs*
> *With his bare feet, so they say,*
> *But he hung around Wild River too long,*
> *And it drove him nuts one day.*

> 2. *Now old Jigger Jones he got pretty tired*
> *Of doin' all of our cookin',*
> *So he says, "If I hear one more guy bitch,*
> *For a new cook you'll be lookin'."*

> 3. *Jones was out in the woods next day*
> *Chasin' a big deer herd;*
> *Coming back to camp without any luck,*
> *He slipped upon some fresh moose turds.*

4. *He scooped 'em up in his old game bag,*
   *The grin on his face was sly;*
   *He thought the boys would surely bitch*
   *If they tried a piece of his moose turd pie.*

5. *The boys come in for supper that night—*
   *Their appetites were high;*
   *They chawed their way through a ten-course meal,*
   *Then they started in on the moose turd pie.*

6. *One by one the boys turned green,*
   *Their eyeballs rolled to and fro;*
   *Then one guy hollered as he sank to the floor*
   *"My God, that's moose-turd pie!*
   [Shouted] *Good, though!"* [cheerfully, with eye-
      brows and one finger raised]

The song has been heard in many parts of the country, but I think it is not widely sung anymore; at least I have not found anyone who sings it all the way through. Occasionally someone will mention that they are aware of another punch line, such as "Just the way I like it!" or "Just like Mom used to make!" It is impossible to say, I think, whether the song was made up by someone who knew the story, or whether the story came about as a spoken version of the song. Most people today who are aware of this cluster at all have usually heard it as a story and not a song, but this proves little, for it parallels the general situation in the United States, where song traditions seem to have been on the wane while spoken narrative traditions have continued to develop. For our purpose, how- ever, it is enough to note that the idea has survived with clever articula- tion both in spoken narrative and in song. That it can be phrased in either way, according to the dictates and assumptions of each genre, indicates that generic matters are here part of the vehicle rather than central aspects of the item itself; the item we are discussing is here the recurrent folk idea, not its surface structuring in any particular kind of performance.

Of course, with a little study you can come up with any number of good examples that suit the case here. Generic distinctions will always be use- ful, but we must never let them become lockers in which we try to confine the live materials we study. At a special conference on legend, Professor Robert Georges of UCLA astounded his colleagues and his audience by suggesting that the symposium had started at the wrong end: Scholars had been inclined to decide first what legends were, and then to study only those items that fell within that standard definition. One angry member of the audience demanded later, "How can we study anything if you guys keep jerking the rug out from under us and making us suspicious of the terms we need to use in the study itself?" Professor Georges was polite enough not to respond with the obvious counterquestion: "If we are studying live and dynamic traditional performances, how can we understand anything if we use only lifeless and rigid terms?" The secret is that generic terms are not mutually exclusive; take the making of Ukrainian Easter eggs. Is it an art? A craft? An aspect of folk belief and superstition? Folk symbol? Folk religion? Custom? Is it considered, potentially at least, beautiful? The answer is yes.

# ✒ A MATTER OF TASTE: FOLK AESTHETICS
For many people, art is understood to be a conscious attempt on the part of an individual to produce an aesthetically pleasing expression in a form recognized by society. What is recognized and what is aesthetic are of course the cruxes of any tighter discussion of the subject. We are all familiar with comments like "That's not art, that's junk!" and "That's too imitative to be real art," and "That's too ugly to be art" (which I overheard a woman say while looking at a Dali painting). True enough, no one has come to a final definition of *art* and *aesthetic* acceptable to everyone (and we might well hope that the day never comes when such a defintion becomes possible). Nonetheless, several central concerns are almost always encountered in a discussion of art, at least of what people call fine art. For example, usually there is a concern about the artist as a unique individual developing his or her own vision within the possibilities of a recognizable genre (e.g., painting, musical composition, architecture). There is a concern for the genre itself, especially if it has classical and refined aspects within which the artist works and against which creative expressions may be judged. There is a concern for the judgment, which is informed by a refinement and education in the classical aspects of the art. Finally, there is the underlying implication that the artist is trying to elevate his art into the ranks of those whose unique visions have already been recognized as worthy of praise.

We are well aware that developments in the formal arts are more easily perceived from the present looking back in time, for many artists were not recognizably within the accepted canons of taste in their own eras, so far ahead of their contemporaries were they in their pursuit of their vision. We often have a better sense of Rembrandt the painter, Mozart the composer, Edward Curtis the photographer, long after their deaths. We also recognize an attitude of exclusivity about art that suggests, for many, that the more popular something is the less founded on refined tastes it must be. Thus, detective fiction, fantasy, science fiction, and Westerns are not usually given much serious attention by literary specialists. Art historians often concentrate on the highest achievements in art, the most impressive demonstrations of the artistic spirit combined with the highest examples of personal talent in the execution of an art object. The most beautiful examples, judged by educated taste, are put on display in art galleries, museums, literary anthologies, or musical programs. Often their innovative aspects are stressed.

Folklorists, on the other hand, are interested in precisely those expressions that most members of a close group know and to which they respond. They are equally interested in the mechanisms by which the group develops and transmits its tastes over time and space in multiform ways. Thus, while many folklore studies focus on one person as the exemplar of a kind of folk expression, it is usually to the avowed purpose of revealing more about the tradition and about where the artist stands within the tradition that folklore addresses itself. Innovation is not important here except as an index of how far *away* from the tradition an artist may be.

FOLK ART AND FINE ART   Nothing seems to infuriate art historians, art collectors, and museologists more than folklorists who insist that the process by which an artifact is produced and the community taste it represents are more important than a question like "Is it suitable for framing?" Similarly, nothing bulges the eyes of folklorists faster than art historians, collectors, and museum folk who concern themselves with single artifacts (often described as unique) because they "come up to" the expectations of the art critic as worthy of display. The professional art people feel the folklorists are concentrating on sociology, not art; the folklorists feel the art historians are being elitist (and stuffy). Both are probably correct in their own way, and the reason they disagree is not easy to deal with. It starts because art for the art historian is based on a study of objects that are related to an ever-developing intellectual sense of proportion, design, and individual creativity held by—and judged by—people of educated and sophisticated taste. Art is held to be an important part of life, of course, but an exceptionable and not an everyday part, something classified along with other intellectual aspects of cultivated sophistication like good manners, appreciation of good literature, good taste, and complex aesthetic judgment.

For most folk artists, I think we can say that folklore represents the expression of the aesthetic factors central to their everyday lives. Folk artists are not unaware of their own aesthetics, as we shall see in the examples cited later in this chapter, so we cannot fairly call them naive (as many art historians do). Nor are folk artists untrained, for they often spend years, a lifetime perhaps, trying to learn and perform well their genres and styles. For example, Bess Hockema knows what a good afghan is and has worked years to be able to "perform" one well, yet she would be the last to claim she had produced a perfect one—or a unique one, for that matter. Not a perfect one because first of all she is modest, and community decorum would prevent her from bragging; moreover, it is the community's (in this case primarily her family's) taste, not her individual creativity running in its own direction, that exercises the judgment. Not a unique one because the whole point in folk art is to produce an excellent performance within a customary form, not far out and away from it.

For this reason it is just for Albert B. Friedman to say of folk ballads, "Any rare or subtle figurative expression in a ballad would make its genuineness suspect, for the language of ballads is a tissue of commonplaces, stock figures, stock symbols, and formulaic phrasing." Some students of the ballad have taken Friedman's comment to be derogatory, but of course it is not. It represents the plain fact that ballad aesthetics are based on a continually shared battery of expressions known and used by the ballad-singing communities, not on the unique poetic brilliance of particular recognizable composers. For this reason, ballads, afghans, and all the other folk expressions we have been discussing represent community taste more than individual genius. It is not a comment on any lack of talent on the part of the folk performers, but a recognition of an entirely different dimension in aesthetic background.

This is where the distinction between these two types of art should become clear: Folk art is produced from and judged by the tastes of the close group for which and in which it is performed. If there is any "foreign" criterion involved, it is brought by the people themselves from their earlier place of abode. If we are dealing with Ukrainian folk art in America, it is made up of those Ukrainian aesthetic traditions still operating among the Ukrainians who brought them here in the first place, not of intellectually exercised ideas taken from formal studies of Ukrainian art. Neither is Ukrainian folk art to be judged against any other standard than its own.

Fine art is usually judged from the vantage point of the professionally trained, from the intellectually aware person for whom the field is a study geared, not necessarily to the everyday life of home folk, but to the inspired work of creative individuals often performing outside their own close groups and often using models of inspiration foreign to their own close group. Fine art is thus another kind of art, with other rules, other focuses, other tastes. It often looks upon expressive items outside its own realm as lesser than "real art." Terms like *primitive, untrained, self-taught,* and (curses) *folk art* are used in a generally condescending way, as if to imply that some artifacts from the past and some artistic processes uninformed by formal training and intellectual awareness of classic art traditions may occasionally be of interest to us for display. This may seem an elite viewpoint, but it is really only narrow-minded. It is insisting on judging all cats as if they must be Siamese in order to qualify as cats, but allowing that a few lesser kinds of animals, by virtue of fur color or regal bearing or tone of meow may occasionally be of interest to those who know what cats really are meant to be. Siamese cats themselves would no doubt concur in such a judgment, as would their owners and breeders, but the owners of all the alley cats of the world would respond that their cats are just as good as any Siamese, and some would argue that the robust tabby of nondescript background has an even greater vitality than the carefully cultured purebred. In this discussion, as with art, there is no reliable final authority on which is better, for we are comparing two different things: on the one hand, a consciously applied, formal, and selective kind of breeding for one result, and on the other, a kind of breeding with entirely different, informal restrictions for a different result. Fortunately, we need not resolve the dilemma: *"De gustibus non disputandem est,"* said my uncle Toby, and he was right.

Of course some high art is elite, in that it is produced for and bought by those with such large sums of money that it is out of the reach of average people. I once took a college class of Native Americans to the Oriental art museum on our campus. They were not moved by the delicate jade carvings, the immense thrones, the detailed Japanese lacquers, or the extensive embroidered tapestries, but they were enthusiastic about prints by Hiroshige and Hokusai and ecstatic about an exhibit of boats, oars, and masks from New Guinea. Primitive? Naive? I think not. They were quick to point out to me that the Asian treasures were pleasing to the eye but "that's not really art," they said. "You can tell that it's stuff some rich man could afford to have made for him, to suit his own likes. This other kind, these pictures and these masks: You can tell that the guys who made these were satisfying themselves and people who were just like them." My students might easily have made similar negative assessments of many of those paintings, musical creations, buildings, and sculptures that have been seen by historians as important formal steps in the development of Western art. One cannot deny the impact and the importance of formal art in the development of any culture; equally so, one cannot deny the existence of various kinds of art, judged by different standards and addressed by and to differing audiences.

Folk art, of whatever genre, is not the uninspired or naive production of items that might have been done better had the artisan only been properly trained. It is not the humble outpouring of rural, backward, or underdeveloped genius, nor is it the coincidentally attractive making of practical items by people unaware of what they are doing. The folk artist is not a bumpkin standing at the scholar's back door, gumming the brim of his cap, saying with awkward embarrassment, "Shucks, folks, I don't know whatcha mean by all this es-thetic stuff. Why, I just carves out them duck decoys and goes a-huntin' with 'em," before lighting the corn-cob pipe and bowlegging away, elbows out. Rather, folk artists are likely to be fiercely aware of what is good and beautiful in their areas of expression, and even more aware of what the close group will think about it. Guided by a sense of community aesthetic which is usually unspoken because it is functional, not intellectualized, subscribing to a sense of decorum that prevents bragging and discourages the overarticulation of the obvious ("hot air"), the folk artist is likely to place more focus on the item being produced than on his own abilities. One hears: "Oh, I really like that song; my dad always used to sing it," or the opposite, as when Maggie Hammons Parker finished singing "In Scotland Town" (Child #17, "Hind Horn") for Alan Jabbour and said, "They claim that's a good one; I don't like it too well. . . . I never did care much about the tune to it, now."

The folk arts, which we may see as synonymous with what we have been calling folklore in general in this discussion, are not excerpted from everyday life for special scrutiny or elevation of taste or intellectual curiosity. On the contrary, what makes folk art different from fine art is precisely that it is based on the aesthetic perception, expression, and appreciation of the community adventures of everyday life. Folklore is dynamic in large part *because* it is totally integrated with the dynamics of life in a close group, a situation that encourages unspoken group awareness of what is considered pleasing and discourages individual (oddball) expressions of creativity. In a letter to John Greenway, folk singer Aunt Molly Jackson put it as well as anyone can: "This is what a folk song realy is the folks composes there own songs about there own lifes an there home folks that live around them."

BEAUTIFUL LANGUAGES   A few examples will show that folk aesthetics are far from naive or primitive for the tradition-bearers. We will notice further that aesthetic comments are not all based on the same sets of criteria: Some are commentaries on function, some on content, some on style. All of them seem to recognize, some more overtly than others, the integration of aesthetic judgment with the processes of every day life.

Ida Moffet, of Springfield, Oregon, decorates Easter eggs in the Ukrainian tradition, having learned it from her mother while growing up in her Ukrainian family. Drawing fine lines of melted beeswax on an egg with a small stylus, she uses the batiklike process of applying continually darker dyes to the egg until, graced with a number of colors and designs, it is put on display for Easter. Her designs include the rose, the ram's horn, a fish, symbols of Lent and the Dead Sea, ladders to Heaven, the Blessed Mother's tears, eternity, the Holy Trinity, and sometimes animals (including, for fun, three-eared rabbits). Probably her favorite single design is one she learned from her mother; it clearly has a deep meaning for her because it grows directly out of the circumstances of everyday life. For their family, wheat symbolized life, and Ida comments, "There's something about the wheat [symbol] that I like. Maybe it's because I remember Mother's scolding if we dropped a crumb of wheat on the floor, 'cause wheat meant a lot to people in Europe. That was life, and as long as we had wheat we had nothing to worry about. Mother always said it was life, 'cause wheat was life to her. 'Cause I know when we kids would drop even a crumb, we had to pick it up. We could not throw half a slice of bread away to the dog because she used to say, 'As long as you have wheat you can live.' " Who can doubt that wheat, as a family symbol for life, is not superimposed on Ida Moffet's eggs with the Christian concept of everlasting life symbolized by the wheat that is made into the communion wafer? This interpenetration of art, religion, and daily life is not rare in folk arts, and it is a fine example of the basic aesthetic of which we speak here.

"He uses those pretty languages." In these words, the daughter of a Navajo narrator tried to explain to me the especially beautiful archaic vocabulary her father uses in the recitation of Coyote stories. I was trying to solve the puzzle of why the Coyote stories as told by the Navajo seemed to be easily understood by family members of all ages, even the youngest, while non-Navajos with twenty years' experience in the Navajo language were often dumbfounded by the vocabulary. What I began to surmise through my conversations with some of the Navajo narrators is that there is a special old-fashioned-sounding vocabulary used prominently in the Coyote stories, and because the stories are told so often during the winter months, everyone learns this special language as fully as everyday Navajo. Whether the vocabulary is actually archaic or not I cannot say, especially since contemporary speakers of Navajo all understand and use this vocabulary. At any rate, it is clear that the special vocabulary, which is considered stylistically beautiful and fun to listen to, is an integral part of telling the Coyote stories.

On the practical level, this is of course one of the vexations in providing English translations of the Coyote stories, for the beauty of the vocabulary, its special feel, along with all the deep associations in the minds of the listeners, all disappear in translation. Since, as we have seen previously in Chapter 3, the meaning of the Coyote tales is seldom overtly stated, we must assume that at least a good part of the meaning must reside in the style of the narration. And if we accept the narrator's insistence that hearing the stories will help young people become good folks (while not hearing the stories will incline them otherwise), we may begin to perceive a hazy, perhaps undefinable, link between aesthetic response and meaning. The Navajo concept of perfection, often interpreted as long life and good health, is most fully summed up in the word *hozhǫji*, literally, "in the direction of beauty" or "along the path of beauty" or "the way of beauty." In other words, quite the most special condition imaginable by Navajos is described with a word that speakers of English would identify with aesthetics. It seems to me arguable that the "pretty languages" (by which my informant's daughter simply meant the especially beautiful words) of the Coyote stories may have a direct therapeutic relationship to the more all-embracing Navajo concept of well-being. Thus, the narrator of a Coyote tale, using beautiful language to express ideas conducive to a beautiful life (from a Navajo point of view), actually engages in that sense of well-being and applies it to his listeners as the story is performed.

Sometimes beauty can be a reflection on the aesthetic appreciation of the most common daily task. In his presidential address to the American Folklore Society in November 1974, Dell Hymes suggested that the truest exposure to aesthetic experience as a part of everyday life might be gained "by an accounting of the satisfaction in the voice of Mrs. Blanche Tohet of Warm Springs, Oregon, when, having finished fixing eels to dry one evening, she stood back, looking at them strung on a long line, and said, 'There, i'n't that beautiful?' " Eels are a favorite food of Indian people from the Columbia Basin and plateau areas, so part of Mrs. Tohet's assessment must be seen in her recognition of the eels as a highly prized ethnic food. Obviously, too, something about their preparation is involved here, because her comment came when her job of preparing the eels was finished. In this, do we not see her own appreciation of herself as a competent participant in traditional modes of food preparation? In addition to her comment that the object of her scrutiny was beautiful, we need most of all to remember Dell Hymes's request that we account for the "satisfaction" in her voice; the way she made the pronouncement, the style in which it was enunciated, was a part of what was being said.

All of these aspects provide common grounds for folklorists to discuss, for they are all provocative markers of folk aesthetics. However, it will be a while before the Museum of Art ever mounts a display of drying eels. And even if such an exhibition did take place, I imagine Mrs. Tohet would not find the result beautiful, for the item out of its traditional context would certainly not make much sense or provide much beauty. The same thrill of participating in a tradition in a meaningful way within its usual context was registered by an old woman who stopped singing in the middle of a song and seized Cecil Sharp by the lapel of his coat, saying, "Isn't it beautiful?" The referrent of "it" in the old woman's urgent question, and the referrent of "that" in Mrs. Tohet's sigh of satisfaction, are far more complex entities than a song or a string of eels as physical objects can account for.

John Palanuk, the Ukrainian hammered dulcimer maker mentioned in Chapter 3, does not speak of his instruments themselves in any aesthetic terms. Rather, his comments run toward the kind of wood used and its utility in holding its shape, the difficulty of finding iron rods that can be cut down to tuning pegs, the virtues of fishing wire versus piano wire for strings, and so forth. Mr. Palanuk is modest enough not to refer to the finished product as a beautiful instrument. On the other hand, he is fond of snapping a heavy fingernail down onto a set of strings to test the liveliness of sound projected by a given instrument. If the volume and timbre suit his ear, he comments, "Now that's a pretty one, isn't it?" Since Mr. Palanuk does not himself play the instrument, his judgment is based on his perception of the ability the instrument will have in projecting its distinctive sound when it is being played in a small orchestra at a Ukrainian dance. Where the crowd makes a good deal of noise, and where other instruments are often electrified, the ability of the ethnic instrument to hold its own and to provide a distinctive ethnic sound for a distinctively ethnic celebration is paramount. Thus when John Palanuk says, "That's pretty," he is singling out a particular aspect of his traditional art for focus. It would be difficult to perceive how an art exhibit might handle such a matter, for in a gallery the instrument would be on display, not its distinctive sound. Of course, with this traditional art as with others discussed here, the central question does not come down to how an item may be best displayed in a museum. In the case of a hammered dulcimer, we might suggest that a museum display several of them and then hire a musician to play appropriate tunes for passers-by. Still, one suspects that John Palanuk would rather have one of his instruments played in a small orchestra at a Ukrainian wedding than to see it or its sound enshrined in a marble hall.

Sometimes aesthetic judgments in folk arts are based on evaluations of practical function, and it is possible for several aesthetic bases to be used simultaneously. Michael Owen Jones's chairmaker, "Charley," referred to his grandfather's chairs as stressing one kind of quality over another: They "weren't comfortable, but one thing about it, my grandfather's chairs—if you could see one today—it'd be good an' stout. They didn't make for the beauty part, they made for the lastin' part, he did." His grandfather's chairs, he felt, "don't set good but they last good," and his uncle observed of the same grandfather, "Buddy, when he threw one together, hit was together." Here the aesthetic basis is not visual recognition of design or style, but rather a high evaluation for a piece of furniture that would last, obviously of considerable importance in a mountain culture in which the passing on of family heirlooms is important and in which money for continual buying of new furniture is limited. In distinguishing between his own chairs and his grandfather's, moreover, Charley makes it clear by implication that while his grandfather's "last good," his own probably "set good." That is, two different criteria can be applied to the traditional chairs in this family, neither of which is based on surface beauty in design.

In the Pacific Northwest, one often hears traditional woodworkers and boatmakers refer to a particular kind of work in which surface aesthetics are subordinated to the practical necessity of an indestructible item (such as a small boat to be used in heavy surf or a cabinet to be used in someone's shop or garage): "It ain't much for purty, but it's hell for stout." Here, aesthetic considerations are openly admitted, as are their conscious subordination to pragmatic use. At the same time, language of a distinctly nonelite variety is used to show that the artisan is not trying to "talk over anyone's head."

Some folk aesthetics are based on recognition of the proper way of doing things. The logger's derogatory reference to a Coos Bay splice is based on the assumption that such a splice is made the way a seaman would do it, not the way one of *us* would perform the task. Even though the splice might be perfectly acceptable, perhaps even a superior job, by sailors' standards, the loggers' recognition that it is done by an outsider according to other rules provides the basis for a negative aesthetic judgment. Said one Norwegian grandmother to her granddaughter when asked her secret for lefse, "You must spend twenty years in Norway and bake it every year for eighty years." This is of course a hyperbolic statement of the proverb "Practice makes perfect," and it is found as the basis for aesthetic judgment in many kinds of folklore. The point is that if you don't know how to do something right, if you have not had extensive experience in actually doing it among those whose taste is valued, you can hardly be expected to do it very well.

I once took some teachers with me to visit some Navajo friends in the wintertime, and when the inevitable string was brought out for string games, one of the teachers, a woman in her forties, tried to learn one of the more complicated designs from a teen-age Navajo girl. The teen-ager kept insisting that the string be approached from certain directions, and when loops of the string had to be removed from one hand and placed on the other that it be done in a certain order and laid out on a certain knee. The teacher, however, thought she had noticed a way of doing it more handily for her own manual dexterity and proceeded to try it her own way. Time and time again the Navajo girl patiently insisted that the string had to be placed on the left knee, not on the right. Finally, in exasperation, the Navajo girl asked, "What is it you say you do?" "I'm a teacher in the public schools," my friend replied. "You sure don't learn very well," the Navajo girl observed. "Now put this string on your left knee and do as I say." Here the proper way of doing something, in this case the Navajo way of doing something, had become far more important than the final outcome. Somewhat coincidentally, when my friend finally did it exactly as told, the string figure did come out looking more like it should have, which the Navajos in the room attributed as much to doing it properly as to practice.

Other kinds of aesthetic judgment in folk art tend to be based on proper content. The following is a transcription, with only some minor excerpting and modification (interruptions by the telephone, by visitors at the door, by cats, and by pudding spilling over on the stove), of a conversation I had with Mrs. Clarice Mae Judkins, a traditional singer in Eugene, Oregon. She was telling me about a young man she had met who had been collecting folk songs in the rural areas nearby and had found one that featured some wording she entirely disapproved of.

MRS. JUDKINS: My sister taught at Crow, on the Siuslaw River, and that was where most of those songs came from. When this, uh, young man went looking for them several years ago. Well he said there was one or two old men out there at Siuslaw. I remember arguing with him bitterly about one song that I had learned and it was about the, uh, corn and why of course, why corn was, uh, but anyhow, what was the line? Well anyway, it went to the effect that, uh, when he was harvesting, he wasn't harvesting corn. But anyway it was something you could only do to wheat or oats but not corn. I tried to explain to him I came from the Midwest where we raised wheat and corn. And I knew that, what was it now? That he, that line went—and this old fellow at the Siuslaw taught it to him. And, uh, but I said you don't, what was it now? You fallow and you husk, but you don't—

TOELKEN: Thrash?

MRS. JUDKINS: No, the word wasn't thrash. It was just like something like mow, yes mowing corn. And that outraged me, right entirely because I knew you couldn't mow corn. And I said the man's got it mixed—it's *hoe* corn. And, uh, no he said, he, he took the old fella's word for it. Boy, I said, you'll just be laughed at if you find anybody lived in the West and you go around singing about mowing corn. I said that's just foolish. But that was the way he learned it and he insisted on keeping it. But, uh, this is about this young man that, uh, and I knew the song anyhow myself. This young man went a-courting to his next neighbor's door:

> [She sings:] *Where he'd often been before,*
> *And then the subject came along,*
> *Asking if he'd hoed his corn.*
>
> *No, madam, no, and I'll tell you why.*
> *He bowed down his head and began for to cry.*
> *No, madam, no, and I'll tell you why,*
> *Truly my corn has grown up too high.* [laughter]

And so then she told him of course that he couldn't come courting. That she wouldn't marry a man that couldn't support her and he'd have to go home and hoe his corn. And so this old fellow in Siuslaw had the song but when he sung it he sung it "to mow his corn." And I kept telling, what was that young fella's name? Anyway, he had it all wrong, and people would sure laugh at him if he stuck to "mowing" his corn.

[She recites:] *He hung down his head and began to cry,*
*No madam no, and I'll tell you why*
*I tried and I tried and I tried in vain,*
*And I don't think I shall have a single grain.*

*So why do you come and ask me to wed,*
*When you cannot earn your bread?*
*Single I am and single I'll remain,*
*For a lazy man that won't maintain.*

Mrs. Judkins was clearly unaware that the word *corn* in England refers to grains like wheat and oats, and the term *mow* would have been quite appropriate in English versions of the song. Thus she could not have known that the old man out at Siuslaw might have been maintaining a song tradition more directly related to England than that which she herself had participated in. At the same time, she was certain that in her understanding of the word *corn*, one could only hoe it, not mow it. Hence her negative value judgment on that version of the song, and her general contempt for anyone who would maintain those words even in the face of proper information.

In a parallel instance, I took George Wasson, a Coos Indian, with me to visit my friend Yellowman, a consummate narrator of Navajo Coyote stories, and after we had listened to a number of Yellowman's stories I suggested that George tell a few Coos Coyote tales to show the Navajos what kind of episodes Old Man Coyote experienced in the Coos tradition. George and I had previously agreed that many of the stories seemed to us very much like the Navajo stories. But when George told a fairly lengthy and humorous story from his tribe, Yellowman's question to me was, "Where did he learn that story from, missionaries? Or from a book? That's not a Coyote story." We asked why Yellowman did not consider the story proper, and he responded it was because Coyote was described eating fish. I explained that the Coos were fish-eaters, which brought an involuntary shudder to Yellowman and a grimace to his face. He politely changed the subject.

Still another kind of aesthetic judgment may be based on what we can call ethnic style. For example, the Japanese New Year foods described in Chapters 2 and 4 are often said to be beautiful, based on their arrangement, their color, the design of their ingredients, and the way in which they are laid out on the table. In this way, a Japanese person might enter a room and see all the proper items on a table but might recognize that they had not been placed there in an aesthetically pleasing way by someone who shared the same ethnic background. In his books on urban Black folklore, Roger D. Abrahams notes the extent to which style forms the basis for personal evaluations. Calling someone a cool cat is actually an aesthetic value judgment based on the recognition that a person's actions and the style with which he carries them out are done so well according to esoteric standards that they require singling out for commendation. A Black friend of mine tells of an incident in which he and other Black musicians were "jamming" after hours in the back room of a San Francisco nightclub. Several prominent jazz men were there, including a very well known jazz trumpeter. A white teen-ager begged to be admitted so he could sit in on the drums, and he was so sincere and so obviously interested in jazz that the group invited him in briefly, even though the presence of a minor in the nightclub environment was illegal. The young man took over the drums and impressed everyone with his virtuosity for the next couple of hours. At the conclusion of the jam session, the prominent trumpeter walked over to the young white man and said gravely, "You a *baad* motherfucker, Jim," at which the young man broke into tears—not tears of rage but of surprised pleasure at having been singled out for such high praise. In this case the material being performed was not folk song, but the style with which it was rendered in jazz improvisation was so traditional, so ethnic in its articulation, and the young man had mastered it so well, that the Black jazz players' only appropriate response was through their own folk speech. Such aesthetic judgments are to be found in all ethnic groups in America, and their focus may range from evaluations of personal action to styles of performance to distinctive ways of arranging furniture in the living room of a home.

We should listen closely and ask questions when such phrases as "That's a slick job" or "He's a good hand" or "That's just like Mom used to make" are used in what might otherwise seem to be casual conversation. In most cases, we will find that the evaluation is only seemingly a simple one; it is usually based on a perception of a style, or of content or of application and function, that is valued highly by members of a close group precisely because it is shared by many and because the particular person who is its medium at that moment has reperformed in a creditable manner, working from and within the recognizable folk ideas and genres of the group.

The folk artist is, then, a medium for community concern, decorum, and traditional standards; the traditional artist knows this, as does the audience. When a community sees excellence in one of its own folk arts, it is because the performer has exercised community taste in a recognizable and praiseworthy manner. The repertoires of the folk artist and of the fine art artist may occasionally overlap, of course, but the canons of taste by which they are fairly judged seldom do.

## ◪ BIBLIOGRAPHICAL NOTES

The standard interest in genre as a basis for organizing the field of study in folklore is evident in such works as the Aarne-Thompson *Types of the Folktale,* Dorson's *American Folklore and Folklife,* Brunvand's *Study of American Folklore,* Ben-Amos's *Folklore Genres,* Wayland D. Hand, ed., *American Folk Legend: A Symposium* (Berkeley: University of California Press, 1971), and Hand, *American Folk Medicine: A Symposium* (Berkeley: University of California Press, 1976), as well as in articles such as Linda Dégh and Andrew Vázsonyi, "The Memorate and the Proto-Memorate," *Journal of American Folklore,* 87 (1974), 225–239, in which personal narrations are seen in both their generic and "pregeneric" dimensions.

Over the past few years an increasing number of studies have focused on the dynamics of tradition for a particular folk performer or a particular kind of folk performance. Out of them all, one should at least consult Roger D. Abrahams, "Creativity, Individuality, and the Traditional Singer," *Studies in the Literary Imagination* [Georgia State University], 3:1 (April 1970), 5–34, as well as his and Almeda Riddle's *A Singer and Her Songs: Almeda Riddle's Book of Ballads* (Baton Rouge: Louisiana State University, 1971), and David Evans, "Techniques of Blues Composition Among Black Folksingers," *Journal of American Folklore,* 87 (1974), 240–249, noting especially his comments on rephrasing, p. 248.

N. Scott Momaday's story about the arrowmaker is only one episode of many traditional vignettes in his important collection of Kiowa lore, *The Way to Rainy Mountain* (Albuquerque: University of New Mexico Press, 1969), p. 46. Bess Hockema's expression about putting the big pot in the little pot is a fairly common one in the South, but with a certain important difference: F. R. Smith and C. R. Smith, in their pamphlet "Southern Words and Sayings" (Jackson, Miss.: Office Supply Company, 1976), say that "put the little pot in the big pot" means "company's a-coming; water it down." Walter McCulloch, *Woods Words* (Portland: Oregon Historical Society Press, 1958), says "Pulaski" is named for "Ranger Pulaski, U.S. Forest Service, famed for his lifesaving work on the big 1910 fire in Idaho," an equally vague derivation as the one mentioned here, though closer to the facts of history. A version of the nuns and the forest fire is mentioned by Brunvand in *The Study of American Folklore,* p. 88. The legend of Yoho Cove is given by Dorson in *American Folklore* (Chicago: University of Chicago Press, 1959), 130–131; the Yeahoh story ("Origin of Man") is in Leonard Roberts, *South from Hell-Fer-Sartin* (Berea, Ky.: Council of the Southern Mountains, 1964), p. 162.

In his headnotes to ballad #155, "Sir Hugh, or, The Jew's Daughter," Francis James Child provides a rather full background for the medieval European version of the mutilated boy story. A briefer account of the legend, detailing Chaucer's possible source for his use of it in the Prioress's Tale, is given by F. N. Robinson, *The Works of Geoffrey Chaucer*, 2nd ed. (Boston: Houghton Mifflin, 1957), pp. 734–736; a greater range of comment is given by C. Brown, *The Miracle of Our Lady* (London: Chaucer Society, 1910). An unusually detailed study of the whole complex, with reference to the employment of the legend by Chaucer, Joyce, and Malamud, is provided by Faith Hippensteel, " 'Sir Hugh': The Hoosier Contribution to the Ballad," *Indiana Folklore*, 2 (1968), 75–140.

For further explorations on multiple or overlapped genres and repertoires, see Adrienne L. Keppler, "Folklore as Expressed in the Dance of Tonga," *Journal of American Folklore*, 80 (1967), 160–168, in which traditional dance is described as existing simultaneously in other traditional dimensions such as cosmology, legends, heroic exploits, information and connotation about sacred animals, recollections of local events, and the like, all interwoven in a communal, gestural reaffirmation of cultural allegiance. William A. Wilson, "The Paradox of Mormon Folklore," mentioned several times previously in this book, demonstrates the existence of formal and "unofficial" religious stories side by side. Warren L. d'Azevedo, "Mask Makers and Myth in Western Liberia," in *Primitive Art and Society*, ed. Anthony Forge (London: Oxford University Press, 1973), pp. 126–150, discusses creativity, magic, ritual, and art as mutually inextricable elements of cultural expression. Vivian De Sola Pinto and Allan Edwin Rodway, eds., *The Common Muse* (New York: Philosophical Library, 1957), suggest that the broadside ballads and traditional ballads of England were and are mutually invigorating and occasionally identical, even though their format, diction, and contexts were often quite dissimilar. Linda Dégh calls it symbiosis in "Symbiosis of Joke and Legend: A Case of Conversational Folklore," in *Folklore Today: A Festschrift for Richard M. Dorson*, ed. Linda Dégh, Henry Glassie, and Felix J. Oinas (Bloomington: Indiana University Press, 1976), pp. 101–122.

For introductory purposes, the two most useful and informative pieces on the subject of folk art are Henry Glassie's chapter, "Folk Art," in *Folklore and Folklife: An Introduction*, ed. Richard Dorson (Chicago: University of Chicago Press, 1972), pp. 253–280, and Holger Cahill, ed., *American Folk Art: The Art of the Common Man in America, 1750–1900* (New York: Museum of Modern Art, 1932). The latter work is probably the first book on American folk art to deal with the subject not in condescending terms of quaintness and whimsy but with direct recognition of its own status as a species of community-based aesthetics. Although Cahill occasionally uses such terms as *primitive, childlike, quaintness, innocence,* he admits the term *primitive* has inappropriate implications and finally insists that "the work of these men is folk art because it is the expression of the common people, made by them and intended for their use and enjoyment. It is not the expression of professional artists made for a small cultured class, and it has little to do with the fashionable art of its period" (p. 6). Glassie points out that we usually assume if a traditional item has chiefly utilitarian purposes the artifact is called an aspect of craft, where if pleasure predominates in its production it is called folk art. We can see how easily genres can overlap under these circumstances, if we consider that many old hand-held and locally made plows have been later used as mailbox supports by the descendants of the original farmer. It may be the same plow, the same family, the same region, but clearly it is the aesthetic process involved in the local usage that determines the position of the item in the community at any particular moment. Albert Friedman's comments on the lack of "subtle figurative expression" in ballads are found in the Introduction to *The Viking Book of Folk Ballads of the English-Speaking World* (New York: Viking Press, 1956), pp. ix–xxxv, esp. p. x; his remarks have been mistaken by many to represent an elite view toward oral tradition. This is as good an indication as any of how difficult it is to speak of aesthetics in a language where that very discussion has been carried out chiefly by people of elevated social class. Unfortunately, the English vocabulary carries evaluative connotations about aesthetics that often impede the process of clear discussion. Maggie Hammons Parker's quotation may be found in the booklet accompanying Alan Jabbour and Carl Fleischhauer, *The Hammons Family: A Study of a West Virginia Family's Traditions*, Archive of Folk Song Records L65 and L66 (Washington, D.C.: Library of Congress, 1973), p. 27. Aunt Molly Jackson's clear and unpretentious definition of folk song is quoted by John Greenway in his *American Folksongs of Protest* (Philadelphia: University of Pennsylvania Press, 1953), p. 8. Anyone unfamiliar with Aunt Molly Jackson as a singer and songmaker may find remedy in Chapter 8 of Greenway's book.

Further information about the "pretty languages" used by Yellowman may be found in my article of that title in *Folklore Genres*, ed. Dan Ben-Amos (Austin: University of Texas Press, 1976), pp. 145–170. Mrs. Tohet's comment is quoted by Hymes in his article, "Folklore's Nature and the Sun's Myth," *Journal of American Folklore*, 88 (1975), 346.

Michael Owen Jones, in *The Handmade Object and Its Maker* (Berkeley: University of California Press, 1975), places more stress on the individual's own direction in his folk art than on the role of the close group in providing the aesthetic framework, as demonstrated through the works and character of the man on whose craft this book is based. Beyond this the book is extremely informative and helpful and the notes to each chapter are extensive.

The fishermen's attitude toward the knotwork of farmers can be inferred from such comments as the following: Farmers "always think they're working in the 'lower forties' and they tie farmers' knots, which can't be untied in a hurry . . . they think the tree line at high water is caused by the sea cows' biting the twigs off, and they tie up the vessel like it was the *Queen Mary*." This and similar attitudes may be found quoted and discussed by Suzi Jones, *Oregon*

*Folklore* (Eugene: University of Oregon, 1977), pp. 16–23 ("The Oregon Coast"). The comment on the extended apprenticeship in making lefse was made by an immigrant Norwegian grandmother, Mrs. Helge Ledahl, in a collection made by a folklore student, Tamara Stenshoel; it is filed in the Randall V. Mills Memorial Archive of Northwest Folklore with the collections of December 1976.

A brief but fascinating consideration of an urban folk art form is given in Elaine Eff, "The Painted Window Screens of Baltimore, Maryland," *The Clarion* [published by the Museum of American Folk Art, New York City], 6 (Spring 1976), 5–12. For a few examples of the varying ways in which the aesthetics of folklore may be approached, one can consult the following pieces: Tristram P. Coffin, "Mary Hamilton and the Anglo-American Ballad as an Art Form," *Journal of American Folklore*, 70 (1957), 208–214, reprinted in *The Critics and the Ballad*, ed. MacEdward Leach and Tristram P. Coffin (Carbondale: Southern Illinois University Press, 1961), pp. 245–256; Daniel J. Crowley, *I Could Talk Old-Story Good: Creativity in Bahamian Folklore*, University of California Folklore Studies, no. 17 (Berkeley: University of California Press, 1966); Warren L. d'Azevedo, "A Structural Approach to Esthetics: Toward a Definition of Art in Anthropology," *American Anthropologist*, 60 (1958), 702–714; Alan Dundes, "The Henny-Penny Phenomenon: A Study of Phonological Esthetics in American Speech," *Southern Folklore Quarterly*, 38 (1974), 1–9; Michael Owen Jones, "The Concept of 'Aesthetics' in the Traditional Arts," *Western Folklore*, 30 (1971), 77–104; Jones, " 'There's Gotta Be New Designs Once in Awhile': Culture Change and the 'Folk Arts,' " *Southern Folklore Quarterly*, 36 (1972), 43–60—since folk art is a manifestation of culture and a direct outgrowth of the tastes of both artist and audience, it changes in response to ongoing cultural developments; therefore folk art does not cease to be "folk" when modern machinery is used, as long as the traditional aesthetic system of performer and audience is still intact; Jones, "Violations of Standards of Excellence and Preference in Utilitarian Art," *Western Folklore*, 32 (1973), 19–32; Alan Lomax, "The Good and the Beautiful in Folksong," *Journal of American Folklore*, 80 (1967), 213–235; Robert Jerome Smith, "The Structure of Esthetic Response," *Journal of American Folklore*, 84 (1971), 68–79, reprinted in *Toward New Perspectives in Folklore*, ed. Américo Paredes and Richard Bauman (Austin: University of Texas Press, 1971), pp. 68–79.

# 6

# FOLKLORE

## AND

## CONNOTATION

ONE OF CHAUCER'S MOST INTERESTING CHARACTERS IS THE WIFE OF BATH; SOMEWHAT OVERDRESSED AND PROCLAIMING LOUD HER INTEREST IN AND ABILITIES at sex, she is described as riding along on a religious pilgrimage with one eye open for a potential husband. When Chaucer says, "She had passed many a foreign stream" and "She knew a lot about wandering by the way," we feel fairly secure in assuming that he is speaking metaphorically—that these are not only denotative records of her geographic travel but that they are simultaneously connotative of her sexual wandering. When Chaucer mentions her knowledge of remedies for love and says, "She knew the old dance of *that* art," we can be confident, again, that the author wishes us to register *dance* with a somewhat wider and deeper application than the word normally would suggest (saying "She danced a beautiful waltz" would surely miss Chaucer's intent).

# PLAYING WITH LANGUAGE Yet, we

may ask, how do we know Chaucer's intent? Isn't this an example of reading something into the author's work? After all, Chaucer himself said *wandering* and *dance;* who are we to come along six hundred years later and be so certain of what he meant? And if he meant something else, why didn't he just come out and say so instead of confusing us? These are common questions in folklore and literature classes; they are often asked by people who believe that the authors themselves don't know (or remember) what they meant, by those who believe the world's problems would be solved if all communications were denotative, and by those who do not allow themselves to play (the same kind who interrupt the first line of a traveling salesman joke to demand the salesman's name and company, the date and place of the occurrence, then—when you've made up an answer to get on with the story—state triumphantly that the Filstrup Brush Company did not sell in Oklahoma until 1952). The question is often asked by serious students who have been brought up to believe that texts are sacred and who are just finding out that one may indeed ask into such matters. At the other extreme, others are ready to assert that a piece of literature can mean anything the reader feels it means. That, too, is unfair to the author, the work, and the shared knowledge of the culture.

First of all, connotation (the attitudes, value judgments and implications associated with words) is a common aspect of language. Many animals communicate; as far as we know, only human beings use connotation. Some have argued indeed that connotation, especially in the use of metaphor, is more basic to human language and meaning than is denotation (the dictionary meaning of a word). In our daily conversation we are more likely to use words like *pig, cow, monkey, cherry,* for their figurative power than for their regular definitions. And we are not confused when others do it; we are ready to perceive the *real* meaning via implication because usually we are talking of matters that are not susceptible to denotative discussion.

Consider: "That party was a real blast!" First, unless a bomb went off, it probably was not a real blast. Was the party, then, noisy? Well, that's part of it, perhaps. What else lurks in the meaning that is not part of the denotation but that is central to the declaration? The idea of fun. The term is a value judgment as well as a description, and the effects of both levels are meant to be simultaneous, with a stress on the connotative, not the denotative, level.

PIGS AND RED STOCKINGS  Consider this complaint overheard

in a school hallway: "Sam fixed me up with a real pig last night." A real pig? Not unless Sam is a practical joker. More likely it means: "A friend of mine arranged an evening engagement for me with a young person of the opposite sex whose physical, moral, intellectual, and habitual attributes struck me as being objectionably on the negative end of my scale of values." Yet I know of no high school student who would make the latter statement in the hallway (at least not seriously). Not only is it stuffy, but it omits the personal revulsion easily suggested by the word *pig*. Now, in recent years, it might be that a smoker had been fixed up with a narc, and was complaining about that, still using the connotative power of the language to carry the value judgment. Thus, while the declaration can have a number of meanings, the one we assign to it will be the one we see as obvious in the particular context, using the terms as members of the group would use them. The denotation has little to do with the real meanings here.

While denotation is easily translated into other languages, connotation is not; this should be a clear signal to us that connotation is a strong part of a shared sense of "we" as it is found in language usage. And this is true in larger national and cultural terms as well as in the very local setting of a close folk group. Remember that *lumberjack* is a positive, masculine term in some parts of the United States, but among Northwest *loggers*, the term is used in derision.

One of my own experiences in teaching a Chaucer class may give an example of the cultural differences in connotation. I had given a quiz that asked students to speculate briefly on why Chaucer had described the Wife of Bath as wearing red stockings—neatly tied, at that. Everyone came up with something: If other pilgrims could see how neatly tied her stockings were, she must have had her dress pulled up immodestly; *red* stockings might suggest sensuality, passion, sex, maybe even danger. Two very sharp students from Formosa, however, sat totally puzzled by the later conversation. How could we assign those meanings to red stockings? What's wrong with displaying a woman's legs? The rest of us succeeded immediately in pointing out that dress customs were different in those days; for the Chinese students there was no problem there. Then we started giving analogies for our connotations of the color red: red light district, sins as scarlet, *The Scarlet Letter*, I saw red, and so on. The Formosan students were still puzzled. "What do you think of first when I say *red*?" I asked. "Good luck," they responded. "Would a bride in Formosa wear a red dress?" "Of course, what else?"

Now, of course, my students had no way of knowing whether red had exactly the same connotation for Chaucer as it had for them; in fact, most of their analogies were quite recent. Yet we can speculate that, since the color and its meaning do seem to enjoy widespread connotation in the society on the informal, folk, level, *perhaps* it may be traced back through a considerable time to the Middle Ages. In this case, we do not know for certain that Chaucer so intended the color of the Wife's stockings to register on the reader, but we can use the data we have to speculate on the matter, bolstered by the knowledge that such a construction is congruent with the rest of the Wife's description. Our shared connotations can lead us to fruitful questions about how meaning is shared by members of a close group, and how, because of folklore, things can actually mean more than they initially seem to. And it forces us to recognize how culture-specific connotation is: We can share it more easily with Chaucer in spite of a great span of time than we can with contemporaries from a distinctly different culture.

Connotation is not limited to spoken or written language. Any communicative event can—and no doubt will—have a connotative level, whether everyone is aware of it or not. Eye contact during conversation can be seen as an observable fact; as connotative meaning, it may be responded to positively (as in most Western cultures, where it is read as a sign of interest, integrity, assertiveness) or negatively (as in many American Indian tribes, where it is read as insolence, mistrust, intrusion). A hand held up, palm forward, may be a cheerful greeting in one culture and an obscene gesture in another. Not only may the meaning be different, but the associated emotions and responses may be sharply opposed.

THE CONNOTATIVE MOOSE NOSE Sometimes an entire situation carries such a strong set of understood meanings (especially in a high context setting) that the mere presence of someone will come to have a connotative function, especially if the person is a visitor who does not fully share the context. One snowy December evening I had enjoyed a sweat lodge ceremony with some Indian friends on a small reservation in the Pacific Northwest. As we left the sweat lodge behind, someone suggested we visit an old man who enjoyed singing the old traditional songs. A new drum had been consecrated, and we would surely be welcome to join in the singing. I was told not to worry about not knowing the songs; I would catch on to them easily.

We received a warm welcome at the old man's small frame house, and almost immediately the group fell into sharply defined traditional activities: A middle-aged woman gathered the children together on the far side of the room and led them in beadwork; the men and older boys sat in a circle around the drum, had a cigarette and told a few jokes, then began singing; the old man's wife stayed by the stove and kept everyone in the room supplied with coffee.

Each singer held a drumstick; the group sat around the drum, drumming and singing simultaneously. The old man sang the first phrase of a song, which provided everyone with the tempo, the tune, and the words or vocables, then everyone joined in on the next phrase, singing in a strong falsetto. I was able to pick up the tunes easily enough, but I could not sing as high as the others, so I settled on an octave below. As the singing went on, the old man was becoming visibly more and more amused, although I couldn't tell whether he was smiling because I was joining in with them or laughing because I could not sing in falsetto tones. I was sure that I was doing all right, in any case, because I was keeping to the tunes faithfully.

The old man called for a break, and, after mopping the perspiration off his face (partly to hide some further chuckling), he said, "You know, this reminds me of the time a few years ago when one of our girls here got married to a guy from another tribe from down south on the coast somewhere. They got married up here, you know, and they decided to go up to Canada moose-hunting for their honeymoon. So anyway the girl's father decided to go along, too, and he really liked moose hunting, see. So they went on up there and they were camped out up there in Canada someplace, and they started in hunting for moose. Well, after about two or three days, they caught sight of a real big moose, a bull you know, with a real big rack on him. So the son-in-law takes a careful sight on him and lets him have it. Got him on one shot. Fell flat right there. And before the kid knew what was going on, the old man runs right up to the moose and starts kicking it in the nose. As hard as he could just kicking that moose's nose. And the kid runs up to him and says, 'Hey Dad, what are you doing that for?' "

General heavy laughter in the room indicated that we had reached the end of a funny story, but I sat puzzled. "I guess maybe you didn't understand that joke," the old man offered, trying to stop laughing. "Absolutely right," I said. "Well, it's like this. The kid was from another tribe, see, where they didn't know about eating moose nose. You have to soften it up—tenderize it, I guess you'd say—while the moose still has some blood in his head. You have to bash it with a rock, or kick it, or something, and it gets all swollen up. Then you cut it off, and boy it's a real delicacy. But, see, this kid didn't know all that. So all he could say was something dumb like, 'What are you doing *that* for?' " More laughter from the old man, echoed by everyone in the room.

"Oh, I guess I see, then," I said cautiously. "It's a joke about how dumb outsiders are, right? And here I am an outsider, too, right?" "It's nothing personal, see," he said, "but it's just that outsiders don't know what they need to know. It's not their fault. You might even like them—like that kid that married our girl in that joke. But there are just some things you don't know." Trying to be objective, I asked if my singing had been off. The place collapsed in laughter. What remained unanswered was the question of *how* I'd been off: Was it that bad to sing an octave below everyone else? And what was the relation of the moose nose story to singing; that is, why did the old man choose that particular story as the epitome of what was happening?

For a while I had no answer to these puzzles of meaning. Clearly, the members of that group had understood and had enjoyed something keenly based on their response to the meaning of the story as it was made congruent to the meaning of the immediate situation. But just as clearly, the totality of meaning did not reside denotatively in the story or in the situation, for I had been there and had heard it, and had not understood. Some weeks later, when I shared the anecdote with some Native American friends in another town, they doubled up with laughter, and one remarked, "Boy, they really put one over on you, didn't they?" And to my baffled silence he added, "Nobody over there eats moose nose!"

At this point I was now sure that I had been originally told a story about how "dumb" outsiders are, one that was so ludicrous that it could be told to an outsider who would then be so naive as to think people really ate moose nose and who actually would believe that he had been able to understand the nature of the joke. In recognizing myself as a parallel to the young man from another tribe, and by articulating it there in front of insiders, I had become an embodiment of outsider naiveté, made the more funny by the fact that I had swallowed the explanation of the joke along with the joke. In this hypothesis I was partially correct.

Subsequently, I found out that among the tribes on that reservation there were long-standing differences in food customs, and that moose nose was one of the local ways to tell tribal differences: Some tribes had eaten moose nose, some had not. Those who did felt that those who did not were somewhat backward; those who did not felt that anyone who would must be warped. The group I had been singing with had been eaters of moose nose in the past; my friends who had later explained the joke to me were from the abstainer tribes. Still further, I found that in the tribe who had been my hosts at singing, moose nose had been primarily a food of women. Now what emerged was the possibility of a double joke: It was as funny that the *father*-in-law so avidly ran up and began preparing the moose nose for eating as it was that the young man had no idea what was happening. The old man in the joke had been playing a joke on his son-in-law, who had not understood. But still, what had all this to do with singing?

The last piece of connotative evidence came into place about four years after the original situation. I was retelling the anecdote to some old women from that same reservation as we spoke of singing styles. I asked what would have been so funny about my singing an octave lower than the other men. They considered this for a few minutes, then said, "Show us how it went; we'll sing, and you join in." As we sang they suddenly began laughing, and one stopped to say, "Oh my, you were making them sound like women!"

In the customary singing styles of some of these tribes, the women sing an octave above the men. Apparently as I had been singing with the men, they had suddenly realized that they were an octave above me and felt very odd about singing the "women's" part. The moose nose joke not only broke the tension by allowing the outsider to be singled out as the unwitting cause of the dilemma, but it also provided an extremely accurate depiction of the entire episode: The naive outsider takes a masculine role (shooting the moose, singing in a lower register) and the knowledgeable insiders are put in the role of women (preparing the moose nose, singing in a higher register). The laughter, we may suspect, was directed at themselves as much as toward me, which makes the joke a complicated one indeed. Yet, for all its complications, it was immediately understandable to members of the in-group, for whom all these strands were already parts of a total context of custom, attitude, food lore, and esoteric contrast.

Sharing these ideas through multifaceted traditions of the folk group (in this case tribal) constitutes a dynamic reservoir of potential meaning that can be brought forth and focused by someone skilled in those traditions. We justly call this kind of meaning connotative, for it resides not in the item or situation or in the denotation of the words, but in the feelings people have about the items, situations, and words. Since these attitudes are usually culture-specific, the deepest meanings seldom arise automatically from the text but need to be extrapolated from ethnographic evidence as well as from further discussion with the tradition-bearers themselves.

What my Indian friends understood and relished in a few moments took me over four years to understand. Yet it was only one joke. In order for us to perceive the enormity of the folklorist's task, we need to multiply this incident (theoretically) by all the texts, genres, and situations possible within that folk group.

The possibilities for connotative richness are enormous in folk groups, where closely associated members are in constant touch with each other, sharing continual references, attitudes, and information. Among such groups the most basic statement or performance may elicit a tremendous depth of meaning. As a Papago singer remarked to Ruth Underhill, "The song is very short because we understand so much."

## ◤ INTENTIONAL CONNOTATION: IMAGERY
While some kinds of connotative events may take place inadvertently, as in the last example, we also have abundant evidence that the evocative powers of connotation are commonly used consciously by succeeding generations of tradition-bearers. The following ballad circulates in oral tradition in many parts of the English-speaking world; it seems to have had its origins in England in the Middle Ages, at least as far as its ballad formation goes (it is based on a far older apocryphal story, which no doubt circulated in oral tradition long before anyone made it into a song). Denotatively, the song tells a very simple story about a brief episode in the lives of Joseph, Mary, and Jesus; it is the moment at which Joseph discovers that Mary is expecting a child. Although Joseph is at first doubtful about his wife's announcement, the unborn Jesus speaks miraculously from his mother's womb to certify her story.

THE OXYMORONIC CHERRY We notice that the ballad is phrased, however, in one of the stereotyped situation comedies of the Middle Ages: An old man married to a young beautiful woman discovers by chance that his wife is pregnant and, doubting that the child can be his own, raises trouble about it. Thus, as we listen to the song, we are confronted with an odd juxtaposition between the standard religious seriousness of the moment from a theological point of view and the potential comic misunderstanding inherent in the situation from a medieval literary point of view.

> 1. *Joseph was an old man, an old man was he;*
> *He married pretty Mary, the Queen of Galilee.*
> *He married pretty Mary, the Queen of Galilee.*
>
> 2. *While they were out walking, said Mary so mild,*
> *"Go gather me some cherries, for I am with child.*
> *Go gather me some cherries, for I am with child."*

3. *Then Joseph got angry, so angry grew he:*
   *"Let the father of your baby get your cherries for thee.*
   *Let the father of your baby get your cherries for thee."*

4. *Then out spoke little Jesus, so loudly spoke he:*
   *"Bow down low to my mother, bow down oh cherry-*
   *   tree.*
   *Bow down low to my mother, bow down oh cherry-*
   *   tree."*

5. *Then the cherry tree bowed low down, so low to the*
   *   ground,*
   *And Mary gathered cherries while Joseph stood around.*
   *And Mary gathered cherries while Joseph stood around.*

6. *Then Joseph, he took Mary all on his right knee,*
   *Saying, "Tell me, little baby, when your birthday*
   *   it'll be."*
   *Saying, "Tell me, little baby, when your birthday*
   *   it'll be."*

7. *"On the sixth day of January my birthday it'll be,*
   *And all the stars in heaven will twinkle with glee.*
   *And all the stars in heaven will twinkle with glee."*

Folklorists will notice almost immediately that part of the action in this ballad turns on a well-known item in folk medicine: Pregnant women crave certain foods that they must often ask their husbands to provide for them. Yet, curiously enough, the particular food craved in this ballad is a fruit, and the craving for fruits in folklore seems widely connected to the idea of sex and self-indulgence (examples of this attitude are to be found ranging from the widespread folk notion that it was an apple that was eaten in the Garden of Eden to the famous and sensuous banquet scene in the movie *Tom Jones*). Moreover, it is interesting to speculate why the cherry, over other possible fruits, has been maintained as the key object of craving in this ballad. Proving that the cherry was commonly used in the Middle Ages as a metaphor or symbol for virginity (as it has been in more recent years) may be impossible; but it is also impossible to ignore the tenacity of this one fruit in this particular ballad, knowing the constant variations that can occur in orally transmitted poetry. We are justified, for this reason, in suspecting that the cherry has something to do with the idea of the song as it has been passed along in tradition. What might explain this, and how can we account for the function of the cherry?

First of all, we note Joseph's surprise when he learns of his wife's pregnancy through her craving for fruit. He assumes he is not the father, and he thus responds to her request with sarcasm: "Let the father of your baby get your cherries for thee." If we work from the premise that the reference to cherries carries an implication of virginity, we see an even greater irony in the scene, for of all foods a young pregnant wife could crave, certainly the symbolic virginal fruit would be the least likely under the circumstances. In this light, of course, Joseph's reference to the "father of your baby" becomes doubly rich, for the audience realizes that the father of Mary's baby is God; the listener is therefore prepared for some sign from God to that effect. When the unborn Jesus speaks from the womb (and of course in the medieval view Jesus, God, and the Holy Spirit are one), not only is Joseph's sarcasm carried out on a serious level (father = son), but if cherry = virginity, there is implied a direct relationship between the father, the unborn Jesus, and Mary's virginity.

At this point it should occur to us that according to the Christian view Mary is both pregnant and a virgin: Both the pregnancy and the virginity are central to medieval Christian theology. When Joseph is described as so dumbfounded that he can only stand around while his wife gathers cherries from the bent tree, we can imagine that his astonishment derives as much from the contemplation of a miraculous virgin birth as it does from the miraculous movement of the tree. It seems to me that no other fruit is available in English folklore that could so powerfully stand for both aspects of Mary's situation, and that may be precisely why the cherry has remained central to this ballad.

The potentially funny cliché of the *senex amans*, the old man married to the beautiful woman, is used as an ironic setting for Joseph's enlightenment. We, the audience, know something about the potential outcome of the story because we recognize the names of the participants. If their names were Jim and Maizie, for example, we would have no grounds upon which to understand the miraculous behavior of the unborn child and the tree. The medieval setting of the garden in which fruit trees grow is of course a well-known parallel to the Garden of Eden, and it reflects the common medieval notion that the earliest of gardens was itself a scene of an essentially sensuous event. Thus, even in Chaucer's working of this motif, the Merchant's Tale, where Old Man January and young May stroll through a walled garden that encloses a pear tree (that in turn conceals a lover), there is the same possible double level; even though the garden is the scene of sexual activity, the event itself causes enlightenment as the old husband regains his sight through the actions of a man in the tree. This juggling of physical and spiritual imagery is well known in medieval European poetry, and we see the same kinds of juxtapositions running through this ballad. Certainly, such complex uses of sexual and spiritual connotation cannot be explained away by chance or coincidence. Rather, they testify to an ongoing concern for the evocative properties of shared language. Making such an observation does not require us to believe that every ballad singer who has ever sung this song understood the delicate relationships; on the other hand, enough primary singers of the ballad must have had some strong notion of the real meaning of the song, or there could not have been such a faithful retention of the central connotative elements.

CONNOTATIVE WORD PLAY: THE DOUBLE-ENTENDRE CHERRY   In the summer of 1952, I was invited along with some friends to a southern mountain family picnic held in Grassy Branch, North Carolina. In addition to a fine, old-fashioned dinner on the grounds, there was a good deal of singing: old, traditional songs people had learned from their grandparents, hymns old and new, and a few popular "country" songs from the radio. I was particularly struck by a song I had heard hundreds of times before, however. "The Riddle Song," a bit too sweet for my taste, was being widely sung on the radio by Burl Ives and other professional singers, but it was sung on this occasion in Grassy Branch in such a distinctive way that it popped into another focus for me. A young couple newly engaged to be married sang the song as a duet, with much nudging of each other to the accompaniment of delighted smiles and knowing looks from their relatives in the audience. I had never heard it sung in this manner before, and I have never encountered it in this fashion since. It would be attractive to suppose that they were carrying on an old tradition that maintained some striking connotations inherent in the song; on the other hand, perhaps their performance was their own attempt to insinuate their own situation into the obvious connotations of the song for local effect. In either case, the resultant song was far more meaningful than the sum of its denotative parts:

> *She: I gave my love a cherry that had no stone;*
> *He: I gave my love a chicken that had no bone;*
> *She: I gave my love a ring that had no end;*
> *He: I gave my love a baby with no cryin'.*
>
> *He: How can there be a cherry without a stone?*
> *She: How can there be a chicken without a bone?*

He:   *How can there be a ring without an end?*
She:  *How can there be a baby with no cryin'?*

She:  *A cherry when it's bloomin' has no stone;*
He:   *A chicken in the egg has no bone;*
She:  *A ring when it's rollin' has no end;*
He:   *A baby when it's makin' has no cryin'.*

We can assume that the song has existed for a long time on both sides of the Atlantic not entirely innocent of implications of pregnancy; Sharp, for example, notes that a Mr. Thomas's version had for the last line: "When the baby's in the belly, there's no cry within." Thus, even though the denotative message of this song seems quite innocent, we are justified in looking further to see if there are not, on the connotative level, other possibilities that may add to the total meaning. We see, of course, the cherry, with its possible connotation of virginity; there is the egg, a widely used fertility symbol; the ring is often found as symbolic of sex, fertility, and, of course, marriage. In addition, many other versions of the song include other words and refrains that are themselves suggestive of sexual processes and anatomical parts; the periwinkle, mentioned in some versions, has been used both as an aphrodisiac and as a low colloquialism for the vagina. It is, of course, impossible to say that all these possibilities have been present in the minds of all the singers of this ballad; on the other hand, given the common understanding of these terms in colloquial language and folk speech, given that they all seem to relate somehow to sex and marriage, it would be rash to dismiss them as a coincidental cluster. And who, knowing the courting customs of the rural Old World and of the American frontier, would suggest that the sequence cherry (virginity), egg (pregnancy), ring (marriage), and baby is an accidental combination? We should note that if indeed cherry here is meant to connote virginity, it is an appropriate gift for the woman in the song to give; similarly, if the egg refers to impregnation, it is an appropriate gift for the man to give; if the ring refers on the physical level to a metaphorical or anatomical view of sexuality, or of the inception of a family circle, certainly it makes a fitting gift for the woman to give the man as a physical counterpart of the wedding ring; with the reference to the baby in the final line, of course, both levels of the song come neatly together.

Yet, on the surface level of the song, the questions and answers are phrased in such a way as to resemble riddles, so that the person answering uses an innocent word that satisfies the demands of propriety and yet at the same time implies the meaning of the song. It is not accidental that such riddles can be humorous, for of course one of their literary functions is to bring up at least two possibilities at once in the minds of the audience, yet to solve the dilemma with an answer that everyone recognizes but does not outrage public sensibilities.

The connotations discussed thus far have been seen as the workings of shared associations about a word or an image by people in a close group. In the case of the moose nose incident, a particular event gave rise to the use of a connotative joke in which the meanings shared by the close group about moose nose were focused in such a way that the story had a rich meaning for them (and almost no meaning at all for the hapless outsider who had unwittingly triggered the episode). At the same time, had the old man simply said "moose nose," the meaning might not have been so clear to the insiders. So in addition to our understanding that colors like red and fruits like the cherry may have splendid connotative power, we need to recognize that occasion and structure will also function as determiners of appropriate meaning.

## ◢ CONNOTATIVE STRUCTURE A good

part of the connotative meaning in "The Riddle Song" derives from structural position. The riddles are juxtaposed and given meaning by being parts of a dialogue; by themselves they would mean little, while in combination they reflect meaning on each other. Connotative structure can be found on even more complex levels: Whole parts of long narratives may have the same reflecting capacity, and entire tales in a cycle may reflect on other entire tales (as when a Native American Coyote tale is told, for it assumes the audience has heard all the others as well). In *The Red Swan*, John Bierhorst suggests that many Native American myths are double, that is, they tell the same story or incident twice, the second telling adding a connotative dimension to the narrative that provides a depth of meaning it did not have before.

DOUBLE STRUCTURE IN MYTH   Bierhorst sees the Arapaho tale "Raw Gums and White Owl Woman" as one of these double myths: A monster baby born with teeth sneaks out of the lodge at night to eat old chiefs, and later in the story as a young man he saves his people by killing the spirit of winter. In Bierhorst's view, these are complementary retellings of the same story, providing the listener with two enactments of the same struggle: the overpowering of older, deadly forces by youthful energy, first in frightful physical fashion by using the mouth for chewing human flesh, second by using the mouth in a battle of wits with White Owl Woman. There is a clear distinction between the earlier, fierce oral urge by the baby to *consume* human flesh (an analogy to breast feeding?) and the later, socialized urge to save the people from winter by *speaking* judicious answers to culturally important riddles. Looking at the story sequentially, there is indeed a development from infantile to adult processes; but looking at both halves simultaneously there is a further impact: a deep and complex enactment of the normalcy of violence, qualified by context. For the youth who saves his people from winter in the second part does so by bashing out White Owl Woman's brains after she had treated him with food and hospitality. Is there a difference in the quality of the killings? Only by bringing both halves of the story together, reflecting on each other, can we have the "proper" cultural meaning of the story—a meaning that, although we as outsiders may never fully comprehend it, clearly resides not in praise of actual bloodshed but in a kind of mythic metaphor, a sacred equation perhaps, about youth and the production of food. The baby had consumed fellow human beings; the youth he grows into brings about the season of vegetation by vanquishing the killing effects of winter. Like so many myths, this one says more in its simultaneous enactment than the commentator can say in summary, and more than the structure will reveal by itself. Probably this is one key to the function and survival of myth.

Be that as it may, I want to suggest that this double structure is a prominent feature of Northwest Indian myths and that our appreciation of that fact can help us to derive even fuller meaning from the grand myth achievements of the American Indian. Here I would like to focus on a particular matter that goes beyond structure: the folkloric process in which structure is but one mechanism for transmitting connotative meaning. In the case of these double myths, for example, I think it is of the utmost importance to recognize that the story would seldom have had an unknowing, naive audience. Not only would the typical listener have heard the particular tale many times, perhaps often through his own narration of it, but the listener would also have been familiar with the same formulas, attitudes, motifs, numbers, sequences, colors, characters, and other expressive narrative features from innumerable other tales. Thus, while the modern reader of such a myth might register it as a linear story, the native auditor would have been able to apply "the second half" to the first half while the story was being told, and thus the feeling would have been a simultaneous perception of complementary qualities rather than a string of events. The result is quite similar to the perception of metaphor therefore: Two (or more) concepts are juxtaposed in such a way as to create a mutual reflection and enrichment of meaning that is fuller than the single concepts taken separately. One result of perceiving a metaphor is the creation of an emotional response or an evaluation of the quality of things as suggested by the reflection.

THE SUN MYTH: STRUCTURAL CONNOTATIONS OF MORALITY  In his presidential address to the American Folklore Society in November 1974, Dell Hymes presented a scholarly landmark: the rephrasing of a Native American myth in a way that restored as much as possible the mode and style of presentation lost when an oral narrative is presented in written prose. The myth Hymes used is a Kathlamet Chinook text narrated to Franz Boas in the 1890s by Charles Cultee, one of three surviving Kathlamets at that time. The myth is a very powerful one, not the least for its spare style and stark imagery. It concerns the destruction of a people through the selfishness of a chief whose fascination for a bright object clouds his sense of responsibility to his people. Hymes is convinced that for Cultee the story must have been a chillingly real re-enactment of the demise of his own tribe—perhaps through their own ruinous fascination with the bright and powerful things of the new world around them. That topic—the destruction of a people because of someone's attachment to a bright and overwhelming object—has been of course a matter of universal interest in Western literature from the story of Pandora's box to the abduction of Helen of Troy to the theft of the dragon's treasure in *Beowulf* to the preoccupation with money and power in modern literature.

On the mythic level, however, one wants to find out what the internal meaning of this narrative might have been, aside from modern literary perceptions. Can we see in the myth some dynamic reference to forces or attitudes that had sacred power for the Kathlamets in earlier times, long before the whites brought about a new physical reality, a sudden, terrible congruency between myth and daily life? Approaching the narrative as a double myth may afford some clues, although the analysis here is un-informed by any extensive ethnographic data on the Kathlamets. These speculations are thus subject to correction; they are based primarily on suggestions drawn from the text itself, using the hypothesis that the two parts may represent equivalents rather than (or at least in addition to) a linear episodic progression.

The broad outline of the story may be summarized quite simply: A chief leaves his home, arrives at another place, and stays. Later, he leaves that place and returns to his home. Hymes divides the story into two parts, which may be recounted as follows:

1.
   a. A chief is so fascinated by the sun that he wishes to travel to look for it.
   b. His wife remonstrates with him, scoffing at the idea.
   c. Nonetheless, he is determined to go, and, in spite of her reservations, she equips him for the journey.
   d. He travels for ten months, using up as many moccasins and leggings.
   e. He reaches a large house.
   f. Inside, a prepubescent girl is surrounded by tremendous wealth that is to be given away when she is mature enough to be married. Great detail about the many items is provided.
   g. He "takes" her, and settles down there to live.
   h. Among the things in the house is a shining object that he likes.
   i. An old woman (the Sun) daily brings them gifts.

2.
   a. The man gets homesick, and the old woman notices he wants to return home.
   b. She tries to offer him proper items for the trip.
   c. Nonetheless, he is determined to have that shining thing, and after showing him everything else the old woman finally hangs it on him and gives him a stone ax, making it clear that it is his own responsibility.
   d. He travels for an undetermined time.
   e. He reaches his home.
   f. There, as he approaches his uncles' towns, the stone ax begins to shake, and he utterly destroys the five towns and their inhabitants, the last one his own village. Great detail is provided, with fivefold repetition.
   g. He tries repeatedly to rid himself of the ax, to no avail.
   h. The old woman appears, takes the shining thing from him, and leaves.
   i. Alone, he builds a house, a small house.

Hymes suggests the following gross structure:

*Part 1:* Desires (a, b, c)
         Travels (d, e)

THE DYNAMICS OF FOLKLORE

Discovers (f, g)
Stays (h, i)

*Part 2:* Desires (a, b, c)
Travels (d, e)
Discovers (f, g)
Stays (h, i)

A careful reading shows that these are not simply sets of parallel structural elements, they are just about homologous. For example, both parts begin with the man at home thinking of going away. In both, a shining thing is the prominent object of his attention. In both, women represent the forces of cultural reason: In Part 1 the chief should have been attentive to family and tribal needs, not to a selfish curiosity; in Part 2, he should be sensible enough to take the proper items (skins, blankets, armor) offered him, not the shining object that the old lady (the Sun) obviously does not want to part with. Both parts end with the man settling in a house.

However, the second part does bring in some differences that indicate that something qualitative is being developed or suggested. In the section referred to by Hymes as "Discovers," Part 1 shows the man surrounded by goods that he obtains by creating a family relationship (marriage), while Part 2 shows him destroying his own goods and family; in the section labeled "Stays," he is given gifts in Part 1, has the shining thing taken away in Part 2; in that same section he settles in a large, wealthy house in Part 1, in a small and obviously poor house in Part 2.

| | *Desires* | *Travels* | *Discovers* | *Stays* |
|---|---|---|---|---|
| 1. | Sun | ten months | acquires goods, takes girl | marries, inhabits large house |
| 2. | "Shining Thing" | presumably same distance, but travel is compact in description | destroys towns, kills relatives | is alone, builds small house |

The contrast between the two houses is perhaps the easiest to deal with because of the obvious irony. A chief has devastated his own life and those of his people through selfishness; the small house at the end is a fine image for the loss he has brought about. Especially since his selfishness was focused on the goods in Sun's opulent house—in particular on the shining object—the small house he builds for himself at the end seems a fitting moral comment. The image would have suggested a considerable contrast for the Chinookan people, in whose society the chief would normally have enjoyed a large house, complete with extended family, surrounded by the rest of the village. So the small house not only provides the stasis necessary to the end of the story, but it epitomizes the condition of a man brought low by his own willfulness.

The section labeled "Discovers" is probably, on both levels, the center of mythic meaning in this story. In both Parts 1 and 2, this section is the richest in detail and repetition, and it seems to be the most important aspect of the story. But can the amassing of goods on one level be equated with the destruction of relatives and their towns on the other? I think so. Hearing the two levels together, one is struck by the idea that what the chief does in his personal selfishness is in fact destructive to family, fortune, and the whole social fabric, and this is consistent with our sense that the chief has abandoned social obligations by leaving his family and tribe in the first place.

In taking the young girl, he has apparently appropriated to himself the many items that should have been given out to others at the time of her maturation. He has thus intervened in the normal social order of delicate gift relationships. This certainly puts his earlier search for the sun in sharper focus by confirming in specific terms his great selfishness: first the dereliction of cultural duty, now personal acquisitiveness outside the normal means of distribution—in fact, even in direct denial of custom. Moving from this stage to his almost hypnotic attraction to the shining thing (which is never precisely named) is only a matter of still sharper focus. It is important, I think, that this attraction is mentioned right at the end of Part 1 and the destructive consequences of it are followed up in Part 2. The shining thing seems to be thus the link between the two levels. It is the epitome of his lust for treasure in Part 1 and the driving force behind his killing of relatives in Part 2. For this reason I think the equation is justified. There is also the possibility that taking a prepubescent girl to wife is another factor in the total sense of social deterioration, but I have no direct ethnographic evidence of this. We do know that among the Clackamas Chinook the highest bride prices were paid for the girls who were at puberty. This may bring in another possibility for a moral or social flaw: Why does the chief not offer a payment for the bride—is he in the wrong in this? Why does he marry a prepubescent girl? Clearly for her goods. Since the Chinook were acquisitive people, I think we can assume that amassing a fortune is not in and of itself bad, but the methods and propriety of obtaining goods were of extreme importance, and that is the connotative focus here. I think that even in the absence of fuller data, we can infer that something is totally amiss in his trip to begin with, in his taking the girl, in his selfishness generally. And the meaning of equating these defects with his willful destruction of relatives in Part 2 is that such actions, undertaken by a chief, *will* destroy the society utterly. The equations, then, suggested by the chart above, might be stated as follows:

1. Desiring the sun is equivalent to wanting an object that is not proper for you to have.
2. Arduous travel toward such a selfish goal is the surest way to come directly into conflict with your family.
3. Acquiring goods under these conditions is destructive to the society.
4. Being married improperly, even though in prosperity, is really personal, moral, cultural impoverishment.

But, as I observed earlier, merely stating these meanings is far from approaching the real power of the myth. One would have the same sense of inadequacy in hearing *King Lear* summarized with the statement: "Things aren't always what they seem." It is of course the dramatic interplay and connotation made possible by the mutual reverberations between levels that provides the actual power of the myth.

TRIPLE LAYERING   To make it clear that the structural metaphors discussed here are not simply unconscious appearances of a widespread binary system, I would like to show a more complicated example of the phenomenon, in hopes both of indicating that the concept of doubling may be in some cases not accurate enough, and of demonstrating that the layering of meaning is a part of the narrative art, a conscious way of producing meaning through connotation. In his essay "The Wife Who Goes Out Like a Man, Comes Back as a Hero," Jarold Ramsey reprints with commentary a striking Coos tale collected by Harry Hull St. Clair in 1903 from Jim Buchanan, "The Revenge Against the Sky People."

What I will call Part 1 deals with the murder of a man by someone from the sky. Part 2 deals with the man's younger brother getting revenge. Specifically, the incidents in Part 1 are repeated almost identically in Part 2 twice, as I shall show. First a bare-bones summary of the story:

*Part 1:* A canoe maker is working one day when a stranger comes along and asks what he does with his canoes when they are finished. Without looking up (an incredibly naive or stupid omission, considering the usual wariness toward strangers), the canoe maker answers that he sells them. The stranger hits him on the neck, beheads him, and makes off with his head. The villagers discover the body, and decide from the actions of the man's dog that the murderer went up in the sky. The younger brother pursues, on a chain of arrows.

*Part 2:* The younger brother is directed to the murderer's wife, whom he finds digging fern roots. He asks her detailed questions on how she relates to her husband, how she prepares the roots, and so on. Without question, she answers him. He kills her, skins her, and, wearing her skin, masquerades as the murderer's wife when the husband comes to pick her up.

At the murderer's home people are dancing "for the head" of the canoe maker, which is fastened to the ceiling. Everyone in the household goes about doing normal chores, including the "wife," who is nearly found out a number of times. In this section the disguised intruder is referred to throughout as *she,* forcing us to adopt the view of the onlooker within the story. As "she" climbs to an upper level in the house, a young boy, the murderer's brother, says, "My sister-in-law looks like a man." He is hushed by his grandmother, who tells him that "the women from there look just like men! You must keep quiet!" No one heeds the boy's words. Under "her" pillow the "wife" has hidden a knife. After walking about outside, during which time she cuts holes in all but one of the tribe's canoes, "she" goes to bed with "her" husband and late at night "she" beheads him, escaping with his head and that of "her" murdered brother. The body is discovered and the people of the village give chase, but their canoes sink; "she" escapes in the one sound canoe.

*Epilogue:* The younger brother returns home, his brother's head is restored to its body, and the older brother recovers. These people are said to be the woodpeckers because of the blood on the neck. The story ends: "You shall be nothing. You shall be a woodpecker. The last people shall see you."

Obviously the epilogue functions the way many such tags do: not so much to give a point to the story as to bring the story up to historical times, to the era of present human beings, the last people. We would be hasty, then, to conclude that this story tells how the woodpecker got its red head. The meaning lies rather in the connotations of the main body of the story. Note the parallels:

*Part 1*

    a. A man is doing normal, traditional things.

    b. A stranger intrudes, asks a question.

    c. A naive or unquestioning response is given.

    d. The man is killed by the stranger (beheaded).

    e. The body is discovered by the family.

    f. The murderer is pursued.

*Part 2*

    a. 1) A woman is doing normal, traditional things.

       2) A stranger intrudes, asks questions.

       3) A naive, unquestioning response is given.

       4) The woman is killed by the stranger (skinned).

       5) The body (that is, the skin) is seen by the family but not recognized as dead.

       6) [Discovery and pursuit expanded on in b.]

    b. 1) A man (husband) is doing normal things in his home.

       2) A stranger ("wife") intrudes in disguise.

       3) The family naively leaves the matter unquestioned, even though the "wife" makes some errors and even though "she" is discovered by the young brother-in-law.

       4) The man is killed by the stranger (beheaded).

       5) The body is discovered by the family.

       6) The murderer is pursued.

*Epilogue*

    a. The first murdered man is revived.

    b. The world is brought to its current status.

Here it seems clear that Part 2 is fitting as the revenge for Part 1, for it is phrased in almost identical terms. But it is interesting that Part 2a, obviously a mechanical way of setting up the revenge, is phrased in almost the same ideational sequence, too. It seems to me that this argues rather strongly that the narrators used a particular style that insured the congruency of parts in a myth.

Where is the equation in this one? I think the inevitabilty of revenge itself is the answer. The revenge is shaped properly in exactly the same terms as the original murder, and those same terms are further noted even in the setup for revenge, except that the violence is doubled. This is a concept like "an eye for an eye" escalated by connotation to a more dramatic level. Naiveté about strangers, improper precautions against intruders, paranoia about others, are all dynamically enacted. Further return revenge (and thus an imbalanced story) is thwarted by the inability of the Sky People to pursue the victorious younger brother: The last we hear of them is: "They could not follow him."

Conclusions and generalizations on the basis of such material must necessarily remain guarded and tentative. Here are only two tales out of many thousands, only one tale from two different tribes out of hundreds in the Northwest. Nonetheless, certain particular "architectural" details are prominent in these stories, and a check of numerous other myths indicates to me that these details, as features of dramatic meaning, are quite common in the narratives of the Northwest tribes. Bierhorst has written (in private correspondence) that he feels the double structure may be a regular feature of American Indian narratives generally, unnoticed by scholars because the halves may not be obviously congruent (in length or meaning) to outsiders.

In any case, the feature seems widespread, and it may be—as I have suggested—far more complicated than mere doubling would suggest. Whether there are two or more simultaneous levels of meaning, their function seems to be a direct outcome of ongoing oral tradition, not a matter of prodigious memory feats. The listener, steeped in continual myth recitals using the same or similar features, having heard particular myths numerous times previously, would have been able to apply several possibilities of meaning to each part of a myth. Such devices as were catalogued by Melville Jacobs and others (number, time of day, sequence, personalities) are the particularizing items that focus the listener's attention on meaningful clusters within the tale in contradistinction to all other possible meanings for the action.


Without ethnographic evidence of the fullest sort (so we can approximate the cultural meanings of these items on the idea, word, and phrase levels and hence the people's likely response to them), without an appreciation of the mechanics of oral tradition, the prose narratives left to us by scholars like Boas must remain stark skeletons. We can say, I think, that at least as important as order, sequence, and structural patterning are the inevitable effects of evaluation and qualitative response that occur when two related concepts are brought into each other's sphere of influence in a performance. Most of the real meaning in these myths seems to take shape "between the lines," in the dramatic tension set up between congruent layers of narrative.

This chapter has dealt mainly with connotation in verbal performances, but the inquiry cannot end here. What of textural and structural connotation in other traditional genres and folklore events: Are there connotations in an unpainted New England barn? In a Japanese woman wearing a red dress? In a Slavic woman showing the soles of her feet while dancing? In the number of ingredients in *sushi*? In a wink?

## ✎ BIBLIOGRAPHICAL NOTES

There are now many editions of Chaucer's works available, including some very serviceable translations. The standard single-volume text for university-level work in Chaucer remains F. N. Robinson, *The Works of Geoffrey Chaucer*, 2nd ed., cited in Chapter 5; Chaucer's description of the Wife of Bath appears in lines 445–476 of the General Prologue, on p. 21 of Robinson's edition. Because Chaucer uses a great number of puns, and due to the delicate nature of connotation itself, anyone interested in Chaucer's connotative use of language must always read the material in the Middle English, not in modern English. The Merchant's Tale appears on pp. 115–127.

Munro S. Edmonson, in *Lore: An Introduction to the Science of Folklore and Literature* (New York: Holt, Rinehart and Winston, 1971), feels that folk groups can indeed be defined as those peoples who share culture-specific connotation: "the connotative meanings that constitute a lore grow up in patterns held in common by populations with an intensively shared history" (p. 3). Pointing out that the color yellow implies mourning in Russia, sanctity in Thailand, maturity in Yucatán, and cowardice in England, he suggests that the entire expressive output of any culture can be considered its lore as long as it is phrased in the codes understandable mainly to insiders. Recognizing the culture-specific aspect of connotation, Edmonson says that "it is a basic feature of lore that it is not easily communicated." I would add: "to people outside the close group." Geoffrey N. Leech talks of the importance of connotative power to poetic expression in a very tightly condensed but totally lucid statement, *A Linguistic Guide to English Poetry* (London: Longmans, Green, 1969), p. 41.

Although I present the moose nose story as if I have arrived at a final explanation for it, there are a number of details in the story that beg further study. Alan Dundes has pointed out to me privately that we may expect to find further meaning in the fact that the incident occurs on a honeymoon, suggesting that father-in-law and son-in-law are shown in a competitive relationship. Is there a parallel between the father kicking and severing the bloody nose and the new son-in-law's implied defloration of the bride? Why does the father want to go on the honeymoon in the first place? These and other questions may indeed bring up other levels of connotative meaning for the joke, each of which should be properly accounted for in terms of its relationship to the singing situation that occasioned the joke in the first place. Edward T. Hall's concept of the high context group certainly comes to mind in this discussion as a way of describing the intensity with which unspoken meaning is shared by people who operate in a long-standing cultural system. The remark to Ruth Underhill by the old Papago woman, Maria Chona, may be found in *The Autobiography of a Papago Woman*, ed. Ruth Underhill, Memoirs of the American Anthropological Association, vol. 46, 1936, p. 23. To experience the esoteric richness of what the Papago lady meant, one might consult Donald M. Bahr, *Pima and Papago Ritual Oratory* (San Francisco: Indian Historian Press, 1975); in this work, Papago texts are presented in direct, line-by-line translation. A phrase like "then reached the sun-drinking water" (p. 43) is not shrugged off as a mere awkwardness in translation, but recognized as representing tremendous connotative power for those who know the language and its cultural references.

The story of "The Cherry Tree Carol" derives from the apocryphal Pseudo-Matthew Gospel, Chapter 22. Francis James Child gives a brief account of the story and its background, along with several texts, in *The English and Scottish Popular Ballads*; the "Carol" appears as #54 in the Child collection. The text for the version cited here was sung to me by Daniel Hoffman, near Black Mountain, North Carolina, in the summer of 1952. For an even more complicated usage of double-level sexual riddles, see "Captain Wedderburn's Courtship," Child #46, in which the sexual connotations of the riddles themselves are placed within a structural situation featuring an aggressive courtship and an eventual sexual domination by the male character. See also my article "'Riddles Wisely Expounded,'" *Western Folklore*, 25 (1966), 1–16. For examples of the way in which folk song collector Cecil Sharp felt obliged to translate sexual connotation into something more acceptable to the Victorian taste, see James Reeves, *The Idiom of the People* (New York: Norton, 1958). There are interesting connotative riddles in Old English: see W. S. Mackie, ed. and trans., *The Exeter Book*, part II, Early English Text Society, no. 194 (1934), especially riddles 25, 44, 45, 54, 62.

John Bierhorst's anthology of Native American narratives, *The Red Swan: Myths and Tales of the American Indians* (New York: Farrar, Straus and Giroux, 1976), is an excellent collection containing a number of tales that are almost intimidating to us because of our inability to respond to the connotative suggestions. "Raw Gums and White Owl Woman," an Arapaho myth, appears on pp. 141–148. Bierhorst's comments about double myths appear on pp. 10–14. See also his article "American Indian Verbal Art and the Role of the Literary Critic," *Journal of American Folklore*, 88 (1975), 401–408. The full reference for Dell Hymes's article on the Sun Myth is provided in the bibliographical section of Chapter 5. Jarold W. Ramsey's brilliant article, "The Wife Who Goes Out Like a Man, Comes Back as a Hero: The Art of Two Oregon Narratives," *PMLA* (January 1977), 9–18, is a landmark in scholarship on Native American traditional expression, not the least for the very fact of its appearance in a journal that has seldom if ever paid attention to Native materials.

Other works that relate to this chapter are Benjamin Lee Whorf, *Language*,

*Thought and Reality* (New York: Technology Press, 1956), which deals with cultural connotation as real meaning; Marcel Griaule, *Conversations With Ogotemmêli* (London: Oxford University Press, 1965), which discusses the relation of metaphor to the Dogon culture; James Fernandez, "The Mission of Metaphor in Expressive Culture," *Current Anthropology*, 15 (1974), 119–133, plus discussion, 133–145, in which the author holds that metaphors convert "pronouns" from inchoate references to distinct concepts with large social and cultural identities; Peter Farb, *Word Play: What Happens When People Talk* (1974; reprinted, New York: Bantam, 1975), pp. 99ff., for a discussion of obscene puns.

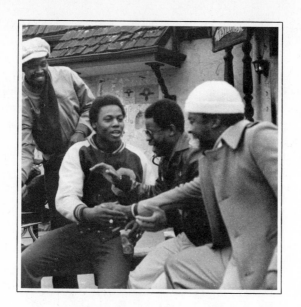

# 7

# FOLKLORE

## AND

## CULTURAL

## WORLDVIEW

**"WORLDVIEW" IS A GENERAL** **WAY OF REFERRING TO THE MANNER IN WHICH A CULTURE SEES AND EXPRESSES ITS** RELATION TO THE WORLD AROUND IT. WHILE EARLIER students of culture were certain that similar conditions would impress any human eye and soul in similar ways in widely separated circumstances, there is now evidence to the contrary; that is, objective reality (as we like to call it) actually varies widely according to the viewer's means of perceiving it. Often those means are affected by cultural and linguistic factors that have been so deeply engrained in the mind that they have actually become a particularized method of thinking. For example, a UCLA research team working on the Hopi reservation found by brainwave analysis that Hopi children use the right hemisphere of the brain for speaking and hearing the Hopi language and the left hemisphere for English. The researchers concluded that there is solid support for the concept that people speaking different languages "may perceive things in basically different ways." Such an observation does not waste time on the comparatively superficial idea that people in different cultures may disagree with those of other backgrounds; likewise, it does not take up the common occurrence of disagreement among people of the same culture. The point here is that each culture has a distinctive way of thinking that it passes on to its young, and this way of thinking is made up of codes so deeply represented in language that they become, as Dorothy Lee pointed out some years ago, the only way in which people of that culture can understand anything.

CULTURE AND MEANING    The same kinds of codes found in language are also found in the way we experience things visually, even under the most objective circumstances. In *Patterns of Discovery*, Norwood Russell Hanson says, "We are set to appreciate the visual aspects of things in certain ways. Elements in our experience do not cluster at random. . . . Seeing is not only the having of a visual experience; it is also the way in which the visual experience is had." In the area of linguistic theory, this idea has been heavily discussed by Benjamin Lee Whorf, Edward Sapir, and more recently by Edward T. Hall. It is fair to point out that the linguistic discussion is far from settled, and so it is not possible for us to use it as a convenient touchstone on which to base observations on such a general notion as cultural worldview. However, taking some leads from that linguistic debate, and drawing our observations from a great variety of traditional expressions, we may still be able to provide ourselves with some important perspectives on the ways in which insiders of a culture view and express the world around them through their folklore. Beyond the world of language, although not totally divorced from it, we find a great variety of human behavior and expression that is culture-specific. In *The Hidden Dimension*, Hall points out that "significant evidence that people brought up in different cultures live in different perceptual worlds is to be found in their manner of orienting themselves in space, how they get around and move from one place to the next."

The researches of Hall, John Adair, Sol Worth, and many others indicate that the members of any given culture perceive reality in terms of culturally provided sets of ideas and premises, and that the world of reality is processed somewhat differently from culture to culture. Not only are the incoming data interpreted according to the pattern of a particular culture, but expressions and communications with others are based on those same perceptions and premises. The human mind keeps producing —in miniature, as it were—the worldview that has formed its conception of reality by creating analogs and parallels on all levels of human expression, from houses to myths. Thus, the artifacts and artistic expressions of any culture will reflect rather strongly the codes that that culture sees as representing the premises of reality.

Since folklore is comprised of those artistic expressions most heavily governed by the tastes of the group, we should be able to find in folk performances a continual tableau or paradigm more revealing of cultural worldview than we might find in the expressions created independently by individuals. Nonetheless, as students of culture have shown, in terms of worldview the distinctions between so-called high culture and folk culture are not as sharp as one would have imagined; apparently, little is exempt from the functionings of cultural worldview. In this chapter we will not be able to take up all the ramifications of this idea, for they need to be followed into philosophy, architecture and art, music and literature on all levels. Here, our focus on folklore will ask us to consider those aspects of cultural worldview that may be seen as transmitted and performed in the same manner as the other folklore we have been discussing.

WORLDVIEW AND TRADITION AMONG EUROPEAN-AMERICANS: THE PRIMAL CONTEXT  As remarked in Chapter 1, every child grows up surrounded by a number of cultural, personal, and physical features that provide its first—and perhaps its most lasting —set of perceptions about the world and its operation. In the earliest years, the child is learning more about its language than it will ever learn again; at this time of life, just as much is learned about cultural context and physical surroundings. For our purposes, we need to know which aspects of this learning are culture-specific. That is, what might be experienced by a child in one culture at this age that would not be universal to all children? We might suspect that every child has some kind of family surrounding it that could be called fairly universal; at the same time, we must recognize that the concept of what a family is and who comprises it varies widely from one culture to another, and therefore the effect upon a newborn child varies considerably as well. We can assume that in most cases around the world the child will have some kind of physical context that may be called a home, some kind of shelter provided by the family. Just as quickly, however, we realize that not all these shelters look alike, and so their visual impact on a newborn child will vary from one place to another. If we were to take a look at several key contextual features for the European-American child, what sorts of physical and cultural surroundings would we find that might be considered formative of cultural worldview?

First of all, for physical surroundings, most babies in America find themselves lying alone in a room made up primarily of straight lines. The child may be placed face up or face down during sleeping, but is almost invariably placed face up during waking hours. Above the child the ceiling provides a large flat surface with corners. Around the child, more close at hand, are the vertical and horizontal slats and corners of the crib. How early the child notices the presence of these straight lines is probably not possible to determine, but it is a moot point, for there are few other things for it to look at. Presumably, the setting simply impresses itself upon the mind as the basic surrounding for the individual. It is also difficult to say at what point a baby begins to be aware of aloneness, but the situation is simply basic for the individual.

Contacts with other human beings at this early age are chiefly with parents, who must seem to come from some invisible place above as they hang their faces over the edge of the crib to investigate the condition of the baby. Often these visits from above are unannounced, but often they come in response to the appeals of the child. Many doctors feel that within a few hours of birth a baby can learn how to make these appeals and make them work in bringing comfort and succor from above. This ability is developed still further when, as a growing child, the individual learns to compete for attention among other siblings or playmates. If language is being learned so quickly at this time of life, it would be strange indeed if these other visual and interactional patterns were not also being absorbed as basic sets of human experience. It does not take a great stretch of the imagination to suppose that these experiences, perceived as normal ways of life, must provide a strong basis for certain ideas found in more sophisticated form among adults in this culture: the idea, for example, that the individual is the basic unit of society, that straight lines and grid patterns constitute a sense of order, that help from invisible sources above can be had if the proper appeal is made, that competition—and especially the use of wit and sharpness in competition —is an indispensable and praiseworthy means to confront the problems of life. These ideas not only provide a foundation for action, but as the individual grows older and has children they become almost basic philosophical necessities: for example, the insistence that "the baby should have its own room" and the later encouragement of the child in competitive endeavors that are thought to "build character." As we will see more fully in this chapter, these ideas also become ways of judging other people who act differently: Consider the opinion widespread among many European-Americans that people who do not provide separate bedrooms for each member of the family are overcrowded, underprivileged, immodest, or even backward.

In addition to physical surroundings and human interactions that may be said to have their foundations in cultural attitudes, the young child is also bombarded with a number of oral traditions. Folktales provide examples of how some younger brother was able to compete with wit and valor and gain the hand of a princess; proverbs teach the merits of culturally appropriate ideas or behaviors; lullabies may help to relax the child for sleep. But what are the deeper messages of some of these traditions? To whom, for example, is the lullaby addressed? Bess Lomax Hawes has shown convincingly that a good many lullabies sung in America are really laments about the mother's fear of losing the child or her husband. We might add that some other lullabies seem to stress the father's continual obligation to support the child ("Papa's gonna buy you a . . ."). Through these subtle means, the child is trained in the underlying "facts of life" that separate people into distinctly individual categories of obligation and hierarchy.

All of these observations are typical of the basic contexts experienced by European-American children. I have not considered the more complex ideas of Freud and Jung here because I want to stress those aspects of the cultural scene that we can see more clearly through artifact and performance. If we were to add those inborn tendencies discussed by psychologists, the subject would become far more complicated.

INDIVIDUAL ORIENTATION   By using the basic patterns learned in the earliest childhood context, a child in any culture learns how to get oriented in space and time. Among European-Americans, the concepts of orientation are simply extensions of the rudimentary straight lines and grid patterns experienced in the nursery. From a child's knowledge of the crib and its placement in the room, it develops an expanded sense of the placement of rooms within a house (along with their specialized functions, which are not to be confused). On a still larger scale, one learns the arrangement of houses and streets in the neighborhood, the pattern of streets and avenues around an entire city; in rural areas one learns about boundary lines, acres, range and section coordinates, and so on. On a smaller scale, one also learns the typical expression of these concepts in material traditions; the similarities between a patchwork quilt and a view of rural America from the air are more than coincidental or superficial, for as cultural designs they are based on the same premises of evenness, symmetry, predominance of straight lines, distinctive measurements. Jagged edges, disparate measurements, asymmetry, and incompleteness are considered intolerable in both areas of expression. There is something deeper than a pun in the statement made by the old New England farmer to his wife: "I'm glad I don't reap the way you sew."

Ways of orienting ourselves in space can be both imaginary and physical. In the wilderness we can use a compass line, and the imaginary course set for us by straight lines projected over a map can bring us safely to our destination (even if in actuality we come out of the woods down the road from where we expected to). In a physical sense, our cities, classrooms, graveyards, and coliseums all use straight lines and symmetry to order the relationships between people by use of regularity in discrete spaces, whether they be large vertical spaces for people storage, arenas for great numbers of people to focus on a single occurrence, or final "places of rest." The effect of these grid patterns on our behavior will be discussed later in this chapter; at this point we need only note that using coordinates such as these, most of us can find our way even in a city we have not visited before. These are assumptions about the use of space that are so ingrained in our culture that it is ludicrous when someone gets lost. Yet getting lost is a common occurrence, especially when one moves from one set of grid assumptions to another. New Yorkers laugh about strangers who don't know the difference between uptown and downtown, and farm people the country over love to make fun of the wandering tourist who can't find his way back to town ("Come to think of it, mister, you can't even get there from here").

The coordinates we recognize in keeping time are very similar to those we use to measure space. Our very interest in arriving on time, our concern about wasting and saving time, our penchant for eating meals at measured intervals, and our continued anxiety about "what time will bring" are strong indications that we see time as a lineal structure, a path along which we move (preferably ahead at all times). The cultural conviction that we move forward on a single line of time has led to a concept of future, the anticipation of future events, and a high evaluation of anything that lies in the future. Conversely, since time is single-stranded, it does us no good to look backward and "cry over spilled milk." Even the study of history is justified by many, not in terms of its inherent value, but because of its capacity to teach us what to avoid in the future. Alan Dundes has followed this topic through a study of the aphorisms, figures of speech, metaphors, proverbs, and customs that saturate American life: our demand for happy endings, our concern with the future of children ("What do you want to be when you grow up?"), our concept of a person's worth in terms of his potential (categories like "rookie of the year" or "most likely to succeed"), membership in clubs like Future Farmers of America and Future Homemakers of America, our interest in the news, the number of shopping days before Christmas, future rewards in heaven, and future payments on credit buying. One might also add matters ranging from the sophisticated to the everyday: financial investments, weather forecasts, and greetings like "What's new?"

The grid patterns of space and time have become so important for European and American culture that they dictate nearly everything we do. It may well be that some of these patterns had their origins in practical necessities or as helpful aids for the interests of the culture or particular people in it. Nonetheless, as Thoreau pointed out, after the discovery of fire there arose the necessity to stand by it; similarly, after the development of the clock there arose the necessity to go by it, and one now finds widespread in Western culture the general assumption that there is such a thing as time, that it moves forward, that it is measurable, and that people must relate the events of their lives to the clock. So deep is this assumption that if clocks are taken away from people anxiety results. On the positive side, using these coordinates, any number of us could agree to meet on the corner of First South and Second West in Salt Lake City, on July 24 of any specified year, and we could all find our way there even though we had never been there before. As we shall see further, however, there are cultures in which such precision of time and space would be meaningless (even ludicrous), and this capability would not necessarily register as a positive advantage.

INDIVIDUAL DEPORTMENT As I have indicated, much of our deportment in life as individuals is based on where we conceive ourselves to stand in time and space, for our concepts of appropriate behavior rest on these perceptions. One thing a grid pattern seating arrangement provides for a group of people in our culture is a behavioral set. The audience is in its place, and the speaker or entertainer is in another place before them. If the members of the audience leave their places, they are considered unruly or unmanageable; through this we can see a direct relationship between the use of space and a sense of appropriate regulated behavior; and we can surmise that the grid pattern seating found so often in school classrooms is as much related to pre-established concepts of behavior as it is to the practical seating of a certain number of people in a limited space. In fact, many teachers who have broken their classrooms up into circles have found that the janitor has come through shortly after to "put the room back in order." Even though the individual may be the basic unit of Amercian society, then, he or she must learn the appropriateness of behavior in time and space with respect to other individuals. Part of this behavior has to do with predictability, and the grid pattern seating arrangement helps to provide a stability of behavior in which whole crowds can be more or less predictably disposed toward appropriate behaviors.

On the personal level, we want younger people to know their place, we expect people to be direct, we hope they are "out front," we admire a young man who knows where he's going, and we advise people to be logical enough to take one thing at a time. We expect a person to show up on time for an appointment, and we expect everyone to be concerned about personal identity. We are encouraged to "do our own thing," and to "look out for number one." We are thus encouraged to extend the competitiveness learned in the nursery, and to measure our worth in progress against or alongside others' progress by besting them or being bested by them. We measure the length of our lives very carefully and we celebrate a long succession of birthdays, some of which have special significance in determining our entrance into larger spheres of activity (twelve years old, eighteen years old, twenty-one years old) that involve development, independence or activity, and later in life (sixty, sixty-five, or seventy), our entry into a condition of "reduced" usefulness to the society, the retirement we have been encouraged to look forward to.

Because we are expected to be direct and forthright, in our conversation we are supposed to move directly to the point and make our lines of reasoning clear, often by using parallels. Eye contact and body gesture are important. If proximity forces us into very close (amorous) distancing, we compensate for it (because of the demands of law and order) by facing the same direction as the other person (on crowded elevators or movie lines or buses, in which body contact can occur as long as people are not looking into each other's eyes). In a personal conversation, the speakers are expected to maintain eye contact most of the time in order to indicate sincerity and attention. In a classroom or church, the speaker makes contact by looking down at the audience; they signify their attention as well as their subordinate role by looking up at the speaker, ordered carefully by their seating. To break up these patterns is to create, for the typical European-American, a sense of disorder in which the predictability of human thought and action is considerably lessened, and in which the responsible individual then is guilty of suspicious behavior.

CULTURAL DEPORTMENT  In addition to general support for these ideas through the various rewards given an individual for excelling in them, there is a broader corporate use of such premises as the basis for society's actions and as an explanation for its history. For example, there seems to have been a generalized high evaluation for the concepts of sub-duing the wilderness, driving back the frontier (that place characterized by disorder), the bringing of law and order to the Wild West, and the establishment of townships and governments all subject to similar rules of time and space. Modern government planning, the establishment of timetables by railroads and airlines, the setting of deadlines for applica-tions to granting agencies, and so on, are similar current applications of these concepts. Within the culture, they are perfectly sensible modes of operation.

Nature, on the other hand, is often dealt with as if it stands quite separate from the created systems. Spring comes and goes when it pleases, not by government schedule. Thus, much of our cultural deportment is aimed at the regularization of nature, the reduction of its "hazards," the harnessing and directing of its energies, and the utilization of its "re-sources." It often seems as though nature, to fit into our system, must be subordinated to our values. Even during wartime, when armies try to camouflage themselves, they often give themselves away by maintaining a grid pattern on a larger scale; it is said that German fighter-bomber pilots were told to bomb anything they found in a straight line—where there is a straight line there are bound to be human beings. This cultural recognition, that the straight lines in time and space are means by which we can prove our presence, our validity, or our domination over nature as well as over people, is testimony to the extent these premises are felt throughout our cultural existence.

European-American tradition values time and space in proportion to the ways in which they can be ordered, measured, planned, timed, and thus weighed. Actions that are "off the wall," statements made off the top of the head, enterprises undertaken at the spur of the moment, are generally less seriously taken than impact statements, 1980 plans, pros-pectuses, well-planned activities, and completion of work by deadline, even when the substance of the former group is exciting and creative or the content of the latter group is totally boring or inconsequential. The individual who wants to get along in American society is therefore en-couraged to plan the future, not to daydream.

CULTURAL PHILOSOPHY AND FOLKLORE   As Alan Dundes has pointed out, we see multiform examples of folk ideas being expressed through cultural traditions. Folk tales very often transmit for the mem-bers of a culture a set of unstated yet obvious rules for the kind of de-portment leading to success within the value system of that culture. More overt are the various proverbs and figures of speech we use to express our cultural attitudes toward the behavior of others rather than our own assessment. Phrases like "First come, first served," "The early bird catches the worm," "He who hesitates is lost," are ways of asserting the positive cultural value of rapid movement along the linear path of time. Related to this, Dundes feels, is our great interest in youth and staying youthful, along with our abhorrence of old age and of getting old; our wish to be avant-garde rather than "old hat"; our not wanting to run out of potential; our fascination with new frontiers, new directions, future promise, and so on. It probably lies behind our feeling that death and old age are something to be confronted and coped with rather than features of life in which we are fully and naturally involved.

Beyond this, we recognize that the very concept of logic and practicality in our society is based on this same set of notions. In logic, usually $a + b = c$, and in mathematics certain linear relationships in algebra are felt to be basic to learning more advanced computations. The linear order in spelling and alphabetical systems, filing systems, essays (usually with an introduction, a body, and a conclusion), novels with linear plot structure, marching (the most underrated folk dance of our society) and square dancing, linear concepts of productivity (resource, production, product/waste), and assembly lines are all examples of linear use of time and space to achieve ends considered practical and logical by society at large. Indeed, if one derives anything from an idea to a vehicle from just putting stray bits of important items together, the product is considered shoddy, crazy, or incomplete. That is, our notion of what is objective, logical, and regular is also very much dictated by parallel premises.

These ideas are experienced and expressed further through the common use of expressions like "keeping things straight," "getting straight," "being direct," "staying in line," "toeing the line," by keeping our thinking "level-headed," our "quarters" squared away, and our behavior "on the straight and narrow." When we want to indicate that someone else is crazy, it is often by making a gesture directly opposed to the linear perspective, that is, by making a circle around the ear with the forefinger.

This well-known gesture may be one of the most important examples of the issues raised in this chapter, for it is a conscious usage in a folk gesture of a "different" pattern to indicate not simply disagreement with another person but total negative evaluation of the other person's approach or behavior. Conversationally, we may say, "He's talking in circles," "You're crazy; your logic is circular," or "That idea makes me dizzy" (recalling that dizziness is described in cartoon form by a spiral drawn over the affected person's head). It is in this matter of folk expression that worldview studies can be of tremendous importance to our understanding of the modern world. For one thing, we recognize immediately that many of the patterns discussed here as European-American are found primarily in northern Europe, several parts of the Middle East, and in America. Not all people who are American citizens, however, share these patterns equally, for their transmission goes more closely along ethnic, folk, and national lines than through the channels of formal citizenship. We should realize equally that many other cultures in the world do not share these patterns at all, and still others recognize them but value them differently. If it were simply a matter of recognizing diversity in the world, if one could approach these dissimilarities on the intellectual level of curiosity only, the problem would not be so complex. Perhaps it is unfortunate that our own worldview gives us such a secure sense of logic in our daily encounters with the world that our sense of normalcy depends on it when we encounter something radically outside its pattern. In such a situation we react emotionally rather than intellectually, often as if we had been deeply and personally challenged.

As Hall has pointed out in the case of proxemics, if an Arab, coming from a culture that encourages close body contact among people of the same sex in conversational situations, approaches an American, who comes from a culture that discourages physical body contact except under amorous or sports conditions, each one will feel something has gone wrong. The Arab is likely to feel offended by the American, who seems "totally disinterested in what I am saying or who I am," while the American may feel that there is something sexually aberrant about the Arab and recoil in horror. The least likely occurrence on such an occasion is the intellectual; the participants have not said to themselves, "This is very interesting indeed; that other fellow there seems to have a different set of proxemic customs than I have been brought up with." Rather, each one has said to himself, "My God! What's wrong with that guy?" An American, looking over the rather general account of worldview given in the first part of this chapter, might well feel throughout, "Well of course, how else would anybody do it?" And a Navajo or an Eskimo listening to the same account might well say, "What's wrong with those people; are they crazy?" It is precisely because the members of each culture consider their worldview to represent normalcy, a system of reality that can be experienced in all traditional forms from proverbs and tales to physical artifacts, that folklore provides us with one of the most valuable and reliable ways of entering the subject. A person being interviewed on his front doorstep would perhaps give his own intellectual answers to a quiz on his concepts of people outside his own culture group. If he is suddenly plunged into a circumstance in which his traditions are suddenly juxtaposed to those of another culture, however, his expressions, attitudes, and actions will reveal more fully the powers of tradition.

# ◪ WORLDVIEW AND TRADITIONAL MATERIAL ARTIFACTS OF THE NAVAJO

THE PRIMAL CONTEXT   The widespread creation of folk artifacts by a broad segment of the population is not as prominent among European-Americans as it is among some other peoples. Even though I have tried to make the point that all productions within a culture bear strong relationships to the cultural worldview, a study of artifacts and how they represent the basic premises of the culture is easier if we can refer to a group of people where traditional artifact production is more common, and where the premises may therefore be seen through a wider variety of expression. There are many such cultures, but I choose the Navajo because of my deeper acquaintance with it than with most others. Before looking closely at a few typical Navajo artifacts and their relationship to the Navajo worldview, however, I would like to mention the basic circumstances in which a Navajo child first perceives its surroundings, so that the objective world in which a Navajo grows up can be seen in contradistinction to the one described for a typical white American earlier.

The Navajo child, at least one brought up traditionally, is not only born at home but begins life within and among the family, not alone. The one-room Navajo hogan, made of mud, stones, and cedar poles, contains the entire family in circular fashion. The baby spends much of its time bound up in a cradle board, which is thought to give it the feeling of being held at all times. In addition, the baby is often held or placed upright within the family group; its perspectives of other people from earliest times, then, are of being surrounded by family members, not separated from them in space. When the baby is on its back, looking upward, its view is of the domed inner roof of the hogan rather than a flat ceiling.

Most of the family's activities within the hogan are related to the center of the room, where a fire burns almost continually for warmth in the wintertime and where most cooked meals are prepared. Family members often group themselves around the fire, with the various sexes aligned to certain cardinal directions. The door of the hogan always faces east, and so the family is, as the child learns when somewhat older, oriented to the movements of the sun and the cosmos.

Living space and ritual space are not rigidly separated from each other as they are in the European tradition; rather, the sacred healing ceremonies take place in the same hogan where the patient lives. The fire is extinguished and its place in the center of the hogan is taken by the sand paintings that depict the holy people, the *Yei*, who, although depicted with long rectangular lines, are arranged to reciprocate each other by color, direction, arrangement, and function. In short, nearly every patterned experience coming to the young Navajo child, whether featuring round or straight lines, is described in essentially circular rather than linear terms.

The Navajo concept of time is most similar to European concepts of space; insofar as the Navajos talk about anything like time at all, it is not seen as a pathway along which one moves but a context in which things come to pass. The flowering of a plant, the birth of a horse, the maturation of a tree, the building of a home, all have their own time surrounding them and are not measured off against each other on a single scale. For this reason, ancestors who might be considered remote by Europeans are often discussed as if they are near at hand by Navajos. One Navajo confided to me that he thought the whites were unfortunate because they lived "so far" from their ancestors while "ours are all around us."

INDIVIDUAL AND CULTURAL ORIENTATION The individual craftswoman, instead of standing on a straight ribbon of time leading from the past to some future point, stands in the middle of a vortex of forces exerted in concentric circles upon her by her immediate family, her extended family, the clan, the tribe, and the whole living ecological system within which she lives and functions. Instead of planning the future as if she were separable from nature, she negotiates with those forces presently around her; instead of looking toward a future product, she looks to the past for patterning, for advice and wisdom. As we might expect, her expressions, whether oral (religious or secular) or material (artistic or practical), are created according to the circular reciprocating designs that are models of her concept of the human position in nature. Time surrounds her, as do her dwelling place, her family, her clan, her tribe, her habitat, her dances, her rituals. The Navajo feels that one's proper position with respect to nature has to do with one's reciprocal responsibilities to it, and that maintaining this proper position in turn maintains and occasions good health, which is the central part of Navajo religious concern.

INDIVIDUAL AND CULTURAL DEPORTMENT  Because of this reciprocal model of reality, each person is brought up to act in ways that are not only harmonious but that match the concept of how life actually operates. For example, one avoids competing with relatives and peers; one avoids any aggressive actions or gestures which might cause undue focus to fall on a particular individual; one relates to the world around him as if it were made up of interlocked, concentric circles beginning with the immediate family, surrounded by the clan of the mother (and, peripherally, the clan of the father), the people who live in the locality, other Navajos in general, and, finally, "other people."

As in any culture, deportment includes all of those things people do which are considered culturally recognizable modes of action. Many of these modes are what we would call expressive in nature: they seek in various ways to express those models and systems which "make sense" to the people who share that particular worldview. The various genres of folklore could hardly exist unless in their expressiveness they participated heavily in references to those ideas, philosophies, attitudes, and logical patterns which are held in common by the group for whom the folk performances take place.

CULTURAL ART AND ARTIFACT  In order for an item to be recognized as Navajo by a Navajo, it needs to reflect the Navajo circular, reciprocal, negotiating view; but the word *reflect* does not fully describe the Navajos' own recognition of artifacts themselves as models of worldview. Perhaps today the juniper seed necklace provides one of the best examples of this recognition.

The brown seeds in these necklaces are found inside the blue juniper berry. The tree drops the berry to the ground, where it is picked up by chipmunks and other ground animals and taken to partly underground burrows. Navajo children, mostly girls, search for the hiding places and take those seeds with one end chewed off, carefully replacing the rest so the animals will have their normal food supply. The beads are taken home, where the hole in one end serves as a guide for punching a hole in the other end with a needle. Colored beads are obtained from a nearby trading post or mercantile store, and the results are necklaces sometimes called ghost beads by the whites who buy them. One Navajo term for them, however, is *gad bi naa'*—literally, "juniper's eyes." Because the seeds represent a partnership among the tree, the animal, and the human, they stand in the Navajo mind for the delicate interrelationships between various departments of nature whose harmony produces good health. A Navajo will say that one who wears the juniper seed necklace will not go astray in the fog, get lost in the dark, or have bad dreams.

However, Navajos whom I have quizzed on this subject have assured me that they do not believe that the necklace itself actually has magical properties; that is, the necklace as a physical item does not produce the condition of harmony necessary for good health. Rather, it epitomizes it in such a way that it acts very strongly as an external, physical representative of an internal frame of mind that the Navajo considers absolutely necessary in maintaining natural harmonies. If a person lives harmoniously with the natural world, he will be healthy. If he is healthy, he will not get lost or have bad dreams. In this respect, the necklace is primarily symbolic, or it acts as what a literary critic might call an objective correlative; in and of itself it is a physical model of some deeper reality, one that must operate in our own relationship to our total natural context.

The beads are strung in sometimes simple, sometimes complex, ways, but always with the same meaning for the wearer. One further dimension is sometimes added: In those juniper seed necklaces that feature circles with pointed figures, there is a representation of the cosmos, the stars, which deepens further the physical reference to total context for a Navajo. No Navajo of my acquaintance, living in Navajo country, goes without carrying juniper seeds, although not everyone wears them as necklaces. Making these necklaces for sale, especially featuring brightly colored beads from the trader, is probably an innovation encouraged by the Utes, who have used beadwork more prominently than the Navajos. It seems also to be based on the widespread Navajo belief that whites like bright colors.

Another model of worldview is seen in the weaving of Navajo rugs or blankets. It is important to remember that the Navajo do not normally weave rugs for themselves, but produce them to trade for food or to sell directly for income. Thus, the Navajo could conceivably produce rugs in ways that do not distinctively represent their worldview. But inquiry into the matter suggests that in this craft, as in others, the Navajo *way* of doing things is very much a part of their total processing of data through the worldview, showing that their concern is with process more than with products.

In Chapter 4, I referred to the incident in which Professors Sol Worth and John Adair gave movie cameras to a group of Navajos and asked them to produce their own films. In Susie Benally's film on rug weaving, there were only the briefest glimpses of someone actually weaving and only a few minutes devoted to full shots of rugs. This seemed rather puzzling to those whites who first viewed the film, but in fact it represented very well the Navajo attitude toward weaving: The weaving itself is the least Navajo part of the production. Rather, the interaction of people with plant life in the gathering of herbs for dyes, the movement of people and animals across a familiar landscape, are matters that deeply absorb the Navajo as aspects of their reciprocal relationships with the environment. These are the central elements of weaving. I suspect strongly, too, that the reciprocating geometrical designs in the rugs (suggesting a balance of the four cardinal directions) are also a reflection of a basically circular attitude produced on a flat plane, but they may be as well functions of a style of weaving that is done on slants by counting so many vertical strings across for each movement in the pattern. The same slanted weave is sometimes called a lazy line by whites.

Some years ago, my adopted Navajo sister wove a rug that she gave to my family as a gift. It would probably be termed a *Yei* rug by many buyers (*Yei* in Navajo means something like holy people, or spirits, or something approaching the idea of department heads of nature). The figures in this particular rug, however, do not represent generalized holy spirits; rather, they are *nashǫ'i*, or reptile people. The weaver would rather have used four figures (the Navajos' special number is four, as compared to our three), but she wanted to let these figures represent my five children: The two on each end are alike because my oldest and youngest are both girls. The next two are alike because they are twin boys. My fifth child, who is actually the second oldest, is depicted in the middle as different from the rest because he has no one else in the family who matches him; he is set apart by four feathers on his head.

But why should my adopted sister depict my five children as lizards? It is because reptiles in general, and lizards in particular, are symbols of longevity and good health, and by superimposing on the idea of my children a concrete expression of longevity and health my sister was creating a physical model for an abstract health concept, offering it as a gift that reflects her attitude toward my children. But the rug goes far deeper than that; as we talked about it, I found that the wool represents in and of itself an important interaction between the sheep and the human herder, as well as between the sheep and the shearer, the spinner of the yarn, and the weaver of the rug. In addition, nearly all the colors in this rug are taken from plant and herb dyes that had to be gathered over the span of an entire year because some of them are from the same plants, whose roots produce different colors in different seasons. Thus the rug itself represents not only the interaction of humans with animals and of humans with plants, but of humans with the continuing cycle of natural seasons, and all of these, too, should be applied to the total model of longevity and health for my children.

Further, some of the plants used are associated with particular medicines. The design, as I have suggested already, also represents an interaction between all of these factors and the human agent, the weaver, who had all of these possibilities in her conceptualization of the rug. Moreover, in spinning the yarn, the spindle must be turned in a sunwise direction (we call it clockwise), for since it represents the direction of the sun's movement, to spin the yarn by turning the spindle "backward" would be to produce yarn that represents the reverse of the normal state, yarn that will "come unraveled," "won't stay in the rugs," and "might cause sickness." It matters little whether the yarn might really physically unravel, for Navajo health beliefs are ritual and psychosomatic: The idea of unraveling is a greater reality and therefore a greater threat to health and stability than mere physical fact.

It is important to note, also, that in Navajo tradition it is from the woman that fertility and power emanate. The woman owns the hogan, the children, and most of the livestock, and weaves the blankets and rugs. This particular rug, given by one mother to another, is a powerful and eloquent articulation of human and natural relationships that language can only begin to describe. An artifact that we might normally say reflects the tastes and artistic premises of a culture actually embodies far more deeply the whole set of beliefs underlying the weaver's cultural worldview, thus ordering and giving power to her traditional expressions.

The production of Navajo moccasins is an analogous situation with respect to man's responsibilities to his other relations in nature. When deerskin is to be worn as part of the clothing, such as in moccasins, shirts, or cradleboards, according to older custom the deer's hide should not be punctured in the killing. Accordingly, the hunter must find a deer, chase it into open country, and pursue it until it is exhausted. While a deer will run in great bursts of speed for short distances, it cannot endure very long in the open or semi-open desert. The hunter eventually catches up, throws the deer over onto the ground gently, and holds its nose and mouth shut, suffocating it (often with sacred corn pollen) while singing a chant that apologizes to the deer for taking his life and hide and that thanks him for giving his substance to the welfare of the man. Other more complicated ritual acts follow, but I have been asked not to share them.

The reason such ritualism was obligatory, I am told, is that while food is a natural right of man, clothing is in another ritual category, and thus requires extra apology and a greater sense of direct responsibility in the killing. This is, of course, very close to Hopi custom in the pursuit and killing of deer; my friend Yellowman informs me that not long ago most traditional Navajos would have tried, at least, to obtain hides to be used for any kind of body cover in this way. Yellowman himself still occasionally gets his deer in this manner, but since he is now afflicted with back trouble, he is more inclined to use his bow and arrow. This seems not to pose a traditional dilemma for him, however, for the moccasins he makes nowadays are chiefly bartered to a local trader for sale to white tourists. Apparently the same rules of responsibility need not be so efficiently carried out when one is producing clothing for non-Navajos, just as brighter commercial dyes are often used in rugs for trade when the buyers ask for them. Yet, in Yellowman's earnest discussion on these matters, one can see that his role as hunter is still very deeply imbued with cultural attitudes running far deeper than the practical aspects of simply killing and skinning a deer.

Yellowman further points out that the moccasins (made of animal skin), and the dye (some of the ingredients of which come from plants), and the tanning process (which uses the brains of the same deer), and the man with his foot inside compose a typical Navajo combination of cooperation among plant, animal, and man. It is especially with reference to the moccasin that this coalition is important, because the word for moccasin is exactly the same as the word for foot (ke'); in the Navajo mind, the moccasin becomes a part of the individual wearing it and partakes of some aspects of the person's physical being, the most noticeable of which are the indentations of the toes and the shape of the foot that are distinctively inside each moccasin. The old adage of not criticizing someone else until one has walked a considerable distance (I think we have added the mile) in his moccasins is widespread in many tribes, including the Navajo, and carries more meaning than our comparatively superficial metaphor: "If the shoe fits, wear it."

The bow and arrow are still another complex of cooperative elements.

The bow is made of wood, of course, and the bowstring of braided animal hide (in his bow Yellowman uses cowhide). The arrows, too, come from the plants, but are guided by the feathers of birds and are tipped by arrowheads made by man. The arrowheads today are made of nails pounded out between rocks and then shaped. (Stone arrowheads are made by reptiles and are left on the ground by them for us to use in medicine.) On the arrow, at the end grasped by the fingers, are two bands of color; one of them is always red, from herb dyes, and represents danger and death. Inscribed on each arrow are lightning designs, which represent both speed and death.

The arrows are straightened from their original crookedness by two means. One is a ram's horn through which two holes have been pierced in such a way that they provide a strain on the arrow being passed through them. The arrow is soaked and is then continually bent through these holes until the original crooks and bends are worked out of it. The older method, used in conjunction with this helper from the animal world, is the human mouth; the arrowmaker makes minor adjustments in the arrow's straightness by biting it with his teeth. Thus on the arrow itself are the toothmarks of man, the feathers of birds, lightning from the cosmos, colors derived from the vegetable world, all applied to a piece of wood.

Yellowman, describing the workings of the bow and arrow, refers to all these things as necessary points of interaction, not only in the production of the arrow itself, but in the development of an instrument to be used quite carefully and specifically in one of the most delicate areas of man's interaction with his ecological environment. One further gestural dimension should be noted here: When Yellowman uses his bow, it is not held vertically, but horizontally; the hand drawing the arrow is brought back to the front of his chest, where it lies briefly over his heart before the arrow is released. In this way, in addition to all the cultural considerations mentioned, the hunter makes one final gestural commitment to his task, which, if all other ritual aspects have been successfully completed, is reciprocated at the other end by the entrance of the arrow into the heart of the pursued animal. The arrow is thus a link between man and animal, a form of communication and communion.

We could make similar excursions into nearly every aspect of Navajo material culture, and we would find that in most cases the premises upon which each artifact is made are also found behind the myths, tales, and religious commentaries. Not only is the hogan the living space for the

Navajo, it is also where rituals occur. It is created in the shape of rituals, its round floor and east-facing door are parts of the total alignment of human beings with the world of nature to which their rituals are addressed. Ritual space is not separated from daily life but integrated into it. The hogan, not surprisingly, is made of a combination of plants (trees and branches used for the internal structure), animal substances used in the lashing of materials together, dirt from the earth covering the outside, corn pollen rubbed along the main beams inside when the hogan is blessed, and the whole combination created for, and lived in by, people whose concept of their position in the world is expressed in terms of circles and interaction with those various departments of nature. The great sand paintings on the dirt floor of the hogan provide a two-dimensional diagram for the forces of nature. When the patient walks on the sand painting, the ritual creates a four-dimensional world where one is surrounded by and related to the holy powers; the same ideas are found in connection with the juniper seed necklace, the rug, the moccasin.

It is safe to say that it would be nearly impossible for a Navajo woman to take a close look at any of her own artifacts and not recognize in it the epitome of the larger realities governing the world about her. Similarly, it would be impossible for her to look at any natural scene without responding to each plant and color as potential symbol or helpful substance.

Our study of material culture can give us access to the deeper levels of any culture's premises and worldview if we are willing to go beyond the artifact itself into the set of abstract data it represents. The search is often aided by the people under scrutiny. Let us go back to the rug briefly. Many, not all, Navajo rugs have a border. In many, not all, cases, this border is interrupted by a gap, called—in Navajo—*ch'indi bitiin*, "road of bad spirits." The specialist claims that the Indians believe all rugs must have a "flaw," that every blanket needs such a road for its evil spirit to escape. I have asked many weavers about this and have received this reply: There is no spirit in the rug and thus nothing to be let out. Rather, there is a bad condition in the mind of any weaver who believes a design can be finished off, completed. If a mistake occurs, it is left there as a good sign; if not, a "spirit road" can be provided. For it is the mind and the culture of the weaver, not the rug itself, that remain the Navajo concern. Never the same from rug to rug, the designs fluctuate as reference points to the weaver's continual reperformance of premises that reflect the basic worldview. The rug is a product, and when it is completed it is sold. The flaw is a reference to the weaver's unclosed mind. What we are speaking of, then, is a cluster of cultural and artistic codes that occasionally reach expression in a rug (or string figure, hogan, moccasin, bow/arrow, necklace) but that really exist primarily as traditional assumptions. So the real tradition is not the artifact itself, for it is a particularized statement of traditional premises and assumptions. The tradition is that dynamic process by which these premises are shared, performed, understood, and transmitted through time and space among members of a close group.

We must learn to watch beyond the thing, beyond the rug, the turquoise, the moccasin, for there—with proper visual and aural training—we will begin to perceive another reality. This reality will not be discovered through chemicals or Sunday witch-hunting trips to obscure mountain villages, but through the rather more difficult path of language acquisition and sensitivity to a culture's most delicate expressions of itself. We may find many separate realities along the way, for each culture will yield forth its own, and we will perhaps have the good fortune, then, of better witnessing the dynamic kaleidoscope of traditional thought and expression.

## ⬛ WORLDVIEWS IN MULTICULTURAL AMERICA   Every group that has shared a distinctive ethnic or national background for a considerable period of time will have a correspondingly distinctive worldview. Its premises are expressed in a number of ways, ranging from terms of relationships, customs in proxemics, the use of gesture, the arrangement of furniture in a room, attitudes on the proprieties of food and food consumption, and designs of houses, settlements, and cities.

ETHNICITY AND WORLDVIEW: BLACK AMERICANS   In any discussion of worldview, we need to remind ourselves continually that we are not seeking stereotypical behavior (where every individual is assumed to act and feel like all others in his group, and where those actions are responded to very often with a value judgment from the outside observer). At the same time, we must remember that most ethnic groups do indeed have widespread ideas among themselves about how other ethnic groups seem to act, think, and relate to the world, and that these ideas are very often accompanied by value judgments. For many people, therefore, one uncomfortable aspect of the study of folklore is recognizing that there are many traditions about "other people" that may be rejected intellectually by any single member of a group while they are nonetheless transmitted widely among that group's members. For the purpose of this book, we need to avoid those value judgments ourselves, but it would be foolish to overlook the unfortunate presence and vitality of ethnic prejudices that are transmitted and maintained in folklore.

We cannot say that every European-American is highly motivated to compete, is continually interested in the evaluation of the passage of time, or that each European-American believes himself or herself to be a distinctly independent individual. Nonetheless, those elements are widely encouraged and believed in by members of that very large category of people in America. Similarly, many Black Americans share some distinctive traditions about human interactions and performances that, although they may be said to be distinctively Black and thus perhaps represent a distinctive worldview, cannot be used to define the roles or attitudes of any particular Black American.

As Roger Abrahams and others have shown, there is among urban Black Americans a distinctive use of a style of interaction that some have called the conflict model. This term is unfortunate, for it implies a negative evaluation of this interactive style. I prefer the term *antiphonal,* for it is based on the recognition of a constant interaction between two sides in every performance frame. In the urban folklore of Black males, as Abrahams has shown, there is the custom of "playing the dozens," in which a series of insults is traded by two participants, beginning with aggressive remarks about each other and escalating to derogatory comments about each other's mother. Such an interaction ends, in the words of a Black acquaintance, in "fight or flight." Certainly, under the conditions of stylistic interaction encountered on an urban street corner, this behavior would seem like a conflict model to an onlooker. However, we must realize that the same kind of interaction can be seen in many kinds of Black expression, ranging from rural to urban, from secular to sacred. For example, it is an integrated part of many Black Protestant church services, in which the congregation responds continually, in many cases to each single line or phrase, to the preacher in his sermon. It is also found in many kinds of Black music, perhaps most distinctively in blues, where a line or phrase of human singing is responded to by an instrument or another voice. It is found in many of the Black work songs and jail songs that use the call-and-response style. One detects the rhythmic application of this idea in much of modern jazz, with its strong attention to the upbeat of a song (as compared, say, to white fiddling, and its strict attention to the downbeat).

Some people have suggested that the conflict model is prevalent in Black American folklore because Black life in America started in disequilibrium, and that the Black rhythms of life ever since have reflected that formative stage. While this may certainly be true on the psychological and sociological levels, it is also worth pointing out that in many of the traditions of the African tribes themselves there is this same stress on a call-and-response style. In fact, this particular stylistic tradition may be one of those few Africanisms to survive the horrible processes of kidnap, transportation, murder, and slavery that characterized the beginnings of Black life in America.

This quick survey has of course only scratched the surface, but the reason for bringing it up here is to point out that such a distinctive style, which may be extremely meaningful to our understanding of the expressions, customs, and attitudes of a group of people, will be registered by folk and other groups as a defining feature as well; in many cases, the exoteric perception of such a style can result in a stereotypical value judgment of it. For example, among European-Americans, who believe that one thing should occur at a time, who want each person "to have the floor in order to speak," where we tend to submit rather readily to the deliberations of legal groups (committees, juries, regional legislatures, and so on), the Black style of interaction with its exciting antiphony may be seen as talkativeness, aggression, tendency toward argumentation, or simple lack of manners. That is, the very device that may be positively distinctive to those who share it may be thought of as negatively distinctive by outsiders.

A high school principal once confided to me that he would be able to get along perfectly well with his Black students if only they would "not shout at me all the time." I learned that he was altogether unaware of the antiphonal style in Black music and conversations, and equally ignorant of the custom among Black males to use a wide variety of intonations during conversation. Conversations with Black friends have convinced me that many Blacks are equally uncognizant of the custom among white Americans to use modulated tones in formal conversation in order to avoid any variation in volume that might imply the speaker is "losing control." This broad difference in the daily application of traditions concerning culture-specific speech events has led many whites to believe that Blacks lose control of their tempers easily, that they won't let a person finish his statement, that "they just won't listen." It has convinced many Blacks that whites are not interested in conversation (or in the issues represented therein), that whites never really get committed to anything conversationally, and that "they just won't listen."

If we add to this the common ingredient found in worldview discrepancies—a kind of fear or paranoia concerning those who process reality and human expression differently—we get a faint glimmer of how the study of folklore relates to racial and social dynamics in a multicultural country such as America; for whenever fear enters such relationships, especially when that fear is founded upon and nourished by folk traditions that believers feel represent normalcy and stability, merely rational approaches will not suffice for the discussion and resolution of resultant conflicts and problems.

ETHNICITY AND WORLDVIEW: SPANISH-AMERICANS AND MEXICAN-AMERICANS  An equally brief (but I hope not unfair) look at Mexican-American custom and lore reveals a distinctive set of expressions that mirror a cultural attitude about the world and the way we must cope with it. In addition to the strong retention of the Spanish language, which of course favors maintaining an esoteric system, Spanish-Americans and Mexican-Americans place a very heavy stress on family ties and community obligations. There may be occasional strife between families in a community, but in general there is the widespread assumption that traditions hold the village together against the onslaughts of the outside and aggressive world. Sickness may come about when another person threatens us by coveting something we own. The condition brought about by this situation is called evil eye, and an insider knows enough to touch the other person when paying a compliment to take away the possibility of causing illness or death. Other kinds of evil can be visited upon a community or a family from without; *susto,* "shock," is one of these, only one of several kinds of malevolent effects of witchcraft. The community deals with these matters by its own internal means: There are traditional ways of trying to ward off evil, evil eye, and shock, and there are internal, traditional ways of curing their effects when contracted. *Curanderos* or *curanderas* are folk healers who know the language, the customs, the medicines, and the attitudes of the people. Many Mexican-Americans would prefer to go to a *curandero* than to a licensed physician precisely because the folk healer knows more about the psychosomatic elements of the malady and knows how to deal with them in culturally recognized and accepted ways. A member of your close group is more likely to cure you than a stranger who scoffs at your ways.

There are now several examples of clinics or other services that have been set up by Anglo-Americans to aid Mexicans (for example, in migrant labor camps) and that have failed because the physicians or the lawyers or the social workers did not know enough about Mexican folklore to keep themselves from slipping into the category of an outside threat. For example, a Mexican worker with an injury comes to see a doctor at a free clinic. Following his tradition, he brings his entire family with him, and they wait patiently in the outer lounge while the doctor provides his services. When the doctor and patient emerge, the doctor attempts to show how friendly he is toward Mexicans by complimenting the worker's children on their good looks or health or pretty clothes. In the usual Anglo manner, he does not circulate among them and touch them as he makes his complimentary remarks, and thus he unknowingly exposes them to the effects of the evil eye. Later, when one of the children has an accident or becomes sick, the family may feel that it was brought about by the strange actions of the doctor. When several such incidents occur, the word gets around that the clinic is not a good place to go if one wants to stay healthy; business fall off; the clinic closes.

For the doctors involved, who have selflessly donated their time in addition to their regular duties, this is easily interpretable as lack of appreciation on the part of the Mexicans, or it may be attributed to anti-Anglo feelings, political designs, or laziness. In other words, the conditions can only be logically judged from the observer's cultural point of view. Even if the Mexican attitude is explained to these doctors, they may very likely become contemptuous and respond with something like, "Well, if they're going to let their superstitions stand in the way of good health, then they get what they deserve." Similarly, the Mexican people involved will interpret it according to their own worldview traditions and will see that their own avoidance of the clinic has protected them and their families from potential illness brought about by outsiders. Each group may end up resenting the other for what has happened.


The study of varying worldviews among ethnic and national groups in America remains one of the most important unfinished tasks for folklorists and anthropologists, for these matters are very seldom expressed when we give rational, personal answers to questionnaires, surveys, and other formal attempts to gauge the nation's feelings. Rather, since these concepts are shared most heavily with those people we have the greatest identity with, they tend to become integral parts and premises of our folk performances and beliefs. Thus the folklorist and the anthropologist are much more likely to discover their forms and meanings as they exist in the events of traditional life than are other investigators. And, as shown earlier, in even the most brief discussion of these elements of culture we see that they are of more than passing interest: They seem to underlie the daily events that determine our political, economic, educational, and—in many cases—personal decisions and conflicts.

We find we get along best with those folk groups whose worldviews most closely approximate our own on some problem issue. Thus Asian-Americans have a reputation for being quiet and law-abiding citizens largely because their strong concept of family identity and filial piety, coupled with an apparent reverence for formal authority, seem to make them the epitome of behavioral characteristics we would like to see in all "law-abiding citizens." One juvenile judge confided to me that he almost inevitably awarded probation to offenders of Asian backgrounds because he considered them exceptions, and because he knew their families would take care of the disciplinary problems ahead properly; at the same time, he bragged rather forcefully that it was typical for him to give strong sentences to Black youths because he believed they were typical of their group, that they were basically aggressive and insubordinate, and that therefore the larger community needed to make an example of them. In a case like this (and such instances are far from rare in this country) justice is based not so much on the individual or on the crime as on feelings generated by similarities or dissimilarities in worldview.

One finds them multiformly on an international level as well, such as in the famous argument at the Paris peace talks that tried to settle the Vietnam war: The North Vietnamese required that a round table be used so that negotiation could take place, and they interpreted American resistance to this plan as a sure sign that the Americans would not sit down in good faith. The Americans, on the other hand, insisted on a square table, taking the Vietnamese resistance to this "logical" proposal to indicate that surely the Vietnamese had not come with serious intent. It is easy to imagine that the diplomatic, economic, and religious history of the world is more fully characterized by squabbles over the shape of tables, the nature of time, the ownership of land and water, the existence and nature of God, than it is by famous names and "rational, objective" thinking. It is probably not the job of a folklorist to unscramble and solve all these matters, but certainly it does seem within the reach of this field to help us understand the dynamics of traditional worldview more fully than we have in the past.

# ◤ TECHNOLOGY AND WORLDVIEW

Although technology and machinery in general may not seem at first blush to have much connection with folklore, in a general way we may see the function of technology (in the way it is used, in the extent to which it means something) as a larger analogy to the observations made earlier about the Navajo production of particular material items reflecting certain cultural attitudes. Technology does not arise simply because one culture can invent a helpful or useful item while another culture doesn't see the possibility. Rather, items are developed that fit into the assumptions of worldview. It would be absurd for a culture to devise a machine to perform some function that the culture thought abominable. It is no coincidence, for example, that the tremendously sophisticated technology of modern warfare has been under continual intensive development precisely in those cultures where physical property has been considered valuable (and therefore its destruction would be a meaningful act) and in which occupation and ownership of another's land constitutes a meaningful resolution of a culture's dilemma. In cultures where such dilemmas are settled more satisfactorily by bashing in someone's head, the instruments of war that provide that particular function are articulated with brilliant inventiveness. Those cultures that have more recently become interested in such processes as land acquisition have of course become more interested in the technology with which to accomplish it; in such cases, no doubt because of the good offices of American and European education, there seems to be more worldwide interest in almost any usable airplane than in the most beautifully articulated war club. But as I hope to point out, such technological borrowings are not often accomplished without a heavy price being exacted from the stability of the recipients' culture.

## FROM CORN GOD TO TRACTOR IN NORTHERN EUROPE

Technology as we know it in Europe and America is in some part an extension of some common worldview features once shared by many people. If one imagines trying to accomplish the processes of agriculture in northern Europe in early times, one can imagine how beautiful the earliest agricultural machines must have seemed. The growing season is short, the winter long. Food supplies must be laid up for a long and intense winter, yet planting and harvesting must be carried out under the most limited and trying circumstances. One imagines that work itself must have been highly valued simply in terms of survival. Future planning would have become absolutely necessary as an increase in the number of people placed continually greater demands on those involved in agriculture. People would certainly have looked forward to the winter solstice as that magical hint of eventual return to warmth and fertility. Under these circumstances, almost any invention that would have made plowing, planting, fertilization, and harvesting more efficient would have been considered something close to a religious blessing. From what little we know of the mythological evidence of those early days in northern Europe, we know that fertility of plants was one of the most central concerns. Just as the priests of the river cultures in the Middle East gained stability for their cultures and power for themselves by learning to predict the annual floods, so must any inventor of an agricultural implement have gained personal prestige and an added margin of survival for his people in those dark grainfields of northern Europe.

But as in all traditions, the conservative element tends to dictate what is actually extended or developed. Thus there has always been a driving compulsion to develop a better plow, and it has very likely been because the plow was considered basic and necessary. So even though soil experts have recently concluded that plowing earth is one of the more certain ways to reduce the longevity of the soil, we continue even today to build larger plows and larger, more powerful tractors to pull them. In the modern tractor and plow we can see a physical, technological extension of a set of ideas that really reflect folk attitudes and worldview concepts of a culture that has survived through the development of agricultural processes.

"I'LL BE DOWN TO GET YOU IN MY ONE-EYED FORD" (FROM A CONTEMPORARY NAVAJO SONG) Another example of how technology may extend a cultural idea rather than conflict with it can be found in the current use of pickup trucks by Navajos. Despite their stalwart ethnocentrism, Navajos have always been quite willing to adopt quickly the use of any item from any other people that can be used in a Navajo way or that can extend one's capabilities of being

Navajo. One of the most central ideas in Navajo grammar, folklore, and religion is the metaphor of movement. Central to almost all Navajo conversational expressions, it receives even heightened attention in the rituals, in which the patient is described as moving in various ways among the holy people. The Worth and Adair experiment, it will be remembered, brought forward several movies in which the Navajo filmmakers had used the movement of people and animals across a landscape as the basic framework for an entire idea. The well-known Navajo ritual phrase for completeness, beauty, longevity, and good health is phrased as a wish that beauty may be ahead of us, behind us, on both sides of us, above us and below us, as we go along. In former times, the Navajo riding on horseback provided the physical counterpart of this religious image: the self-contained harmonious individual, related to other live elements of nature, taking reality along with him as he went. Today the pickup truck has allowed for an easy extension of this metaphor in everyday Navajo life. Thus, even though a given Navajo may choose to retain Navajo hair styles, costumes, and language, he may feel no hesitation at all in buying a pickup truck as a means of transportation, for it is much more than the practical element that makes it functional in his life. Additionally, the current widespread use of Citizens Band radio in Navajo trucks allows for an even more significant extension to take place. Tourists driving through the Southwest in recent years have tried in vain to contact aloof Navajos on their CB radios. But those who have monitored bands in that area have noticed that when a Navajo call goes over the air, the channel comes alive with Navajo responses. The pickup truck allows for an extension of the Navajo metaphor of movement into the realities of the modern world; the CB radio allows a similar extension of the Navajo language across space, but primarily for Navajo-style contacts and interactions with other Navajos.

THE AX, THE ALPHABET, AND THE TV    The borrowing of other cultures' technological devices does not always have a salutary effect on the borrower, however. There is the now well-known and melancholy story of the introduction of steel axes into Australia by missionaries and shopkeepers. In a culture where stone axes were produced by painstaking labor over long periods of time, they had been for many tribes the symbol of a patriarchal system, the basis for family stability, the center in many cases for religious meaning. When steel axes became widely available, all of these important cultural features were demolished within a few years for the tribes concerned. Even more extensive than the advent of the ax itself, of course, is the desire and demand it creates for other implements, such as sharpening stones, extra handles, and the like, which create the need for further and more articulated contacts between the cultures. Since in a case like this the advantages are almost always on the side of the culture that controls the technology, such contacts can result in corrosion or downright destruction of the worldviews of the recipient of technological charity.

This seems to have been the case for many of the Indian tribes of the northeastern United States and Canada. Formerly restricted in their killing of animals by rigid taboos and regulations which provided that certain animals could be killed only by certain means at certain times of the year, the Indians had enjoyed for generations untold a constant food supply ready to hand. When whites interested in beaver pelts began to supply the Indians with firearms, when the local medicine men were at the same time so incapable of curing the new European diseases that they and their religious views were easily subordinated, and when this considerable bombardment to the local sense of stability was strengthened by Christian missionaries preaching individual salvation and hard work, it did not take long for the Indians to begin competing with each other for beaver pelts, driving the animals almost to extinction, and unwittingly sealing the fate of their own cultural worldview.

Not many years ago the government of Malaysia decided that it might communicate more readily with the widespread villages in the countryside by installing small TV sets in a central public location where announcements could be made, helpful programs could be aired, and a sense of national togetherness could be fostered. In these villages there had existed an institution, more properly a place called a *wakaf*, a small, separate-standing, verandalike structure in the middle of the village where different groups of people could meet during the day, usually separated in their timing by sex and age, to discuss various important subjects. Many of the people in Malaysia are Moslems, and the sexual separation on these occasions reflected for them a religious as well as a secular custom. The installation of small TV sets in the village coffee shop did provide the government with almost instantaneous contact with its own villagers. At the same time, however, it attracted people away from the traditional communication system provided by the *wakaf*. And, since TV watchers are all facing in the same direction, not talking to each other, the presence of males and females in the same room was found to be tolerable.

Thus began not only the gradual disintegration of a village communication system that had operated since ancient times, but also a secularization of human relationships within the village that had been regulated by religious precepts. Additionally, the TV programs offered in both film and animated form continual representations of the human body, something that orthodox Islam has always opposed as a kind of sacrilege. Because the item through which this irreligious experience occurred was not of their own making, the villagers apparently had no way of working out for themselves the impact it was providing subtly for their own lives.

More recently, Malaysian communications experts have lamented that while the TV program has been useful in the strictly technical sense, it has endangered, rather than strengthened, the sense of unity that authorities had hoped would be a foundation for national pride and development. A Malaysian professor pointed out bitterly at an international conference on traditional communications that "we have had to learn that we cannot expect to adopt the machinery of the Western world without adopting the philosophies and worldviews upon which that machinery is predicated." He went on to warn other nations to recognize that a technological object is not merely an object, but an item of cultural communication; he asked fellow participants to scrutinize the concept that technology itself is benign, that it can be utilized the way the user sees fit. Along with the thing comes its idea, and the idea is often culture-specific. Without the idea, without the worldview it represents, the object is often of little value or use.

Educational TV systems had been offered to the Malaysian government as positive elements to help them build a stronger culture, as devices to aid them as independent participants in the world community. Instead, many Malaysians now feel that the introduction of village television may be only a thinly masked intrusion of American political philosophy into Southeast Asia. Whether or not such an effect was intentional, we may see in this example the beginnings of the kind of fear and resentment that I have suggested are common when worldviews clash. We may expect them to be especially strong feelings when it seems as though one worldview is trying subtly to obliterate or modify another. We have no right to congratulate ourselves for wiping out patriarchal systems in Australia, "primitive" hunting and "pagan" religion in America, or sexual segregation in Malaysia, even though such ends may be consonant with our high moral concept of ourselves and our sense of advanced liberation. Wanton destruction of other cultures, for whatever lofty purpose, should be added to the list of deadly sins and capital offenses.

The tensions, frictions, and outright clashes that have characterized the history of Africa, Ireland, the Middle East, and many other places are as much the outgrowths of conflicting worldviews as they are of conscious political, religious, and economic factors. For this reason, they are not susceptible to easy resolution through the objective application of political, religious, and economic principles. The study of folklore will very likely not produce a resolution to these conflicts either, but it may certainly help alert us to the foundations of ethnic and national malaise, and, more importantly, it can help us see that in each case a worldview is internally valid, consistent among its parts, and effective as a means of relating the mind of the individual to those larger occurrences of the world around. From fist fights to international war, conflicts seldom occur between Good Guys and Bad Guys, or between Right and Wrong; more typically, battles occur between two parties who are both right in their own estimation. Insofar as folk tradition, in the form of ethnic or national worldview informally transmitted among members of close groups, constitutes the background or matrix of situations arising around us in the world, these matters do indeed become important aspects of our field of study.

# ✍ BIBLIOGRAPHICAL NOTES

The study of cultural worldview is far more complex than this chapter can afford to admit. These references are therefore grouped into the areas of concern brought up in the chapter; I assume the reader will take the subject far beyond the meager suggestions offered here. The minority peoples discussed in this chapter are perhaps the easiest to see; but the same considerations must be applied to the immigrants from European cultures, to the tremendous variety of Indian tribes, to the varying Black communities, to the different Asian groups, and so on. I have referred to the peoples and studies I am most familiar with; you must do the same: Study the urban Greek community, the Russian Old Believers, the Irish in New York, the Italians in Chicago, the Scandinavians in Minnesota, the Basques in the Great Basin, the Spanish colonial descendants in New Mexico, as well as the later immigrants from Mexico. Each group is likely to exhibit a distinct worldview that may be encountered in its language, customs, proxemic rules, folk arts, jokes, and songs. Florence R. Kluckhohn and Fred L. Strodtbeck show how differently five close groups in the American Southwest perceive and express their relationship to the same ecological surroundings in *Variations in Value Orientations* (Evanston, Ill.: Row, Peterson, 1961). The importance of this kind of observation cannot be underestimated.

Some general comments on worldview, especially as it relates to topics of concern to folklorists, may be found in the following works. William Bascom suggests, in "Folklore, Verbal Art, and Culture," *Journal of American Folklore*, 83 (1973), 374–381, that in a nonliterate culture, folklore is synonymous with the culture; this might provide a beginning for the discussion of how to approach *a*literate cultures like ours (in which many people are literate, but in which we continue to transmit many of our cultural views orally and gesturally). Ruth Benedict, *Patterns of Culture* (New York: Penguin, 1934), while somewhat outdated now, is a basic study. Alan Dundes, *Every Man His Way: Readings in Cultural Anthropology* (Englewood Cliffs, N.J.: Prentice-Hall, 1968), presents an outstanding array of essays on cultural differences, most of them related to matters of worldview. See especially Dorothy Lee, "Codifications of Reality: Lineal and Non-Lineal," pp. 329–343; Alan Dundes, "The Number Three in American Culture," pp. 401–424; Horace Miner, "Body Ritual Among the Nacirema," pp. 433–438; Laura Bohannan, "Shakespeare in the Bush," pp. 477–486. The works of Edward T. Hall are almost all related to the topic of worldview, and they contain innumerable comparative examples; his books *The Silent Language, The Hidden Dimension,* and *Beyond Culture* (Garden City, N.Y.: Doubleday, 1959, 1966, and 1977, respectively) are basic and uncomplicated. His three-level system, put forward in the first book, is illuminating, but probably oversimplified. In *Patterns of Discovery: An Inquiry into the Conceptual Foundations of Science* (Cambridge: Cambridge University Press, 1958), Norwood Russell Hanson shows the extent to which even our most scientific observations are channeled and defined by worldview. Harry Hoijer, ed., *Language in Culture* (Chicago: University of Chicago Press, 1954), presents a series of essays on the relationship between cultural worldview and language. Johan Huizinga, *Homo Ludens: A Study of the Play-Element in Culture* (Boston: Beacon Press, 1955), shows how a particular kind of expression— often one overlooked because of its everyday aspects—relates to cultural views. Benjamin Lee Whorf, one of the principal proponents of the hypothesis that language shapes and is shaped by culture, presented his views in *Language, Thought and Reality* (New York: Technology Press, 1956); most scholars today do not accept the whole argument, yet many, including Hall, have based their theories on the general proposition brought up by Whorf (and discussed by Lee, above): An individual sees chiefly what his culture (including his language) has trained him to see.

Relationships between worldview, culture, and childhood are discussed by Erik H. Erikson, *Childhood and Society*, 2nd ed. (New York: Norton, 1950); see especially his comments on the tenacity with which Native American schoolchildren retain customs and attitudes formed at home in spite of the well-intentioned efforts of both teachers and parents to change them when school problems arise (p. 131). The effects of the lullaby, both in function of music and content of words, are discussed by Bess Lomax Hawes in "Folksongs and Function: Some Thoughts on the American Lullaby," *Journal of American Folklore*, 87 (1974), 140–148. See also Mary and Herbert Knapp, *One Potato,*

*Two Potato: The Secret Education of American Children* (New York: Norton, 1976), and Ione and Peter Opie, *The Lore and Language of Schoolchildren* (London: Oxford University Press, 1959), especially ch. 8, "Code of Oral Legislation," pp. 121–153. Both books deal with the powerful ways in which children learn an entire way of life from their peers through the dynamic processes of tradition. Although the Opies omit reference to "crude" materials, which they consider unrepresentative of the good child, the Knapps apparently have had better advice from their young informants.

For discussions of folk ideas and their relation to custom, behavior, and culture, see at least the following: Alan Dundes, "Folk Ideas as Units of World View," *Journal of American Folklore*, 84 (1971), 93–103; reprinted in Paredes and Bauman, *New Perspectives*, cited previously, and Dundes's "Thinking Ahead: A Folkloristic Reflection on the Future Orientation in American Worldview," *Anthropological Quarterly*, 42 (1969), 53–72. Edward T. Hall, who originated the term *proxemics*, discusses the traditions of where we place ourselves in relation to other people in space in "Proxemics," *Current Anthropology*, 9 (1968), 83–108 (including discussions and a valuable bibliography); his "impressionistic" observations on Arab and American proxemics (Arabs stand closer to each other than do Americans) is confirmed in Michael O. Watson and Theodore D. Graves, "Quantitative Research in Proxemic Behavior," *American Anthropologist*, 68 (1966), 971–985. The idea of leaving a flaw in a rug (Navajo) has parallels in related crafts among other cultures: Suzi Jones found the same idea among quilters in Oregon, where there is a common notion that perfection in a quilt would be presumptuous, for the quilter would not be humble before God. See *Oregon Folklore* (Eugene: University of Oregon, 1977), p. 113. Jones notes that the construction of a quilt is so complex that the quilter does not need to strive for humility.

For an elucidation of how the Black American worldview is expressed in folklore, see, of course, Roger D. Abrahams, *Deep Down in the Jungle* and *Positively Black*, both mentioned previously. Also illuminating are the many essays in Alan Dundes, *Mother Wit from the Laughing Barrel: Readings in the Interpretation of Afro-American Folklore* (Englewood Cliffs, N.J.: Prentice-Hall, 1973). For more texts of the "toasts," along with perceptive remarks on their meaning and context, see Bruce Jackson, *Get Your Ass in the Water and Swim Like Me* (Cambridge, Mass.: Harvard University Press, 1974). Langston Hughes and Arna Bontemps, *The Book of Negro Folklore* (New York: Dodd, Mead, 1958), and J. Mason Brewer, *American Negro Folklore* (Chicago: Quadrangle, 1968), are both fine collections of Black folklore done by Black scholars; they omit much of the "obscene" folklore that characterizes the traditions of most young urban people of all groups today, with the result that the collections seem slanted toward the older kinds of folk performances. A good collection of Black folk tales is Richard Dorson, *American Negro Folktales* (New York: Fawcett, 1967), although since it contains tales collected by a white from Black informants, it is difficult to determine how fully representative it may be of the Black worldview; there is always the possibility that the stories are those that Black people felt most like sharing with an ethnic "outsider."

Folkloric studies of Hispanic-American culture are rare. The reader might start with the "Southwest Mexicans" section of Dorson's *Buying the Wind: Regional Folklore in the United States* (Chicago: University of Chicago Press, 1964), pp. 415–495, along with the companion section in Dorson's *American Folklore* (Chicago: University of Chicago Press, 1959), pp. 101–112 ("Spanish New Mexico"). Sylvia Ann Grider studies a particular form of urban Chicano folklore in "Con Safos: Mexican-Americans, Names and Graffiti," *Journal of American Folklore*, 88 (1975), 132–142. Joan W. Moore, *Mexican Americans* (Englewood Cliffs, N.J.: Prentice-Hall, 1970), provides a succinct and compelling account of Mexicans in America with a considerable focus on traditional customs and beliefs, though folklore, by name, is not overtly discussed. In the Foreword and the Introduction to his *Folktales of Mexico* (Chicago: University of Chicago Press, 1970), pp. xi–lxxxiii, Américo Paredes provides a most helpful account of major themes in Mexican narrative folklore that distinctly mirror culture-specific views. Irwin Press, "The Urban Curandero," *American Anthropologist*, 73 (1971), 741–756, demonstrates the vitality and function of urban folk healers in Bogotá, Colombia. There are many studies of folklore in the countries of Central and South America, of course, but few of them are available in translation. Until North Americans shake off their reluctance to learn the most prominent neighboring language, these works will remain essentially beyond our reach—as will most of the traditional performances of the Mexican-Americans, who now make up the largest "minority" group in most of the western states.

Books on the Native American have appeared as regularly as stacks in the local pancake parlor, and most of them are as hastily produced. I do not have the space here to evaluate the many frauds and the few triumphs in this area. For some guidance in the area of worldview, the reader should consult Walter Holden Capps, ed., *Seeing with a Native Eye: Essays on Native American Religion* (New York: Harper & Row, 1976), and Dennis Tedlock and Barbara Tedlock, eds., *Teachings from the American Earth: Indian Religion and Philosophy* (New York: Liveright, 1975). For revealing accounts of particular tribes, see Joseph Epes Brown and Black Elk, *The Sacred Pipe* (1953; reprint ed., New York: Penguin, 1971), which discusses the seven sacred rites of the Oglalla Sioux in relation to the Sioux worldview; Alfonso Ortiz, *The Tewa World: Space, Time, Being, and Becoming in a Pueblo Society* (Chicago: University of Chicago Press, 1969); Edwin Wade and David Evans, "The Kachina Sash: A Native Model of the Hopi World," *Western Folklore*, 32 (1973), 1–18. Popular among Indian faddists have been Hyemeyohsts Storm's *Seven Arrows* (New York: Harper & Row, 1972) and Frank Waters, *Book of the Hopi* (New York: Viking, 1963). Both have been repudiated by the tribes concerned.

The relation of cultural worldview to our concepts of environment and to the way we deal with the environment (as in farming) can be profitably studied by noting how our European ancestors felt about nature and fertility: see Sir James George Frazer, *The New Golden Bough*, ed. Theodor H. Gaster (New York: Criterion, 1959). With regard to plowing, the *National Geographic* of July 1976, p. 45, shows studies that indicate that eight inches of topsoil will last an average of 36 years if plowed in straight lines, about 104 years if contour-plowed, and about 2,224 years if the seeds are "drilled" through unplowed turf. Yet one expects that the tractor companies and the farmers will not want to give up what they consider to be normal practices in order to "go back" (note the linear concept) to what they consider primitive farming methods. For further remarks on worldview and the way we register our environment, see David Lowenthal, "Geography, Experience, and Imagination: Towards a Geographical Epistemology," *Annals*, Association of American Geographers, 51 (1961), 241–260, reprinted in *Man, Space, and Environment*, ed. Paul W. English and Robert C. Mayfield (New York: Oxford University Press, 1972), pp. 219–244, esp. pp. 233–240. Equally important is Wilbur Zelinsky's fuller treatment of cultural patterns in relation to patterns on the land, *The Cultural Geography of the United States* (Englewood Cliffs, N.J.: Prentice-Hall, 1973); Zelinsky makes some pointed remarks about American linearity in time and space. Two other works already mentioned in other chapters bear repeating in this list: Yi Fu Tuan, *Topophilia* (Englewood Cliffs, N.J.: Prentice-Hall, 1974), and Lewis Mumford, *The City in History* (New York: Harcourt, Brace and World, 1961). In Chapters 1–4 of the latter, Mumford provides an exciting view of religion, ritual, and worldview as they relate to the concept of early villages and cities.

In the area of culture "contact," acculturation, colonization, or direct friction between worldviews, the following are enlightening. Of course, to begin with, the reader will want to become reacquainted with William Hugh Jansen, "The Esoteric/Exoteric Factor," reprinted in Dundes, *The Study of Folklore*, pp. 43–51. In addition, Don Adams, "The Monkey and the Fish: Cultural Pitfalls of an Educational Advisor," *International Development Review*, 2 (1960), 22–24, reprinted in Dundes, *Every Man His Way*, pp. 504–510; John H. Bodley, *Victims of Progress* (Menlo Park, Calif.: Cummings, 1975); Pertti J. Pelto, *The Snowmobile Revolution: Technology and Social Change in the Arctic* (Menlo Park, Calif.: Cummings, 1973); Robert Tonkinson, *The Jigalong Mob: Victors of the Desert Crusade* (Menlo Park, Calif.: Cummings, 1974); Calvin Martin, "The European Impact on the Culture of a Northeastern Algonquian Tribe: An Ecological Interpretation," *William and Mary Quarterly*, 31 (1974), 3–21; Francis E. Dart, "The Cultural Context of Science Teaching," *Search*, 4:8 (August 1973), 322–327. Dart, a physicist, found that different cultural views of nature and knowledge, different cultural organizations of evidence, affected the learning process of students forced to think, perform, and compete academically in a system not their own. The colonial role of television in Malaysia came to my attention in a fascinating paper given by Mohd. Dahlan HjAman at an international conference on traditional media held at the East-West Communication

Institute, Honolulu, July 7–August 1, 1975; Dahlan's presentation was entitled "The Sociocultural Significance of Traditional Gathering Centers in Peasant Fishing Communities in Malaysia," and should eventually appear with the proceedings of that conference. A hint of the psychological aspect of cultural differences may be gained by reading "Language Differences," by Warren Ten Houten in *Behavior Today*, March 3, 1975, p. 407, which gives a brief account of the UCLA study on Hopi children (right brain–centered).

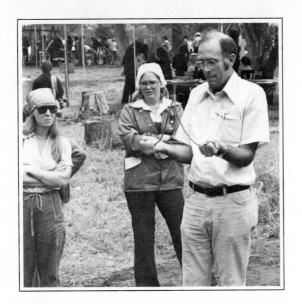

# 8

# BEING

## A

# FOLKLORIST

**APPROACHING ANY FIELD,**
ACADEMIC OR OTHERWISE, THE NEW-
COMER BECOMES AWARE OF WHOLE MOUNTAIN
RANGES OF ESOTERIC BOOKS AND ARTICLES THAT
seem to require conquering and digesting before any claim to proficiency
—even legitimacy—can be made. True enough, it is impossible to study
any subject seriously that has enjoyed a long history of scrutiny and commentary without coming to grips with at least the high points of those
discussions. Yet we recognize that being a doctor involves much more
than scholarship in medical school or the mastery of Latin; being a professor calls for more than a graduate degree; being a mechanic requires
more than owning a set of tools. Being a folklorist requires more than
climbing (or creating) alps of Germanic scholarship. Fortunately, the
basic requirement for being a folklorist—a fascination with and an appreciation of culture-based expression—is something most of us already
possess. Whether you are a folklore student planning further work in the
field, a curious beginner, a retired and jaded professor, or an intellectual

tourist, you have already had extensive exposure to and training in folklore.

## ✍ EVERYFOLK

Nearly everyone is a folklorist; some are professionals at it. To put it another way: Although some people choose to study folklore and obtain the training necessary in that profession, all of us, to one extent or another, learn, collect, and use folklore as a natural consequence of being members of close groups. The millworker needs to learn and use the hand signals that allow communication in a noisy shop; the college student needs to know how long to wait for a late professor; we all learn how late is late—at a cocktail party, a wedding, a class, a picnic; we need to know what connotations are available to us in our language (or else risk not understanding most of what is said to us); we need to know what a joke is and where the punch line goes (or risk exasperating our friends and losing out on fantasy and enjoyment); we learn the proper food for breakfast and the proper dress for supper ("Junior, don't you dare sit down to the table without your shirt"). All of these and many more "rules," customs, mores, observances, and communicative traditions we learn and use through the dynamics of folklore. Indeed, unless we "collect" and perform the folklore of our close groups, we may be thought of as nearly outsiders. Just to belong to a close group we need to be amateur folklorists, then; how rapidly we become members of new close groups and how deeply we remain members of others will probably lie in direct proportion to our command of the group's folklore.

LEVELS OF FOLK INVOLVEMENT   There are two kinds of involvement with the processes of folklore: cultural and intellectual. By cultural involvement I mean that gut-level personal relationship to the close group felt and acted out by the individual in the very performance of folklore under normal circumstances. The performances and responses in this kind of involvement are geared more to the group—the culture—than to the individual. In the intellectual, intentional engagement with folklore, the individual stands aside with some objectivity, actually studying and analyzing those dynamic processes that, as a member of the close group, he may have participated in culturally without self-consciousness.

Unfortunately, the jump from cultural to intellectual involvement is farther than we may suspect, and many people are not willing or able to become objective about those matters so closely related to their own sense of cultural propriety, personal stability, ethnic identity. For this reason, people are often more willing to study the folklore of others than the traditions of their own group. Until recently, folklorists and anthropologists had an inclination to run off to the South Sea Islands, to Africa, to the Native American reservations in the United States, and to immigrant colonies to study their folklore. Probably this is related to the continued interest in rural folklore by urban-bred and university-trained folklorists, too. And it probably relates to the terminology one finds until recently in the study of religion: ours is religion, theirs is myth—with the corollary that we can be objective about them and their myths while we simply accept our own as truth.

FOLKLORE AND EMOTION   I bring up this interesting dichotomy for a double reason. First, as amateur, everyday folklorists—as folk—we may resent it when someone analyzes our folklore; that is, when we suddenly are forced to see some of the reasons behind our customs or sense that our views are not as unique or as universal as we had assumed. As professional folklorists, we need to recognize that when we analyze or study those expressions that are deep aspects of other peoples' cultural involvement, we run the risk of offending them by bringing these intellectual considerations into focus as if they were more important than the real functioning of the folklore in its habitat.

These are obviously opposite sides of the same coin, and they represent one of the greatest potentials for misunderstanding in the field of folklore: People often become angry when their cultural involvement is held up for intellectual scrutiny. This means that people who seek to become intentional folklorists must realize that they will be dealing with the most delicate and potentially volatile of human expressions: those that relate the individual solidly to a close group—those that can therefore undergird such dynamic matters as the frictions between Celt and Saxon in Ireland, between Arab and Israeli in the Middle East, between soldier and marine on leave, between logger and millworker on weekends, between Black and white in the ghetto, between feuding mountain families, between Hopis and Navajos, between "the U" and "the Aggies," between kids and adults, between men and women. For, regardless of other psychological, economic, political, or historic factors, membership in any of these groups is also a matter of involvement with that group's folklore, and a demonstration of belonging lies in the expression of shared tradition as much as it does in intellectual pronouncements of philosophy and personal opinion. Question these deep allegiances, or be condescending about them, at your own risk.

THE CULTURAL CEMENT TRUCK DRIVER During our friendly discussion of urban belief tales, a university administrator told me he knew of a similar story which was "actually true," for it had happened in his home town. He told me of a cement truck driver who stopped home one morning to have a cup of coffee with his wife. To his surprise, he found a strange car there, and being a suspicious sort, he assumed his wife was having an affair and filled the strange car with concrete. The car could still be seen at a certain gas station in his town, but more important, the episode demonstrated how men in his community dealt directly with a marital threat. "He didn't see any more of her after *that*," he concluded proudly.

I made the mistake of responding on the intellectual, not the cultural, level. Instead of registering the story as an amusing confirmation of a man "in the driver's seat," I cheerfully pointed out the widespread occurrence of that story across the United States and noted the various outcomes I had heard. My acquaintance immediately felt that in front of his own colleagues his honesty had been questioned (along with the integrity of his home town, I now believe) and became very irate, insisting that we step outside to settle the matter. I narrowly avoided a fight by apologizing and noting the possibility for coincidence. I told him I would value highly a picture of the "real car" so that I could put it in along with other versions of the legend that I had collected, and he loudly promised one, by God, before the end of the month. Now, fourteen years later, I have begun to lose hope. Perhaps he forgot. But I have not forgotten the lesson: He was telling me the story not because I was a folklorist, but because I was a man and we were sitting with a group of men. I had awakened the legend in his mind by referring to some similar anecdotes, but he was clearly telling me the story because he thought I would be interested in what it represented. He was operating on the cultural level, I on the intellectual level, and the immediate result was outrage.

The folklorist, amateur or professional, must demonstrate a personable interest in the traditions being shared by any folk performer, but to analyze those traditions in front of the performer is to ask for trouble, not because the performer is intellectually incapable of such discussion, but because analysis and comparison seem to bring the veracity of the tradition-bearer into some question.

CULTURAL PSYCHOLOGY AND FOLKLORE Because folklore operates primarily on what I call the cultural level, because its aesthetics, choices, and performances are dictated more by the group than by the individual, the expressions themselves reveal more of group values than of individual opinions—as I have already suggested. In fact, a person may even disagree on the intellectual level with something he is used to expressing on the cultural level. Some years ago I myself passed on the cement truck driver story to a number of people because I was totally convinced by a close and trusted friend that it had actually occurred in Moscow, Idaho. Why did I tell that story so many times? On the intellectual level, I do not believe that filling someone's car with concrete necessarily resolves a marital problem, especially when it is done without checking on the details. What if, as one version tells it, the car actually belonged to the man's boss, who came over to arrange for a surprise party celebrating twenty years of faithful service to the company? In my own mind, I realize that if I saw a strange car in front of my house, I would not seek to damage it, even if I were suspicious of skullduggery.

Nevertheless, I recognize that on the cultural level I belong to a society in which marital infidelity by women is considered a massive threat to masculine pride and position. Thus, for the cement truck driver to triumph in a symbolic way represents, on that cultural level, a successful resolution to the psychological threat posed. I think when I told that story with relish to a number of friends, of course adjusting the corroboration of the story a couple of steps so that the anecdote related an event that had happened to a friend of a friend of *mine*, I was participating psychologically with my culture, not expressing my own opinion on how a rational male should deal with a situation he does not understand. One aspect of the intellectual approach to folklore is that now, having heard versions of this story all over the country, having seen cute advertisements for cement companies illustrated by a grinning truck driver loading an old jalopy with concrete, having read of numerous pranks in which people's cars were filled with concrete, I am in a position, as a student of folklore, to make some analytical remarks about that story that I never would have thought of back when I believed the story represented something that had actually happened in a nearby community.

THE BLACK ELEPHANT  Folklorists Alan Dundes and Roger Abrahams once made a study of the designs, topics, and categories of the well-known elephant joke craze of the early 1960s. They noticed that if all available versions of elephant jokes were compared, certain broad categories emerged, such as the supersexual elephant or the elephant who tries to disguise himself by an absurd use of color (Why do elephants wear red tennis shoes? So you can't see them hiding in the cherry tree), or the intrusive elephant (whose tracks are found in the peanut butter, or whose presence is felt in bed or in the bathtub). Clearly, all of the elephant jokes depended for their effect on a basic set of absurdities: Elephants were always described hiding in places that could not possibly hide an elephant, being found in places obviously too small for elephants, being attracted by totally impossible sexual partners, and so forth.

At least one element of the elephant joke that anyone would recognize would be its play on absurdity. However, Abrahams and Dundes felt that there were a number of other features that were too prominent and too timely to be overlooked. For example, they wanted to know why the elephant joke craze had swept the country at that particular time. They wanted to know why certain categories were so prominent. They wanted to know, in short, what the elephant might symbolize for those who were telling the jokes at that time, for certainly there were many other absurdities available in the world.

They noticed that the categories of the elephant joke matched very accurately the categories found in comments and feelings about other races, especially about Blacks; for example, the absurd disguise with color seemed to parallel the widespread white notion that Blacks are absurdly interested in lightening their color, straightening their hair, buying cars associated with white affluence, and, in short, acting the "wrong" role. The supersexual elephant with gigantic anatomical parts and eclectic tastes seemed to mirror the widespread sexual folklore about Blacks encountered commonly among whites. The intrusive elephant, described as being found in the refrigerator, bed, and bathtub—in all the most personal and private places—seemed to be an analogue to the widespread fear by whites that Blacks were moving into areas of housing and employment that were not proper for them. Another category, one in which we are asked how one takes power away from elephants, usually featured some aspect of castration: How do you keep an elephant from stampeding? You cut his stampeder off. This category seemed an obvious counterpart to the fear-inspired castrations, in reality and in story, in which whites symbolically took power away from Blacks who threatened them.

Using Freudian psychology, Abrahams and Dundes argued that humor often functions in such a way as to allow a joke teller to bring up a topic of some anxiety among the members of a group and then to demonstrate or experience superiority over the implied threat by reducing it to something laughable. In other words, jokes may well represent traditional symbolic experiences with precisely those matters that bother us on the group level.

If that is so, how can the elephant possibly symbolize white anxieties about Blacks? And what does that have to do with the timing of the elephant joke fad? First, the authors noted that in the popular imagination of Americans, elephants come from Africa (even though in fact the elephants we see at circuses come from India). They also noted that the elephant joke craze took place precisely at the height of the civil rights movement across the country. They argued, cogently, I think, that the elephant jokes provided an outlet for fear and anxiety among whites.

In order to find out for myself whether this interpretation was noted by people on the cultural rather than the intellectual level, I asked a friend of mine from Philadelphia (which has a large Black population) whether he had heard Black people of his acquaintance telling elephant jokes during the civil rights movement. His answer was both curious to me and supportive of the Abrahams and Dundes hypothesis. He said, "You know, that's really an interesting question. I have a Black secretary, and when I came in one day and told her a really funny elephant joke I had just learned from a friend, she said to me—really sarcastically—'You folks used to call us monkeys; how come you changed it to elephants?'" Of course, this one bit of testimony does not prove the theory, but it does indicate a certain validity that the authors could not have known. I do know that the elephant jokes are not particularly funny or even understandable to people of other ethnic backgrounds. For example, once when I was struggling with the problem of what was funny about a certain Navajo joke, one of my Navajo friends said in exasperation, "I'll tell you what's funny about this if you can tell me what's funny about elephant jokes."

What is funny about elephant jokes? Is it only their basic absurdity? If so, why did they start during the civil rights movement and fade as that era faded? I think Dundes and Abrahams go a long way toward explaining what happens in ethnic, esoteric humor; it is all the more valid because it ties in with what we may notice in other kinds of joke fads in our culture. And it is important to know that different groups of people find different things funny; therefore we cannot make the simple assertion that these matters are universal.

Nonetheless, my experience with mentioning this theory to people is that they immediately become angry and deny that it has any validity. "Well, I told lots of elephant jokes during the sixties, and I myself was involved in the civil rights movement!" In other words, we will find that the very people who were telling those jokes are not only not in a position to analyze them according to any larger system such as that suggested by Abrahams and Dundes, but they also resent, on the intellectual level, any implication that they might have been joking about a subject of such passionate philosophical meaning to them. But of course this is exactly the point. As intellectual individuals in a culture that encourages individuality, we may expect that in discussion people will bring forth those ideas that represent them in public, among friends, or among their professional colleagues. When we are acting or performing as members of a folk group, our expressions will be less geared to the personal, intellectual statement than they are to the feelings of the entire group. The country was gripped by excitement and anxiety over the civil rights movement during the 1960s, and the elephant joke illuminates the fact that regardless of our intellectual orientations, we did not escape in any way the ramifications of membership in a larger culture that was very much threatened by the racial issue.

If we were to list the most common jokes told in our culture, I believe we could relate most of them to anxieties, threats, and concerns felt by different groups at different, noticeable periods of time in our history. Probably the bulk of American jokes concern sex, politics, religion, and ethnicity—just the very subjects that cause us continual malaise in conversation, the topics our mothers told us never to discuss in public. I think it is too much to place on the shoulders of coincidence that all these joke topics continue to parallel the ongoing emotional concerns of society. Can it be coincidence that moron jokes were circulating in the 1940s just as IQ tests were becoming so common that they were almost obligatory in every child's life? Is it not possible to see the moron jokes as an expression of anxiety among parents about where their children would fall on the grand chart?

What about the dead baby jokes that were being told, even at the table, recently by pre-teen-age children? When I became incensed at my own children for telling these "jokes" at supper, I was told indignantly by one of them, "Why do you care about dead babies? Nobody wants babies anymore." It suddenly occurred to me that dead baby jokes, as circulated among children, might well have been a similar kind of symbolic playing through of anxieties occasioned by the sudden public discussion of contraception and abortion. Similarly, a few years ago, when disabled children began to enter the regular school system in some numbers, we were flooded with Helen Keller jokes, MR jokes, and others ("Mrs. Smith, can Billy come out to play?" "No, of course not, you know he doesn't have any arms and legs!" "We know! We want him to play second base!"). And who is the traveling salesman but perhaps the symbol of that marital threat felt by many men, also experienced to some extent in movie characters like Shane and serial heroes like the Lone Ranger? These homeless wanderers move into other people's towns, sometimes solving the local problem, often threatening the men and entrancing the women. It is important to note that the traveling salesman is outrageously funny only insofar as he remains in the joke; if he arrives on our front doorstep, the joke is over.

THE RACIAL POLACK   Not long after the elephant joke cycle came the so-called Polack joke, a kind of ethnic slur focused on one particular group, but made up of attitudes and phrases found throughout Europe and America wherever esoteric-exoteric ethnic factors exist. One finds the same jokes today in Yugoslavia, where the Serbs use them in referring to people who live in other parts of the country. The Germans tell them about the Italians, the Danes tell them about the Germans, the Romanians tell them about the Russians. In the United States, the people in Montana tell North Dakota jokes, the people in Texas tell Aggie jokes, and so on.

If we keep all these things in mind, and if we remember that the word *Polack* has an older history than it has had as American slang for Polish (in the Slavic languages it refers to a person who lives out on the land, a country bumpkin), if we recall that a good many of the Polack jokes were told in the 1930s as "nigger" jokes, and if we make the same category analysis as suggested by the Abrahams and Dundes study, we may be able to see that the Polack joke is not about Americans of Polish descent but probably about ethnic minorities in general, especially of the non-white variety. The main categories are stupidity, strength, and dirt. These are the most recurrent topics in ethnic slurs across America; they are most commonly applied by European-Americans to non-European-Americans, sometimes to any immigrant group.

Just as the traveling salesman joke is not about salesmen, so the Polack joke is not about Polish people; rather, it is a symbolic ethnic slur, the ingredients of which call up, on the cultural level, stereotypical assessments of groups outside the majority. Any number of ethnic groups could have been named in these jokes; I suspect that it is because Polish-Americans have become so Americanized that it is clear to most people that the reference to the Polack is only on the most superficial joking level, while the more serious levels of the joke, which may indicate anxiety and tension about an unskilled labor force threatening jobs in industry, do not represent matters of concern about Polish people.

Those who tell Polack jokes would assure us that they had no negative feelings about ethnic minorities, though some will admit that they feel Polish people are dumber than others. Again, our point about cultural psychology is that very often, as members of a culture, we may be responding to and expressing ourselves in a series of traditional idioms that really belong to the group. For this reason, if someone comes door-to-door with a questionnaire or survey, we are likely to give our intellectual answers to the questions that relate to our feelings about other groups. If we collect our jokes, on the other hand, we may get an entirely different cultural answer about the dimensions of intergroup feelings and tensions.

THE ETHNIC THREAT    The story of the castrated boy mentioned in Chapter 5 is another good example of how folklore represents the feelings of a culture. One of the things we noted about that story was its ability to exist in a number of different generic frameworks while still passing on the same ethnic information: one of "our" innocent people has been mutilated by members of the locally feared minority group. One need not ever have heard of Freud to be aware that castration has been widely used as a symbol of taking power away from someone. We have stories in which other people's aggressions toward ourselves are described in terms of castration, and there are stories, legends, and even factual occurrences that detail how castration has been used in retaliation to such aggression. Moreover, the accounts of a number of cavalrymen and American Indians from the frontier days of the United States tell us that castration of enemy dead and dying was a standard procedure. Yet we can assume, I think, that castration is more common in story and song than in reality. Again, without even inquiring of the standard works on psychology about the nature of this symbolic action, we can assume from the records available in folklore that such an image as castration may stand as a startling kind of tableau that can express for a close group the most horrible aspects of interracial strife.

On a somewhat broader level, but related nonetheless, we noted that feared ethnic groups are often depicted as being "out to get us" sexually. One hears the urban legend, sometimes circulating as rumor, that all the illegitimate children in a local high school had nonwhite fathers. One hears that Blacks, Indians, and Jews want nothing more than to cause someone from "our" group to become pregnant. There is the story "Goldilocks on the Oregon Trail": On the way across the Plains, grandmother (who was then young and beautiful) was almost bought by an Indian chief (this story is not in any of the family journals of the trip, no matter how exhaustive their entries; nonetheless, it is told as true by at least a dozen unrelated pioneer families). And of course the image is often used in popular literature and in the movies: The young, innocent, light-skinned heroine is threatened, tortured, or even sexually attacked by an animallike, darker, aggressive male.

In the psychology of ethnic folklore, the majority group symbolizes its anxieties about minority groups by seeing them as sexual threats to "our" innocent males and females. The virtue is on our side, the aggression on theirs. One is motivated to inquire into how these themes can be so vitally and continually passed on in oral tradition if indeed it is true that "nobody believes them." Here, I think, is the confirmation of the double level of the folk involvement I suggested previously in this chapter. As our culture has become increasingly intellectual in the way it rears its individual members, we are reared in at least a double view of reality; included, of course, are all those codes, attitudes, connotations, and traditional patternings that we picked up as members of our ethnic, familial, regional, and occupational folk groups. Included also are all those individualized patterns and philosophies that we have been encouraged to develop for our own view. These two kinds of involvement exist simultaneously in most of us; being a folklorist does not exempt anyone from the effects of both levels.

Being a folklorist involves recognizing that one cannot escape from tradition merely by studying it. One belongs to a particular ethnic group and perhaps has deep connections with the regional, occupational, and national groups of parents and relatives. Being a folklorist on the level of cultural involvement is a simple matter of participating in those expressions and customs that relate to the group's sense of being. Being a folklorist on the intellectual, intentional, level of involvement thus does not imply that one can in any way claim an intellectual superiority or an aloofness over folklore and other bearers of tradition. We need to be able to realize that we are at one and the same time participating members of a culture in which the elephant jokes made sense a few years ago and as individuals who can, because of our particular interest, stand back and scrutinize our own position in those traditional networks. Anyone is free to hold a personal opinion on such matters as race, sex, politics, and human rights; at the same time, it would be naive to deny the effect tradition has on any society in exactly such matters as these. The folklorist therefore needs to distinguish between personal opinion and the powers of tradition. The larger importance of this can be grasped only if we are capable of noticing that the two kinds of involvement exist daily side by side.

Currently, there is a very strong move toward equal rights for women; many people have spoken out forcibly on one side or another. Regardless of the particular position taken by individuals, however, we still must recognize that we live in a society that tells jokes about mothers-in-law, that relates jokes and legends of women's alleged inability to understand mechanics or money, that thinks it funny to ask someone "Have you stopped beating your wife?" and in a society whose members still laugh at ballads like "The Farmer's Curst Wife" and "The Wife Wrapt in Wether's Skin." It would seem clear, considering these elements of tradition, that the final determination of women's rights will very likely not be made on the basis of shifting opinions of individuals but, if at all, on the development of another sense of propriety within the culture. Such changes come slowly, especially when pressure is applied from without. The folklorist is in a position to see and appreciate how cultural involvements impinge upon timely matters that might otherwise be thought of as entirely political, personal, or philosophical.

FOLK MEASUREMENTS   A less ominous example of how we all participate in a cultural and intellectual use of folklore is in our traditional measurements. Even though we are pleased to believe that our measurements are exact and reproduceable, and even though we may believe they are based only on scientific exactitude, it is interesting to know that our most commonly used measurements are based on rather inexact foundations that reveal more about our culture's earlier attitudes than about scientific precision. For example, our foot seems to have been based originally on the average size of a man's foot. Similarly, a rod was the length of the left feet of sixteen men in the 1500s. Our word *mile* comes from the Latin *milia passuum*, one thousand paces. *Yard* comes to us from the Old English *gierd*, by way of the Middle English *yerde*, a rod or staff. A furlong was the length of a farmer's single furrow in a field.

In due time, of course, these measurements became standardized, and once they became formal entities within the intellectual framework of science they developed a sanctity that is now almost impossible to shake loose, for the foot has become so believed in as an actuality in nature that recent attempts to change over to the metric system have been greeted with suspicions of an international conspiracy against our culture. These measurements are therefore a part of our cultural bearings as well as building blocks in our intellectual connections as we study the formalities of weights and measurements. This is not only a good example of how folklore and formal culture interpenetrate continually, but it is also testimony to the necessity for the folklorist to realize that we live in a world in which people share traditions and in which the intentional intellectual use of those traditions can be developed to a high art indeed.

Many scholars have pointed out how concepts of time in Western culture developed in pretty much the same way. We are aware that there was not even a future tense in Anglo Saxon (Old English), the forerunner of modern English, which was spoken from about A.D. 700 to 1000. Not only did northern Europe and some cultures in the Middle East develop the concept of measurable time, but some of these cultures became exceedingly interested in future time. We have become so intensely involved in measuring time that we actually believe that time exists as a separate entity in and of itself, that it can be counted upon, that it can be followed like a ribbon. Yet the concepts leading up to this current situation, in which we can measure microseconds, probably have more to do with cultural attitudes and traditions than with scientific observation.

It is illuminating that our folk speech today contains a great number of measurements that seem to the scientific eye very inaccurate, or at least inconsistent, and yet we use them on a daily basis perhaps more readily than we use more specific measurements. For small quantities we have just a tad, a smidgen, a touch, a skosh (no doubt brought back from Japan after the Second World War, for in Japanese the word for a small quantity is *skoshi*), a dab, a dash, a thimbleful, a pinch, a bit, a little bit, and, for evenly distributed but sparse objects, a smattering.

A small, undetermined period of time is referred to as "just a minute"; the implication of the term is that although a small amount of time will elapse, the person waiting is not to take it seriously. This can be contrasted with the statement, "It took hours for you to get here." A short distance can be referred to as "only a whoop and a holler down the road." Terms like "just a little ways," "a little bit farther," and "pretty soon" indicate small measurements whose precise dimensions are not required in order to gain the knowledge we need.

Some particular occupations have what might be called hyperbolic folk micromeasurements. In logging, when gigantic logs are being loaded onto railroad cars or logging trucks, it is often necessary for the person guiding the loader to indicate how much farther the log needs to be lowered or placed to one side or the other. In order to indicate tiny movements of the log, measurements such as BCH, YCH, and RCH are used, based on the supposed difference in diameter of female pubic hair. The colors black, yellow, and red, indicating increasingly fine measurements, are used by loggers in preference to such terms as "eensy-weensy" or "just a teeny bit more," either of which might bring gales of laughter from one's colleagues or, worse, aspersions cast on one's masculine credentials.

Measurements for larger amounts include such terms as scads, a gang, a whole bunch, a whole raft, a pile, the whole shooting match, and the whole kit and kaboodle. In Ireland one sometimes hears the term "a clatter of people," an appropriate measurement that indicates not only a large group but also the noise it makes.

As people who are culturally involved in our own folklore, we use such terms as these every day, even though we like to think we are very precise and practical. As intentional folklorists looking to intellection as a way of interpreting some of these matters, we may be in the somewhat more complicated position of being able to study such measurements further, making complete lists and definitions, and finding out thereby how our culture actually uses the concept of measurement on a day-to-day basis. These measurements convey something accurately or they would not be used. As with the jokes mentioned earlier, daily concepts of measurement may differ quite distinctly from what people think they think about measurements.

Another step for the professional folklorist, of course, is to compare the measurements used commonly by one's own culture with those used by others. An interesting way to start is to apply the measurements directly to situations experienced in the other culture. An old friend of mine, the Reverend Baxter Liebler, a long-time Episcopalian missionary to the Navajo, tells of his first adventures in Navajo country when, riding an old bony nag across the desert, he tried to locate a certain area where he thought he might found a mission. He met a Navajo riding nearby and inquired if the man could speak English. He said he did, so Liebler asked him how far it was to the place he sought. The Navajo sat his horse thoughtfully for a while, looking at Liebler's skinny horse. Then he said, "It's about five miles; on that horse of yours, about ten." Our first inclination is to smile at the well-intentioned inaccuracy of the measurements. Yet it is clear that the man had learned that a mile was some unit of distance, and in this situation he probably had said something far more meaningful than if he had been able to give the precise distance to Liebler's destination.

I tried once to show a small group of Navajo friends exactly what a mile was. We got into a jeep and I inquired if they saw where we were at that moment. They answered that they did. I then drove as straight as I could across the desert until the odometer told me we had gone one mile. I stopped and announced, "Well, here we are. This is one mile." My Navajo friends sat silently for some time, then one asked politely, "Where?" "Right here," I said. "This is a mile." "Oh," they said politely. "Didn't you see first of all that we were way over there and now we are right here?" I asked. "Yes, we see," they said, "but where is it, this thing you are talking about?" Of course, at the time I was exasperated at my friends for not understanding me, but I had failed to recognize that the distance we had traveled, the place where we started, and the place where we ended were all irrelevant in the world they lived in, and there was no reason at all why they should have seen it as important or worthy of any kind of measurement. In fact, so various is the Navajo understanding of our word *mile*, that the term *Navajo mile* has come to have a meaning all its own in the southwestern United States. When used by whites, it means a distance of up to thirty miles. As far as I can tell from my older Navajo friends, their understanding of the term is "way down the road and out of sight." Travelers in Navajo country looking earnestly for a gas station or a restroom, or who pick up a Navajo hitchhiker, would do well to be aware that "Oh, about a mile," is not a sure sign that the goal is near at hand.

I had lived with the Navajo family of old Little Wagon for several months before he politely asked me early one morning what kind of noise I was making on my wrist every day. I tried to explain to him that my watch was a means of measuring time, but of course since the Navajos have no word for time as we know it, and because I was still learning the Navajo language, I had no way to explain it to him. My first impulse was to believe that I could simply describe what time was like and why it was important to know it and where I was in relationship to it, but I was brought up abruptly by my realizing that nothing I could say to the old man made any sense to him at all. I pointed out to him how the hands went around a dial that was marked off in equal sections. I then told him that by watching where the hands were I could determine what kinds of things I should be doing. "Like what?" he asked in Navajo. "Well, eating. It tells me when to eat." "Don't your people eat when they are hungry? We eat when we are hungry if there is food." "Well, yes, we eat when we are hungry; that is, no, we eat three times a day, and we are not supposed to eat in between times." "Why not?" "Well, it's not healthy." "Why is that?" And so on. I tried another tack. I said that this machine told me when I needed to do those things that were necessary in order to make my living (there is no Navajo word for *work* that sets it apart from other useful and normal things a person might do). The old man asked, "Aren't those things that you do anyway? What is it that this tells you to do that you wouldn't do anyway?" "Well, it tells me when to go out and look for rocks [there was no Navajo word for uranium at the time], and then my company will know how much to pay me." "Do you mean if you lost that machine, you would stop looking for rocks?" "Well, no, I guess I wouldn't." Finally, in exasperation, I said that the watch actually was my reference point to some larger ongoing process outdoors, and this seemed to satisfy the old man. But later, when we were outside that afternoon, he stopped me and held me by the elbow and asked, "Where is it? That which is happening out here?" Beginning to be even more frustrated, I said, "Well, the sun comes up and goes down, doesn't it?" "Yes," he agreed expectantly. "Well, I guess I can't explain it to you. It's nothing, after all. It's all inside the watch. All it does is just go around and make noise." "I thought so," he said.

In these adventures, although I didn't know it, I was being asked to be a folklorist in function if not in title. I suppose every person who has worked among the members of a distinctly different culture will have great numbers of similar stories to tell. The point is that when we experience the people of another culture, even to understand them and to encourage them to understand us, we must operate through the world-view codes that are expressed in everything from art to science. When we find ourselves among people whose codes and systems are so different from our own that almost no understanding can take place without further study, we are forced to become applied folklorists and anthropologists even to survive. What many people do not realize, and the point I have been trying to illustrate through several of the examples here, is that we are obliged to be applied folklorists in direct proportion to the extent we try to exist fully within our own close group as well. We may not be so overtly aware of it, not so painfully cognizant of it because of dislocations in meaning, but we are forced to study, learn, and use folklore nonetheless or be labeled oddballs in our own group. By noticing what kinds of everyday measurements we have and do not have, and those that other people have and do not have, we are given one code by which we can navigate in our culture or in theirs a little more clearly. Similarly, by knowing what is and what is not funny in a culture we have one more avenue of relating ourselves to that culture, whether it be that of the Navajo or of our own family.

## ◤ THE INTENTIONAL FOLKLORIST As

I have suggested, the intellectual involvement in folklore, at least for clarification, can be seen as that objectified scrutiny of tradition that is brought about by our awareness of the existence of many versions of a story, the many ways of telling a joke, the variety of barn styles, and so on. In short, once we are cognizant of how tradition functions in lives and close groups outside our own, we can make an intellectual approach to the subject as well as maintain our own personal cultural involvement with the folklore of our own group. There are at least two kinds of intentional folklorists. For our simple purposes here, we may describe them as amateur and professional, but perhaps untrained and trained would be closer to the dichotomy many professional folklorists feel between themselves and others in the field.

AMATEURS   There are two kinds of amateur folklorists: good and bad. The good amateurs are those who, in spite of a lack of professional training, have developed and maintained a real appreciation of the depth of a local tradition. Their attempt is usually to contact the real bearers of local traditions, to interview them in depth, to record their expressions, and to bring their works forth in book form or in educational TV series, commercial records, and the like. In fact, a good many fine records of folk music have been produced by amateurs in folklore who, armed with a personal knowledge of folk music and proper equipment, have been able to provide for amateurs and professionals alike a tremendous range of traditional musical art the likes of which most people are not in a position to experience firsthand.

One recent phenomenon in this area has been the Foxfire project, begun in Rabun Gap, Georgia, by Eliot Wigginton as a class exercise for his high school students. Typically, the students combed their neighborhoods for local traditional artists of all kinds, those with special talents in everything from hog butchering to cabin building, to chair carving, to singing songs and telling anecdotes. The Foxfire project, and the great number of imitative progeny across the land based on it, are exciting not so much for their analytical brilliance as for the obvious local commitment and rededication to those traditions that might otherwise have died out without the strong attention and interest of the younger generations.

The Foxfire students and their adviser do not claim to be professional folklorists whose interests are in the discussion and analysis of tradition; rather, they are local aficionados in the fullest sense of that term, partisans of their own culture who want to see it recorded and properly revered. Sometimes these projects have been taken to task for their superficiality or thinness, but I believe it is better to laud them for the dynamic way in which the public school—certainly one of the most conservative formal elements in American life—has been able to open its perspectives to include the folk arts and traditions of the students' own locale as meriting the same serious consideration as other topics in the curriculum.

Quite the most stalwart and tireless of the people who have elevated our awareness of the traditions of their regions without first obtaining academic credentials has been Vance Randolph, the venerable Ozark folklorist. Long before folklore became a big publishing business in the United States, Randolph was publishing small collections of Ozark tales, retold according to the vocabulary demands of the publishers. *Who Blowed Up the Church House?* and *The Devil's Pretty Daughter* are simple retellings of Ozark folk tales and jokes. *Ozark Superstitions* is a somewhat more formal gathering of beliefs and customs from the Ozark area, gathered by Randolph over a lifetime of active participant observation. His *Pissing in the Snow,* a collection of Ozark folk tales that could not have come into print until now, is an astounding compendium of anecdotal and narrative material, much of which can be traced back to its European origins. Vance Randolph valued his Ozark heritage enough to want to share it with others not of the same close group. Without a formal degree in folklore, without the benefit of grants and government foundations, sometimes in the face of grinding poor health, he has shown us the richness and beauty available in regional folklore when one is dedicated to the conscientious amassing and interpreting of personal traditions.

The bad amateurs are easily identifiable, and I do not intend to name any of them here. They are the ones who insist on cooing over local whimsies and absurdities, pointing out the backward quaintness that "still survives" in the nooks and backwaters of rural America. They would be embarrassed about folklore if it were not possible to describe it in demeaning terms. For such people, folklore is the stuff of children's stories, of cutely reworded anecdotes, of local color uninformed by the richness of live tradition. Many of the bad amateurs are motivated by ancestor worship and a nostalgia for a past that may exist only in the imagination. The materials they concentrate on are therefore often romanticized or given an odd focus; the traditions they mention, insofar as they are recognizable as traditions at all, are usually comfortably juxtaposed to modern times, as if to say: "This is what folks around here were like, back before the highway came through" (implying relief that they are no longer that way).

There would be no harm in this kind of amateur except that such work tends to confirm the misconception many people hold of folklore: It is backward and quaint, it is held chiefly by people of low intellectual ability, it is found mostly in the rural areas where the blessings of technology have penetrated only slowly. Any record or book that portrays local people as hicks who ought to know enough to apologize for themselves

THE DYNAMICS OF FOLKLORE

is essentially an insult to serious tradition-bearers and an impediment to our understanding the most dynamic aspect of our culture. The worst possible effect in this category of folklore is that sometimes the folk themselves will hear such a record or read such a book and concur in the sentiments it projects.

THE PROFESSIONAL   Some people would also divide this category into two sections, the good and the bad, or to put it more technically, the pure scholars and the applied folklorists. The dichotomy is really unfair, and although there may certainly be good and bad professional folklorists, they are likely to be described more accurately in terms of how well they do the professional task they set out to do. At least most professionals are agreed that they have in common the task of encouraging and maintaining not only the field of study called folklore but the traditions themselves that form the basis of the field. Thus, while some professionals as teachers may be boring and others as scholars may be drudges, it is not so simple to divide them into positive and negative categories. Rather, we can observe that most professional folklorists today are either in teaching and research, usually connected with a college or university, or they are employed by public agencies and private businesses who see the need for work in, or exposure to, the perspectives of folklore. Some examples of folklore employment are provided in Chapter 10, "Applications of Folklore." Perhaps here it would be well to describe briefly the nature of some of these jobs for those who may wonder what one can do to make a living as a folklorist.

Probably the most common employment for folklorists today is in the academic setting. A number of major universities in the United States have folklore departments and institutes, but it is more common to find a folklorist teaching a few classes in an English, history, or anthropology department. Usually the professor is interested in a particular genre of folklore, often one related to the specialty of his department: One finds English department folklorists stressing genres such as the ballad and the folk tale, while anthropological folklorists often stress linguistics, custom and belief, Native American oral literature, and so forth.

Most university folklorists spend at least some of their time doing field research, writing up their results for the professional journals, and when travel money is available, reading short papers to each other at regional and national meetings of the various folklore societies. Because the press of academic business and paperwork is always great, however, many folklorists in academe find that they do their research through surrogates—their students. Students in folklore classes are very often found doing field research rather than library term papers. A typical folklore class features some kind of engagement with field research, some theoretical research in the library, and considerable discussion in class as the professor tries to make clear to students from a variety of academic departments what folklore does and how it does it. Collections of folklore made by students are usually kept either in the professor's own files or in a larger archive of the department or university.

It is a fact of the modern academic approach to folklore that much of the basic field research has been carried out by students. This may be one of the few subjects in which a student can do a term paper that does not end its days in the wastebasket or rotting among the discarded Coke bottles, cheese wrappers, and freshmen themes in the professor's desk drawer. Students who took a folklore course because they thought it might be an interesting way to fulfill a general course requirement have found their own research being used by scholars worldwide. A recent book on Oregon folklore is filled with examples of occupational, ethnic, and regional lore, virtually all of it collected by students. This is fortunate for everyone, for it not only forces students to confront the dynamics of tradition and the idiosyncrasies of tradition-bearers directly, but it also allows professional folklorists access to a far wider range of traditional examples than they could ever make contact with themselves. It has a melancholy side, however: Some professors are known to use the fruits of their students' labors without appropriate acknowledgment.

Professional folklorists who work for public and private agencies usually develop and coordinate festivals, social programs, or research in applied folklore. One prominent medical school employs a folklorist on its staff in behaviorial sciences. The Smithsonian Institution employs a few professionals to study family folklore, occupational folklore, and the folklore of ethnic groups, live parallels to the materials found in the Smithsonian's collections. The National Endowment for the Arts employs a professional folklorist as the Director of the Folk Arts Program, a small office that encourages the maintenance of folk traditions and promotes greater public access to them as well as greater public appreciation of them through modest grants. Cities have employed folklorists as coordinators of ethnic heritage programs. Some states have established the office of State Folklorist or State Folk Arts Coordinator. Some companies hire folklorists to train management officials for overseas assignments. Indian tribes have hired folklorists as consultants for heritage maintenance and cultural retention programs. These and other jobs are explained in greater detail in Chapter 10; I bring them in here simply to show that folklorists indeed play a variety of roles in the formal life of

America, and that their job generally requires them to take seriously the matters of tradition brought up in this book and to bring them before the public for a variety of purposes ranging from intellectual scrutiny to personal involvement to social action. The job of the professional is construed, then, not as an attempt to show how quaint folklore is or used to be, but to discuss and analyze its validity in the ongoing culture, to provide greater recognition of its role in our lives, and to encourage people to be more articulate about their role in tradition and about tradition's role in their lives—and to be more aware of the connections between their traditions and the codes and worldview of their entire society.

## 𝕂 RIGHTS AND RESPONSIBILITIES

Keeping in mind that the intentional folklorist is dealing intellectually with material the tradition-bearers themselves deal with personally and culturally, the folklorist presents not only a set of positive functions for tradition (to study, preserve, and provide status for folklore), but also the possibility of a negative impact by intruding upon or mishandling those very personal and gut-level codes that members of close groups share so solidly.

THE RIGHT TO INFORMATION    First, there is a distinct possibility that folklorists might unwittingly become cavalier about other people's lore. Indeed, since it is not our belief, or our song, we may not feel the need to approach it with the reverence accorded it by someone in the close group. In fact, until very recently folklorists and anthropologists assumed they had an inalienable right as fieldworkers to a proprietary interest in the materials they generated. Very seldom in a collection of tales or myth texts does one find an overt statement by the tradition-bearer giving permission to publish the account. Seldom is the tradition-bearer listed as the author of such a book, either; usually the scholar gets the credit for producing the work. Because of this, and because some groups have distinct restrictions on how materials ought to be used and disseminated —restrictions that are not recognized by the print-oriented culture of the scholar—folklorists and anthropologists have earned, to some extent justly, the reputation for taking things away.

Some of my Navajo acquaintances have become very reluctant to share their beloved Coyote stories with anyone who plans to publish them. They reason that these stories should be told only in the winter, and that the telling of them under proper circumstances enables the Navajos to take part in the annual round of seasonal events on a cosmic level. To tell these stories out of season is to challenge the stability of this cosmic system. To have the stories available in print makes it possible for them to be read at any time of the year. My friend Yellowman is convinced that this may be one of the reasons why sheep do not produce as much wool anymore, why there is not as much grass as there used to be, and why people are being bitten more often by rattlesnakes. Non-Navajo researchers might well laugh at these concerns in a cheerfully condescending way and assure the Navajos that, indeed, printing a story has nothing at all to do with rattlesnake bites.

This is all well and good for scholars, but it may not allay the fears of tradition-bearers, who, working from the concepts and premises of their culture, have their own psychological stability to watch out for. They are not likely to find the answer for their dilemma in the codes and systems of another distinctly different worldview. Should we stop publishing Navajo Coyote tales? We could, of course, but there are already so many in printed circulation that perhaps action at this time would be fruitless in reducing the fears of Navajo storytellers. Should we suppress those already in print, burn all books with Coyote stories in them? This course of action runs against our feelings about freedom of the press and access to information. This is a good example of an entirely irresolvable dilemma, one that has grown more acute through the years because folklore and anthropological field researchers have assumed the right of access to traditional materials and have assumed the right to publish or disseminate those materials however they saw fit without regard to the hesitancies, codes, taboos, and ritual concerns of the real owners of those stories. We are now in a position where we cannot retreat or advance without doing injustice to the people who provided the riches of their culture, perhaps too willingly, for our scrutiny. That they feel dislocated and hurt while we only register embarrassment is a clear indication of the differences in worldview. It is also testimony to the abuse of power.

OWNERSHIP   One thing that should be made clear both in the mind of the folklorist and in the perceptions of the tradition-bearer is that even though folk materials are seldom copyrightable by an individual, they should be considered owned to some extent by the tradition-bearer or by his community, not by the folklorist. Folklorists, especially those working in archives, have an uncanny ability to translate the stored materials of others into a respository of facts and data to be disseminated to any interested party at the discretion of the archivist. This can very easily overlook the fact that dissemination of some materials may be embarrassing or shocking to the community that considers those expressions their own. In some cases it may be a matter of simple impropriety, in others a matter of religious outrage.

Albert Lord has observed that some Yugoslavian singers perform certain stories so well—or by special personal inclination—that they are thought by others to own them. Similarly, in many Indian tribes particular storytellers are thought to own the stories and songs by virtue of having been given them by a previous narrator. Even within the person's own village, in a case like this, the story would not be told by anyone else without special permission, or without the narrator "giving the story away." This necessarily means that any folklorists or anthropologists who wish to collect and transmit the stories of such groups as the Tlingit need to be sure that they have been given permission, literally given the tales, before they can feel free to disseminate those narratives. It is a pernicious and corrosive impertinence for folklorists to assume that once the materials are collected the choice of sharing is up to them.

I once talked to an archivist who presided over a collection of Native American anecdotes, reminiscences, tales, and myths being amassed by a fairly large tribe; he insisted that the tribe had no right to tell him which materials could be shared with outsiders and which required special protection and secrecy. He felt obliged as an archivist to disseminate any and all materials to those people he felt were bona fide scholars in search of the kinds of information his archive could reveal. Why else have an archive? The tribe, frightened that it might lose control of some of its precious ritual information, concerned that older tradition-bearers might not cooperate with the project if they felt their stories might come into the hands of strangers, asked for the archivist's resignation. But of course there could have been a compromise between the two in which the tribe recognized that some of its materials were of great scholarly value and might be shared while the archivist recognized that part of his job was to encourage and protect the tribe's special cultural information. Such compromises are not corrosive to folklore; rather, they ask the folklorist to join forces with the tradition-bearer to make sure that the materials are not squandered, misplaced, misunderstood, or mishandled. Surely those who can most accurately delineate the concerns in those areas are the tradition-bearers themselves.

An outstanding example exists of a horrible situation that arose because of a well-intentioned field researcher sharing secret information with outsiders. The folklorist had been accepted warmly into a small tribe on one of the islands in the South Seas. He had become so familiar with the tribe and its people, so trusted by them, that he was inducted into one of the men's societies. For a considerable period of time while he lived there he participated fully in the ritual life of this small tribe, even being allowed to take photographs where none had been allowed previously. Obviously, the people trusted him with these photographs, as they might one of themselves, because as a ritual brother he could be expected to act and respond the same way as others in the group. After his return to his home country, he was urged by colleagues to put out a small book of limited circulation describing the rituals of his adoptive tribe. This he agreed to do, apparently in the belief that the data were so full and rich that the only result would be a positive one: A few scholars interested in this particular tribe and its ceremonies would have a fuller picture and a deeper understanding of the beauty and complexity of those rituals. But as can happen the book was listed in a bibliography and came to the attention of a schoolteacher on the home island. Thinking the students would be interested in reading a book about their own tribe, the teacher ordered it for the school library. When eventually—and inevitably—a young girl from the tribe checked the book out and took it home, disaster struck: There, laid out in pictorial detail, were all the secret ceremonies of one of the central men's societies, secrets that had never before been revealed to the eyes of women or of people outside that ritual group. For one thing, the people believed women would go blind if they saw the ceremonies. But none did. Shock and apostasy followed, and the result of this episode was the near-total dissolution of the tribal religion. One of the practical effects of this misadventure has been that folklorists and anthropologists have been generally barred by tribesmen in that area.

This is not a case of a sinister, calculating folklorist with graverobber mentality, striking it rich with shocking photographs for bookshelves across America. Rather, the researcher tried, perhaps beyond his ability, to limit the circulation to the eyes of those who could best understand those people. Nonetheless, we cannot avoid admitting that the result was chaos and cultural destruction for the people so innocently betrayed.


The folklorist and the anthropologist may be contemptuous of such tribal interests if they want, but they cannot avoid responsibility when it comes to the effects of the dissemination of material outside the control of its usual owners and proprietors. If folklorists are to expand cultural awareness, not be "con artists," we must keep the delicacy of these responsibilities constantly before us in our research.

# ⚞ BIBLIOGRAPHICAL NOTES

In my estimation, the finest modern statement about the field of folklore, its promises, and its responsibilities is in Dell Hymes's presidential address to the annual meeting of the American Folklore Society at Portland, Oregon, on November 2, 1974. It forms the first part of an article already referred to several times: "Folklore's Nature and the Sun's Myth," *Journal of American Folklore*, 88 (1975), 345–369; see pp. 345–356 especially.

Several notes and queries about the cement truck driver story have appeared around the country in regional journals and newsletters. Louie Attebery brings the strands together in "It Was a De Soto," *Journal of American Folklore*, 83 (1970), 452–457. The widely found Northwest family legend about Grandma almost being sold to the Indians is discussed in Francis Haines, "Goldilocks on the Oregon Trail," *Idaho Yesterdays*, 9 (Winter 1965–1966), 26–30.

I have already referred several times to the Abrahams and Dundes article on the elephant jokes (*The Psychoanalytic Review*, 56 [1969], 225–241); the piece contains a very succinct résumé of Freud's approach to joking behavior. Dundes explores other more recent jokes stemming from racial friction in "Jokes and Covert Language Attitudes: The Curious Case of the Wide-Mouth Frog," *Language in Society*, 6 (1977), 141–147. In still another article, Dundes suggests that in the case of jokes employing minority stereotypes there is a transference of what is painful, unacceptable, or taboo from "us" onto "them," an indication that the psychological term *projection* provides a clear way of dealing with the phenomenon; see "Projection in Folklore: A Plea for Psychoanalytic Semiotics," *Modern Language Notes*, 91 (1976), 1500–1533. Of special application to this chapter are his comments on the mutilated boy (pp. 1524–1525), dead-baby jokes (pp. 1525–1526), and streaking (p. 1526).

Other references to the mutilated boy are mentioned in previous sections of this book; consult, at the least, Hippensteel, " 'Sir Hugh': The Hoosier Contribution to the Ballad," *Indiana Folklore*, 2:2 (1969), 75–140, and Florence Ridley, "A Tale Told Too Often," *Western Folklore*, 26 (1967), 153–156. A very fine set of precautions for those who want to use the terms and approaches of psychology and psychiatry is suggested by David Hufford in "Psychology, Psychoanalysis, and Folklore," *Southern Folklore Quarterly*, 38 (1974), 187–197. Hufford notes that many nonspecialists are inclined to misuse terms like *anxiety* and thus lose the force of what they could have shown in their studies. Dealing with psychological realities, such as real dangers and uncertainties on the job, Patrick B. Mullen shows that one need not use a Freudian approach to make the case for a clearly functional set of beliefs and practices based on shared tensions and group dynamics; see "The Function of Magic Folk Belief among Texas Coastal Fishermen," *Journal of American Folklore*, 82 (1969), 214–225.

For a lighthearted example of how far the naming of animals and people in groups can be carried, see James Lipton, *An Exaltation of Larks, or, The*

*Venereal Game* (New York: Grossman, 1968). For the cultural background of our folk measurements, see Hall's three books mentioned previously, especially *The Silent Language*.

Vance Randolph's most recent book is *Pissing in the Snow and Other Ozark Folktales* (Urbana: University of Illinois Press, 1976). Introduced by Rayna Green and with extensive annotations (which do not overshadow the tales) by Frank A. Hoffman, it represents a brave foray against the kind of stereotypification that prefers to view the quaint hill folk as harmless churchy clods with dull wits. Other works by "amateurs" would include *One Potato, Two Potato*, by Mary and Herbert Knapp—already referred to previously as a fine collection of real children's lore—and that of Eliot Wigginton (and his students), whose Foxfire project, for all its focus on their own rural scene, captured the imaginations of people all over the country. On the snobbishness that has sometimes reared its head in spite of these clear examples of valuable work by nonspecialists, read John O. West's impassioned but succinct statement, "The Professional-Amateur-Popularizer Feud in Folklore," *Journal of American Folklore*, 88 (1975), 299–300.

For comments, advice, and good examples of the relationships between folklore researchers and their live resources, see the following works. Richard M. Dorson, in the Introduction to his *Buying the Wind: Regional Folklore in the United States* (Chicago: University of Chicago Press, 1969), provides some very helpful remarks based on his own field experience ("Collecting Oral Folklore in the United States," pp. 1–20). Dorson's comments in the introduction to his *American Negro Folktales* (New York: Fawcett, 1967), pp. 12–64, are also illuminating, for they describe, among other things, the dilemmas faced by a white collector trying to get people of another ethnic group to share their most cherished anecdotes. Alan Jabbour and Carl Fleischhauer, in their work on the Hammons family records referred to previously, provide us with a high performance to emulate: working with several members of an isolated family over several years' time without flagging and without alienating the family. George Carey gives some thoughtful reflections on our ethics, and on our professional debt to "informants," in his deceptively simple "The Storyteller's Art and the Collector's Intrusion," in *Folklore Today: A Festschrift for Richard M. Dorson*, ed. Linda Dégh, Henry Glassie, and Felix J. Oinas (Bloomington: Indiana University Press), 81–91. It is clear from Carey's remarks that while he is not completely sure about the effects his published articles have had upon the lives and reputations of his informants, he is certain of their effects upon him: They have been instrumental in establishing him as a leading professional. Here is a rare and moving example of why vertical distinctions between scholar and folk simply cannot be tolerated. Michael Owen Jones provides another, equally important consideration in "Folk Art Production and the Folklorist's Obligation," *Journal of Popular Culture*, 4 (1970), 194–211, when he warns us of the possible distortion of both art and scholarship by the very nature of intrusion and special focus on a traditional performer. John J. Honigmann argues that relations between researcher and subject need not be restricted to objective, formal modes, however, and he suggests, moreover, that the researcher need not remain totally outside the phenomenon being studied or aloof from its eventual description. In "The Personal Approach in Cultural Anthropological Research," *Current Anthropology*, 17 (1976), 243–250—plus discussion, pp. 251–261—Honigmann puts forth the idea, already well accepted by most folklorists, I think, that the personal approach recognizes the importance of the investigator's own account and evaluation of an event, his interpretation of it, and his conclusions about it (matters often dismissed as too subjective by social scientists).

If you want to meet folklorists and participate in the exchange of views at any regional or national meeting, you can find out how to join the various folklore societies by looking at the fine print in any *recent* issue of any folklore journal. Usually, subscription to a professional journal includes membership; in cases where it does not, the details for application are usually spelled out, often inside the front cover. The annual meeting of the American Folklore Society draws professional folklorists (most of them college professors), other interested academics, graduate and undergraduate students, local history buffs, and, on occasion, some of the folk from throughout the United States and from many other countries. Many of the best papers and reports are given by students, and many of these, in turn, become published papers, theses, dissertations, and books. *Oregon Folklore*, written by Suzi Jones and already mentioned several times, is one of several good examples of a book researched and written by a graduate student in folklore, using her own fieldwork as well as that of many previous undergraduate students at the University of Oregon. A whole issue of the *Journal of American Folklore*, 88:347 (January–March 1975), devoted to the topic of women and folklore, was edited by a graduate student at the University of Texas (and many of the articles were done by graduate students). *Folklore Forum*, a journal of contemporary folklore studies, is put out entirely by graduate students at Indiana University (some of whom also help edit the prestigious *Journal of the Folklore Institute*, also published at Indiana). There are similar examples of other folklore centers around the United States and Canada, but it is unnecessary to mention them all; the point is clear, I hope. Being a folklorist, on the international level, is a collegial activity involving the professional and the apprentice in an exciting partnership of discovery that would be totally impossible to carry off without the aid, charity, and interest of the tradition-bearers themselves, among whom we may occasionally number ourselves.

# 9

# FOLKLORE RESEARCH

**EVEN THOUGH INTRODUCTORY** STUDENTS AND OTHER NEWLY INTER-ESTED PERSONS MAY NOT BECOME DIRECTLY INVOLVED IN FOLKLORE RESEARCH, THEY SHOULD find the details of fieldwork directly related to their understanding of how the dynamic expressions of folklore become available, intellectually palpable, to audiences outside traditional habitats. Were it not for folklore field research, there would be nothing of substance for folklorists or their students to discuss. While at first sight such a statement seems a careless admission that there is a field of study only because we have dredged one up, it is actually an assertion that folklore—like marine biology—is a study founded on items "brought up" for scrutiny. Although folklore surrounds us all the time, it is so enmeshed in all we do and say that we seldom take the opportunity to regard it separately. Folklore field research does just that by focusing on those particular performance activities that can be seen as traditional.

# ▨ FOLKLORE FIELDWORK Research in folklore

can be pleasantly divided into three main categories: gathering, storing, and pondering, or as they are more commonly referred to in the profession, collecting, archiving, and analysis. In collecting, the main participants are the collector (the folklorist out in the field looking for—and recording—folklore) and the informant (the possessor of folklore, whose role is to supply the collector with material). In archiving, there are the archivist (whose role is to protect the collected materials as they are accessioned and stored) and the scholar (who wants to study these materials). In analysis, there are the collector, the archivist, and the scholar, trying together to make critical judgments on the meaning, function, and importance of folklore materials.

COLLECTOR AND INFORMANT  Throughout this process, it is easy to forget that in folklore—in ongoing tradition itself—it is the tradition-bearer, not the collector, archivist, or scholar, who remains the important person. Notice how the terms *collector* and *informant* suggest a certain kind of one-way relationship: One takes and the other gives. If we are to view the field of folklore seriously, we must realize that the collector is doing something far more delicate than capturing rare butterflies, and the informant is giving out something far more difficult to share than an antique chair. Since folklore is made up of the expressions most closely related to personal identity within a close group, its possessors do not simply throw it up on command. Folks do not give out family recipes to just anyone, do not share songs with people whose reactions might be hurtful.

More knowledgeable folklorists have found that they must first establish some kind of warm relationship before people are willing to share their traditions. And once the traditions have been shared, the relationship must not be canceled. The givers of folklore are the basis of our whole enterprise, yet potentially they are placed in the most extraordinarily hazardous emotional position. Consider what happens to the old lady you have been collecting remedies from when she hails you from the front steps saying, "Where have you been? I've remembered a whole lot of cures I forgot to tell you before!" and you answer "Sorry, lady, I'm not into that anymore." The point is a double one, and it needs to be considered seriously by anyone intending to do fieldwork in folklore or anthropology: (1) The very visits of the folklorist may help to jog a tradition-bearer's memory, so that more items will come to mind (along with a flood of nostalgia, especially in older people or people far from their home territory). (2) A friendship between the collector and the informant will have begun, related directly to these traditions (and the informant will try hard to please the friendly visitor by remembering all possible related materials). Betraying this relationship can have not only severe cultural implications, but it may have a devastating effect on the person so affected and on the tradition itself, to say nothing of placing a barrier before all subsequent researchers who may want to study the tradition further. The Appendix gives a moving example of a woman who nearly stopped singing because of a collector. Accepting responsibility for the delicacy of relationship and trust with tradition-bearers must be the basic ethic for fieldworkers. Just as important, the responsibility is passed on automatically to anyone who controls archival materials and to anyone who uses the materials in scholarship.

We might benefit greatly by junking the terms *collector* and *informant* altogether in favor of *researcher* and *tradition-bearer*, but the former words are so entrenched that a shift seems unlikely. In any case we need to recognize that the informant is neither the subject nor the object of our research (even when studies seem to concentrate on traditional individuals, like Roger Abrahams's study of Almeda Riddle, Edward Ives's book on Larry Gorman, or Michael Owen Jones's work on "Charley"). Rather, bearers of tradition are our distinguished colleagues, our most valuable "library" of tradition, our primary resource for the expressions we seek to understand. Without them and their cooperation, many folklorists would be looking for jobs in the five-and-ten-cent store.

Indeed, folklorists have found that their relationships with their traditional colleagues have been among their most intense and personally rewarding friendships. One thinks of Roger Abrahams and "Granny" Riddle, John Lomax and "Leadbelly," Richard Dorson and J. D. Suggs, A. L. Kroeber and "Ishi," Joseph Epes Brown and Black Elk, Jorge Preloran and Hermogenes Cayo. Not all of these people related in the same way, of course, but in every case it is clear that the folklorist learned more from the tradition-bearer than vice versa, and that the learning took place under the most intimate circumstances.

APPROACH TO FIELDWORK: TACTICS   Since most people do not "do" their folklore at the drop of a hat, especially for strangers who request it, the folklore fieldworker may as well start out recognizing that the most practical approach to recording folklore is to plan on considerable reconnaissance and development of rapport with the tradition-bearers most likely to share their materials. The collector cannot expect to walk up to someone's door, hold out a microphone, and say, "Hi there, I'm from the university and I'm collecting folklore. I wonder if you would tell me a few stories or share some of your superstitions." First of all, as we have observed, the frontal assault is hardly the method, and the front doorstep is hardly the place. Moreover, the person at the door may not have the same understanding of the word *folklore* as the researcher does; it may in fact be taken as an insult that some stranger feels that the resident possesses old wives' tales, nonsense, misinformation, or irreligious notions. More consciously, the housewife at her door may well ask, "Who are you, and why do you want to know?" And the slamming of the door, possibly preceded by a hard look, may end this hypothetical scene.

Surely some kind of friendly introduction is in order in a case like this, and many folklorists have found it helpful to do initial work in a community by asking around town concerning the whereabouts of old-time singers, yarn-spinners, using terms that indicate the nature of the material desired rather than professional jargon. Often it will be a local sheriff, minister, or social worker who knows from personal experience who the tradition-bearers are. A doctor may be aware of some old man down the road who specializes in herbal cures, or he may know the midwives in the vicinity. The owner of a local lumber mill may be aware that some of his workers share hilarious stories over their lunch. A policeman may be full of leads about fruit vendors or sidewalk characters along his beat. If the folklorist comes to someone's door, or visits someone's place of employment at the appropriate time, forearmed with the name of a friend, acquaintance, or relative, the chances are far more likely that it will be possible to engage a tradition-bearer in enough of a conversation to ascertain his or her inclination to share folklore. Richard Dorson, trying to collect Black folk tales in a small town in Michigan, found it necessary to hang around town for a week while the local people silently checked out his assertion that he was a college professor looking for folklore. When they finally concluded that the leather patches on his elbows identified him as a professor, not an undercover policeman, they cheerfully referred him to J. D. Suggs, who turned out to be an apparently inexhaustible resource for folk tales.

When you are invited into another person's home, it is at the discretion of and on the terms of the person doing the inviting. It is not up to the folklorist to be pushy, aggressive, or dazzling. Rather, the researcher should try to blend in as cheerfully as possible with that aspect of the context that seems most likely to help induce and support a traditional performance. If you intend to do folklore research among the members of a Mormon farm family, it will not advance the cause to arrive tipsy. If you wish to study traditional fishing procedures with a group of conservative riverboat guides, it will not be appropriate to show up wild-haired, noisy, and passing marijuana around.

If you wish to record an old woman singing ballads, it will probably scare her to death if you arrive with four friends who haul out their banjos and mandolins to give her a taste of what you are looking for. While it is sometimes possible to coax some folklore from a willing person by singing the first line of a song (see the Appendix), it is also possible to overdo it so that the traditional singer denigrates his or her own ability to satisfy you. On one occasion, with hearty references from his friends, I visited an old man in Roosevelt, Utah, and proceeded to sing several songs I thought he might know. Although he was described as "the guy who knows all the songs around here," one who sang them at great length at every gathering, I found he was totally intimidated by my singing. Concluding that his songs would not be interesting to someone who sang as well as I, he refused to sing a single note for an entire day. Some of the examples of inappropriate tactics I have suggested here are outrageous enough to be visible to anyone; but they bring up the consideration that must be made, subtly or otherwise, by all fieldworkers: What is the tradition I seek to record, and how can I put the tradition-bearer in such a frame of mind and personal context to encourage the performance of the things I want to study?

Does this mean the folklore fieldworker must be a hypocrite? I suppose it all depends on your definition of hypocrisy. It seems pretty evident that there are ways of inducing a normal context and ways of inhibiting one. For example, very few midwives of my acquaintance will discuss the details of midwifery with me. No matter what references I may have from friends and neighbors, most women simply feel awkward discussing these matters with a man. Similarly, if one tries to collect logger songs in all their obscene glory from a retired logger, the performances will simply not come about if the man's wife remains in the room or if the collector is a woman. Noting and responding to certain basic inclinations of the tradition-bearers does not require hypocrisy as much as a recognition of those factors that are indeed cultural and psychological parts of the tradition itself. If the fieldworker is not willing to deal with these necessary components of a tradition, it hardly does any good to try to study performances from that tradition.

In my own fieldwork, I usually try to visit a prospective resource person a number of times before I ever bring a tape recorder. I try to get some kind of personal reference to use at the first meeting, if possible a direct introduction by a close friend of the tradition-bearer. Or I may observe someone performing in some tradition, say, at a county fair or a family picnic, and approach the person on the spot and ask if it might be possible to drop around sometime to hear some more stories or to trade some songs. The initial contact made, the next task is to develop the kind of informal footing with the tradition-bearer that will allow him or her to recognize that traditions may be shared with a researcher. I must admit that in many cases only one visit is necessary to establish a friendly rapport, often because the tradition-bearers, especially older people, are pleasantly surprised that anyone would be interested in the old ways they value so highly. Indeed, they will sometimes share their songs and stories with the most idiotic of researchers. Often it is because of an essentially conservative nature that they are already slightly embittered that many of the old ways have passed. In many cases resource people whose folklore stems from their ethnic backgrounds have been seeking ways in which they might remain American and yet still maintain their ethnic traditions. It is often, thus, with a sense of relief that the tradition-bearer hears a folklorist say these expressions are well worth saving and studying. The tradition-bearer often then sees that he or she can play an important role in sharing these valuable expressions with someone who cares about them.

During these first visits, after a rapport is established, I try to see if it is possible to elicit the kind of performance I want to study. This means, for example, that if I were visiting a Navajo family in order to collect Coyote stories, even with the finest rapport I would not be able to hear any performances unless it were winter. In the case of some other kind of performance, say the kinds of songs that farmers might sing at weddings, I would try to show up at a wedding where I might see the performances done in their usual setting. Once I can establish that the tradition-bearer does in fact perform in such a way that warrants further study, I begin to inquire if the person wouldn't be willing to share some of the stories, songs, or traditions with me at a later date. If possible, we try to set a date when the context can be reestablished as close to normal as possible. In other cases, such as in collecting songs and ballads from old-timers, the best approach may be simply to drop by the person's house for some singing in private.

Once the resource person has shared some of his traditions with the folklorist, it is usually possible to ask permission to bring a tape recorder or a camera on the next visit. In the meanwhile, the fieldworker can size up the room in which the singing or storytelling takes place, the shop in which the wood is carved, and so forth. The appropriate equipment to bring can therefore be chosen, and a certain amount of practicing can be done at home where, for example, the tape recorder can be used in a similar-sized room. By the time the researcher returns, a minimum of playing around with volume controls and placing of the microphone will be necessary. The more quickly and simply the machinery can be operated, the less likely it is to intimidate the tradition-bearer, who may be far more accustomed to large live audiences than to electronics.

By the time the fieldworker is actually ready to start recording, he will have become familiar enough with the tradition-bearer and with the immediate surroundings and context for performance that other particular tactics will have become obvious. Whenever I go to talk to an old logger at his home, I invariably take a woman folklorist along so that first, the man's wife will not feel left out of a conversation in her own home (because it is very often the wife whose role it is to be hospitable and conversational when guests are present), and second, to try to detour the wife into another context—perhaps one in which she herself will express some traditions—so that her presence will not inhibit the logger from talking about those matters that cannot be mentioned in front of women. Sometimes under these circumstances I have found later that my accomplice succeeded in recording more folklore from the wife at her quilting frame or in the kitchen making bread than I could garner from the husband. In any case where these tactics do not seem appropriate, where splitting up a husband and wife for conversation strikes the tradition-bearers themselves as so odd that it constitutes a strain on their sense of propriety, I simply do not put the plan into action.

To a certain extent, one can feel free to manipulate the situation when doing so will allow a tradition-bearer to operate honestly and in a way consonant with his own values. Manipulation of the event becomes manipulation of human beings if the researcher pushes people around in their own home just so folklore may be collected. Some kind of tactics will always be necessary, however, but the researcher must keep in mind that they do not represent an unfair pressure on the tradition-bearer unless they are misused. Rather, they are the same kind of tactics one normally follows in any congenial conversation with friends, especially when trying to avoid argument. Certain topics may be dropped and others played up, people may be brought back around to the main subject if they wander too far from home base, examples may be given (such as when the researcher wants to do work with jokes and finds that most people do not tell a joke without being reminded of one by a previously told joke). Obviously "priming the pump" is a necessary, not unfair, tactic.

MACHINERY  Some folklorists collect with pencil and notebook, others with sketchpads, others with their memories. It is safe to say that many kinds of folklore items may be handily written in a small notebook; proverbs, cures, figures of speech, regional dialect, local terminology, and the like do not always need to be put on tape. It is probably fair to say, however, that most researchers today try to use sound recorders and some kind of film equipment in their attempt to capture fully the whole performance. This means, basically, work with a tape recorder and a camera. Videotape is coming into more widespread use now that the quality of cassette-based, highly portable equipment has been improved. Movies, especially with synchronized sound, are still too expensive for most folklorists to afford on a regular basis, although with recent improvements in technology, some Super-8 work is being done (Super 8mm is available with a magnetic strip attached to the film on which sound recordings may be made simultaneously with filming).

TAPE RECORDERS  Two considerations are of utmost importance: The machines used must be of the highest possible quality available, and the researcher must be thoroughly acquainted with their operation. These observations seem obvious, but most Americans are so familiar with tape recorders and cameras that they think they know more about operating them than they do in practice. Indeed, the cassette tape recorder has become so common that many are inclined to believe it will eventually replace reel-to-reel tape recorders. At least in folklore fieldwork, this is not likely to come about in the foreseeable future.

The whole point of tape recording a folk performance is to capture all the stylistic and intonational details that would be difficult or impossible to note by hand; there is also the advantage of being able to capture a performance while it is actually taking place rather than asking the performer to go over it line by line while someone takes notes. It is the former consideration that makes the tape recording most valuable to the folklorist, however, for in it the actual stylistic details of a performance may be captured and studied, thus carrying the researcher far beyond an attention to the mere content of a performance (which, as we have noted previously, may not be the central feature). If the tape recorder cannot produce these nuances of intonation, or if the operator of the machine cannot use the machine's capacity fully, then there is almost no point in making a recording.

In most tape recorders, the fidelity of sound runs in direct proportion to the width of the tape and the speed with which the tape passes the recording head: the faster the speed and the wider the tape, the more likely that the tape recorder will pick up the greatest range of sound with the most careful regulation of constant tone. The slower the speed and the narrower the tape, the less fidelity can be captured. For this reason, studio tape recorders usually use the entire width of recording tape and are operated commonly at 15 inches per second. Thus most fieldworkers prefer to use reel-to-reel tape recorders, operated at 7½ inches per second (this is top speed in most portable tape recorders) and in either full width (single-track) or half-width (two-track). Since all the sound is recorded on the same surface of the tape, the more tracks provided (such as in stereo or quad recorders), the less tape width there is available for the electrical impression to be caught and stored. Obviously, then, cassette tape recorders, which have extremely slow speeds and very narrow tapes, while they may be very handy in size and operation, are not helpful to the fieldworker. Other problems are that the thinner the tape is, the more likely it is to stretch (and thus to distort sound), to break, or to print through, a phenomenon in which the electrical impressions on one layer of the tape eventually seep to the next layer, causing an echo effect. Again, cassette tape is thinner than standard recording tape and so is subject to these problems, as well as to the occasional frustrating occurrence where the tape breaks or snarls and is eaten by the tape recorder.

I do not mean to suggest that cassette tape recorders are entirely useless, for many folklorists find that initial prospecting for materials may be done with a high-quality cassette tape recorder. Moreover, many students do their fieldwork, at least at first, on their own (or their professor's) cassette machine. To prohibit this would restrict folklore fieldwork to the wealthy. Students should be encouraged to use the best machine available, and to operate it where possible on house current rather than on batteries (which can fade and change the tape speed without the operator's knowledge). If the cassette tape is no thinner than the 60-minute variety, if the machine is well made and in good operating condition, and if the person operating it uses a good-quality microphone in the proper proximity to the speaker or singer, the cassette may indeed be more than valuable. Even so, most folklorists will go to an archive as soon as possible and transfer their materials to standard reel-to-reel storage tapes so that at least the fidelity that has been captured will not be lost. Some folklorists prefer to use high-quality cassette machines to record spoken materials, especially where intonation and style are not primary features, and to use reel-to-reel machines for recording folk songs and ballads, folk tales, or any other performances where style and texture are as important as content, or where musical sound is so central that the material would be less valuable for study if it were not recorded in the best possible way.

Recently there have been startling advancements in the construction of tape recorders, and those who can afford them use the Nagra or the Nakamichi; these are outside the financial range of the typical researcher, so I am assuming that we are talking about a more modest line of equipment.

CAMERAS  As with recorders, so with cameras or any other equipment. Since most fieldwork with the camera will not be especially useful if it falls into the snapshot category, the researcher should use a good-quality camera and film with a fine enough grain so that it will stand easy enlargement to 8″ x 10″. Some folklorists prefer to take primarily color slides, which can be projected for scrutiny of detail as well as for use before large audiences. Others prefer black and white so that prints can be produced that will be more easily stored in archives and more available to researchers without damaging the original negative. When taking photographs of folklore performances or folk artifacts, remember that the photograph serves visually the same kind of service as the tape. That is, it should be able to show those surface features of style and texture that allow the researcher to study the particularities of performance of the item or process under scrutiny. Photographs should be taken from as many angles as will reveal these details. The photographer should operate on the assumption that it may not be possible to photograph the same event or the same artifact again; thus, taking more pictures than absolutely necessary is preferable to not taking enough and coming away with only a partial record. Very often the item being photographed will be only one of a great number of similar kinds of items, and thus the researcher will want to gather photographic evidence of as many parallel examples as possible. This makes the work of the folklore photographer a potentially burdensome one, and certainly brings in a financial consideration that should be dealt with before research commences.

Both the tape recorder and the camera to be used in any research project should be practiced with enough ahead of time so that mechanical features will not have to be puzzled out in front of people in the midst of a project. The less obtrusive the machinery, the more likely that the tradition-bearers will not find their use objectionable. Incessant adjustment of tape recorders and playing back of tapes may rattle a resource person, and certainly the popping of flashbulbs close at hand is not likely to be conducive to the ease of a performer. Thus, adjusting levels properly, using film that can capture available light, being at ease with one's equipment (and therefore with one's resource people), all can lead toward a more successful research venture. One last precaution is an obligatory one: Always carry extra film and tape. The interview with Mrs. Judkins supplied in the Appendix ends abruptly at the most inopportune moment only because I neglected to bring sufficient tape for the occasion. There is no way of recapturing traditions lost at such moments.

PREPARATORY WORK    Familiarizing yourself with the machinery and the technology of fieldwork is only part of preparing for a successful folklore research project. If the project is not to be a waste of time, you must also prepare yourself for the general topic by doing a considerable amount of background reading. If you are looking for a particular genre, say folk songs, then extensive reading in that area is obligatory. What kinds of songs are commonly found in tradition? In particular, what kinds of songs, or what particular songs, are found in the traditions of the particular geographical area you are going to study? What kinds of ethnic groups make up the area? When did they arrive? Are some more likely to be participants in a song tradition than others? Have earlier researchers indicated a local song style or preference for certain topics? Do you know some of the songs you might encounter in this area or from a particular singer? Following up on such questions is not simply a theoretical scholarly exercise; rather, it prepares you to ask appropriate questions, to make remarks that might jog a singer's memory, to be able to mention a line or a title that may trigger an entire performance. In addition, it enables you to have some general notion of how the singer being recorded relates to the tradition as it is already known, first as a genre recognized by scholars, and second as a local tradition. Then, if you hear the singer performing songs that have never been collected in that area before, or performing texts of words or music unlike those appearing in other collections, there is some way of judging or analyzing other aspects of the tradition and the singer's position in it. Certain tune families may suggest an influence by one ethnic or national group upon another in the transmission of songs. Certain texts may indicate that in this geographical area one ballad has commonly borrowed stanzas from another because they are recognizable as images of local import. Without knowing what to ask, without knowing which sorts of performances to encourage, without some feel for what else has been done in the field, you may have a high old time listening to a traditional singer but may find yourself frustrated as to what it all means.

Another kind of preparation takes into consideration that there are at least two kinds of folklore research: the general survey and the theoretical project. In the survey, you will be satisfied if the ballad singer you have been referred to is actually a singer of ballads, if the barn builders you have arranged to photograph actually show up and build a barn, if the old yarn-spinner you have made an appointment with shows up and is willing to tell yarns. The survey, in other words, is an attempt to gauge the breadth and depth of different folk traditions and performances within those traditions without trying to solve particular theoretical problems. The theoretical project, on the other hand, usually begins with the formation of a hypothesis: You want to test a particular idea by subjecting it to the data that can be generated in fieldwork. In this case, the preparation not only entails familiarizing yourself with the genre, the geographical area, the potential tradition-bearers, and so on, but it calls for an analytical focus on some particular topic for which further discussion will be expected to provide new perspectives in folklore theory, however small they may be. Hypotheses can vary in focus. A very broad one might be phrased: "No folksongs have ever been collected in this valley; however, most of the settlers are from English-Irish-Scottish families among whom one finds in other geographical areas a considerable song tradition: There must be folk songs here that simply have never been unearthed before." Such a hypothesis may be tested simply by mounting an intensive search for folk songs in that particular valley, with the hypothesis being either confirmed or denied by the results.

Somewhat more specific than this might be the following: "The dairy barns along this river all seem to look different; perhaps the barn designs give some clue to the difference in ethnic backgrounds of the farmers in this area." In this instance, you might go from farm to farm simply interviewing the farmers about their barns, the designs and architectural particulars that are considered traditional, local, ethnic, and so on. During the research, you may indeed find out that from the farmers' point of view the barns are very much alike, varying only in superficial matters such as color and trim. Thus, while the initial hypothesis may simply be unconfirmed or denied, another hypothesis can be constructed in midproject, which says: "While there are many superficial differences in the designs of the dairy barns in this valley, the traditional structural aspects are very much alike; an ethnic similarity may account for these similarities in design." Further research along the same river may indicate that the ethnic similarities are not as close as might originally have been supposed, and that a local sense of barn-ness has actually been the deciding factor. No matter how such a project comes out, you will have been able to narrow the problem and come closer to some workable conclusions for it by testing out various hypotheses with the data provided by field research among the tradition-bearers. Obviously, such a project could not be carried out very thoroughly unless you had previously done a lot of reading into the construction of barns in general and aspects of traditional barnmaking in particular.

For some research projects, both surveys and theoretical researches, it may be necessary for the fieldworker to spend as much as a year in preparation. This means that folklore fieldwork must be undertaken with somewhat more planning, preparation, and thoughtfulness than we are accustomed to giving a picnic or a fishing trip. Unfortunately, due to time constraints and sometimes to a lack of seriousness, some folklorists have indeed carried out field research in their spare time with the zeal and efficiency of Sunday fishermen. While it is possible to record folklore without considerable preparation or development of expertise, that is no argument that this is how it ought to be done. Rather, it is sobering to reflect on the amount of traditional materials, styles, and textures that have remained unrecorded and therefore not well understood because of the hasty and unplanned efforts of folklore fieldworkers, both amateur and professional.

AFTERMATH: TRANSCRIPTION AND NOTES  I suppose that every scholarly enterprise has hidden in it somewhere an element of tedium. For many folklorists it is the transcription of field-recorded tapes. Tapes of any traditional performance worth studying should be themselves preserved, of course, so that we have as far as possible an accurate sound recording of the event with all its textural minutiae. At the same time, it is necessary to have the words for songs, stories, anecdotes, oral history, proverbs, and so on, transcribed from the tapes verbatim. This is not a job to be foisted off on an archivist; it is the final obligatory aspect of the job done by the researcher, for only the person who made the record can be relied upon to interpret indistinct phrases, jargon, or regional dialect, and only the researcher can provide the contextual notes on such matters as gesture or name of speaker or time of day that make the tape a fully functioning document. The further value of a transcription is that anyone looking for a particular text can locate it in the transcription and determine whether it is indeed the item desired; one can determine by its setting in the transcription where it may be found on the tape (while tape recorder manufacturers almost always provide a measuring device for elapsed footage, the systems are not particularly reliable).

The one restriction that most folklorists insist upon in transcription is that the material must be taken off word for word as it is in the original, including pauses, false starts, ungrammatical constructions, and so on. Most transcribers find it difficult to reflect with any accuracy a regional dialect, so most researchers spell phonetically only those words that are distinctly unique variations from standard pronunciation. Some transcribers supply punctuation or other markers of phrasing as well, even though many people do not in practice speak in full sentences. Thus, every transcriber has to come to terms with the peculiarities of the tradition-bearer and must then try to represent those peculiarities as fairly as possible in an exact transcription. In order to carry this out, however, most people find that it takes between eight and ten hours of transcribing to bring off every hour of recorded material. Some archives plan on fifteen hours per hour, including other related paperwork.

Alongside the transcription, marginally or perhaps in footnotes, the fieldworker normally provides notes on elements not recorded but central to the performance: the time of day, number of people present, time of year, gestures, special meanings if not apparent in the oral performance—in short, any data from observation that help to make the performance understandable or that are necessary for the performance to have meaning for anyone else. Transcribing and providing notes are not complicated matters; however, they often constitute the difference between a useful recording of a dynamic tradition and a batch of interesting folk stuff.

The tape recordings, videotapes, notes, and photographs are the primary documents of folklore fieldwork. The transcription is an accurate but not fully reliable account of that document. The serious scholar will always go to the primary document for full detail, for it is only there that the nuances of performance, the particularities of style, and the total natural context of meaning are fairly represented for the traditional performer. Sensitivity to our resource people requires that we collect, archive, and study their traditions in the most accurate way possible.

# ◤ FOLKLORE ARCHIVES

STORAGE  The word *archives* refers basically to any repository of public records, in earliest times those documents relating to the official business of a town or community. It is important to recognize that the spirit of that term remains a part of the concept of a folklore archives, for the whole point of maintaining such a facility is not simply to afford bulk space to store collected items, but also to provide reasonable access to the materials important to our culture. However, it should be immediately apparent, because of the nature of folklore itself, that the materials have to be dealt with in a variety of ways so that they may be safely stored, so that those who shared their traditions with the folklorist will not be embarrassed by what they did or by how their materials are later viewed or used, and so that the materials will represent folklore fairly.

Because the archives must provide both storage space, filing systems, and facilities for playing back tape recordings (at the very least), most individual folklorists cannot afford one in their homes. Most archives are funded by, or at least take refuge in, public institutions of some sort: universities, historical societies, anthropological museums, and so forth. Folklore archives range in size from a filing cabinet or two to entire buildings. The folklore archives at the University of Oregon is housed in one rather large room of the office building in which the English Department resides. Named the Randall V. Mills Memorial Archive of Northwest Folklore (after a professor of English who initiated the scholarly study of the subject at the university in the 1950s), the Northwest Folklore Archives, as it is called for convenience, has a rather simple physical appearance: About twenty metal filing cabinets contain separate field collections done by staff and students in addition to critical papers on folklore, dissertations and theses on folklore—all done at the university— and miscellaneous collections of folklore taken from newspapers, locally published books, student journals, and letters. There is an atlas of Oregon, books on folklore and related subjects, a set of file cards, and a few small artifacts (limited in number because the archives have no safe facility for storing and protecting such items). The furniture consists of a few desks that are used by archivists, student assistants, and researchers using the archives. There is also a locked metal cabinet that contains unused tapes and the various tape recorders and cameras allocated to the archives by the English Department and the University Audio-Visual Services.

Archives of this nature are probably fairly typical of a medium-sized university in the United States that has no extensive folklore program. A far larger and more complex archives exists at Indiana University, where undergraduate and graduate programs are available and where several thousand students study the subject each year. Considerable archives also exist at UCLA, Wayne State University, the University of Maine, Memorial University in Newfoundland, the University of Pennsylvania, the University of Texas, and Utah State University, where students and staff have, through their own fieldwork efforts, amassed sizable collections of folklore. On the other hand, many folklorists have worked in so solitary a fashion for so many years that their own collections are stored in such a way as to inhibit their use by other scholars. For example, for years a small folklore archives existed in Utah, stored away in a cardboard box or two under the desk of a retired professor. For a while its existence could not even be corroborated. Other partial collections have been hidden from public view because of the whims of their collectors. For example, when Robert Winslow Gordon, an early archivist of folk songs at the Library of Congress, left the Library, he took a number of his most special collected songs with him and stored them under his bed for years thereafter. Long after his death, when his collection of folk songs had been given to the University of Oregon by his daughter, we found that a number of texts actually should have been in the Library of Congress. There are probably hundreds of examples of such small or partial collections that, because of personal taste, fear for the contents, or simple lack of money, have been stored in such a way that the physical materials have deteriorated or have been perhaps thrown away or lost by those who had no idea about their contents.

On the other hand, in Europe it is common to find extensive and well-financed facilities for the storage of folklore, especially in the countries that have emerged or re-emerged since the Second World War. In Romania, there is a complex of several buildings in which nearly a hundred government-paid specialists operate a folklore archives and research facility. They have a modern recording studio, the best recording equipment, room after room of books, journals, collections, card files, photographs, movie films, and so on. In many of these countries the collection and study of folklore has been a direct counterpart to the development (sometimes the re-establishment) of a sense of national, cultural, ethnic identity. Those countries that lived under the yoke of foreign domination for years are especially anxious to encourage their own ethnic roots to come forth again after long years underground. In these countries, folklore becomes almost a part of political reality as a nation seeks to demonstrate to itself and to others the fact of its own separate existence. In such a case, folklore and ongoing vital traditions can be much more functional means of cultural cohesion than the economic or political symbols normally represented by official boundary lines or political party.

A similar consideration is now gaining increasing attention from Native American tribes, for in their case as well the existence of ongoing dynamic traditions is a much more accurate marker of ethnic existence than the so-called blood quantum introduced by the government some years ago. Many tribes were convinced that they should vote a tribal definition of what it took to be a member of the tribe. In most cases, with encouragement from the government, tribes voted that a person must be at least one-quarter "blood" of that particular tribe in order to be enrolled and to be thus eligible to vote, to participate in tribal programs, or derive any benefits that might arise from sale of land or resources. This was done even though many tribes already had a long history of intermarriage with other tribes. Thus when these regulations came into existence in recent years, many members of the tribes were already at the minimal level of membership, for although they were entirely or almost entirely Indian, their grandparents came from different tribes; therefore in the next generation children were born who were less than 25 percent of one tribe and who were no longer qualified to be on tribal rolls. If we project this into the near future, considering the recent heavier intermarriage with whites and other ethnic groups, many of the Pacific Northwest tribes will, in technical terms, cease to exist before the year 2000—although they will still be there in even greater physical numbers than they are today. In other words, the Indian culture is still being passed along in each of these tribes, but members of these cultural groups are represented by such a mixture of tribes and peoples that in technical terms they will not qualify to vote and do business in their own tribes. The Colville Confederated Tribes in central Washington, for example, estimates that by the 1990s there may be no new enrollments; that is, young people born into the tribe will not have enough "tribal blood" to qualify for official membership. This in no way means that tribal traditions are fading. To the contrary; among the Colvilles as in many other tribes in the United States today there is an increased awareness and in fact a resurgence of vitality of those traditions that had been earlier nearly obliterated. For many of these tribes, then, the only hope for establishing a sense of ethnic identity, the only hope for "proving they continue to exist," will be the availability of data to document the ongoing vitality of distinctive tribal folk heritage. For these reasons, many tribes are becoming increasingly concerned with documenting and preserving their folklore in archival facilities.

We must then realize that folklore archives represent far more than storage space. Folklore collections are more than merely the playground for scholars, for in folklore archives (whether hidden under the bed or catalogued in several buildings) is the most telling evidence of the vitality of cultural tradition in our country as well as elsewhere. Thus the care and preservation of materials in folklore archives must be approached in as delicate a way as I have suggested previously for our treatment of our traditional resources, our informant-colleagues in the field. Obviously, none of these concerns can be well exercised unless there is room to store our materials, unless we can protect them from deterioration, and unless they can be found again after we have packed them away in the file drawer.

PROTECTION: PHYSICAL   The considerations for the protection of physical materials within archives are staggering in their proportions, and I will not pretend to take up their technical detail here. Rather, I would like to suggest some of the important concerns that every archivist (and therefore every folklorist) must keep in mind to assure that materials garnered at so high a cost in time and sensitivity in the field will not be lost to the ravages of decay. A clean, well-lighted room—even on an antiseptic campus—will not be adequate protection for our materials.

FILING   A good filing system will help particular items from going astray. Things can be lost by being dropped on the floor, by being handled by people unfamiliar with the archives or its operation, or may be misplaced by well-intentioned folks who would like to put things back where they think they found them. The basic operation of an archives, then, involves some kind of restricted access to the materials, so that a very few individuals are allowed to find an item, take it from the file, and return it when finished. If access is unrestricted, things will be lost, misplaced, and stolen, which is what happens in nearly any library or public facility. Recognizing this should suggest some basic and not very complicated operational rules.

MAINTENANCE   The machines used in and by the archives can develop malfunctions. Videotape equipment, for example, can be put out of kilter simply by being carried up and down flights of stairs too often. Not only should access to these sensitive machines be limited to those experienced with them, but they should be stored and handled with extreme caution and care. Moreover, every piece of equipment requires a regular maintenance program: Shutter speeds on cameras can sometimes get out of adjustment; battery-powered light meters and tape recorders can be affected by fading (or worse, leaking) batteries. Electric "bugs" can show up in the magnetic heads of recording equipment if they are not regularly cleaned. In general, people will operate a tape recorder without realizing how their lack of experience may affect their success. The same brashness disappears when it comes to repairing equipment, however, and when faced with the prospect of tinkering around inside a tape recorder, most people grow pale and faint. It is well to admit a lack of expertise in these matters and leave the repairs and technical maintenance to the proper people. At the same time, there are simple, efficient, and inexpensive ways of keeping recording heads clean, lenses dusted off, batteries checked, and so on. People who are not willing to take responsibility in these matters should probably not be allowed to use the equipment. Since that would perhaps place a severe restriction on fieldwork, the folklore archivist must realize that proper maintenance of equipment is a central obligation for the archive itself.

FILM  If unexposed film is stored in the archives, note the expiration dates. The emulsions of color film continue to change, and they will change more rapidly at higher temperatures. Film bought in bulk may be frozen and thus be preserved almost indefinitely. At least the temperature of the archives must be controlled enough so that any unexposed film does not become outdated ahead of its factory expiration date.

If the archives contains color slides, the slides must be protected from being scratched and mishandled. This can be done fairly simply by putting them in slide holders or keeping them stored in carousel trays. There are of course various storage mechanisms, such as sheets of plastic jackets in which the slides can be held in front of a lighted viewing panel. Black and white photographs and their negatives need to be protected not only from each other (since small particles of dust or grime can cause scratches on the surface of pictures), but also from direct sunlight, extreme heat or dampness, or any other situation that can curl, corrode, or alter the materials themselves or the image. Light is a more deadly enemy with older pictures, of course, which can fade very rapidly. If the collections contain pictures, the archivist must have a reliable book on maintaining and preserving photographs.

TAPES  Tape recordings probably require a lot more consideration than we normally give them. As I suggested earlier, it is possible for sounds on one layer of tape to print through to another layer, thus causing an echo. It is also possible for tape to become brittle, especially under unusual conditions of temperature and humidity change. Most professional archivists therefore find it practical to run each reel of tape through a tape recorder at least once a year to check for brittleness or breakage as well as to redistribute the stress on the entire tape that might have built up by partial use or by inactivity. Some people who work exclusively with sound recordings suggest, beyond this, that each tape be redubbed to a fresh tape every so often, perhaps every four or five years, to cut down on the deterioration of the tape itself and to inhibit printing through.

PAPER   One of the deadliest enemies in any archives is the presence of acid in paper. Nearly all paper deteriorates because of the acid residue, which is in turn a part of the process by which paper is produced. Not only is there deterioration of the typing paper on which data is stored, the same problem exists with manila folders and envelopes, cardboard or paper mats and jackets for photographs, and the like. Some kinds of paper have more acid than others, and of course now that archivists are aware of this problem, they can use available "acid-free" papers and folders and boxes. Also available are chemical strips that can be inserted into boxes or folders that will reduce the acid pH of the materials stored. With some papers and cardboards, as the material begins to deteriorate more acid is formed, so the process is hastened, in some cases almost geometrically. While it is hardly likely that paper will deteriorate before our very eyes under controlled conditions in the archives, it is nonetheless a distinct possibility that within a hundred years an entire archives might have to be copied or risk being lost. If we try to imagine the massive and expensive chore that would represent for any archival collection, we can see the necessity of trying to ward off these deteriorating processes before they get well started. Again, a number of books are available on these matters. It is perhaps unfortunate in this regard that most folklore archivists are trained more in folklore than in the physical aspects of document protection; nonetheless, basic first aid may be learned without intellectual pain and with considerable benefit for the archives.

ENVIRONMENT   The total physical environment within an archives must remain under careful control. The best of all worlds is to have a room with a separately controlled heating and air-conditioning apparatus as well as humidity control. This kind of facility is usually available only through the larger libraries, so for many folklore collections it is unrealistic. Failing that, however, anyone working with folklore materials must develop a workable plan for providing as much protection as possible from such ironically destructive forces as sunlight and air. Those who live in cities with considerable pollution will find that the air has a greater propensity to attack all conceivable objects, even paper hidden in drawers. Those who live in relatively pollution-free environments need not feel much more cheerful, however, because direct sunlight and the varying humidity of fresh air flowing through an open window can be just as dangerous in other respects.

For one melancholy example, consider the following: A researcher came to our archives one afternoon and asked to see some black and white photographs of tombstone epitaphs in a pioneer cemetery. These photographs had been stored in a student collection, and, to protect the photographs themselves, the student had placed each one in a clear plastic folder in which had been inserted a dark piece of cardboard matting as a background. The pictures were brought out and left on a desk in the center of the room for refiling with the collection. Before the archivist had a chance to put the pictures away, however, a beam of sunlight had rested on the photographs for perhaps no more than two hours. When the photographs were to be put away, the archivist found a hole had melted in the clear plastic. A specialist in the university library suggested that the acid in the photographs, combined with the acid in the clear plastic folder, enhanced by the acid in the dark cardboard matting—all brought into more rapid action by the direct sunlight—had conspired to burn a hole in the plastic. If such a thing can happen so quickly, consider the destructive processes quietly at work in the darkness of file drawers, in the various levels of light around the archives, and especially under a direct source of sunlight. Considering that paper and photographic materials are likely to become increasingly more expensive, the physical problems of preservation within an archives are enough to cause genuine concern. While nothing can be done about the forces of decay, at least common sense and good advice can help us inhibit those processes that could eventually rob us of the rich examples of folk heritage we have spent so much time obtaining.

PROTECTION: ETHICAL   As if the physical problems were not staggering enough, the archivist (and thus the contributing folklorist) must also consider the fact that the archives is a repository of other people's most cherished inheritances. Thus the archives must be handled with more human sensitivity that the First National Bank, for these materials are not to be cashed in and out without regard to the feelings of the contributors who made them possible. For one thing, when people are talking among friends and telling jokes, recalling celebrative events like shivarees, or giving oral histories of the union movement, they may say things and recall events that they might not share with total strangers. If a researcher publishes these things without regard to the feelings of the person in the field, there is the possibility of everything from hurt feelings to insult to lawsuit.

PROTECTION OF DECORUM   Every folklorist perhaps has favorite examples of this consideration, but I will mention a few that have come up in our operation of the Northwest Folklore Archives. We have one collection of logger songs, most of them generally considered obscene. The retired logger who sang them for us did not mind sharing them, principally because the collectors were accompanied by loggers and one of the collectors had been himself a logger before. Thus the context in which the collection was made was an easy one to deal with, and the materials shared would normally have been shared under similar conditions. Moreover, the old logger was delighted with the prospect that the songs he had preserved in his own repertoire were actually considered important cultural items by anyone else. In addition, he took a humorously devilish delight in realizing that bookish scholars were somehow now trying to deal with what he considered the real world of male experience in a hazardous profession and the expression of the attitudes thus attained in cleverly obscene songs. When the tapes had been made and played back to him, however, he suddenly realized that if anyone else heard him singing these songs he would be embarrassed. He allowed us to keep the songs in the archives, but placed the stipulation upon us that they not be played for any woman under twenty-one. He was concerned, for example, that his granddaughter might possibly come to the university, might possibly take a folklore course, might find herself in the archives and see that there was a collection of songs from her own grandfather, and might thus expose herself to songs that her grandfather had spent his entire life protecting the women of his family from. The logger admitted that perhaps the granddaughter would not be embarrassed, since young people today have a wider vocabulary than they had when he was brought up, and he was well aware that women, especially from logging communities, are not ignorant of the subjects or the terminologies used by the loggers. However, his own moral ethics were such that he could not abide the thought that as a grandfather he should ever sing these songs to his granddaughter.

But of course the case is more complicated than that. Suppose we wait until his granddaughter is, say, thirty, and then we publish his songs in a national journal, identifying the singer and his locality. Is it not possible that a leading patriarch of a community could be in effect libeled by an article that featured him as the articulate and talented singer of "dirty songs"? This is an ethical dilemma for the folklorist-scholar, of course, and it is confronted nearly every day by professionals who seek to publish the results of their research without embarrassing their resources. But it also becomes an ethical consideration for the archivist, who needs to know the nature of the researcher, the nature of the research, and the intended result before making a judgment on the dissemination of some materials. This job will be done more efficiently if such matters are taken up with the field resource people themselves and written into whatever contract may represent the donation of the materials to the archives.

PROTECTION OF OCCUPATION   Another example of a similar concern relates to a particular boat style in the state of Oregon. Several rivers in Oregon have local styles of boats used by local fishermen. One very distinctive such boat is the McKenzie River Boat, and one of the most talented craftsmen at producing this boat, Keith Steele, makes his living doing so as well as by being a river guide for fishermen. We wanted to have photographs and detailed drawings of Keith Steele's McKenzie River Boat in our archives, but we found that the boatmaker himself was extremely reluctant to let measurements be taken and drawn for fear that others might then have access to his plans and thus, perhaps with the best intentions, put him out of business. We assured him, of course, that the archives would never let anyone make copies or detailed notes of his drawings—and in fact we finally used only partial drawings for two views of the boat that we have displayed on the walls of the archives—precisely so that the information would not be available to parties who might be able to memorize enough of it to carry it away. Clearly the archives act in a precarious role here: If we provide the fullest view of Keith Steele's boat, we might become the medium through which Keith Steele can no longer make a living making his own McKenzie River Boat. Rather than celebrating his talents, we might put him out of business, which of course would run directly contrary to the whole point of having an archives.

PROTECTION OF RITUAL SECRECY   Other more complicated considerations come into play when ritual material is collected. For example, a number of Native American tradition-bearers have been willing to be recorded singing songs or telling stories and then have placed restrictions on access or usage. Some do not like the Coyote stories to be available to anyone except during the winter, their usual time of use. In two cases we have become the repository of traditional information from tribes who feel that they do not have the facilities for safe storage on their own reservations and would like to take advantage of ours, but they do not want their materials shared with anyone except members of their own tribe. If we were to disclose their secret rituals to a well-meaning anthropologist doing research on that tribe, we might advance the cause of knowledge, but we would also completely obliterate any sense of trust that tribe would have in our archives, and might in the long run encourage them never to preserve or document their central traditions again. In such cases, I think archives have a perfectly sound basis for demonstrating what Alan Dundes has often referred to as the anal-retentive characteristics of librarians.

Some kinds of traditions are meant to be secret among those who share them, even though they do not necessarily represent any religious or ritual secrets that, divulged, might ruin the structure or the stability of any close group. An example might be information such as that shared by fly fishermen along the North Umpqua River in south-central Oregon. The North Umpqua fly fishermen, most of whom go after steelhead, are a very tight-knit group of people as fishermen, even though they come from an amazing variety of professions and backgrounds in everyday life. While they're on the river, they learn the ways of the stream and of the fish from each other, and this information is placed in a larger framework of practical data that includes the names of fishing spots and holes along the portion of the river that is open to fly fishing only. The names of the holes, the order in which they may be followed downstream, the ways in which they must be fished depending on different water conditions and weather, the kinds of tackle used in each case, are closely guarded secrets. They exist in the oral tradition of all who share that experience, but they are not divulged to outsiders, least of all to bait fishermen, who are looked upon with great contempt. If their secret information, stored in the archives, were revealed inadvertently by a scholar publishing a study of fishermen's language and lore, it would not cause a religious outrage or the dislocation of anyone's cultural bearings. Nonetheless, it is easy to imagine that a fieldworker might ever after have considerable difficulty doing research among fishermen in this area, for they would have felt betrayed by anyone who would have placed scholarly interests over concerns more central to their existence as a close group. While this is not an earth-shaking ethical dilemma, it is a secular variety of the problem inherent in storing religious folklore that should remain secret. To what extent does the scholar or researcher have the right over the proprietary concerns of any group's internal beliefs, customs, and attitudes? If one relies merely on the Freedom of Information Act or the copyright laws, all of the advantages are with the scholar; after all, this is a free country, isn't it? We can publish what we please, can't we? If one is on the side of human sensitivity, which I have argued must be a basic ingredient of folklore field research, then the answer is not so easy.

PROTECTION FROM LIBEL  A prominent university in the Midwest once started to accession a great number of tapes that had been made concerning the oral history and traditions of a particular labor movement. As part of the process of obtaining the tapes, they requested that some lawyers listen to them to see if any legal restrictions should be placed upon them for access and use. The lawyers' advice was that about 90 percent of the tapes should be destroyed immediately, for they contained random observations by people who could be brought to court for libel by a number of parties. For example, someone recalled that the person who founded a certain union local "was a Commie in those days." Now, calling someone a Communist and identifying the person in a public place has already been ruled by a number of courts to be grounds for a libel suit, because it may materially affect the person's welfare, status, and employment. Since archives are, at least in most cases, potentially the repository of publicly available information, it can be construed as information open to, or published to, the public, even when the materials may not necessarily appear in printed form. This is a legal area that is far from solidly defined at this point; at the same time, it does bring up the possibility that our archives may contain comments and statements that, if not properly handled, might be damaging to the people who said them or about whom they are said. Probably a folklore archives, if it is limited to that orientation, is less likely to contain such potentially complicated materials, but since many archives also contain a lot of anecdotal oral histories, it is a question to which any folklorist needs to pay some attention.

PROTECTION FROM THE LAW  Still other problems may arise if the archives contain any information dealing with illegal activities. Students in the past have found a rich store of folk speech, custom, and gesture in close groups whose definition is based on actions or attitudes that might be considered illegal. Such items as "hash" pipes, criminals' speech, marijuana legends; the customs and language of smugglers, prostitutes, and pimps; stories and legends of "crossing the wire" by and about illegal immigrants from Mexico, and the like, are contained in a number of archives. Since investigators can easily gain admittance to stored records in order to glean evidence or clues about criminal activity, the collectors and informants of such collections may be placed in a vulnerable position simply by having their names on record. Some archives handle this problem by obliterating names or by substituting fictitious names in all documents concerning such collections. In this way, the materials are still usable for folklore research, but the archives are not a potential threat to the safety of those who have shared sensitive information or who have revealed their identities. Other archives, feeling that the lack of verifiable names and addresses reduces the scholarly worth of such a collection, simply do not accession such materials, thus avoiding entirely any threat to the people involved as well as cutting down on the number of collections within the archives whose value might be compromised by lack of information.

Sometimes these matters are hard to deal with in advance. During the Vietnam War a student of mine, a conscientious objector in solid legal standing, decided that it would be interesting to collect the many legends, anecdotes, and jokes concerning draft-dodgers. There were hundreds of them in circulation, usually featuring some unique or clever way in which a candidate for the draft had avoided military service, often by eating bits of aluminum foil, consuming great quantities of sugar just before a urine analysis, or by trying to make homosexual advances to the military doctor. The stories were in circulation among many who were not themselves draft resisters, and in many cases names were used that might or might not have been the real names of people trying to avoid the draft. Nonetheless, such activity if carried out in reality was considered tantamount to illegal by the government. Since the student was himself legally exempted from the draft, and since he did not ascertain in his two field collections that the tellers of his stories were in any illegal situation, it seemed to me as though the presence of those collections in our archives would not represent a threat either to the government or to any individual named therein. Nonetheless, during a period of intense student antidraft and antiwar activity, when we were aware that law officers were on campus in great numbers doing undercover surveillance, the two fine collections suddenly disappeared from our archives only to reappear again in their usual places three weeks later. How these collections were taken from the archives and returned is entirely unknown to us. Did some well-meaning and thorough police officer identify himself to a janitor and gain access to the archives after hours to look for such clues? We have no way of knowing. If such an occurrence did happen, however, even under the most discriminating of police officers, the names and addresses generated by such collections would by no means have been a fair set of clues as to the identities of those in the university community who were in fact most actively campaigning against the war. Moreover, while such activity was then considered illegal, it was later considered justifiable, thus indicating that information available in an archives at one moment might be sensitive and at another might not.

Suppose, for example, that an archives contains several collections of traditional processes for homemade beer. Then suppose that five years from now the state passes a law against private beer production (as some states have already done). Would it be fair for authorities to use the archives as a source for a list of people on whom police would like to call to determine if now-illegal activity is still occurring? I think most archivists would consider this an unfair use of folklore archives, yet most law enforcement officers would consider it legal and justified. Since we cannot foretell when something is likely to be sensitive, we may simply need to be aware that it can happen and try to develop some archival rules or responses to such situations.

FILING AND RETRIEVAL   As we move more inexorably into the computer age, some larger archives are developing storage and retrieval systems that are partially or entirely computerized. Eventually these archives may become the terminals of larger interlocking systems that will give researchers around the country access to data that would otherwise require considerable travel and tedious reading. Nonetheless, for most of us in the coming years, the realities of archival work will remain pretty much as they are today: We will need to visit a particular archives and see if we can find the materials we need, and then we will need to find some way of getting them out of the file drawer and onto the table for scrutiny before determining what further use can be made of them. Therefore, each archives must develop a cataloguing system that will assure that when materials are accessioned into the larger collection they may be readily retrieved.

Some archival systems are cross-referenced exhaustively, and the researcher can look up a particular motif or theme or type in an extensive card file or computer system. Other archives are arranged on an intentionally simple model, designed so that the basic larger questions of finding materials can be answered and leaving further comparative and analytical work to the researcher. The Northwest Folklore Archives has a card file that answers the four most common questions asked by researchers: What items do you have of this particular genre or kind of folklore? What do you have from this particular folk group? What do you have from this particular geographical region? What do you have from this particular informant? There is therefore a file of 5- by 8-inch cards classified as *genre*, a category construed very broadly so that it can include particular recognizable structure-based genres such as ballad, legend, proverb, and so on, as well as larger distinctive kinds of folklore like magic and custom, or groupings such as family folklore. Each person who deposits a collection in the archives is obliged to fill out standard cards in which as many genre cards are completed as seem to indicate the range of folklore in the collection fairly.

There is a file designated as *folk group* as well, again a category broadly construed so as to name or define that particular grouping of people that seems most distinctively related to the kind of folklore in the collection. Under this heading there are loggers, well-drillers, residents of the Rogue River valley, Native Americans (always including a tribal designation), women, teen-agers, and so on. There is no suggestion that the folk group necessarily functions as an isolated or rural grouping; rather, the attempt is to find the common denominator that defines that close group in which the folklore under consideration is normally performed.

Another file is designated as *geographical region*, which ranges from the names of particular towns and settlements to definable geographic-cultural areas (insofar as they may be ascertained with any accuracy). There is a distinct Willamette Valley culture in Oregon as there is a distinct John Day Country, and a Central Oregon, and a Coast Range, and a Coastal area. Some counties, as Sanpete and San Juan counties in Utah, may have distinct traditional characteristics. In some places a whole region may be distinctive, like the northern peninsula of Michigan or the Ozarks of Missouri and Arkansas. In some cases, the folklore in the collection may be distinctive of one of these recognizable regions, and this designation may be an index to some further observations on shared traditions on a regional basis. On the other hand, it may be only by coincidence that a number of people have been interviewed in Seattle, Washington, and before researchers go there to do more fieldwork they may simply wish to know what kinds of things have been collected there and from which particular people so that they will not duplicate the work on the one hand or so that sensible recollecting may take place on the other, if that is called for by the research.

Another file is organized as an index of *informants*. I have already expressed some dislike for this word, but in a filing system it seems at present our simplest and most direct term for those individuals who shared their folklore with the field researcher.

In the first three categories here, the file itself is broken down into obvious subheadings: under *folk group*, tabs mark such subdivisions as *occupational, ethnic, religious,* and the like. Under *geographical region,* separate tabs indicate those cards arranged by city, county, state, by particular regions within a state and among states. Thus, in all cases, if someone comes to the archives to do research and says, "Do you have any stories told by Old Man Jones in Coquille?" we can go to three different files to see if, first, anyone has collected anything from Old Man Jones, whether it is the same Old Man Jones being referred to here as in Coquille, and, last, whether anyone collected his stories (perhaps a previous collector found out that he knew some songs but was unaware of a story repertoire or did not have time to collect them). Similarly, someone can ask if there is any folklore from Aurora, Oregon, and can be told quickly, "Yes, there are seven such collections, four of which are available for researchers to use."

On each of these file cards is the title of the collection, the collector's name, and the date of accession. Once we have ascertained that we have something in the area the researcher is interested in, we then consult another card file designated *release*. This is a standard and perhaps too brief form signed by the collector, which indicates that the collection is being donated to the archives and lists any stipulations and restrictions requested by the collector or the informant. For each collection we also have a master card, actually a table of contents typed out on an 8½- by 11-inch sheet of paper. The researcher can find if we do have some folk songs from Aurora, say, and we can immediately tell the researcher, without taking the collection out of its place in the file, what is in it and whether it may be used for study or publication. If anyone must be contacted for permission, that information is at hand and the researcher can then make any approaches necessary to obtain the proper clearance by contacting the collector or the resource person directly. This system restricts wear and tear on archival materials and focuses the initial steps of research on the filing system and descriptive catalogue of the archives. At the same time, such a system certainly throws most of the labor for research and analysis onto the researcher. If someone asks whether we have any stories with a certain motif, we will not be able to give a precise answer, but by looking at the master card for each collection, the researcher can find out whether there are stories that seem to be related to the motif under scrutiny.

All archives have some such system that is basic to the process of cataloguing accessioned materials. Larger archives, which may be able to employ archival assistants, will have developed more fully articulated filing systems than others. Even so, a complicated filing system is not necessarily the best tool for research, for the more designations made in a system, the more decisions have to be made by the archivist rather than by the researcher; probably all folklorists have had the experience of finding items by surprise or luck because they were not filed under the same heading the researcher might have used. For this reason, if for no other, there is a strong argument for maintaining a fairly simple cataloguing system so that broad areas can be defined and retrieved, and where the researcher can make the analytical judgments necessary to the proper pursuit of a given project, unencumbered by others' decisions. And, of course, if the truth were known, there is still a great supply of folklorists who would much rather sit around in an archives for hours, reading innumerable interesting tales in order to find a couple of useful pieces of information, than punch up a lighted or printed display on an electronic marvel.

PAPERWORK AND OWNERSHIP  Filing systems such as those described above are how we try to insure that we do not lose even the smallest item in our large collections. In order for this basic interest to be carried forward, a certain amount of paperwork in the development of the filing system is an obvious necessity. Beyond that, however, there is another kind of paperwork necessary to the proper maintenance and operation of an archives. What, for example, if someone drops in who placed a collection of folk songs in your archives last year and now wants it back? If there has not been some legal agreement that the collection was indeed given to the archives, there is no way this demand can be denied. Or suppose the old man whose dowsing was photographed by a student comes by the archives, having decided that he doesn't want his picture hanging around in a storage facility? Does the archives have any means of arguing that the pictures are very helpful and that they ought to remain where they are? Again, if there is no formal arrangement by which the ownership of the collection and its photographs was handed over to the archives, it is not difficult to see that the person concerned might have a clear and legal right to retrieve his likeness. So, no matter how seldom these situations might occur in practice, most archives assume that it is a basic necessity to have standard forms that indicate who owns what, what kinds of restrictions are placed on use or dissemination, who should be called on any question about the use or intended publication of the materials, and so on. At the least, the thoroughgoing archives will have the following specific items on paper:

1. A letter, or notes on a telephone conversation, or notes on a private conversation, about the initial contact between the researcher and the field resource person. When was the person first contacted? Was there a reply? Does there need to be any advance work done before the first visit takes place? These and other considerations can be charted by having some recorded information about the initial contact if it was

initiated by or at the request of the archives. This particular item may be missing in many collections initiated by students or other people who suddenly find themselves in contact with a grandfather or a neighbor who is willing to tell stories or whittle for the camera or sing songs at a wedding.

2. There should be an official form noting what kinds of equipment have been checked out from the archives for the project, giving such details as serial numbers or identifying marks, any related equipment (microphones, additional tapes, film), and noting the name, address, and telephone number of the researcher. On another part of the same form, or perhaps if necessary on a second form, there should be an equally detailed way of checking the equipment back in, for the protection of both the archives and the researcher.

3. While most archives use a single release form, most commonly signed by the collector, in all fairness there should really be two release forms, the first of which is an acknowledgment by the person whose material was collected that it is being deposited in an archives with his knowledge and permission.

4. Another release form should be an acknowledgment by the collector that the fruits of his fieldwork are being deposited in the archives for standard archival storage and use. In both releases, there should be a clear provision for any restrictions that the collector or resource person feel are necessary for the proper handling of the material. Among these stipulations, we may expect that some ethnic groups will want to note that the materials are owned in a larger sense by the tribe, say, and that the use of certain items must be cleared in advance with tribal authorities. Some researchers and archivists do not like this consideration; nevertheless, cases have been decided in court on behalf of ethnic proprietorship of certain materials. Some tribes like the Hopi perform sacred rituals related to the maintenance of stability and fertility of the entire world. Hopi religious practitioners take these functions and performances seriously, and they are not willing to have Boy Scout troops learn the dances and the songs, for, performed out of context, they represent intrusions on the religious freedom of the Hopi and constitute a sacrilege that we would not expect any religious body to countenance. The standard restrictions and stipulations listed on the two kinds of release forms are, typically, references to whether the material may be published or not, whether the material may be published only by permission of the collector or the informant, or whether the material must be withheld from public use until a certain

date. Other restrictions are possible, of course, and any such release form should allow space for any other conditions under which the material may be most happily deposited in the archives.

5. An accession document of some sort should identify the tape or the photograph or the text or the transcription by the names of the collector and the resource person, by accession date, and should list other kinds of vital information that identify the work, the date and place it was undertaken, and whether all other paperwork has been carried out in full.

6. Although the idea seems initially too formal to some folklorists, there is a good argument for the use of a request form by which a person who wishes to do research applies for permission to have access to certain materials. Such a form accomplishes several extremely valuable ends. First of all, perhaps in a fiscally political way, it serves as a ready reference to the amount of traffic through the archives during any period of time, thus enabling the custodians to indicate to anyone interested the extent to which the archives is used and the breadth of geographical and scholarly background represented by the users. Beyond this, it forces the petitioner to be serious and specific in his request, which tends to cut down on what might be called academic tourists simply looking for an afternoon of congenial reading. In the case of a small archives, which cannot accommodate serious scholars and curious onlookers at the same time, such a form can help the archivist regulate the use of space or intercept at least temporarily those who aren't quite sure what they need to consult. Further, such a form, read and signed by the researcher, creates a formal arrangement with the archives that requires the researcher to acknowledge the archives' rules (which may define ownership, usage of materials, matters of publication, the question of who pays for copies), so there will be no misunderstandings. Although it may not happen often, the existence of a properly executed request form may also give a later clue to the whereabouts of missing materials. Mainly, however, the request form helps to establish a professional attitude toward the use of the archives. It does not require that one be among the leading folklorists of the world to use the facilities, of course; it simply protects the professional interests of folklorists in general, protects the materials shared by people in the field, and encourages the development of a seriousness of purpose in those who might otherwise approach the archives as if it were simply a treasure chest of quaint toys or a cheap resource for children's books.

The best of modern folklore scholarship is an interdisciplinary combination of scholarly fields, sensitive and thorough fieldwork, careful archiving and research, and an acquaintance with those journals, books, and professional meetings that keep the folklorist up to date in the subject. Because of the central roles of field research and archiving in the development of folklore theory, however, some folklorists have come to believe that fieldwork is as obligatory for the interviewees as for the interviewers; that is, the field resource persons are sometimes approached as if they are a natural resource like coal, which has the obligation of being dug up and burned at the discretion of those who need the heat. Similarly, some have dealt with archives as if they are the grave of folklore and not the protective resting place for delicate materials.

However, not all folklore collected gets into archives, and perhaps I ought to admit that not all folklore belongs in an archives. And it may be that some singers and storytellers do not care to be researched. Not everyone likes to be observed, preserved, or encouraged, and the very presence of a folklorist with camera or tape recorder may actually keep a traditional process from taking place. Comments like "No, we don't allow that to be photographed" or "You can't have that recipe—it's only given out to family members" or "Hell, I'm not going to sing with *that* thing turned on" are sometimes heard and must be respected.

One small tribe of Indian people on the Oregon coast decided that while they did want to retain their winter stories, recording them might not really lead to preservation, for it would relieve the people of the custom of continual retelling with at least two other tribal members present, and might thus bring about a condition where the texts would be saved but the live contexts neglected. Their refusal to tape their stories might be thought of as a loss by some folklorists, but in their reasoning lies an important lesson, perhaps the most important of all for any folklorist: The people's integrity and the dynamics of their folklore are realities central to our profession. Our main job is not to pin up a large butterfly collection at any cost but to understand live butterflies more fully and help to keep them in their natural circumstances. My Indian friends on the Oregon coast decided it would be more to the point to insist that all tribal meetings begin with the telling of Coyote stories during the winter months so that all present members could hear the stories and participate in their telling. Any fair-minded folklorist would certainly recognize this as an insistence upon keeping the material alive and functional, and we might even argue that in so doing this small tribe was maintaining for itself a live archives. Under those circumstances, one can hardly lament that the stories are not in fossilized form in a file drawer or on a shelf of tapes. Although the folklorist may be a master of the discipline, it is the larger process of tradition that should always be dominant.

# ✍ BIBLIOGRAPHICAL NOTES

Not everyone approaches fieldwork the same way. While I tend to be sparing with equipment, others carry a tape recorder over their shoulder everywhere they go in order to establish an image of "that guy with the machine"—as if it were another arm that spectators simply must get used to. Either gambit will produce results if sensitively employed. The present chapter, then, is not a prescription for fieldwork technique but a plea for awareness of the human element in fieldwork, archiving, and research. The following works suggest the range of practical and technical advice available to the folklorist who wishes to see that the people and their lore are not insulted, cheated, or wasted in the collection and study of traditional events.

*Approaches to Field Research:* Richard M. Dorson, "Standards for Collecting and Publishing American Folktales," *Journal of American Folklore,* 70 (1957), 53–56. Kenneth S. Goldstein, "The Induced Natural Context: An Ethnographic Field Technique," in *Essays in the Verbal and Visual Arts,* ed. June Helm (Seattle: University of Washington Press, 1967), pp. 1–6. Michael Owen Jones, "Alternatives to Local (Re-) Surveys of Incidental Depth Projects," *Western Folklore,* 35 (1976), 217–226. MacEdward Leach, "Problems of Collecting Oral Literature," *PMLA,* 77 (1962), 335–340. All the foregoing deal with context, consideration for the informant, means of eliciting traditional expressions, and so on. Leach in particular discusses the importance of cultural matrix and provides some interesting remarks on folk vs. sophisticated aesthetics. Richard M. Dorson's standard work, *Folklore and Folklife: An Introduction,* has already been mentioned previously; toward the end of the book fall several sections of particular importance in this discussion: George List, "Fieldwork: Recording Traditional Music," pp. 445–454; Donald A. MacDonald, "Fieldwork: Collecting Oral Literature," pp. 407–430; Warren E. Roberts, "Fieldwork: Recording Material Culture," pp. 431–444. Each of these gives basic observations on the areas mentioned, and each provides a good beginning bibliography. Rosalie H. Wax, *Doing Fieldwork: Warnings and Advice* (Chicago: University of Chicago Press, 1971), is a personable autobiographical account of several field-work projects undertaken by the author and her husband, also an anthropologist. Part I (pp. 3–55) offers some very penetrating comments on fieldwork based on personal experiences, some of which can only be called fortuitous accidents and unintentional blunders; Wax generously shares the dilemmas she encountered as the bases for observations on knotty problems that some fieldworkers fail to take into consideration until they have occurred in mid-project. Albert B. Lord, *The Singer of Tales* (Cambridge, Mass.: Harvard University Press, 1960), is a classic work that shows how hypothesis about the oral composition of epic poetry led to field research in Yugoslavia that in turn led to rich and sometimes startling discoveries about the nature of oral poetry.

*Apparatus and Technique, Especially in Film:* One of the handiest books on the use of film in fieldwork is John Collier, Jr., *Visual Anthropology: Photography as a Research Method* (New York: Holt, Rinehart and Winston, 1967). In addition to dealing with photography itself, Collier's work considers the critical questions behind photographing in terms of what is to be gained and how certain problems may be approached; clearly, the book is as much a suggestion for visualizing a research method as it is a handbook on photos. Karl G. Heider, *Ethnographic Film* (Austin: University of Texas Press, 1976), discusses the ways in which ethnography differs in conception from standard filmmaking. The book lists representative ethnographic films and discusses the techniques and research methods of prominent ethnographic filmmakers. Lenny Lipton, *Independent Filmmaking* (San Francisco: Straight Arrow, 1972), gives a practical description of basic equipment and how-to processes in filming, editing, and visualizing. While it does not deal with ethnographic or folkloristic filmmaking as such, its technical offerings are well worth having for anyone who wishes to pursue any kind of filmmaking independently (as most folklorists are forced to do). In a similar way, Edward Pincus, *Guide to Filmmaking* (New York: New American Library, 1969), gives a useful discussion of hardware and technique. Ivan Polunin, "Visual and Sound Recording Apparatus in Ethnographic Fieldwork," *Current Anthropology,* 11 (1970), 3–22, is a basic and sensible view of the machinery most needed and encountered in fieldwork and provides a rather full bibliography. A fascinating account of a fieldwork project that moved neatly from hypothesis to fieldwork, through further research and analysis, to a rich conclusion is provided by Sol Worth and John Adair, *Through Navajo Eyes: An Exploration in Film Communication and Anthropology* (Bloomington: Indiana University Press, 1972), already referred to several times. Their conclusions are too numerous and complex to summarize here, but it is important to note that they discovered the kind of truth that has dawned on many a folklorist: When research includes the subjects themselves as participants (instead of as mere objects of scrutiny), the conclusions are astronomically richer and often far different from what the researcher might have hypothesized in the planning stages.

*Manuals for Fieldwork:* Although it is very brief and focuses on a particular geographical and political entity, Jan Harold Brunvand, *A Guide for Collectors of Folklore in Utah* (Salt Lake City: University of Utah Press, 1971), demonstrates how folklore theory can be applied to the study of traditions in a well-defined culture area without unnecessary jargon or overproduction of hypotheses. Kenneth S. Goldstein, *A Guide for Field Workers in Folklore*

(Hatboro, Pa.: Folklore Associates, 1964), is much more extensive and theoretical than Brunvand, but does not offer the tight focus on a particular area. Much of the information and advice on mechanical equipment (cameras and tapes) is now of course outdated by the rapid development of transistorized equipment. Nonetheless, the tenor of the advice is still valid, and many of the other comments on fieldwork in general are as timely as they were when the book was written. There is a good deal of basic advice for fieldworkers working away from their own turf. Edward D. Ives, *A Manual for Fieldworkers* (*Northeast Folklore*, 15 [1974]), is an extremely useful technical guide, especially in the details of archival management. Presently being reprinted by the University of Illinois Press, this book addresses the technical and theoretical problems encountered by archives that include oral history, anthropological data, and folklore. Even though folklore is only one of its central concerns, it is easily the most practical and useful of the shorter manuals. A more extensive coverage is provided in Maud Karpeles, ed., *The Collecting of Folk Music and Other Ethnomusicological Material: A Manual for Fieldworkers* (London: International Folk Music Council and the Royal Anthropological Institution of Great Britain and Ireland, 1958). The practical observations on equipment are dated, but overall the manual is very usable.

Another small regional booklet for an area that, unlike Utah, is not so heavily characterized by a single group, is MacEdward Leach and Henry Glassie, *A Guide for Collectors of Oral Traditions and Folk Cultural Material in Pennsylvania* (Harrisburg: Pennsylvania Historical and Museum Commission, 1968), a combined effort to list a few of the most common traditions in various categories and to suggest how those traditions may be sought, found, collected, and preserved. Quite the most exhaustive manual of this sort, no doubt the real ancestor of the regional manuals in America, is Sean O'Sullivan (Seán O Súilleabháin), *A Handbook of Irish Folklore* (1942; reprinted, Detroit: Singing Tree Press, 1970). By giving innumerable examples of the rich and varied traditions of Ireland in the form of questions to be asked potential informants, O'Sullivan's book provides enough leads to keep the fieldworker engaged in conversation for several years. For the American scholar, O'Sullivan's book is primarily useful in suggesting the kinds of questions, topics, and approaches that may be most useful in eliciting traditional information in the field.

*Archiving Considerations:* First, for some discussion of how archives operate, where they are, and how material may be catalogued, the reader might begin with George List, "Archiving," in Dorson, *Folklore and Folklife: An Introduction,* pp. 455–463. *The Folklore and Folk Music Archivist,* vols. 1–10, published at Indiana University from 1958 to 1968 under the editorship of George List, provides brief but illuminating articles on archives and their contents internationally; Robert Georges, Beth Blumenreich, and Kathie O'Reilly, in "Two Mechanical Indexing Systems for Folklore Archives: A Preliminary Report," *Journal of American Folklore,* 87 (1974), 39–52, propose one plan for coding an archives system so that material being accessioned can be categorized according to a multitude of scholarly interests and later retrieved for research. The careful reader of this article will notice that it is as much a theoretical discussion of how folklore may be subdivided as it is a mechanical plan for finding materials in a storage center. Dov Noy, "Archiving and Presenting Folk Literature in an Ethnological Museum," *Journal of American Folklore*, 75 (1962), 23–38, presents still another aspect of how folklore materials relate to particular kinds of storage facilities. *Folklore Forum*, Bibliographical and Special Series, no. 1, November 1968, presented *Folklore Archives of the World: A Preliminary Guide*, compiled by Peter Aceves and Magnus Einarsson-Mullarky, providing a finding list of archives along with current addresses.

*Preservation of Materials:* Every serious archives should be equipped with proper advice about the nature of paper, films, tapes, and other materials that constitute the basic physical media of folklore storage. While the following list is not exhaustive, these books allow an archives to confront the most pressing dilemmas in conservation and preservation in an efficient way: George D. M. Cunha and Dorothy G. Cunha, *Conservation of Library Materials*, 2nd ed. (Metuchen, N.J.: Scarecrow Press, 1972), offers an extensive two-volume treatment of basic conservation and restoration problems and procedures, threats to different types of media, and principles of archival preservation. Volume 1 contains discussions, helpful appendices, subject and author indexes, and references to other literature; Volume 2 contains probably the most extensive bibliography on the topic and a comprehensive guide to the literature of library and archival conservation. Kenneth W. Duckett, *Modern Manuscripts* (Nashville: American Association for State and Local History, 1975), is a basic text on sound archival practices relating to manuscripts. Two chapters are of special interest to folklore archivists: Chapter 5, "Physical Care and Conservation," and Chapter 7, "Non-Manuscript Material," which gives helpful suggestions about films, tapes, slides, and other items. The book includes a long bibliography, a good directory of supplies and tools, and suggestions on where to get special jobs done. Robert A. Weinstein and Larry Booth, *Collection, Use and Care of Historical Photographs* (Nashville: American Association for State and Local History, 1977), is one of the most recent and certainly most practical guides to the technical aspects of old photographs. The book brings up philosophical questions, details on restoration, ideas about interpretation, and preservation. A good bibliography is included. Howard W. Winger and Richard B. Smith, eds., *Deterioration and Preservation of Library Materials* (Chicago: University of Chicago Press, 1970), is a highly informative survey of basic preservation problems relating to the nature and deterioration of paper, environmental problems, and other topics, all of which grew out of an earlier library conference. Each article features an extensive bibliography. Beginning in 1975, the Library of Congress began to issue a series called *Preservation Leaflets*. These contain bibliographical references and descriptions of monographs and articles relating to the problems suggested in the titles and the contents of the previously mentioned books. These pamphlets are available without charge from the Library of Congress, Washington, D.C. 20540. Of course the Library of Congress is our largest archives, and two of its divisions are directly related to folklore: the Archive of Folk Song and the American Folklife Center. These offices are both willing to help fieldworkers with technical and theoretical problems, and they can offer the use of equipment to scholars doing extensive fieldwork. Anyone interested should contact them directly for information on recent programs and directions.

*Research and Application:* It goes without saying that nearly every work cited in this book is an example of some kind of folklore or ethnographic research having been carried through to an analytical conclusion. I will mention here, then, only a few works whose topics suggest areas of research not covered previously. One of the most helpful general research guides for anyone reading in folklore is Jan Harold Brunvand's *Folklore: A Study and Research Guide* (New York: St. Martin's Press, 1976). Chapter 2, "Reference Guide," is particularly handy because its references are solidly representative of the field; they appear in full notation, including Library of Congress call numbers. The book includes suggestions for paper topics and format (Chapter 3) and is an all-around indispensable research help for the beginner. Richard M. Dorson, "The Use of Printed Sources," in his *Folklore and Folklife: An Introduction,* pp. 465–477, suggests how folklore may be gleaned from and studied in newspapers, popular books, and in other print media that might at first not seem rewarding sources for folklore materials. E. Estyn Evans, "The Cultural Geographer and Folklife Research," in *Folklore and Folklife: An Introduction,* pp. 517–532, appplies the resources of folklife and material folklore research to the problems and perspectives of cultural geography. It seems clear from this study that the cultural geographer and the folklorist often deal with identical kinds of information, even though until recently, at least in the United States, there has been relatively little interchange between the two fields on a theoretical level. Louis Gottschalk, Clyde Kluckhohn, and Robert Angell, in *The Use of Personal Documents in History, Anthropology, and Sociology* (New York: Social Science Research Council, 1945), include a chapter on field methods by Kluckhohn as part of a whole section of great interest to fieldworkers in folklore. Personal reminiscences and oral history are as yet underutilized by students of folklore. L. L. Langness, *The Life History in Anthropological Science* (New York: Holt, Rinehart and Winston, 1965), while not oriented to expressive aspects of culture, stresses the individual's concept of his own traditional place in his culture as he sees it, clearly another particular aspect of oral tradition that bears further study. Bruce A. Rosenberg and John B. Smith, "The Computer and the Finnish Historical-Geographical Method," *Journal of American Folklore,* 87 (1974), 149–154, put forward a rather simple means by which a computer can be used to provide a rapid comparison of texts and variations in the same kinds of scholarly study that once took years of careful reading and handwritten notation. Whether such a system will ever be in wide usage may be irrelevant compared to the observation made by the authors that computer work need not dehumanize or change in any essential way the normal operations of folklore research except insofar as years of effort may be saved and analytical problems solved rapidly enough so that scholars in a given generation may apply themselves to the conversation. Many other folklorists are concurrently pursuing the subject of the computerization of folklore collections as well as computer-assisted analytical work. Professor Richard S. Thill, at the University of Nebraska, has been urging the computer as an essential tool in folklore research for several years to a continually increasing and interested audience. Finally, Robert Wildhaber, "Folk Atlas Mapping," in *Folklore and Folklife: An Introduction*, pp. 479–496, describes an analytical procedure that has been carried forward for some years now in Europe but has only recently begun to gain extensive support in the United States. Many European countries have folk atlases that show variations in dance steps, costumes, haystacking traditions, and traditional tools in tremendous geographical detail. It remains to be seen whether the United States will ever develop enough interest in our traditions on the official level to warrant the long-range expenditure of money necessary for such a vast project; in the meantime, a good number of the foremost folklorists in America are developing among themselves the basis for a folk atlas with the help and leadership of Professor W. H. F. Nicolaisen, an indefatigable international folklorist. Of interest to all scholars using, storing, and quoting oral materials is an undated pamphlet by Joseph B. Romney, *A Guide to Oral History and the Law*, available from the Utah State Historical Society, 603 East South Temple St., Salt Lake City.

# 10

## APPLICATIONS

## OF

# FOLKLORE

**THE TERM** *APPLIED FOLKLORE* **HAS BEEN SEEN BY SOME FOLKLORISTS AS AN UNFAIR PEDESTRIANIZING OF THE FIELD. ESPECIALLY FOR THOSE WHO BELIEVE SCHOLARSHIP** and research ought to be untainted by practical considerations, personal involvement, or mechanical application, the concept has had the same ring that applied art or applied literature might have. It seems to smack of job rather than profession, of problem solving rather than theoretical speculation, of the immediate live world rather than the library. It stresses doing more than talking, and the academy has always been uneasy about such subordination of its central role. Academics ask, with justice, "How can there be free inquiry and imagination if our speculations are tied down to definable practical issues?" Their students have often asked, with equal justice, "What's the use of studying something if it can't be applied to identifiable problems around us?"

I am simplifying the issue here, of course, for there are many different understandings of applied folklore, but of the two polar attitudes implied here, I find myself on the side of the students, for I think their question more often leads to real perception and perspective in folklore than does that of the academics. Sadly, the latter position is more often used as an excuse for not rethinking central issues than as a foundation for genuine insight.

# ▨ APPLICATION AND EVALUATION

I like to encourage students to pose of everything they study the hypothetical question "So what?" That is, what is it good for? What does it tell us that we needed to know? What does it open up for us? How does it help us to understand something? "So what?" is not meant to be belligerent but to serve as a kind of field test to see if a mental exercise has paid off. As a student, I once listened to a long, detailed lecture on the real persons on whom Chaucer might have based the figure of the Knight in *The Canterbury Tales*. At the end, I could not come up with an answer to "So what" beyond the simple observation (which the professor could have made in one sentence) that Chaucer may have had a live person in mind. But why did I need to know that or think about it? It did not seem to expand my appreciation of Chaucer's art, or of *The Canterbury Tales*, or of medieval literature. Now, it may have been my fault or the professor's that there was no adequate answer for my question, but it remains unanswered to this day—for me, anyhow.

On the other hand, read Jan Harold Brunvand's article on Shakespeare's use of a folk tale type in *The Taming of the Shrew* and then ask "So what?" There *is* an answer: We now can see that since Shakespeare used folklore as well as his own genius, we need to deal with both before we can make either broad or specific pronouncements about Shakespeare's art. Which parts are his and which parts are the people's? How, and how appropriately, did he use the folklore, and with what presumable effects on the audience? In how many plays did he do it? These questions should lead us to some important perceptions about Shakespeare's art and its meaning. And we can go back over the work of earlier critics who did not think to look at the folklore deeply enough. What do we know now—what can we say now—that improves our abilities to respond to Shakespeare's dramatic art? These are real payoffs, not mere mechanical tinkerings, yet they are derived from an application of folklore study and theory to an existing field of study, in this case literature.

This is not to say that folklore represents the answer to dull classes, but that in any area, the perspectives of another field may be applied to particular problems with more than respectable results. The lecture "Who

Was Chaucer's Knight Really?" was not pointless because it did not deal with folklore but because it did not apply any real perspective to a real problem: It did not lead to a fuller view of the work. Rather, it added yet more painstaking and detailed information to the already heavy pack of data being lugged around in the minds of young scholars. One might as well have a dissertation on the identity of the original traveling salesman, or of Kilroy; if the treatise helps us avoid dealing with what's funny in the jokes, or with how the message "Kilroy was here" spread all over the world in a few years, it cannot stand up to the question "So what?" It is strange that the amassing of facts often passes for real scholarship, while applying the facts to a problem is often thought of as a cheap shot.

Additionally, I think we may want to admit that there is sometimes a class issue behind academic hesitation concerning the practical application of scholarly perspective. It is as if by gearing down their large professional views to the interests of people outside their disciplines, scholars feel they demean themselves—as if they pictured themselves as classical concert musicians being asked to entertain people on a street corner. How can hoi polloi be trusted to understand or deal with an area of expertise without distorting it? This feeling is intensified when we suggest that the stories of oral tradition may have some bearing on formal literature.

Such suspicion of practical application is not as prominent in other professional fields. A medical doctor is someone who applies the scientific knowledge of his field to problems among live people. While some doctors are lecturers and theorists, no one, I believe, looks down upon the practicing physician as providing a substandard function in his field. If doctors stopped dealing with patients just because the common person lacks formal understanding, we would accuse them of a dangerous and unrealistic elitism. Similarly, it would surely be ironic if a discipline like folklore, whose entire existence is based on the everyday person, ever became one in which the information were shared only among the elite, in which the theories became more important than the people.

Since many early folklorists in the United States were scholars trained in language, literature, classics, and so forth, we may expect their works to demonstrate the basic scholarly concerns with detail, the amassing of data, classification, publication—often carried out with admirable objectivity and fairness. As the field has developed, however, newer generations of folklorists have inclined more and more toward the development of theories that could be applied to the dynamic phenomena of the natural world. Right now there is a healthy mix of both orientations, each a little wary of the other, both as necessary to this field as to medicine.

The ways of applying folklore fall into a few rather well defined categories, depending on the situation in which the applying is done: There are intellectual applications, as when folklore is used as an approach or instrument for literary criticism, historical scrutiny, or cultural psychology; there are applications that involve some kind of action being taken, as in race relations, urban setlement, ethnic arbitration, and education. Other applications are in the nature of employment, such as when the Smithsonian Institution hires full-time folklorists to organize a national festival.

## FOLKLORE AND LITERARY CRITICISM

Suppose we wish to examine the ways in which an author uses folklore—not merely to catalogue it but to see its relation to the writer's style, vision, and literary art. How can we apply the perspectives of folklore to the artistic output of an individual author? What terms do we need to invent or use in order to label the phenomena we see, or which terms may we discover in trying to make our study more clear to those with whom we wish to communicate? Finally, and most important, what do we gain by applying folklore to the writings of a particular individual? After all, a novel, short story, or poem written and copyrighted is certainly not to be seen as folklore.

At the same time, we know that many artists have found folklore and myth to be considerably evocative of cultural responses in the reading audience. We need to take a close look at any author's use of folklore, then, and see if indeed the ideas, connotations, and responses that can be related to those folk ideas are appropriate to and supportive of what is happening in the story. In other words, in a large sense, the questions asked about the use of folklore in literature are almost exactly the same ones asked about imagery or symbol: What is the relation between what is said and how it is said? Are the images and symbols related to the content? In the case of folklore, has the author used the materials to deepen and extend his meaning or only for window dressing, for local color? These are the same questions we ask in any close examination of literary style and meaning, but of course they cannot be asked and answered well unless we are willing to develop some expertise in the field.

Earlier we discussed the relationship of the Wife of Bath's red stockings both to folklore and to Chaucer's possible intent. (We need to remember that since a good many authors cannot be brought back to life to testify, we cannot be overconfident about exactly what they meant; this does not prevent us from speculating on the appropriateness of image to content, however.) We have talked about the connotative power of words like *pig*, and *cherry*, and we have recognized that even entire stories may have rich traditional associations that carry meaning far beyond the mere content of the words. We may suspect, because of the considerable cultural power of folklore and the depth with which many people register their recognition of their traditions, that a sensitive writer will not use folklore materials lightly, but will be motivated by the conviction that the use of certain images, phrases, and structures will serve as a powerful emotional link between the responses of the audience and the emotional and moral issues in the literature.

SOME APPROACHES   The main business of literary criticism is to approach the problem of thinking about and talking about works of literature in such a way as to expand the areas of sensitivity between writer and reader. That is, the literary critic does not see his job as telling what a work means; for that, the reader goes to the work itself. Historical criticism tries to present a clear picture of the historical context of a work; biographical criticism, to provide data that show what personal backgrounds might have been factors in an author's development or in the development of a particular work. These and other approaches try, at their best, to circumscribe and clarify the various areas of the author's background, and intellectual milieu that led to the production of his artistic expressions. The critic, in re-creating these areas for study, is simply preparing a number of lines along which the field of references from which an author operates can be shared. Such an axis is not a way of telling what a work means; rather, it operates as a point of access, a way of thinking more fully about, and thus responding more fully and more reliably to, the work.

There have been attempts to use folklore as a critical tool in the study of literature. Some approaches use the appearance of folklore to indicate an author's acquaintance with folksy materials or his ability to use tradition as local color, or as a reference that throws light on a difficult passage. These are not dishonest approaches, especially if they are warranted by an author's superficial use of folklore, but they fail to help us understand the extent to which folklore can inform the spirit and direction of a given work.

Two schools of thought, which may be called the architectural and psychological, are far more usable as critical tools because they provide more than a superficial access to areas of contact between the reader and a work. In the first, to oversimplify its approach, the terms and structures of myth and drama are used to describe, almost like a critical metaphor, how plots are developed and how protagonists operate within them. Here, there is not necessarily the suggestion that an author has consciously used myth or folklore, but the work may be described as having the quality of myth, and then we consider how that conception aids in our critical examination. In the psychological approach, myths and myth-like structures are seen as embodiments of the author's frame of mind, as symbols of repressions, or as images inherited or inculcated. Both approaches are valuable and have been used with spectacular results by a number of modern critics. However, both depend on the use of myth as a clarifying factor essentially outside the work itself, usually with the implication that such areas as the author's art and the audience's reaction may be irrelevant or unconscious (or at least unknowable).

A few critics, like Daniel Hoffman in *Form and Fable in American Fiction*, do deal directly with works themselves in relation to a body of traditional materials used centrally within them. But the resulting critical approaches have been very general, dealing with rather broad matters like cultural views of the authors or beliefs reflected by their characters. What is needed is a more specific and accurate way to talk about, and to organize, our recognition of traditional materials used by authors, and a way to approach more coherently the question of how traditional themes and forms are used artistically and how they may strike their audience.

THE LITERARY USE OF NATIVE FOLKLORE   Many works of literature can serve as models to the kind of study suggested here. For convenience I have chosen a well-known novel because it has striking examples of what I am talking about, and they so saturate the work that without a doubt they are connected to the whole fabric of plot, character, presentation, and theme: Thomas Hardy's *Return of the Native*.

In the first chapter, "The Three Women," we are presented with a great array of traditional items: There are the November Samhain fires—and, indeed, at this point and throughout the novel Hardy overlooks *no* chance to make it clear that all important junctures of human involvement coincide with ceremonies connected with the seasonal cycle (the autumn fires, Christmas festivities, Maypole dancing). The early action takes place not only around one of these fires but on a barrow built in ancient times situated on a hill shaped like a human breast. An old man sings a few verses from the ballad "Queen Eleanor's Confession" (Child #156), and a lengthy discussion develops on the topic of Christian Cantle's oddities, centered on the proverbially phrased birth superstition, "no moon, no man."

As the novel proceeds, we encounter, to name a few: dreams as omens;

brief references to particularly appropriate folk songs (for example, the small boy who has been tending a fire for Eustacia goes home singing "in an old voice a little song about a sailor-boy and a fair one, and bright gold in store," which is no doubt a reference to "James Harris, or the Demon Lover," Child #243, the topics of which are quite appropriate to this novel). There are references to ritual braiding of hair; throwing a shoe after the bride; witchcraft, including sticking pins in dolls and in people; omens such as a sparrow flying through the house on the morning of an ill-fated wedding; folk medicine, in the attempted cure for Mrs. Yeobright's adder bite (frying adders and applying their rendered fat to a wound). One central character is continually described in terms of that haunting figure Robert Graves has since called the White Goddess: Hardy says of her, "Eustacia Vye was the raw material of divinity," and he calls Egdon Heath her Hades. He describes her as a beautiful black mare on one occasion and as a delicate, pale, potentially cruel being on another.

Still another character, Diggory Venn, is seen almost throughout in the role of trickster, whose function is entirely that of a catalyst. Nothing of structural importance in the novel happens without his aid or scrutiny. He is called Mephistophelian, and he is entirely red from the sheep dye he uses, which "spreads its lively hues over everything it lights on, and stamps unmistakably, as with the mark of Cain, any person who has handled it half an hour." In another place we are told, "Among all these squatters and folks of the road the reddleman continually found himself; yet he was not of them." And yet we notice that he is connected with everything that happens in the novel, and he would have disappeared entirely (and properly) at the novel's end but for the insistence of the serial publisher that he be brought back in, washed up, and married to the heroine, a transgression of his traditional role that strikes us as akin to unmasking the Lone Ranger and then marrying him off to the local schoolmarm.

One thinks of other traditional aspects of the novel: an eclipse of the moon at a point where human entanglements have assumed ominous importance; the continual stress on the reciprocity between Egdon Heath, its weather, and its simple inhabitants; the mummers' play, complete with masks, during which main characters are masked and unmasked. One also thinks of the particularly vivid scene in which Mrs. Yeobright, having been refused entrance to her daughter-in-law's home, sits down exhausted on a bank of sweet thyme, watches a heron fly overhead toward the west, and thinks a last thought described as "marked by a streak in the air, like the path of a meteor." As she sleeps (and we remember she has just returned from a garden with a central apple tree), she is stung by an adder. Since thyme was a funerary herb, the bird often a carrier of the soul (and "going west" at that), a falling star a death omen, it would have come as no surprise to a rural British audience that she soon dies. It should not surprise the folklorist, either. But it may surprise an otherwise well informed person, who might resist reading anything into the scene. The real question is, of course, "What can we read *out* of it?"

These and many other traditional references occur in a novel oriented to what might be called a mythic year, the whole action taking place between one November and the next, exactly one year and a day. Hardy's references to folklore (and they abound in his other novels as well) were catalogued by Ruth Firor some time ago, and her book serves as a handy listing. Much more to the purpose of our present inquiry, however, is not the existence of folklore in Hardy, but the question "So what?" What shall we make of all this: That *The Return of the Native* is a folk novel? That Eustacia Vye is really the White Goddess in her waning aspect? That Diggory Venn the reddleman is the Devil? That the novel is really a myth in modern times? No to all of these, because they all make of the work something it quite obviously is not designed to be. Is it possible to conclude conversely that these folk references either are coincidental or are the surface representations of psychological processes too deep for our scrutiny of conscious art? No again, because the correspondences are too neat, the references too many and consistently appropriate to their context, for us to dismiss them from consideration as units of conscious art.

MODES AND METAPHORS  If we approach these references critically, we find they are of varying focuses and applications. Some, like the orientation of the whole novel to a mythic year of seasonal rituals, seem to be concerned with ordering the entire action in terms of something beyond the observable world, perhaps in terms of cosmic forces. Some of the references, however, seem to be more localized in the story; they describe people and events in traditionally evocative ways, and their contexts are limited to the passages in which they occur. The larger organizational assumptions might be termed *modes*, somewhat after Northrop Frye's term. A *traditional mode* would be a conventionalized ordering of literary design according not to the demands of verisimilitude but to the expectations of tradition; or, to make it simple and specific, a traditional mode is a manner of creating an artistic expression according to Olrik's "Epic Laws." There is no assumption that a particular genre, theme, or content will be present. It is simply an observation on the organizational and conceptual assumptions of the author, but with a distinct critical advantage: Since we are dealing with tradition, we can treat the features themselves as recurrent enough to be conventional, and we can assume that they will be familiar to anyone who shares the tradition. By extension, we may say that the critic, who may or may not share in the tradition as a native, can in any case enter the tradition well enough through study to create reliable connotative relationships.

The smaller, more localized units of description and action might be called *traditional metaphors*. In this view, the traditional metaphor is the suggestive, highly charged vocabulary in which the traditional mode reaches expression. The traditional metaphor also comes out of traditional cultural concepts, but its use is not in the ordering of the whole work. The metaphor itself differs from the usual concept of metaphor in that there is no simple analogy but traditional actions, colors, images, symbols, and so on, that have culture-based connotations. The bank of thyme, the heron, and the meteor image, which combine to foretell Mrs. Yeobright's death, are not used to mean simply a bunch of plants, a bird, and an astronomical phenomenon; they appear in such a way as to suggest death by evoking folk beliefs familiar to the audience (and within our reach through research). One would hesitate to call them symbols, and they appear too closely related to the direction of the plot to be thought of as anything but conscious art. They are effective artistic units that call upon our ability to respond to familiar beliefs and to apply them as translations of image to import.

Applying the concepts of traditional mode and metaphor to *The Return of the Native* and to other works of literature that come to mind, however, we notice some further distinctions. We may say, for example, that when Chaucer takes two traditional stories like the Flood story and the so-called misplaced kiss tale and puts them together in the Miller's Tale, which is itself organized very much along the lines of traditional narrative in spite of its sophisticated poetic embellishments, what we have is an entire work of art conceptualized along traditional modal expectations. We have the same kind of organization in, say, *Beowulf*, and in *The Return of the Native*; moreover, in these works the mode seems much more infused with a sense of religious urgency, of commitment to processes in which the main characters are models of deeper human possibilities, conceived of in a mythic way. Thus we might need to subdivide the terms *traditional mode* and *traditional metaphor* and use the term *mythic mode* for the organizational principles that seem to reach toward the ineffable, the Beyond, and the term *folkloric mode* for the organizational assumptions that produce traditional patterns in secular fictive expressions. Of course the distinction is an arbitrary one, usable only in discussion. In reality, many kinds of folklore references might go as easily into one category as another. Superstitions and customs of everyday life (folkloric), if they concern death and burial traditions, may actually be concerned with the Beyond (mythic). In most cases, though, the dichotomy seems to be a fair one to play with.

The same distinction could be made between mythic metaphor and folkloric metaphor. In the mythic metaphor there is the feeling that the image is pregnant with the aura of universal power. The barrows in *Return*, for example, are described as the poles and axes of a mysterious heathery world; the November fires themselves, and the mummers, carry associations that reach far beyond their context, even though their employment in the novel is quite limited. On the other hand, the references to customs (braiding hair and throwing shoes and gathering holly), while evocative, bring up associations concerning local customs, popular beliefs, and observances that simply have to do with participation in a traditional set. These folkloric metaphors are not the less useful to the author, however. Take the singing of "Queen Eleanor's Confession" at the beginning of *Return* as a single example. The whole ballad is not sung, but certainly most people in Hardy's day would have recognized it, and they would have been able to sense, perhaps, that the narrative opening to view was about to concern itself with such matters as disguise, treachery, adultery, and surprise.

The traditional character appears most at home in the traditional mode, of course. The author is able to develop a sense of inexorable movement that, though it is set in motion by the artist, gains its greatest power from the responses of an audience to a customary, not a realistic, concept of cause and effect. Beowulf understandably fights three battles and dies in the third; King Lear quite plausibly asks three daughters a ticklish question and gets from the third the answer that precipitates the rest of the action; we know from the thyme, heron, and meteor that Mrs. Yeobright will die, and from the sparrow in the house that the wedding will fail and that at least one partner will die. And while the omen does not cause the outcome, the occurrence does happen in a way much more clearly related to traditional expectations, to what Olrik called traditional logic, than to our rational observation of real life. This way of ordering and approaching a work of art is what is here called the traditional mode, and it is of course an artistic phenomenon to be found throughout all of English and American letters.

TRADITION VERSUS PSYCHOLOGY   We have been discussing the artist's craft (as opposed to his subconscious or his biography) in relation to the use of materials from a particular culture, which in turn is depicted in the work as the context of human action. We need to admit that one cannot always determine which of an author's references are borrowed and which are original, perhaps coincidentally drawn from a less than conscious awareness of tradition. But one can at least identify common motifs and references from folklore as existing independently of the author, and we can also study an author's familiarity with folklore, his understanding of it, and therefore his method of using it. Moreover, when we know how a certain folk reference or method is traditionally construed (say, a series of three actions building toward an important climax on the third) and we can see an author using it in a way appropriate to the context, we can deal with it a bit more certainly than with a discrete symbol. Since the items we are discussing come from the group rather than the individual, we can speculate more reliably on an audience's reaction to mythic and folkloric stimuli without depending entirely on our knowledge of the author's intent.

According to Jung and Freud and their followers, the images in folklore and mythology can apparently be transmitted by other means than oral tradition; some have even argued that they may be part of the inherited genetic characteristics of entire groups of people or of humanity in general. Regardless of the extent to which this may or may not be so, we must observe that in any case these images also are capable of conscious transmission and reception. It is to this level primarily (though not to the exclusion of effects incident to the deeper level) that our present discussion addresses itself. I would like to use myth and folklore criticism not as an approach chiefly to the author's mind but to his art, and our responses to that art, in as nonclinical a manner as possible. One cannot rule out the deeper psychological levels of human meaning and response, but they are very ticklish to discuss because they so require information from the mind of the author. Thus, psychological approaches very often lie outside the area of folklore while they rest heavily on data inside the mind of an individual. If a folkloristic approach is to have any merit, it should be able to distinguish its own aims and approaches from others, and in any case it should be able to refer to materials and ideas that are available for everyone's scrutiny and discussion.

Folklore has an advantage in that it is based on freely available fieldwork and scholarship. In other words, without interviewing the writer (which may, after all, be impossible), we can study the lore of the society depicted and speculate on its appearance in the work and the effects of it back on the society. The data of folklore, and the theories based on them, are subject to continual clarification and study by other scholars. Since meaning and connotation of folk ideas can be determined by fieldwork and by comparison with other research, we can watch for the significant and coherent application of folklore in an author's work, and we may speak fairly of the author's use of folk material as well as speculate plausibly on its impact on certain audiences that share the references brought forward.

The traditional mode, divided here into mythic and folkloristic modes, can be seen as a manner of looking at things that are communally based and culture-specific, that therefore include the audience as participant, communicant. When the traditional mode is used in literary expression it causes readers to be participants, whether they recognize the specific features of the myth or not, for they respond to a manner of seeing and feeling that they share with the members of the culture and that refuses to let them only be spectators. This involvement is based on the readers' relationship to the traditions of their culture, not on personal opinions especially, and therefore it does not resemble more than superficially the involvement and response we normally refer to as empathy. In short, we are not simply trying to find out whether a given author thinks that red stockings would make a fashionable, chic dressing for a woman character, nor are we asking an author or reader if there is something about red stockings that particularly represents tension (or eroticism), but we are observing that in an entire culture the color red has for so many generations had a heavy connotation of sensuousness, passion, and even sexuality that an individual author can never be totally free to determine what it means or how it is to be applied if his audience is to understand. If you believe you are totally free from this responsibility of tradition, suggest to a woman you know that she wear a red dress at her wedding, or try suggesting to a matador that pink and lavender would make a much prettier cape for him to use in the bullfight ring.


The terms *mythic metaphor, folkloric metaphor, mythic mode,* and *folkloric mode* have been used to label some differences in scope or focus. Do they really aid our understanding? Are they likely to be adopted by folklorists or literary critics in general? I hope the answer to the first question is yes, because in using and supporting the terms, I think I have been able to point out some distinctly observable traits in Hardy's writing that might not have been easily seen otherwise. The answer to the second question, however, is entirely irrelevant to my purpose here, for insight into folklore, and an author's use of it, is a far more important matter than the acceptance of terminology by a profession or the general public. This is not simply self-indulgent modesty; it is, rather, an insistence that we recognize the validity of playing with words in order to clarify our perspectives without enshrining those words on a professional altar that could easily become more of a focal point than the folklore or the literature.

The effects of traditional mode are many. It can broaden and deepen our experiential responses to literature. The critic can approach some works of literature armed with information that, far from being out of sight and uncheckable (as is usually the case with psychological approaches), is continually redefined and informed by reference to its own traditional texts. We need not accept the assertion of I. A. Richards that stock responses based on the reader's own experience and tradition are necessarily wrong or irrelevant. Here, though the response is personal and external to the work, it is occasioned by an author working from the same tradition that molds the reader's responses. As conventionalized as these responses may be, they are of the deepest sort and are quite appropriate to the mode. For the critic or careful reader who does not already share the tradition of the work, the establishment of the field of reference through study of the relevant materials is obligatory; such study will not tell us what the work means, but how it means, and will represent an extremely important way in which we can extend and expand the range of our own emotional and critical awareness of possibilities in the literary art of a given culture, including our own. As well, it is likely that folklore provides one of the very best ways (in some cases, indeed, the only way) to approach the connotative possibilities in the literature of cultures other than our own.

## 🖋 FOLKLORE AND HISTORY For those who

believe that folklore is characterized by an unreliability of factual data, it must seem absurd to suggest a profitable connection between the two. Historians themselves have been comfortable with the material aspects of folklore, for very often dates and settlement patterns can be inferred and studied in buildings and other artifacts. But with the possible exception of oral history, the more abstract and essentially nonfactual aspects of oral tradition have been more of a puzzle for historians. Yet we can assume that since much of history as we know it was formed by and among members of close groups, folklore must have been on the scene.

Is it not possible that the expressions passed along in these close groups might have reflected and even directed the course of events that we now call history?

ORAL HISTORY   Oral history gives us some very distinctive kinds of expression, some personal and some culture-based. One of the valuable lessons we can learn is that the people themselves have passed on in oral tradition a very perceptive—if narrow—set of observations about important events and the relationship of those occurrences to the group. We may not always find what we are looking for in oral history, of course, just as when we read diaries of a certain era we may find one commentator giving copious descriptions of what we now feel may have been major occurrences in the world while another ignores them. The diaries of my great-grandfather were written during the Civil War, yet there is not one reference to that traumatic event; instead, there is a daily record of labor provided to neighbor farmers, cords of wood cut, terse statements like "went a-huckleberrying one pail," and equally parsimonious announcements of family childbirths. I suspect if we had been able to interview him, the same information would have come forth: anecdotes and recollections about the family, about New England farm life, about labor and the scarcity of money in rural Massachusetts, and about occasional pastimes. At first sight we may wonder whether these observations, whether in diaries or in oral reminiscences, can really tell us very much about the historical events we seek to study. On the other hand, what better record have we of the tastes and concerns of the everyday person upon whose back and with whose labor those grand events in history were carried forth?

Oral history represents the feelings of the people accurately: What events are worth remembering and retelling? History has more farmers than generals; historians trying to reach the factual bases for events under scrutiny will of course be forced to deal primarily with those figures about whom there is an abundance of material in print, on stone, or in storage. But most historians know that history as seen only through the lives of great personages gives us only a partial view of the real course of time.

What has oral history to do with folklore? A good deal, only part of which I will take up here. We notice that even when people are telling stories based on their own adventures, they frame the stories in culture-specific styles. For example, the catching of large sportfish is often described in terms of three attempts. This kind of structural device, in addition to a number of motifs, proverbial expressions, attitudes and beliefs, and general notions about what constitutes a good story (and what parts must be left out or stressed) all derive from the storyteller's command of the folklore in his own group. Oral history is usually made up of anecdotes and narratives that give the individual's own view of a familiar life and times. That is, unless the person is a liar, the perceptions and recollections gained are meant to be accurate personal accounts, eyewitness reports played through the sensibilities and sensitivities of a particular individual. The content, thus, is expected to be factual, but the style, structure, and metaphor may be distinctly traditional. This is not to say that the latter considerations are in any way nonfactual, but they relate to expressive codes within the society more than to verifiable data. Just as a historical novel may be factual in its details and still be more interesting to us because of the emotional human elements developed by the author within the historical framework, so oral history strikes us as a mix of fact and expression. We need to realize that the nature of the expression in oral history is as important to our concept of the culture's view of itself as is the fact.

RELIABLE LIES   If we shift our attention to more recognizable genres of folklore, however, we notice that expression takes on a still larger role and factuality in many cases seems to disappear. For example, in every region of the United States there is a great inclination toward telling lies and tall tales about the attributes and characteristics of the locale. Initially, these stories can be quite easily identified as nonreliable information; certainly they represent the kind of data a historian would not normally go to in order to study the verifiable details of life in a given period. Yet, each local tall tale normally has some germ of truth in it, usually by capturing some key feature of the region in hyperbolic description. For example, one farmer on the Olympic peninsula in northwest Washington (where rainfall is among the heaviest in the United States) took me to see a huge wooden rain barrel at the corner of his barn; it had overflowed so violently in a heavy rainstorm that the water undercut the earth below the outer edge of the barrel, tipping it over. "You may not believe this," he said, "but it was raining so hard that the rain was going into the bunghole faster than the water could flow out the open end. So much water got built up in that barrel that it was flowing for three days after the rain stopped." Anyone who has spent time on the Olympic peninsula in the rainy season will realize immediately that it is difficult to tell if this anecdote constitutes a clear lie. We imagine, perhaps, that it is unlikely the water actually built up so heavily inside the barrel; this part of the story we can recognize as hyperbole. At the same time, the story accurately represents a real feature of the region, and, more important than that, it expresses the attitudes of people native to the area.

Along the Rogue River in Oregon some years ago lived Hathaway Jones. Jones was a local character and raconteur who was skilled at telling lies about the locale to outsiders and local folk alike. One of his favorite stories was how he and his father had tried to raise watermelons and squash on the rich farmland in the Rogue Valley. "Problem was that we never got to eat any of the watermelons; that land was fertile, all right, but it was so fertile that the vines grew so fast they just wore them watermelons out draggin' 'em across the ground. We tried building sleds for 'em, and that would work for a while, but when the sun would come up in the morning the vines would move so fast they would just jerk the watermelons right off the sleds and they'd break. Finally we built little carts with wooden wheels, and one of our favorite pastimes was sitting on the back porch watching our watermelon crop drive around the yard. Only problem was, the wheels got to squeaking so badly that we had to spend a good part of the day greasing the axles."

In another anecdote, Hathaway told how he had seen a whole flock of geese lining up at the bank of a nearby stream, but when he took careful aim with Ol' Betsy, his sights were just slightly off, and when he fired the flock flew away, leaving him only "a bucketful of bills." Hathaway and his father were famous for building fireplaces, and several of the stories told by Hathaway, passed on today by others in the area, describe how well the fireplace drew. A typical Jones fireplace drew so well that one had only to open the front door of the cabin and the fireplace would suck firewood in from the pile. Disaster often came about through the efficiency of these fireplaces, however; on one occasion a whole litter of pups was dragged forth to its doom from an expectant hunting dog, and in another case a roaring fire sucked the entire cabin up the chimney. These and other Hathaway Jones stories primarily feature references to the local weather, the fertility of the land, the ferocity of life in the rough mountainous countryside along the Rogue and adjacent rivers, hunting escapades, brushes with state authority, interactions with animals, and the like. In other words, taken one by one, the stories do not provide much of a historical perspective, while taken together they provide a rich kaleidoscope of human, often humorous, response to actual conditions that must have flavored the history of the times and perhaps even influenced the direction of it.

Reub Long of central Oregon was another teller of tall tales, but his specialty was to celebrate the dryness of the land. He claimed he had never seen a rainstorm until he was eighteen years old, and when he ran out of the house to see what the terrible drumming sound was on the roof, he was knocked flat by a big desert raindrop and "They had to throw six buckets of sand in my face to bring me around." He bragged about how when he was a boy the sagebrush grew so large that there was a substantial sagebrush logging operation. When I asked if the climate were dry where he lived, he answered me indignantly that a sample of their rainwater had been sent off to the state university and the report had come back that it was 32 percent moisture. He did admit that the percentage was low, but he said it was because it had taken thirty-five years to collect the sample and probably some of it had evaporated in the meantime. When the weather got really dry in his area, people around Prineville and Fort Rock noticed that the sagebrush began to follow the dogs around town.

Benjamin Franklin ("Huckleberry") Finn, formerly a resident on the McKenzie River in Oregon, was fond of telling hunting and fishing stories. In one retold later by his grandson Arthur Belknap:

> Grandad was quite a one to fish, too, you know. He'd fish for Dolly Varden [trout]. They're pretty big. One day Grandad was fishing and he hooked something and his line broke. So he got a stouter line and then he hooked something and his hook broke. So he got a bigger hook and then his line broke again so he got a half-inch rope and went down to the blacksmith's and built him a big hook. And he used some kind of big bait. Well, he tied one end to an alder tree and went away. When he come back that old alder tree was just a-whippin' the water. He pulled on it and finally pulled the fish out. It was three and a half foot between the eyes [pause for laughter]. Well, his trouble wasn't over then. Booth Kelly [a local logging company] was havin' a log drive and when Grandad pulled that fish out of the water, why the level went down and beached all their logs and he had a lawsuit on his hands.

Finn also loved to hang around the local store and brag to strangers about his prodigious hunting exploits. Once, after telling of several bucks, moose, elk, birds, and fish he had taken that week, two visitors said "Do you know who we are?" "By golly, no." "Well, we're state game wardens." "Well, do you know who I am?" "No." "Well, I'm the biggest liar on the McKenzie!"

Len Henry, a local Munchausen in Lapwai, Idaho, had similar stories which featured his contempt for governmental authority:

> Well, Len came into Heckner and Carlson's store in Lap-
> wai and said, "I want two 30-30 shells." Old Heckner, was
> kinda slow on the think, said he should buy a *box* of 'em.
> Then old Len says, "I only need two; your damned game
> laws only allow me one deer and one elk."

These characters were all real people, and it is important to note that their stories, often passed on by others, and not the Paul Bunyan stories, are the prominent features in Northwest narrative lore. The same can be said of folklore in the rest of the country. Why is this so? Why should a nationwide network of liars actually represent more clearly and consistently the traditional views of the people? If this country is as dedicated to fact and practicality as its officials often claim, why do local lies somehow represent our region for us better than the local chambers of commerce? The answer is quite germane to the question of the application of folklore study to history, for in these anecdotes we have a running record of people's responses to historical occurrences, government, regional characteristics, the vicissitudes of life on the frontier, and so on. We miss the point totally if we see them only as humorous inaccuracies.

I developed a rather deep sympathy for one family who tried steadfastly to keep me from interviewing their Uncle Charley, who, I was told, could not be relied upon to give factual information anymore because he was so senile. I knew from other sources that Uncle Charley was a tremendously funny raconteur and a Munchausen. But his whole family tried to protect the rest of the world from him because they thought he was simply addle-headed. In fact, he was a repository of tremendously interesting and exciting (to say nothing of intensely humorous) stories about his region. In these tall tales we see a reflection of historical reality as it is played through human responses and a sense of humor that prefers to express regional pride in a complicated way: On the surface, people seemed to be complaining about the extensive rain in their region or lamenting how dry it gets, how hard the work is, and how hard the wind blows. But underneath it all lies a strong sense of regional pride. The hyperbole in these stories is laced with a sense of modesty, as if to say, "No, you couldn't stand it around here; it rains too much. Why, I remember the time. . . ." The historical reality represented in traditions of this sort, especially as they reflect regional settlement and local process, should not be overlooked by the historian who seeks to uncover the true attitudes and directions of the people in a particular time and place.

CULTURAL HISTORY IN FOLK SONG   The same kinds of observations can be made from folk songs. An interesting example is in one of the earliest American folk songs:

> *On Springfield Mountain there did dwell*
> *A handsome youth I knew him well.*
> *Lieutenant Merrick's only son,*
> *A likely youth, 'most twenty-one.*
>
> *One day this handsome youth did go*
> *Down to the meadow for to mow.*
> *He had not mowed quite round the field*
> *When a poison rattler bit his heel.*
>
> *He took the scythe with which he mowed*
> *And laid that pesky rattler low.*
> *Then he shouted loud for all to hear,*
> *To take him home to Molly dear.*
>
> *Now Molly had two ruby lips*
> *With which the poison she did sip.*
> *She also had one rotten tooth,*
> *And so that rattler killed them both.*

One can visit the grave of Timothy Merrick in Wilbraham, Massachusetts, and can ascertain the historicity of the event. On the other hand, as students of this song have found, the story in the ballad does not match the events of history. For one thing, Merrick's fiancée was not named Molly, and whether or not she applied the folk medical treatment of sucking the poison from the wound, Sarah Lamb did not die but two years later married a Captain Dwight in nearby Belchertown. In this case we can see how pedestrian real life is when compared to an artistic achievement based on real life. We have almost the same kind of development of a good story from an actual occurrence that we find in a good historical novel. The songmaker and its subsequent singers have been apparently more motivated by passing on a story that has its own beginning and end than by recording and reporting life as it actually occurred.

In addition to this preference for a good story over real life, we need to note some other important details about the song itself before we can see its application to our study of history. The earlier versions of the song do not mention the girl, but follow the style and content "rules" for a New England funeral elegy: a focus on young Merrick, his lineage, the misfortune, the effect of his death on his survivors. As a song, however, it apparently caught on in Wilbraham, and for years it was sung by the people at reunions and picnics. Newspaper accounts and local pamphlets describe the elderly people singing it with gusto. Later it became a stage comedy song, and by that time young ladies named Molly, Susan, Betsy, Polly, Nancy, and Mary Ann had begun to appear as characters replacing the boy's father. While music hall audiences responded to the humor of a sometimes lengthy exchange between Molly and the dying Timothy, I think New Englanders hearing the song in oral tradition continued to relate it to the familiar tombstone verse in local cemeteries, much of which is humorous. But the song was, as a story, more complete now, for the ending could be seen as a direct outgrowth of the drama: Using a standard and easily recognizable folk treatment, a young girl brings about her own death and the couple is united—a motif that seems quite similar to other English ballads. Our knowledge that this song was made up in Puritan times (the 1700s) in New England allows us to speculate on whether the death of this young couple through the aggressions of a snake might not have been seen as a subtle parallel to the Garden of Eden story. Indeed, this may very well be why the death of the young woman is as important as the death of the young man. If we add to this our knowledge that in earlier times the song was often sung to the tune of "Old Hundred," otherwise known as the doxology ("Praise God from Whom All Blessings Flow"), we can perceive that at least for some singers of this ballad there was the additional level of Providence, an idea very central to early Puritan thought, which held that all occurrences come from God as part of His Providence to humanity, whether those situations were classified as good or bad by their human recipients. It seems to me that we can claim that such a ballad is a complex and revealing item for the historian, for again, instead of concentrating on date and fact and an identifiable personage, the song has expressed a complex of ideas held in common by an important group of people (historically speaking), whose real impact on the events in America is as much to be measured by their attitude as by factual detail. This is not to say, however, that facts about the Puritans are unimportant; rather, folklore may be used to enrich the record by providing that extremely important undercurrent of human thought, feeling, and expression without which the dates remain tombstones.

Widely sung in the American West at the turn of the century was the following song; very likely from music hall tradition, it moved quickly into oral circulation and can still be heard in the repertoires of older singers. Some of my students first heard this song sung by a retired logger, Henry Tams, in Moscow, Idaho. I have since heard it sung in Florence, Idaho, and other old-timers have indicated to me that it was heard in most parts of Oregon as well, especially in areas where gold mining took place.

*Old John Martin Duffy was judge of the court*
*In a small mining town in the West;*
*Although he knew nothin' about rules of the law,*
*At judgin' he was one of the best.*

*One night in the winter a murder occurred,*
*And our blacksmith was accused of the crime.*
*We caught him red-handed and gave him three trials,*
*But the verdict was guilty each time.*

*Now he was the only good blacksmith we had,*
*And we wanted to spare him his life,*
*So Duffy stood up in the court like a lord,*
*And with these words he settled the strife:*

*I move we dismiss him, he's needed in town,*
*Then he spoke out these words which have gained him*
*    renown:*
*We've got two Chinese laundrymen, everyone knows,*
*Why not save the poor blacksmith and hang one of those?*

Students of the American West will recognize immediately that the situation described here is far from fictitious: We know, for example, that Chinese laborers were very prominent in gold mining towns, sometimes making up the bulk of the population. While in some areas they became leading citizens and put down deep roots, in other places they were not allowed even the most basic freedoms or dignities and were much abused. Old-timers in the mining country around Baker, Oregon, have told me that it was common to hire a gang of Chinese to work in the mines and then not to pay them. After a considerable period of time, when the Chinese began to complain about their pay, a convenient explosion was arranged in order to remove the problem. Such heartless treatment of minorities has characterized several aspects of American settlement, and traditions among these ethnic minorities recall, through song, story and anecdote, those frightful times. In this song, however, the perspective is that of the majority group, which proclaims humorously that since Chinese are expendable, it is much more sensible to retain the services of an important and useful citizen rather than to have an over-supply of Chinese laundrymen. Historically, then, the ballad is ethnically accurate, even though it may not describe an actual event, as its singers usually claim it does. I have been told that the incident actually occurred in Florence, Idaho, in Jacksonville, Oregon, and not far from Nespelem, Washington. The people who sang me the song, or fragments of it, presented it as about something that had happened "right around here" some years before.

Just as it is clear that such an incident could not have happened precisely in identical ways in those three areas, so it is obvious that the kind of situation described by the song represents a widespread attitude about the Chinese among other settlers and miners, who by this time in history considered themselves owners and proprietors of the land. The song voices tensions about minority groups that are often felt when those groups can provide labor so inexpensively as to threaten the economic and political power of others in the system. And, as I suggested in Chapter 8, when these psychologically tense subjects are expressed in tradition, they very often take the form of humor, or attempted humor, as if to recognize that some of the situations that make us the most nervous and that cause the greatest ethnic anxiety can be dealt with by laughing them off so that we may feel momentarily superior to their effects upon us.

How does this affect the study of history? Again, I would point out the importance of knowing the attitudes—whether they are made up of tensions or joys—of the people who were engaged in those very processes that are so often displayed to us only through the interpretation of dates and places and prestigious people. The mood of the country, the spirit of an area, the sense of a group of people, shine forth strongly from their folk traditions. If we do not apply these traditions and the wealth of perspectives they provide to the story of history, we run the risk of stressing fact over substance. George Armstrong Custer carried out a campaign against the Indians and became famous for his last stand. But his actions and his meaning cannot be understood apart from the context of the tradition and attitude concerning Indians and westward expansion and gold that saturated American culture at that time. Custer did not invent Indian wars; rather, his exploits, and his continued existence to this day as a folk hero in proportions far beyond the merits of his actions, testify to the power of traditions in how a culture views its own history from its own distinctively ethnic perceptions. Custer is as much an element of folklore as of history; without the perspectives of both fields his position would be impossible to understand.

These applications of folklore to such fields as literature and history are only brief and rather superficial examples for the sake of discussion to indicate that applied folklore is, basically, made up of an easily understandable and perfectly sensible attitude: One may fruitfully apply the materials and approaches of one field to those of another. Our examples are what we must call intellectual or scholarly applications, for they normally take place as part of the ongoing scholarly concern with the development of further knowledge and perspective in academic fields. This is not to say that these perspectives cannot be used in everyday life, however; it simply recognizes that most people who talk about these matters at any length are academicians or writers.

## ◤ APPLIED FOLKLORE AS A BASIS FOR ACTION
Applying the resources of folklore to daily problems in life, politics, medicine, and so on, becomes a more touchy affair, for it implies to many that the folklorist is saying, "If you only knew about this kind of information from the field of folklore, you would do your job better." That is, seen in its active form, applied folklore can seem to be persuasive, avuncular, condescending, and didactic. Especially since people do not like to change their minds about matters so close to home as those elements normally dealt with in folklore, cultural liberals and conservatives alike are inclined to get testy when someone tries to instruct them about how they might get along better with other people, how they might help their government approach problems less chaotically, how they themselves might see their own potentially destructive role in interpersonal relationships. Edward T. Hall, in *The Silent Language*, acknowledges that he was originally asked as an anthropologist to develop some perspectives that could be used by political, economic, and agricultural advisers going to other cultures. In many respects, we can see his books as a form of applied folklore, for they advocate that anyone dealing with other cultures should know a considerable number of the gestures

and customs of those cultures so as to stave off the possibility of unintentional cultural disaster.

Yet some people argue that human beings are alike the world over, under their skin, and that if we all simply could learn the same language or adopt the same religion or believe in the same political system, everything would be rosy. Until such a millennium occurs, however, it seems apparent to most folklorists and anthropologists that people are culturally not alike the world over, and there is no use ignoring it. We simply do need to know each other's folklore before we can get along very easily. As noted earlier, an American needs to know that an Arab man will probably stand much closer to another man while talking to him than the American is accustomed to. If the American interprets this as an aggressive gesture, or if the Arab interprets the American avoidance as a reluctance to converse, it suggests that any delicate conversations between these two people will not come off very well. One aspect of applied folklore, then, is to discover the traditional codes that characterize certain groups of people and then to instruct others so that insults can be avoided and harmony promoted.

FOLKLORE AND MULTICULTURALISM   Other kinds of application require that we notice what sorts of medical or psychological or social processes are strongly traditional in a group of people in our own country so that we may use those processes in our dealing with those people. For example, one aspect of applied folklore on the Navajo reservation in recent years has been the practice of medical doctors working for the Public Health Service to study and become familiar with Navajo concepts of medicine and then to invite Navajo medicine men ("singers") into the hospital to help in the treatment of disease among the Navajo. This is not simply superficial or symbolic; rather, the doctors have noticed that the Navajo customs concerning health stress the psychological aspect more strongly than the physical aspect of human welfare. A Navajo patient is likely to be severely troubled on the psychological matters of his treatment even though the physical aspects may be well cared for in the hospital. Doctors tell of patients coming in with burns, for example, whose wounds were treated and were in the process of healing, yet the patient died. What the doctors have been trying to do, in effect, is to learn how the tribal traditions may be used fruitfully in scientific attempts to provide adequate medical treatment for the Navajos. If the psychological or psychosomatic aspect of medicine is stronger for the Navajos, then it is certain that from a Navajo perspective hospitals do not normally provide proper treatment. By incorporating the medicine man into the system, the doctors are insuring that Navajo traditions are upheld; the patient is more at ease and more willing to believe that an actual treatment is taking place, and, if verbal reports are any indication, the program has met with considerable success.

RACE RELATIONS   Another possibility for applied folklore of this sort is in race relations. Many whites are unaware of the tone and volume variations that are standard in American Black speech events. Moreover, many are put off by the essentially antiphonal, heavily interactive mode of speaking, especially on issues of great moment among Blacks. For this reason, if a racial crisis occurs in an area populated chiefly by whites and Blacks, there are very few ways open for negotiation, for in using its own traditions, each side will assume that the other side is trying to gain an unfair advantage in one way or another. That is, the suspicions on each side can be deepened since under crisis situations each group will play its role according to its own traditions. Folklorists have sometimes been able to help by giving in-service training to teachers, race relations workers, city officials, and the like, demonstrating the traditional basis of different kinds of communicative and interactive modes. Once people are aware that the actions of another group are products of the same kinds of tradition their own responses stem from, the explosiveness of racial friction can be considerably lessened.

EDUCATION   Education is a particularly important place for the application of folklore to potentially troublesome dilemmas. Not only does each close group develop certain traditional codes for expression, but as we observed earlier, these codes are very often the basis for how people learn, what they learn, how they go about learning it, and what seems logical or sensible to them. For this reason, especially in a multicultural country like the United States, it is possible that in every classroom there are people from traditional backgrounds whose ability to learn is incapacitated not so much by personal weaknesses (or by what some well-meaning people have labeled cultural deprivation) but by the mismatching of traditional codes: a discrepancy between the codes they bring with them and those used by the teacher.

Let me suggest the complexity of this area by mentioning only a few traditional dilemmas that have been shared with me by friends in various Native American tribes. One of the most commonly mentioned problems relates to eye contact. In a good many American Indian tribes, young people are taught that to stare in the eyes of an older person while receiving instruction is a sign that the older person is not being believed.

In other words, looking into an older person's eyes in a learning situation implies disrespect, distrust, and disinclination to learn. You will probably recognize immediately that this tradition is almost exactly opposite the one employed by most European-Americans, in which eye contact is seen as a sign of being interested, involved, paying attention, being honest. We ask our children to look us straight in the eye when they tell us something, and we expect audiences—including student audiences—to look continually at the teacher during a lecture. Lack of eye contact for most whites is a sign of disinterest, distrust, or disinclination to learn.

Thus a white teacher, trying to make sure that the class is paying attention, may require Indian children to do something that is essentially considered an insult or certainly impolite. Suppose, for example, that white children were confronted by a teacher who yelled at them, "Pick your noses while I'm talking to you!" It might well be that some students would be willing to swallow their pride and traditional training and spend the year picking their noses, but most the students would probably hesitate to do such a thing. Yet, eye contact, for many American Indian tribes, is more embarrassing than picking one's nose.

In many Indian tribes, children are brought up not to speak of themselves as fully developed individuals until they are old, until they have "become someone." Many tribes do not believe in talking about death. A good many tribes inhibit people talking about the future by one means or another, for in the view of some the future is an impractical and unknowable subject, for others a totally imaginary situation that does not make sense. Most tribal systems the world over rigorously suppress competition unless it is ritually expressed. Thus, while many tribes use sports as a means of competition, in the classroom or in daily life it is rigorously wiped out. Now look at several of these factors together. Suppose the teacher assigns the students a theme in which they must write a personal description; suppose the teacher asks for a paper on "What I want to do when I grow up"; suppose the teacher requires the students to study epitaphs or to write their own epitaphs; suppose the teacher tries to praise one student in class for having done a good job or tries to call on another because that student probably has the answer? All of these instances, quite common as they may be in the classrooms of whites, will provide one or another sort of cultural panic for many Native Americans.

In some Indian classrooms, the student who tries to set himself forward by answering a question will simply be drowned out by the noise of other students ("shaming him out," some Sioux youngsters call it). Even more likely, the student so singled out will give the wrong answer on purpose so as not to appear competitive. Basketball coaches at Indian schools have told me in exasperation how their team will go out on the floor and play a spectacular game during the first half until they are well ahead, then throw the game in the second half so that they will not win. Usually a coach feels that this is a kind of betrayal, a losing of interest in the reputation of the school, or a lack of pride, when in fact it usually boils down to a wish on the part of the team to show that they play well together and then to make sure that they do not come out better than someone else.

Most Indian children are brought up to be very quiet on all occasions; indeed, in some tribes, anyone who talks all the time is simply dismissed as someone who has nothing to say. Silence, rather than noise, in conversation is thought of as wise, sensible, and normal. Thus, if an Indian student is called upon to talk or to converse at length with the teacher, the teacher is often upset to find that the student is reluctant to speak. The teacher often takes this as a sign of disinterest or petulance. Such a confrontation can of course be extremely painful and embarrassing to an Indian student as well, and the typical situation is for the two people to part company considerably more frustrated than at the start. One puzzled high school teacher confided to me that a certain young Indian boy would come to his office every noon and just sit there without talking; when I pointed out that being together with someone in silence was considered a kind of conversation, the teacher was put much at ease. Yet that kind of information was incredibly easy to find out locally; the answer had been close at hand all the time. The teacher had simply not thought to ask into it but assumed that there was something aberrational about the actions of the student.

Indians in many tribes believe that if you laugh or smile at a stranger, it will mean you are making fun; thus it is rather typical among Indians not to smile when first meeting someone or to show any overt emotion when strangers are present for fear they will misunderstand and feel they are being laughed at. This is a point of great delicacy in most tribes, and yet it earns Indian people the reputation for being stoic, unfriendly, inscrutable. At the same time, Indian people have told me in confidence that they never can tell what white people are thinking "because they smile and laugh at you all the time."

If all of these matters were simply interesting facts for the intellectual tourist, it would not be worth bringing them up in a discussion of applied folklore. But in fact very often education does not take place in our schools precisely because the traditional expectations of the teacher are not met by the traditional expectations of the students. Very often the teacher takes the position that if the students are going to get on in the world they need to give up all these old beliefs anyhow, and learn to act normally. Nothing can be further from the truth. Educational specialists continually find that children of any sort do not learn well if they are put off balance and made to feel afraid or embarrassed in the learning situation. All one does by ignoring or denigrating the student's traditions is to make it even more certain that the student will have problems in school. By the time the student reaches high school or college age and has intellectualized the culture differences he has experienced, the topic can become explosive, personally hurtful, and politically sensitive. Learning simply does not take place very efficiently if the learners are angry or embarrassed.

A former student of mine, trying to teach a class in writing to a group of adult Navajos, found that for the first third of the course almost no one would pass in any papers. Finally, one of the older students took her aside and pointed out what the problems were. She had assigned them a paper in which they were to write their own epitaphs; she had read some papers in class noting how well some were written; she had forcefully confronted individuals in the class who had not passed papers in, and to show how earnest she was, she had maintained eye contact with each person she talked to. The woman who took her aside for cultural instruction gently told her, "After all, you know, we don't like to talk about death, and we don't like to compete with each other." My friend now sums up her adventure by saying: "I had to learn not to mention death, not to cause competition, not to use eye contact, not to give direct orders, not to put someone on the spot. After that, they wrote some very interesting and beautiful themes."

This situation has been duplicated all over the country: Once people are put at ease by being able to operate within their own traditional expectations, they do better in an educative situation on the intellectual level. Just as an American does not have to apologize about being American or give up his religion and language just to learn the German language and culture, so an Indian, a Black, a Chicano, a farm boy, or a South Carolinian need not give up home traditions in order to be properly educated. Folklore can be applied in these circumstances precisely because it is one of the ways in which we can discuss exactly those traditions through which people normally learn. The application of these ideas can be made on a number of levels: Teachers, doctors, lawyers, public officials, who know these traditions can use them in their professional functioning. In addition, professional folklorists can often be employed for in-service training, for developing community seminars, for studying traditional health practices of immigrant groups that can then be passed on to doctors, and so on. The doctors on the Texas border whose clinic folded because they inadvertently caused the evil eye clearly needed to learn folklore along the way if they expected to apply their technical expertise to a cultural situation. Lawyers and judges who work in areas of considerable Mexican-American or Spanish-American population must know about the in-group, often in-family, justice system that operates among Hispanic-Americans. And why should urban planners, architects, and city fathers continue to deprive themselves of the traditional knowledge developed by many Black people for living in a crowded urban environment? Although the living experiences among Blacks have not always been pleasant, urban Blacks in America have developed extensive means of surviving in the city, not the least of which is an extended street family of brothers and sisters bound together by oral tradition and custom. May we not assume that these traditions and customs express accurately the emotions of those who live in the cities and may suggest patterns that could be emulated by others as we try to keep cities alive?

CULTURAL RELATIVISM    Perhaps the most important personal application of folklore to dilemmas such as those suggested here is the payoff available to the individual who can understand the traditional differences between his own group and others so that those differences are no longer the basis for value judgments. Folklorists study the traditions of each particular culture or group or region without considering which one is right or best. It is instructive for us to know, for example, that American Indians have passed along an impressive body of medical and scientific knowledge in the form of oral traditions that we call folk tales and legends. Not only are certain herbs recognized and their usage codified in such stories, but the relationships between people and nature are epitomized. When Jacques Cartier was icebound in the St. Lawrence River in 1535, all his men were in the process of dying from scurvy. Local Indians came and cured them by the application of what we have come to recognize as vitamin C. Surely we can see in this incident, and there are many of them, that neither the Europeans nor the Indians can be judged as being primitive or advanced. Cartier had sailing ships; the Indians had medicine. Knowing the validity of each of these areas of cultural concern, how can we ever say that one culture is superior to another? We should remember that Pueblo Bonito had eight hundred rooms in it, and was built from about 919 to 1130; it contained some twelve hundred persons and was abandoned in about 1300. It was the largest apartment house anywhere in the world until a bigger one was finally built in 1882. Africa had kingdoms while Europeans were still roaming in small bands bashing each other on the head. Before the whites came to Central and South America, the Incas and the Aztecs had vast domains where people were not allowed to go hungry or unclothed.

It is clear that we need to get rid of the notion of cultural deficit, because cultures the world over come and go, and at any single time any culture may have developed ideas, customs, traditions, and institutions that were not developed by others. It is impossible to measure the merit of any of these cultures in relation to each other. Rather, we need to recognize that each culture has its own valid way, and much of that way has passed on through the traditions of its people. Thus even while stereotypes that evaluate others based on the norms of one's own group are often rooted in folklore, applying folklore on the individual or corporate level can help us understand those stereotypes for the false judgments they represent. Studying the validity of the folklore of each group can lead us away from stereotypes. We will notice sometimes that the same action will be highly prized by one society and abhorred by another. For example, one often hears whites complain that Indians misspend their money: "If you give an Indian a thousand dollars, he'll go out right away and waste it on groceries and liquor for his family and friends." One hears almost exactly the same story from Indians, that is: "White people waste money; if you give a white man a thousand dollars, he'll go and waste it by putting it in the bank where his family and friends can't share it."

Indeed, the following story is widespread in Indian reservations across the United States. An old Indian man was sitting in the shade in front of a Bureau of Indian Affairs office one noontime when he was joined by a white administrator who had come outside to eat his sack lunch. Just as the white man began to unwrap his sandwich, the Indian man blew his nose the old-fashioned way, snorting down on the ground, wiping his nose off on his finger, and flicking the excess off by a rapid flip of the wrist. The white man was repulsed and sickened, and threw his sandwich back into his lunchbag, saying, "You Indians are just crude! You haven't learned any manners at all since we've been here. You don't even know how to blow your noses properly. This is just like everything else that's happening around here; we come around and try to give you all the education we can, but you all still insist on doing things the wrong way. That's just sickening. Why don't you people ever wise up and do things right?" According to the story, the old Indian man declined to reply, but sat watching the horizon. Later, when the sun came around the tree a little farther and shone into the white man's eyes, he sneezed, pulled out his handkerchief, blew his nose on it, and returned it to his pocket. The

Indian turned and said, "My God, you white people save everything, don't you?"

The very fact that Indian people have made this circumstance into a joke is a strong indication that what the anecdote represents is really something that may cause people concern. It is also true that in a number of Indian tribes selfishness and the storing up of items is seen as a sure symptom of witchcraft. Many Indians, still living in an essentially tribal orientation, therefore bring up their children to value interaction, reciprocation, and the sharing of all items, especially food. Thus it is very easy for Indians to see and represent the attitudes of whites as essentially defective and selfish. That is, whites act the way witches act, therefore whites are in general to be avoided and not taken very seriously no matter how moral they try to appear.

Similarly, it is not rare for whites to look at Indians as reckless with their money, incapable of managing their own affairs, and as poor planners. In white society these are considered negative attributes and are often used to rationalize the continued white jurisdiction over Indian affairs of all sorts. We can see how easily actions turn into stereotypes, for it is quite true that many Indians will indeed share their money and their food at all times with friends and relatives rather than putting them away for their own use. It is also true that it is highly valued among European-Americans to save, plan ahead, and manage their fiscal lives well. In fact, in both instances a person's real economic situation may be held in secret: The Indian perhaps has some money or goods stored away and the white may be nearly ruined by overextended credit.

What a folklorist would suggest by a thorough study of both cultures, however, is that each position is perfectly valid in terms of the cultural bearings it represents. Therefore one cannot easily level a finger at one group or the other and suggest that the attribute mentioned is right or wrong or backward or advanced. In other words, the kind of knowledge generated by folklore study, which seeks to relate traditions as they are performed to the worldview of the group in which they are performed, causes us to focus on internal validities and internal logic rather than measuring things against some presumable objective truth (which usually turns out to be an oversimplification of one's own worldview anyhow).

FOLKLORE AND POLITICS    There are many other applications of folklore as well, both promising and sinister. Many of the emerging countries, especially in central Europe, after suffering years of domination by outsiders, have tried to express and retain their own sense of ethnic unity by purposely collecting, archiving, and disseminating to their own people certain key aspects of their own folklore. In this venture, often certain features are considered less than important while others are given a focus beyond what would have originally been theirs under normal traditional circumstances. Here, even though the folklore presented may accurately depict the costumes, say, of a particular region or the dances and songs of another, there is a stagecraft involved that has strong nationalistic and political overtones. There is always the chance under these conditions that the real traditions in folklore will finally be subordinated to political ends, and that has sometimes happened, lamentably.

Probably in recent world history Hitler represents the most sinister use of nationalistic folklore for baldly political ends. In his pursuit and extermination of the Jews, he counted upon a considerable amount of anti-Semitic folklore among the people for support. In addition, he and his writers fashioned a lot of folkloric-sounding legend and political myth to provide an antique and grand cultural context into which these local stereotypes and prejudices could fit. The result was a partly traditional and partly manufactured cultural set in which subsequent barbaric actions struck most of the participants as perfectly normal. Hitler's regime provided a macabre example of how certain traditions, channeled carefully by propagandists, can provide a mental stage for actions that might otherwise be considered inhuman and inhumane by the same people. There is no overlooking the deep power of folklore in such cases.

Commercial applications of folklore show the same manipulation, ranging from the whimsical advertisements for lumber companies in the manufactured stories of Paul Bunyan to the more subtle onslaughts upon our imaginations through folk symbol in the hands of television and magazine advertisements. An awareness of the possibilities in applied folklore would surely seem to be one of the best antidotes for the misapplication or the misunderstanding of folklore.

FOLKLORE AND THE PUBLIC SECTOR   There are other, more formal, applications of folklore as a field of employment. Various government agencies, private foundations, companies, and community groups have found folklore increasingly interesting to their needs and directions. For some years the Smithsonian Institution has sponsored the Festival of American Folklife on the Mall in Washington, D.C., in an attempt to provide the nation with a live counterpart of the kinds of exhibits found within the Smithsonian's museums. The director, Ralph Rinzler, has hired fieldworkers and coordinators around the country, not only to locate tradition-bearers nationwide, but to bring forward those willing to come to Washington to share their traditions out of context. Performances are accompanied by contextual explanations so that there will be little danger of hurting the pride of the performer or the integrity of the tradition. Nonetheless, even with expert folklorists on hand as buffers, some tradition-bearers feel they are in a circus. For most of them it is worthwhile, because it allows a national, public focus on traditional arts that many thought had died with the Revolution. All the same, quilting, singing, raising barns, and fiddling while jets from National Airport roar overhead and thousands of people look on could easily create an affront to the traditional arts. Had Rinzler and the folklorists not been involved, the festival would truly have been a human disaster.

The National Endowment for the Arts, originally established by Congress to support the arts in the United States and to provide increased public access to them, now has a separate program in the folk arts, which gives grants to people and agencies all over the country who wish to develop ways of maintaining and presenting the traditional arts in their own contexts; this attempt can be interpreted as an inclination on the part of the Endowment to allow as much validity for the folk arts as for the more formal arts (although funding in these two areas remains colossally out of proportion).

Several states have established the office of State Folklorist or State Folk Arts Coordinator. Organizers have been increasingly interested in providing a strong component of distinctly traditional performers for community and national festivals. The United States Forest Service and the Park Service have found folklore to be helpful in some of their programs. For example, the Forest Service has jurisdiction over thousands of acres of land that contain certain locations sacred to American Indian tribes. With the help of anthropologists and folklorists, impact statements can be developed, special sites can be ascertained and protected, and names and signification clarified. During the North Coast Folklife Festival in Astoria, Oregon, in the summer of 1977, one of the most active functionaries was the county extension agent, who felt that the occupations of the area, chiefly fishing and logging, were vastly aided both in their own sense of themselves and in their public image by the exposure of their traditions to public view in the festival format. The American Folklife Center and the Archive of Folk Song, both in the Library of Congress, are government agencies employing folklorists in the job of canvassing, collecting, and preserving the folklore of the country.

Applied folklore is certainly not limited to ethnic or national differences, but these examples should show the central concerns when one takes the identifiable traditions of one group and applies them as perspectives to a particular problem that requires action. Sometimes folklore is used as an introduction to literature in the schools, especially where ballads and folk songs can provide a vivid example of poetic and musical talents of people in general that can offset the notion that poetry can be made up— and understood—only by strange geniuses. Folklore is sometimes used in retirement homes where people can maintain mental exercise and a sense of cultural stability by sharing jokes, anecdotes, songs, and historical reminiscences that express the validity of their own lives. Folklore can illustrate the richness and the complexity of a culture outside one's own, either on the personal level or in public education. Throughout, the point is that folklore as an area of research and discussion is seen as more than an interesting topic; it is a reservoir of powerful human responses that can suggest ways for us to solve, or at least to approach more appropriately, the dilemmas of our day.

All the activities described in this chapter fall under the category of applied folklore because their functions rest on the assumption that one must go beyond the simple intellectual discussion of folklore to gain certain ends. Whether those ends are served by massive government programs on the one extreme or by individual folklorists acting as consultants to schools, companies, and other groups who need cultural perspectives, applied folklore exists as a very broad field of knowledge in action. As a set of possibilities that show the continued importance of folklore study in the modern world, applied folklore allows for a great number of meaty answers to that hypothetical question, "So what?"

# ✍ BIBLIOGRAPHICAL NOTES

Every teacher of folklore has favorite examples of good and bad books, of pointless and inspiring assignments, of boring and exciting mentors. John Matthews Manly, "A Knight Ther Was," *Transactions and Proceedings of the American Philological Association*, 38 (1907), 89–107, while it is not dull and boring, is still a detailed study that ends only with the timid suggestion that Chaucer had a Sir William Scrope in mind as he wrote his famous description of the Knight. Jan Harold Brunvand, "The Folktale Origin of *The Taming of the Shrew*," *Shakespeare Quarterly*, 42 (1966), 345–359, on the other hand, is a clear example of what careful folkloric analysis can offer for a fuller understanding of a text whose author can no longer offer elucidations of his own.

One of the very best essays on folklore and literary criticism is Roger D. Abrahams, "Folklore and Literature as Performance," *Journal of the Folklore Institute*, 9 (1972), 75–94. In it he encourages the reader not simply to look for traditions and customs within written literature but to consider how the traditional materials convey a cultural environment imbued with vitality. Among the hundreds of articles and books written on literary relations of folklore, the following are among the most useful; the more recent ones are likely to be more concerned with interpretation, while the older ones are mostly addressed to matters of identification and terminology. Russell K. Alspach, "The Use by Yeats and Other Irish Writers of the Folklore of Patrick Kennedy," *Journal of American Folklore*, 59 (1946), 404–412; Tristram P. Coffin, "Real Use and Real Abuse of Folklore in the Writer's Subconscious: F. Scott Fitzgerald," in *New Voices in American Studies*, ed. Ray B. Browne, Donald M. Winkelman, and Allen Hayman (West Lafayette, Ind.: Purdue University, 1966), 102–122; Carvel Collins, "Folklore and Literary Criticism," *Journal of American Folklore*, 70 (1957), 9–10; Robert C. Cosbey, "The Mak Story and Its Folklore Analogues," *Speculum*, 20 (1945), 310–317; R. M. Dawkins, "Presidential Address: Folklore and Literature," *Folklore*, 40 (1929), 14–36; Alan Dundes, "The Study of Folklore in Literature and Culture: Identification and Interpretation," *Journal of American Folklore*, 78 (1966), 136–141; Dundes, " 'To Love My Father All': A Psychoanalytic Study of the Folktale Source of *King Lear*," *Southern Folklore Quarterly*, 40 (1976), 353–366; Richard M. Dorson, "The Identification of Folklore in American Literature," *Journal of American Folklore*, 70 (1957), 1–8; William R. Ferris, Jr., "Folklore and the African Novelist: Achebe and Tutuola," *Journal of American Folklore*, 86 (1973), 25–36; John T. Flanagan and Arthur Palmer Hudson, eds., *Folklore in American Literature* (Evanston, Ill.: Row, Peterson, 1958); Daniel G. Hoffman, *Form and Fable in American Fiction* (New York: Oxford University Press, 1961); MacEdward Leach, "Folklore in American Regional Literature," *Journal of the Folklore Institute*, 3 (1966), 376–397; Max Lüthi, "Parallel Themes in Folk Narrative and in Art Literature," *Journal of the Folklore Institute*, 4 (1967), 3–16; Bruce A. Rosenberg, "Folklore Methodology and Medieval Literature," *Journal of the Folklore Institute*, 13 (1976), 311–325, one essay in an entire issue devoted to folklore and literature.

The critical school I have termed *architectural* is represented by Northrop Frye, *Anatomy of Criticism: Four Essays* (Princeton, N.J.: Princeton University Press, 1957), in which "modes" and "archetypal meaning" are used to describe organizational assumptions and dynamic structural aspects of literature. The area of study I have termed *psychological* is represented in literary criticism by such books as Norman Norwood Holland, *The Dynamics of Literary Response* (New York: Oxford University Press, 1968), which deals less with elements of structure and mode in the work and more with the receptivity and responses of the reader. Robert Graves, *The White Goddess: A Historical*

*Grammar of Poetic Myth* (New York: Vintage, 1958), is both exciting and frustrating. Since Graves does not support any of his thousands of matter-of-fact assertions, folklore and myth scholars have been justifiably suspicious of his theories. Nonetheless, his insights are penetrating and brilliant and are well worth reading for the perspectives they provide. His passion for the subject supplies an exciting element missing from more reliable, objective studies in myth and folklore.

Ruth A. Firor's *Folkways in Thomas Hardy* (Philadelphia: University of Pennsylvania Press, 1931) is one of those exercises D. K. Wilgus has called "zebra counting"; Firor locates and names several hundred traditional references in the works of Thomas Hardy (missing quite a few along the way) and then provides almost no commentary on why the knowledge is worthwhile. More modern scholars, foremost among them Donald Davidson, have been working much more seriously with Thomas Hardy's folklore; the rather superficial treatment of Hardy presented in this chapter is not meant in any way to reflect a summary of their complex and rewarding work. Axel Olrik originally published his famous essay as "Epische Gesetze der Volksdichtung," in *Zeitschrift für Deutsches Altertum*, 51 (1909), 1–12; it is reprinted in English as "Epic Laws of Folk Narrative," in *The Study of Folklore*, ed. Alan Dundes (Englewood Cliffs, N.J.: Prentice-Hall, 1965), pp. 129–141.

This brief excursion into traditional aspects of history does not pretend even to scratch the surface of the broad and complicated field now called oral history. Folklorists and historians have tended to approach the subject from different directions anyway, the folklorists paying more attention to the expressive element of reminiscence and the historians fastening upon details, date, and information. From a folkloristic point of view, the following are illuminating and helpful studies: Richard M. Dorson, "Oral Tradition and Written History: The Case for the United States," *Journal of the Folklore Institute*, 1 (1964), 220–234; Ronald Grele, ed., *Envelopes of Sound* (Chicago: Precedent, 1975), a symposium of specialists discussing method, theory, and practice in oral history; Edward D. Ives, "Common-Man Biography: Some Notes by the Way," in *Folklore Today: A Festschrift for Richard M. Dorson*, ed. Linda Dégh, Henry Glassie, and Felix J. Oinas (Bloomington: Indiana University Press, 1976), 251–264; W. Lynwood Montell, *The Saga of Coe Ridge: A Study in Oral History* (Knoxville: University of Tennessee Press, 1970). The tall tales presented in this chapter are quoted from the articles mentioned under that designation in Chapter 3.

Typical versions of the ballad "Springfield Mountain" are provided by Albert B. Friedman, ed., *The Viking Book of Folk Ballads of the English-Speaking World* (New York: Viking, 1956), pp. 302–307. Because of the humor on some of New England's oldest tombstones, however, I do not accept the argument that the comic element entered the song only after the stage comedians of the 1830s and 1840s began using it as a parody of New England rusticity. "Judge Duffy" was collected by two of my students, Marion Cupp and Cliff Michel, near Pullman, Washington, in August 1959. Bruce A. Rosenberg discusses Custer traditions in a number of places, among them "Custer and the Epic of Defeat," *Journal of American Folklore*, 88 (1975), 165–177.

I am indebted to Thomas Duncan, M.D., for sharing with me his insights on the current treatment of Navajos in Public Health Service hospitals on the Navajo reservation; Dr. Duncan served for three years at the Tuba City hospital on the western Navajo reservation. A revealing study of how the materials of folklore may be applied to the predicaments encountered by southern mountain people when they move to a large city is Ellen J. Stekert's excellent essay, "Focus for Conflict: Southern Mountain Medical Beliefs in Detroit," *Journal of American Folklore*, 83 (1970), 116–155; reprinted in *The Urban Experience and Folk Tradition*, ed. Américo Paredes and Ellen J. Stekert (Austin: University of Texas Press, 1971), pp. 95–136, including discussion from the floor. For an international view, see Margaret Mead, "The Application of Anthropological Techniques to Cross-National Communication," *Transactions of the New York Academy of Sciences*, series 2, 9:4 (1947), 133–152; reprinted in Dundes, *Every Man His Way*, pp. 518–536.

Hitler's use of folklore is discussed by Christa Kamenetsky, "Folklore as a Political Tool in Nazi Germany," *Journal of American Folklore*, 85 (1972), 221–235. Creative and developmental uses of folklore in the life of the individual are treated, from a largely psychological point of view, by Bruno Bettelheim, *The Uses of Enchantment: The Meaning and Importance of Fairy Tales* (New York: Vantage, 1977). Throughout their years of publication *Southern Folklore Quarterly* and *Folklore* (the journal of the English Folklore Society) have carried brief articles, many of them excellent, on the application of folklore to literary and historical problems. Clearly, applied folklore is nothing new in the scholarly world; it is when particular applications aim at the tender political, economic, and racial ideas that lie close to our hearts that some people are inclined to be offended.

# APPENDIX

## A Fieldwork Transcript

### ⚡THE FOLLOWING IS A NEARLY⚡ VERBATIM TRANSCRIPT OF A TAPE-RECORDED INTERVIEW WITH MRS. CLARICE

MAE JUDKINS MADE IN EUGENE, OREGON, ON September 9, 1966. Mrs. Judkins came to my attention through some friends who had heard her sing a few years earlier. I had also seen an article about her in *Western Folklore* that was written long before I arrived in Oregon. I was anxious to find out if she still sang and if her songs had changed in the meantime; I also wondered where she had learned them. She was in her seventies and an absolutely warm, hospitable person who insisted on making tea and talking at great length about her family and her early life. Although she was in no way senile, it was clear to me that singing was not as important to her—at that moment—as it was to me. She kept digressing (to more important matters) and I kept pulling her back to songs.

Not until I listened to the tape more carefully did I begin to realize that part of her initial reluctance to sing was founded on some disappointing experience with a previous collector—whose name, mercifully, she had forgotten. I would like to offer the following excerpts (interrupted here and there by her making tea, letting cats in and out, rescuing food from the stove) as a sample of a folkloric document and a warm testimony of one person's life within a folk song tradition.

Notice some of the following broad features:

1. I try to get her to sing older ballads, but in most cases she sings what she wants to.
2. She recites some verses and sings others.
3. Often she does not sing the whole song and I ask her a question about further verses.
4. In several instances I pretend total or partial 'ignorance of a song so that she will go ahead and sing it.
5. She makes occasional reference to someone whose name she cannot recall. Watch how this builds to a later lament about having been abandoned by a field researcher.
6. She refers continually to a professor, a person she admired very much, who made her feel proud to be a tradition-bearer. The professor was an important person in her life, even if one of his students had had a negative effect on her. I have not used the professor's real name because I have no way to check on the accuracy of Mrs. Judkins's observations, especially those that attribute comments and attitudes to the student, who could have been identifiable.
7. She sings a wide variety of numbers including traditional, stage, "coon" and "heart" songs typical of the tastes and attitudes of her generation.
8. She freely admits to learning some songs from books, and mistakenly insists that one of her traditional ballads, "Lord Lovell," was in a book she had on hand.
9. One song, "Babes in the Woods," gets started only when I supply the first line.
10. Even though I miss a chance to ask about orchard workers' songs, my question about "The Farmer's Curst Wife" reminds her of an important song.

TOELKEN: What about the uh, what about these older ballads, these things like "Barbara Allen" and ballads like that?

JUDKINS: Oh uh, well that was pretty well known—the one that this uh, professor—I used to laugh at them for it; the one that he took up and he taught his glee club young men and they traveled all over the state giving programs of that song—well, that was about the earliest song I knew. Seems in the early times in Boston when the ships came in, the boats, uh, the young men would go through the docks to find a girl. And they soon learned that it was the girls with the striped stockings on that were going to go with them [laughter]. So this song was written about the girl with the striped stockings on. The chorus was:

> [She sings:] *She was always out if the wind blew high,*
> *If the weather was wet she would walk or die;*
> *By the raising of her skirts as she passed by,*
> *I saw she had striped stockings on.*

And so then of course—

> [She recites:] *The color of her hose was red and yeller,*
> *Says she I think you're a mighty fine feller.*
> *So I escorted her home under my umbreller,*
> *The girl with the striped stockings on.*

[Laughter]   Well, the professor made that song very famous. He took his band all around over the two or three states with that song.

TOELKEN:   Is that, is that all there is to it?

JUDKINS:   Oh no, let's see:

> [She sings:] *One rainy day, I'll ne'er forget,*
> *The prettiest girl that ever I met;*
> *And as she raised her dress in the wet,*
> *I saw she had striped stockings on.*
>
> *She was always out if the wind blew high,*
> *If the weather was wet she would walk or die;*
> *By the raising of her skirt as she passed by,*
> *I saw she had striped stockings on.*

In those days they were wearing very long skirts and if she showed even the tip of her shoe, well that—

> [She sings:] *The color of her hose was red and yeller,*
> *Said she I think you're a mighty fine feller;*
> *I escorted her home under my umbreller,*
> *The girl with the striped stockings on.*

*And when we parted in the rain,*
*She said we would never meet again;*
*And so she took my watch and chain,*
*The girl with the striped stockings on.*

So that was a song written in the early times, when the sailors would come off the boats. They had this group of Boston women that would [laughs] meet them on the wharf and they were a light fingered bunch. Soldiers didn't have any money on them—only watch and chains—well that was the last—well, I don't know why the Professor liked it so well but he just thought that was wonderful so he taught his glee club to sing it—and they sang it all over Oregon and Washington.

[She sings:] *She was always out if the wind blew high,*
*If the weather was wet she would walk or die;*
*By the raising of her skirts as she passed by,*

[Spoken:] That was the chorus

*I saw she had striped stockings on.*

There were the only three verses. "Says he I think you're a—the color of her hose was red and yeller"— In those days I guess they wore gayer stockings and this was a girl with the striped stockings.

• • •

TOELKEN: Were there any Irish songs in Oregon?

JUDKINS: Yeah, I 'spect there were some—that's where the boys picked up a good many of their dance tunes was from the Irish. We, uh, they moved in and we moved out [laughs]—Father had a great time. He was also looking of course for the cheap land for his family to settle on and uh, my mother's uh, father was quite well to do in Illinois and he left Mother, gave Mother forty acres of ground in Illinois but that wasn't enough for Father. He'd come down from Canada to get in on the lots of ground. So then he moved, in the first place he moved to Iowa and we settled in the same town that Hoover was uh, born. And I laugh now when I hear about, uh, everybody talking about Hoover and taking him back there to be buried. Mother said of all the miserable disreputable places she ever lived in her life, that was the worst. It was terrible. Well, it was settled by a class of people called the "low Germans" and uh, they talked a different language from what we did. But afterward we got acquainted. My brother married a German girl and they called her—her grandmother called herself, her mother just called herself a "high class" German. He said there were high Germans and low Germans and they were not to be confused with the kind of people [laughter] that settled on the west branch. Well, I was born on the west branch. My brother went to school—the same school that Hoover went to. Hoover wasn't uh, I don't remember whether he was born there or not but he uh lived with his grandfather when he was eight years old. His mother died. And his father lived out here in Newburg. And I don't know whether, but I think he was born on the west branch. And he was just as old as my oldest, as my next oldest brother, Burt. And they went to the same school. He remembered Hoover quite clearly.

TOELKEN: To change the subject a little, one thing I was going to ask you—do you remember a few years ago, uh, someone got some songs from you and they put them in *Western Folklore*. Do you remember that?

JUDKINS: I don't know. The only thing this other fella had to prove—this was a young man from California and he went to California. He was a young man who wanted to graduate and he was married and he and his wife came out and, uh, finally the professor sent them out. So he found so many folk songs that I knew that he told the professor and then he came out. And he used some of them for his glee club. Things like that. But the young man simply wanted to graduate. And so after he went to California, why different people called for his address to write to him and I asked the professor about it, and he said yes, I'll give you his address but he said I know that he said he was definitely through with folk song work. That all he used it for was because it was something he could use to get his degree. And he wasn't interested in it a t'all and he didn't want to hear anything about it. Yes, I would have thought he would have gone on being interested but apparently he didn't care anything about it. What he wanted was to get his degree and get his job and that was that.

TOELKEN: Yeah, well I just wondered not so much about him but I just wondered if you remembered any of those old songs. Somebody apparently collected a bunch of songs from you and, and they put them in, uh, *Western Folklore*. I wondered if you could sing me a few of those.

JUDKINS: Well, I don't know what they did with them but I went up to what they called the, the, is it called the humanities room up there at the University?

TOELKEN: Oh, yeah, it could be.

JUDKINS: I, uh, then the professor came here and I, uh, sung a number of songs that they had recorded. And what they did with them I don't know because he told me from the start that he didn't expect for me to make any money out of it. And he said since they had already been published on this other young man. The young man wrote back and told him he wanted nothing more to do with it—it was all work. He had his job and that's what he wanted.

TOELKEN: Uh, that's too bad.

JUDKINS: I hated that, yes. Because we spent quite a lot of time with him, the professor and I did, and one of his friends did, to get him along with it. And we thought it would be nice if he did, uh, put a book out of songs, but he apparently had no idea of it. As far as I was concerned it would have been all right. I didn't expect anything out of it. But, uh, he never did apparently and the professor told me, he's a member of the church, same church I am, so I see him every now and then, but he hardly says anything more about music. He asked me once if I was doing anything about it and I said no I wasn't. So I don't sing anymore as you observe. [Pause.] I did have quite a bit of trouble with the flu and I had rheumatism for a couple of years. I'm getting better now but, uh, uh, so I don't try— I used to be in choirs and work in music with the idea of teaching and I had the piano working and so on. I studied up here at the university awhile, but I never completed anything.

TOELKEN: When, uh, when you sing these older folk songs that you, that you learned from family and friends and so forth, do you always try and sing them using the same words every time?

JUDKINS: Yes I do, I, uh, I tried to bring them the way they were. And that was one thing that the professor appreciated at least. He said that so many people learn songs and then some group would put them to other music and things like that. And so he felt that, that uh, well he told the young man he struck a gold mine because he couldn't have found anybody else that knew these songs right from the start and sung them when I was young. Of course most people don't sing and take much interest in music. But, uh, we always did as a family. In those days you know we didn't have motion pictures [laughs] and everybody tried to have music and tried to have good books.

TOELKEN: Some of the uh, some of the folk singers I knew in North Carolina and the Ozarks, uh, made a practice of singing the song the same way each time, you know, telling the same story, for example, but changing the words a little bit each time—the way they happen to feel at the time.

JUDKINS: The way they happen to feel at the time. I guess so. Uh, did you know that old uh, it isn't too old a song. When I was first married and that's quite a while ago, Edward's uh, my husband's cousins came up from California and, uh, one of the boys, George—he's been dead a long time—he was quite a hand to sing at various occasions you know. And, uh, he sung about "Whistling Rufus." Did you ever come across that?

TOELKEN: No, I've never heard of that one, no.

JUDKINS: And—

[She sings:] *Down in the south where the sly old possum,*
*Hides in the sycamore tree,*

[She says:] I don't think I sung this for the professor either.

*There lives a coon called Rufus Blason,*
*Black as a nigger could be.*

*Rufe had a head like a big sledgehammer,*
*And a mouth like a terrible scar;*
*But nothing could touch him in Alabama,*
*When he played on his old guitar.*

*Don't make no blunders, you could lose him,*
*A perfect wonder they had to choose him.*
*A great musician of high position,*
*Was Whistling Rufus, the one man band,*

*Miles he would tramp to a ball or a party,*
*Rainy weather and fine.*
*There they would give him wealth and hearty,*
*Out came the chicken and wine.*

*When he was done with the wine and the*
*    chicken,*
*He'd play and he'd whistle so grand.*
*You'd think that the angels on harps was*
*    a pickin',*
*They called him the one man band* [laughs].

That was quite old. I learned that when I was just a little girl. But, uh, the professor was strict about one thing. About the young man. He didn't want to learn anything that had ever been in print. It was pretty hard to scratch around and find a folk song that'd never been in print. So I guess he learned more from me than he had from anyone 'cause he went ahead and graduated. 'Cause he was anxious to graduate and somebody told him that folk song work was the best thing to take up now. That it would give you quite a number of, what'd you call them, that you get when you study?

TOELKEN: Credits, you mean?

JUDKINS: That's right. Credits. And yet it didn't require a great deal of work. So that was what he did. He came out here and his wife and they, uh—and I sung him the songs and they recorded them right away. I know that when I did the folk song work, why then the various clubs that I was a member of asked me to come and give a talk on it and sing some songs. Quite awhile afterwards, I was rather amused, there was a group that met at Pleasant Hill. I think they were called the County Federation. It'd been years since I had done any folk song work and they dug me up [laughs]. I can have a good dinner and meet with people—I said why yes, I certainly will go because my sister lived there for years so I was up and gave them a talk about the folk songs. They remembered Edwin and the family. He was my—uh, brother-in-law was, uh, sort of, he wasn't a caretaker, he was uh, he took care of a great big prune orchard for a doctor. The doctor owned the biggest prune orchard anywhere around and he was supervisor of it—hired the men and saw to the drying of the prunes. They sold the prunes dried at that time. And, uh, that was also a time when the workers, the workmen would get together at night and sing songs.

TOELKEN: Did you ever hear of one called "The Devil and the Farmer"?

JUDKINS: No uh—

TOELKEN: The Devil takes the farmer's wife down to hell with him and can't get along with her so he has to bring her back.

JUDKINS: Well, I wonder if you knew the one about the, uh—I haven't sung you that and I think that's about as old as any I know. Uh, "The Sheepskin"?

TOELKEN: Oh, uh—

JUDKINS: I don't know, the young man thought that was so funny. He just had me sing that over and over about the fellow that:

> [She sings:] *Billy got a wife and he brought her home,*
> *Jenny go gently, rosamarie.*
> *Better for him had he left her alone,*
> *The dew flies over the green valley.*

You can see how old it is with those sayings.

*When Billy came home from followin'*
  *the plow,*
*Jenny go gently, rosamarie.*
*"Oh have you any dinner for me just now?"*
*The dew flies over the green valley.*

*She called him a villain and a dirty whelp*
*Jenny go gently rosamarie.*
*"If you want any dinner just get it*
  *yourself,"*
*The dew flies over the green valley.*

You've heard it I suppose.

TOELKEN:  I've heard another version of it.

JUDKINS:  Another version?

TOELKEN:  Do you know any more about that?

JUDKINS:  Yes, uh, Billy went out and he got his whip and he stretched this—this is the one that— What was that fella's name? He thought that was, he got the biggest kick out of that song. And anyway, he brought in a sheepskin and he hung it on—he had a sheepskin hangin' on the door of the wood house or something. So he brought it in and laid it over her back. And the, uh, the whip that he had went "wickety wak." And then she said he wasn't to whip her. He said, "I'm not whipping you, I'm tanning my own sheepskin. I guess I've got a right to tan my own sheep-skin!" [Laughter.] Well anyhow, she didn't talk sassy to him anymore. And she got up and said, "Yes sir" and "No sir" and set the board and cooked his dinner without a word. That was very old also. I don't know why that young man, I suppose he hadn't been married a great while— [laughter].

TOELKEN:  That's a good song.

JUDKINS:  He liked that more than anything. But, uh, I can't remember when I learned that. That's very old.

  [She recites:]  *Billy got a wife and he brought her home.*
                *Better for him had he left her alone.*

I expect you've run across it in various—

TOELKEN:  I've just heard another one that uh, let's see, what's it called? Well, I'm familiar with the Burl Ives version, that tells a similar story. I like your tune better.

JUDKINS:  Well, all Burl Ives did was to go over the country and pick up these things and change the tune enough so that they couldn't—I don't suppose anyone would have tried to accuse him of plagiarism and all that sort of thing—copyrights and things. But he was very careful to change the tunes. They were always comparing, the professor was and this young feller, the tune that I knew to the tune that they heard somewhere else. And mine were never in print. That's what he had to have, were folk songs that were not in print. No matter how old they were or how definite they were, but they must be songs. There used to be one that I thought was very pretty and I don't remember—I don't think I ever gave it to him because I couldn't be sure—at least he didn't take it. Couldn't be sure that it had never been in print. But I don't believe it ever has. Not long ago, when I was reading a Western story I came across just a chorus of it. But I don't know of course what tune. It was just a story of this fella singing this mournful song. I wonder why the mountain people always sing such mournful songs. And, uh, that was very pretty.

· · ·

JUDKINS: And then there's that other old one about the, uh, about the man that's going away and, uh—he was, that was an English lord too. And this girl, he met this girl and she asked him where he was going and so, uh, he was going to some town somewhere far away. And she said, "When will you come back?" Oh, "Lord Lovell," yes.

> [She sings:] *Lord Lovell he died at the end of the war,*
> *He was shot by a Yankee gunner.*
> *At his head there sprouted a red, red rose,*
> *And at his feet a scarlet runner, runner,*
> *    runner oh,*
> *At his feet a scarlet runner.*
>
> *"Oh where are you going, Lord Lovell?"*
> *    she said.*
> *"I'm going away dear Nancy Bell."*
> *"And when will you come back, Lord*
> *    Lovell?" she said.*
> *"When will you come back?" said she.*

And Lord Lovell said, "It might be a year and it might be three." So then she pined away you know and died and at the foot of her grave—why uh, they buried—uh, at the head of *his* they buried a rose. Was that it? And at his feet a scarlet runner. Yeah, and she died when he was gone.

TOELKEN: Do you remember how any more of the verses go?

JUDKINS: Well, I don't know. It ought to be in some of these old books.

TOELKEN: What was that first verse about? The Yankee gunner—

JUDKINS: Well that was the last verse. He was, uh, shot by a Yankee gunner. I don't know whether you ever had this book or not. There are a lot of those old songs in here. My older sister had one. When I was a little girl and later on I went to a sale, an auction market and I found it. My husband laughed at me because I kept on bidding and bidding for it. He said, "What on earth did you want that little book for? Why did you make that fella—"

TOELKEN: What's the name of the book?

JUDKINS: *Heart Songs*. And my sister, older sister bought it for her children when they were little so they'd learn music. They had their piano, or organ lessons it was then. So there's a lot of those old songs in there. I think your "Lord Lovell" song's in there if I'm not mistaken.

> [She sings:] *"Where are you going Lord Lovell?" she said,*
> *"Oh where are you going?" said she.*
> *"I'm going away dear Nancy Bell,*
> *Far lands for to see,*
> *Far lands for to see."*

TOELKEN: Oh yeah, I've seen this book, but I don't think "Lord Lovell" is in it.

JUDKINS: Oh, you *have* seen it. When I was south and visiting my son, I was surprised to find that they didn't have the same music and the same tunes that we did here a t'all. It was where my son lived that they are the ones, the only ones that follow the old five-note. And uh, the Scotch people did too you know. And they were supposed to have brought it from a place in the Orient, as I learned it. Mrs. Campbell told me that. She said the Scotch people were really an Oriental people. They were not Japanese or—I remember making Allan furious, my brother, because he was proud of his Scotch heritage but if you stop to think of it, the Scotch have high cheekbones and they're dark and they were driven out from where they were by people like the Japanese and the Hindus. Nobody knows what all they were but they were Oriental. They know it because their musical instrument is the bagpipe. And they have the five-note songs.

TOELKEN: Do you know any of those five-note songs?

JUDKINS: Well, I don't know; any Scotch song I s'pose.

> [She sings:] *Oh bonny lassie oh where—*

[Speaks:] Oh anyhow, he asks her where she's going.

[She sings:] *Truth I didn't ask yourself for to blame.*
*Tra la la la la la literalarry.*
*Truth I didn't ask yourself for to blame.*
*Tra la la la la literalarry.*

*My bonny lassie,*
*Where was your soldier laddie gone?*

Well he had gone to the wars. And the last verse, "What should you say if I were the man?" And then she goes ahead and tells him she knew it all the time [laughs]. But that's uh, but of course a long time ago when the Campbells—they had, we had what we called a Scotch Burns night at the church. So they dug up all the Scotch songs they could and I know some of the ones I sung they didn't approve of a t'all and insisted they weren't Scotch. And what was that one? The one that Mrs. Campbell didn't like. Well, anyway, it was very gay and flirtatious and something she didn't like. How *does* that thing go? [Sings tune to herself.] It's real cute. Oh "Whistle and I'll Come to You Me Lad."

TOELKEN: Oh, I haven't heard that one.

JUDKINS [sings in a strong Scottish dialect]:

*Oh whistle and I will come to you me lad,*
*Oh whistle and I will come to you me lad.*
*Though father and mither and all should get mad,*
*Oh whistle and I will come to you me lad.*

*But, umm, when ye come to court me.*
*And come as though ye cared not a flea.*
*But give me the wink of your bonny black e'e.*
*And come as you were not coming to me,*
*And come as you were not coming to me.*

*Oh whistle and I will come to you me lad,*
*Oh, whistle and I will come to you me lad.*
*Though father and mither and all would get mad,*
*Oh whistle and I will come to you me lad.*

Well I don't know where I learned it. But my folks learned every song that came across there anyhow. Well, Mrs. Campbell was giving a program and so she asked me to sing a Scotch song and I sang it nicely. Well they called me back for an encore and she hadn't provided for an encore and I just remembered that one and I sung it and it brought the house down. She was so shocked she didn't [laughs] want that kind of song on her program at all. She took a fit about it. But the audience seemed to like it.

TOELKEN: Would, would you sing part of that "Lord Lovell" again? I think that's a wonderful song.

JUDKINS: Well, the words to that is in that book!

TOELKEN: Well, uh, I didn't see it listed but uh—

JUDKINS: Listed? Well Lord Lovell uh—

> [She sings:] *"Oh where are you going Lord Lovell?"*
> *she said.*
> *"Oh where are you going?" said she.*
> *"I'm going away dear Nancy Bell,*
> *Far countries for to see—"*

So when she asked him how long he'd be gone, he says, "It may be one year or it may be three." Well she pines away and dies while he's gone. And so why then he comes back, he's so brokenhearted over it that he dies. And so that was, the last ending of the song was, at his feet they planted—*her* feet they planted a red, red rose, and at his a scarlet runner because he had run away from his true love. And then the other version says it was two roses. And the white rose and the red. Well there was a legend long years ago about England you know. The white rose and the red—there was a fight between the two. I don't remember what time it was. In the early times when the English kings all got beheaded or beheaded somebody else.

TOELKEN: Will you sing that last verse again? Something about the Yankee gunner. I've forgotten how the words went.

JUDKINS: Yes.

> [She sings:] *Lord Lovell he died at the end of the war,*
> *And he was shot by a Yankee gunner.*
> *At his head there sprouted a red, red rose,*
> *And at his feet a scarlet runner, runner,*
> *runner,*
> *At his feet a scarlet runner.*

Well there was another song that, uh, I knew that one. But Mrs. Campbell taught me one that was very sad about this—it was a girl or a young man that was ill, yes—and she was really very unkind to him. And so when she passed where he was, she said, "Young man I think you're dying." And so sure enough he did die and so she was so unhappy about it that she pined away. And so that was another version of this idea that at his feet was the red, red roses.

TOELKEN: Roses. Yeah, that *is* in a lot of songs. Did you ever hear of a song called "Babes in the Woods"? Two babes in the woods?

JUDKINS: Yes, yes. An old lady sung that for me long, long years ago. And I didn't remember much about it. She didn't have much of a tune to it. And, uh, these two babes were sent away with their stepmother. It was taken from a fairy tale, you know. And they wandered around. Let's see, how did that go? They wandered and wandered and finally they cried. Laid down and cried themselves to sleep. And I don't remember the mournful ending to that story. Did they starve to death?

TOELKEN: Yeah, they die in the woods and then the birds, robins come—

JUDKINS: Yeah, now I should know the tune to that. And then the birds came—

TOELKEN: The one tune that I heard was:

[He sings:] *One day as I remember a long time ago,*
[She sings:] *When two little babes, their names I don't know.*
*They wandered away one bright summer's day,*
*And never came back so some people say.*

*And when they, they sobbed and they cried*
*And those two little babes, laid down and died.*

*And when they were dead, a robin so red,*
*Brought strawberry leaves and over them spread.*
*And all the day long they sang their sweet song,*
*Those two little babes who were lost in the wood.*

I remember a ridiculous thing about that because my older sister lived in Pleasant Hill. When her children were going to school they learned that song. And she said, "How ridiculous to talk about birds covering them with strawberry leaves." And she made them sing it, "bright maple leaves" [laughs]. She thought that would be better.

TOELKEN: Wouldn't take as long that way [laughter].

JUDKINS: Well I found out afterwards the maple leaves [end of tape].

THE DYNAMICS OF FOLKLORE

What was the point about bright maple leaves Mrs. Judkins was making when the tape ran out? I was so engaged in turning the machine off (and being angry with myself) that I never registered what she said. Yet it could have been the most important item in the interview. This old song, descended from one of the most popular British broadsides of all time (whence our proverbial expression "innocent as babes in the woods"), may have had a really distinct Oregon variant not found elsewhere. Nevertheless, I can't prove it with any of my material from Mrs. Judkins, for even if she knew of another version, she never sang it for me or for others who collected from her. Her own version of the song, not remembered fully in the interview above, goes as follows in four other performances:

*Oh do you remember a long time ago*
*When two little babes, their names I don't know.*
*They wandered away one bright summer's day*
*And were lost in the woods, I heard people say.*

*And when it was night, so sad was their plight*
*The moon had gone down and the stars gave no light*
*They sobbed and they sighed and bitterly cried*
*And those two little babies laid down and died.*

*And when they were dead, a robin so red*
*Brought strawberry leaves and over them spread.*
*And all the day long they sang their sweet song,*
*Those two little babes who were lost in the wood.*

Even if we have plenty of tape, no single transcribed interview will tell us all we want to know about a given tradition. For example, in this interview, Mrs. Judkins sings only a part of the song she called "The Sheepskin." Did she know more verses? It is unclear from the tape. Indeed, I found out later that it was one of her favorite songs, and she never tired of singing it. My friend Ray Scofield arranged a friendly gathering and asked her to teach us the song. The following is a composite version of "Billy's Wife" ("The Wife Wrapt in Wether's Skin," Child #277) taken from thirteen performances by Mrs. Judkins among that group of friends on the afternoon and evening of February 3, 1968. Although Mrs. Judkins's own perception of her art included an attempt to sing songs exactly as she had learned them (see her comment earlier), the alternations here show that some lines and phrases were "open" to immediate variation while others were not. Poor memory cannot be cited as the reason for these variations, for they were done within a few hours (in several cases within minutes) of each other. Moreover, there is a certain pattern in the kinds of words and phrases available for variation in addition to a clear preference for (assumed from the preponderance of) some key phrases.

The refrain was retained exactly in all thirteen performances, and will be dropped here after its first appearance so that we can concentrate on the variant features. Numbers in parentheses indicate the number of appearances out of thirteen performances.

1. *Oh (6) Billy got a wife and he brought her home,*
   *Jenny go gently rosamarie;*
   *Better for him had he left her alone,*
   *The dew flies over the green valley.*

2. *She would not card and she would not spin,*

   *'Fraid (9)* ⎡ *of soiling her lily white* ⎤ *skin (9)*

   *Afraid (2)* ⎣ ⎦ *hands (2)*

3. *Into the kitchen she would not go*
   *'Fraid of soiling her new kid shoes.*

4. *Now (1) when Billy came home from followin' the*
   *plow,*
   *"Have you any dinner for me just now?"*

5. *She called him a villain and a dirty whelp:*

   *"If you want any dinner just* ⎡ *get (12)* ⎤ *it yourself."*
   ⎣ *fix (1)* ⎦

6. *He* ⎡ *got (8)* ⎤ *the* ⎡ *sheepskin (10)* ⎤ *off of the* ⎡ *barn (7)*
       *took (3)*        *horsehide (3)*              *wall (1)*
       *cut (2)*                                      *house (3)*
                                                      *woodhouse (1)*
                                                      *shed (1)*

$$\text{Cut him a} \begin{bmatrix} \textit{hickory (5)} \\ \textit{whickery (2)} \\ \textit{hickory bough (2)} \\ \textit{willow (1)} \\ \textit{willow switch (1)} \\ \textit{hickory stick (1)} \\ \textit{whip (1)} \end{bmatrix} \text{as} \begin{bmatrix} \textit{thick (6)} \\ \textit{long (4)} \\ \textit{big (3)} \end{bmatrix} \text{as} \begin{bmatrix} \textit{his (7)} \\ \textit{your (6)} \end{bmatrix} \text{arm.}$$

7. And (1) he $\begin{bmatrix} \textit{laid (10) the sheepskin} \\ \textit{put (2)} \\ \textit{tied (1)} \end{bmatrix} \begin{bmatrix} \textit{across (8) her back,} \\ \textit{over (4)} \\ \textit{to (1)} \end{bmatrix}$

· The $\begin{bmatrix} \textit{hickory bough (5)} \\ \textit{hickory stick (3)} \\ \textit{hickory whip (1)} \\ \textit{whip (1)} \\ \textit{leather whip (1)} \\ \textit{willow switch (1)} \\ \textit{willow twig (1)} \end{bmatrix}$ went whickety-whack.

8. "I have brothers one, two, three—
   If they were here you'd not whip me."

9. "What care I for your brothers ten?
   I guess I'll tan my $\begin{bmatrix} \textit{own (10) sheepskin."} \\ \textit{ol' (3)} \end{bmatrix}$

10. *She cut the loaf and spread the board—*
    *"Yes sir, no sir," every word.*

11. *Now Billy leads a* ⎡ *happy (10) life—*

                     | *virtuous (3)*

    *He has him (4) a* ⎢ *gentle (8) obedient wife.*

                     | *dutiful (2)*

                     | *mindful (2)*

                     ⎣ *kind (1)*

We may well ask *why* some features here were open to change and why some stayed remarkably stable. Since Mrs. Judkins is not available for such questioning, we must speculate on the basis of our evidence.

We notice, for example, that even though the variations are not always metrically equivalent, they are ideationally parallel in most cases. A horsehide is not a sheepskin, but either one may be tanned by beating. Gentle is not necessarily dutiful, but both are stereotypically good qualities in a wife. The exception to this observation is in the similar-sounding words *own* and *ol'* in verse 9. In the version most preferred by Mrs. Judkins, Billy insists that it is his sheepskin and he can tan it any way he pleases. The use of *old* (as in "good ol' Charlie") is not inconsistent with that meaning, even though it is not, as a word, equivalent.

Other features necessary to understanding the story line are less variable. The verses setting up the idea of a new marriage, a wife disinclined to dirty herself at work, Billy's demand for supper, and her rejection of that demand are all done with little variation. The same is true of the later verses, in which she threatens to tell her family she has been beaten, his assertion that he is only doing normal, acceptable chores, her (implied) recognition that he will continue to so treat her, and her subsequent capitulation.

The verses that describe the disguised beating are most open to variation, we may suppose, because the exact hide, its whereabouts, his instrument for tanning it, are all comparatively superficial matters as long as they go along with the story line. Obviously, not every change would be acceptable: We would not expect *sheepskin* to be replaced by *suitcase*, *hickory bough* with *gasoline pump.* Rather, the central ruse must be followed: Some hide has to be tanned by being beaten with something in order for the trick to "work." David Buchan, *The Ballad and the Folk* (London: Routledge and Kegan Paul, 1972), p. 39, offers a different, perhaps complementary, notion of why some features of ballads change more than others.

How about the refrain? Is it only a hypnotically repetitious formula the singer need not think about while recalling or phrasing the words of the verse? Perhaps so, basically. But I find it interesting that at least three elements in the refrain may be construed as out of kilter with the action going on in all verses but the last two. "Jenny go gently," if it refers to the otherwise unnamed reluctant wife, may be a continual undercurrent of advice that matches the woman's actions only when she has been properly "tamed." If so, we might suggest that there is a kind of tension set up between the lines of the verse and the lines of the refrain; the tension is resolved on both levels at once in verses 10 and 11.

If we had only this version to judge from, we would have to let it stand at that. But there are many other versions of the ballad available, and in them we find gillyflower, gentian, and other herbal or floral references that, along with rosemary, are often found in folklore as aphrodisiacs, in love potions, and in romantic divination. Here we might focus on *rosamarie* and on *dew*, which James Reeves (in *Idiom of the People* [New York: Norton, 1965]) has found as common sexual references in British folk song. This is another possible undercurrent of tension in the ballad: Where we would expect romantic warmth in a song about newlyweds we find a case of strife and marital dislocation (as well as insubordination). To the accompaniment of a refrain that continually refers to gentleness and sexual harmony we see the tension resolved in the "proper" subordination of the wife. Presumably the last two verses suggest total marital harmony, not merely that Billy finally got his supper.

Was Mrs. Judkins consciously aware of these possibilities? My hunch is that she was not. At the same time, she had sung the ballad for years among people who likely knew other versions of it. Here is where the continuity of community taste may be seen taking a rather large role in the conservation of folklore in all its diverse and complex possibilities. Mrs. Judkins sang the song the way she wanted to, of course, but at the same time she did not apparently feel free to alter the story line or the refrain. No matter what reasons we give for this, the outcome is the same: Mrs. Judkins, like all other traditional performers, made only those adjustments that she felt allowed her to stay within the tradition.

Such questions as those pursued here may arise from a close reading of any transcript. Following up on them in subsequent interviews with the same traditional performer can lead to some very revealing insights into the traditional art, its meanings, and its place in the life of the tradition-bearer. Be friendly and relaxed; don't try to correct the performer or censor the performance; don't overwhelm the performer with your knowledge; and bring plenty of tape!

# ⚜ INDEX ⚜

Barry, Phillips, 87
Bascom, William R., 19, 34, 257
Basket, as folksong, 155–156
Bauman, Richard, 19
Belknap, Arthur (storyteller), 347
Benally, Susie (Navajo filmmaker), 128, 148, 240
Ben-Amos, Dan, 19, 147
*Beowulf*, 173, 213, 339
Bierhorst, John, 211, 220, 222
Bigfoot, 173
Black Americans, worldview, 245–248
Black Elk, 43
Black folklore, 192–193
Boas, Franz, 145, 213
Boise, Idaho, 177
Brand, John, 15
Brown, Joseph Epes, 43
Brunvand, Jan, 13, 94–96 *passim*, 326, 328
Buchan, David, 34
Buchanan, Jim (Coos narrator), 217
Buckeye Cove, North Carolina, 157
Bunyan, Paul, 362
Bushnell, Clif, 173
Butchering, 161–162
Bystander audience, 108

Cahill, Holger, 195
Cameras, 300–301
  in fieldwork, 300–301
Campbell, Joseph, 14
*Cante-fable*, 142–145
Carey, George, 288
Cartier, Jacques, 359
Castrated (mutilated) boy story, 176–178, 272–273
Cement truck driver (legend), 266
Central audience, 108
Chaucer, Geoffrey, 176, 199–200, 201–202, 208–209, 339
Cherry (fig.), 206–211
"Cherry Tree Carol, The," 207–208
Chinese, in America, 351–352
Christensen, Chris (whittler), 153–154
Coffin, Tristram P., 17, 46, 106
Collecting, 292–304
Collier, John, Jr., 325
"Communal re-creation," 87
Connotation, and folklore, 200–223
Conservatism, *see* Twin laws
Context, 49–51
  folk group as, 49–52
  in proverb event, 103

in storytelling event, 94
Coos Bay, Oregon, 164
Coos (Indian tribe), 164, 192
  tale, 217–220
Coquille, Oregon, 165
Costume, loggers, 53
Coyote tale, 167–170, 186–187, 192, 283–284
  *see also* Navajo storytelling
Cray, Ed, 21
Crow, Oregon, 191
Cultee, Charles (Kathlamet Chinook narrator), 145, 213
Cultural audience, 109
Cultural relativism, 359–360
Culture, and meaning, 226–227
*Curandero*, 248–249
Custer, George Armstrong, 352–353
Custom
  Japanese-American, 78–79
    food calendar customs, 79–80
  loggers, 69–71

Danville, Vermont, 114
Davidson, Donald, 366
Deference, 158–159
*Devil's Pretty Daughter, The*, 280
Djupedal, Knut, 90
Dorson, Richard M., 7, 13–20 *passim*, 173, 258
Dowsing, 114
Dozens, playing the, 246
Duncan, Thomas, M.D., 367
Dundes, Alan, 9–29 *passim*, 230, 233, 267–269, 314
Dynamic process, 10
Dynamics (of folklore), definition, 49
Dynamic variation, 32, 34–39
Dynamism, *see* Dynamic variation

Eble, Kenneth E., 11, 20
Edmonson, Munro S., 221
Education, 11
  and applied folklore, 355–356
Elephant jokes, 267–270
"Emotional core," 106
"Epic Laws," 338
Epitaphs, and family, 84–85
Esoteric dynamics, 51–91
Esoteric vocabulary, 54–56
Ethnicity, 73–86
  Arab, 235
  Asian-American, 250

Black American, 115–116, 245–248, 355, 359
  Chinese, 351
  ethnic jokes, 267–272
  European-American, 227–235, 355–356
  Japanese-American, 73–86, 136–141
  Mexican-American, 248–249, 359
  Spanish-American, 248–249
  Swedish, 57
  Ukrainian, 110–112, 114, 186
  see also Native American
Event, 123–149
  dimensions of, 129–131
  induced, 141–145
  inventory of, 124–129, 131–136
  Japanese New Year as, 136–141
  Thanksgiving as, 131–136
European-American, worldview, 227–235
Evolutionary model, 41

Falassi, Alessandro, 9, 20
Family, folklore, 82–87
  "ethnic," 86–87
  "horizontal," 83
  "immediate," 82–83
  "vertical," 83–86
"Farmer's Curst Wife, The," 274
"Fatal Flower Garden, The," 177
Field research, 291–329
  equipment
    cameras, 300–301
    tape recorders, 298–300
  informants, 292–293
  preparation, 301–303
  tactics, 293–297
  transcription, 303–304
  see also Appendix
Filming, theoretical, 126–131
Finn, B. F. "Huckleberry," 112, 347
"Finnish school" (comparative method),
  7, 18
Firor, Ruth, 338, 366
Fixer, The, 179
Fleischhauer, Carl, 288
Florence, Idaho, 351
Folk aesthetics, 9, 20, 158, 181–194
Folk art, and fine art, 14, 182–194
Folk group, 33, 50–91
  religious, 115
Folk ideas, 171–181
Folk language and logic, 24
Folk learning, 25–27
Folklife, 170

Folklore (journal), 367
Folklore
  applied, see Applied folklore
  "biology" of, 41–43
  description of, 27–32
  as discipline, 3–10
  distinguishing characteristics, 10
  and history, 343–353
  and language, 24–25
  and literacy, 39–40
  and literary criticism, 334–343
  misuse of term, 6
  process of, 32–41
  transmission of, 39–40
Folklore and Folklife: An Introduction,
  7, 13, 15
Folklore research
  emotion, 265–266
  involvement, 264–265
  ownership, 284–286
  psychology in, 266–274
  race in, 271–273
  responsibilities of, 283–284
Folklore theories (schools, approaches),
  3–10
  anthropological, 14
  antiquarian, 15–16
  artistic and art historical, 14–15, 20
  contextual, 8–9, 19–20
  ethnological, 7, 19
  functional, 8, 19
  heart-throb, 9–10
  linguistic, 15
  literary, 14
  performance, 7–8, 19
  psychological, 14, 20
  textual, 7
Folklorist
  amateur, 279–281
  being a, 263–286
  professional, 281–283
  rights and responsibilities of, 283–286
Folkloristics, 1–21
Folk measurements, 274–278
Folk medicine, 359
Folk poetry, loggers, 64–65
Folk song, 165–167
  cante-fable, 143–145
  central ideas, 173–176
  community aesthetics, 185
  cultural history in, 349–352
  as custom, 154
  in family repertoire, 165–170

Karpeles, Maud, 152
Kathlamet Chinook, 145, 213
Kimball family Thanksgiving, 131–133
Kimball, J. Golden (Mormon leader), stories, 116–117
Kirshenblatt-Gimblett, Barbara, 146
Knitting and crocheting, 162–163
Kotkin, Amy, 90
Krappe, Alexander Haggerty, 16

Language
   Japanese-American, 76
   logger folk speech, 54–56
   see also Folk language and logic
Lapwai, Idaho, 348
"Lass of Roch Royal, The," 174–175
La Terra in Piazza, 9, 20, 149
Leary, James P., 148
Ledbetter, Huddie "Leadbelly," 175
Lee, Dorothy, 226
Legends, 180–181
   castrated boy, 176–178, 272–273
   cement truck driver, 266
   escape from forest fire, 171–172
   "Goldilocks on the Oregon Trail," 272–273
   urban belief tales, 11
Liebler, Reverend H. Baxter (Episcopal missionary to Navajo), 276
Lincoln, Abraham, 5
Literary criticism
   and folklore, 334–343
      architectural approach, 335–336
      psychological approach, 336, 340–342
      literary use of native folklore, 336–340
      tradition versus psychology, 340–342
Littledale, Reverend R. F., 5, 17
Loggers, 52–72
   beliefs of, 69–72
   and camp, 65–67
   esoteric recognition among, 52–54
   expressions, 64–65
   humor, 57–61
   pranks, 62–64
   and sex, 67–69
   vocabulary, 54–56
Long, Eleanor, 45
Long, Reub (Oregon storyteller), 346–347
Lord, Albert, 285, 325
"Lord Lovell," 381
Los Angeles, California, 178
Low context groups, 51–52
Lullabies, 229

McKenzie River (Oregon), 347
McKenzie River boat, 313
Malamud, Bernard, 179
Malaysia, 254–255
Marshall, John (filmmaker), 126
Material culture, Navajo, 236–245
Mead, Margaret, 128
Medicine, 162, 359
Merrick, Timothy, 349
Metaphor (traditional, in literature), 338–340
   folkloric, 340, 342
   mythic, 340, 342
Mexican-Americans, 248–249, 359
Mode (traditional, in literature), 338–339, 342–343
   folkloric, 339
   mythic, 339
Moffet, Ida (Ukrainian-American folk artist), 186
Moose nose, 202–206
"Moose Turd Pie," 179–180
Mormon folklore, 106, 115, 116
Moscow, Idaho, 267, 351
Motif-Index, 171
Mullen, Patrick B., 287
Müller, Max, 5, 6
Multiculturalism, and applied folklore, 354–361
Munchausen, see Tall tales
Myth
   double structure in, 211–212
   misuse of term, 6
   Native American, 211–220
   structural connotations, 213–217
   "The Sun Myth," 213–217
   triple layering, 217–220

National Endowment for the Arts, 363
Native American folklore, 11–12, 167–170, 202–206, 306–307
   and cultural relativism, 359–360
   see also specific tribes, e.g., Navajo
Native Americans
   traditional behavior codes, 355–358
   worldview and technology, 254
Navajo
   concept of distance, 276–277
   concept of medicine, 354
   concept of time, 277
   storytelling, 93–103, 124–125, 186–187, 192, 283–284
   string games, 95–96, 190